THE

TERRORISM LECTURES

Third
EDITION

THE

TERRORISM LECTURES

A COMPREHENSIVE COLLECTION FOR THE STUDENT OF TERRORISM,
COUNTERTERRORISM, AND NATIONAL SECURITY

Third
EDITION

JAMES J.F. FOREST

www.nortiapress.com

contact@nortiapress.com

Publisher's Cataloging-in-Publication Data

Names: Forest, James J. F., author.
Title: The Terrorism lectures : a comprehensive collection for the student of terrorism , counterterrorism , and national security, third edition / James J. F. Forest.
Description: Includes bibliographical references and index | Montgomery, AL: Nortia Press, 2019.
Identifiers: LCCN 2019941963 | ISBN 978-1-940503-16-5
Subjects: LCSH Terrorism--Prevention. | Terrorism--Case studies. | Terrorism--History--20th century. | Terrorism--History--21st century. | BISAC POLITICAL SCIENCE / Terrorism | POLITICAL SCIENCE / Political Ideologies / Radicalism | POLITICAL SCIENCE / Security (National & International) | SOCIAL SCIENCE / Violence in Society
Classification: LCC HV6431 .F666 2019 | DDC 355.02/18--dc23

Text design by PerfecType | Nashville, TN
Cover design by Marc Whitaker (www.MTWdesign.net)
Author photograph © 2019 by Adrien Bisson (www.AdrienBisson.com)

Printed in the United States of America
by employee-owned Worzalla, Stevens Point, WI

CONTENTS

Part IV: Contemporary Challenges

Part V: Concluding Thoughts

TABLES & FIGURES

TABLES

FIGURES

ACKNOWLEDGMENTS

As this revised and expanded 3rd Edition of my lectures book goes to press, I am reminded ever more about the debt of gratitude I owe to so many people who contributed to my own understanding of terrorism. Indeed, it has taken many years, and the contribution of many people, to make a book like this possible. When I first began teaching courses on terrorism at West Point many years ago, I knew only a fraction of what I know today. Thankfully, I was guided in my journey of learning by several pillars of the terrorism studies field, including senior colleagues at the Combating Terrorism Center (CTC): General (ret.) Wayne Downing, Distinguished Chair; Professor Bruce Hoffman, Senior Fellow; Ambassador Michael Sheehan, Senior Fellow; and most especially Brigadier General (ret.) Russ Howard, Founding Director of the CTC and Head of the Social Sciences Department at West Point. After General Downing's untimely passing, General (ret.) John Abizaid accepted the position of Distinguished Chair at the CTC, and it was an honor to work with him until I left.

Just like many young academics, I studied the works of the world's most respected international experts in the field, like Martha Crenshaw, Brian Jenkins, Alex Schmid, Leonard Weinberg, and David Rapoport. Over the course of the last decade, I have had the privilege of professionally collaborating with each of them, and I thank them for the indulgence and encouragement. Of course, my colleagues and friends at West Point were instrumental in expanding my learning about terrorism and counterterrorism, and none more so than Jarret Brachman, Assaf Moghadam, Colonel Joe Felter, Colonel Kip McCormick, Colonel Scott Womack, Colonel Cindy Jebb, Colonel Isaiah (Ike) Wilson, Colonel Suzanne Nielsen, Lieutenant Colonel Matthew Sousa, Lieutenant Colonel Gingee Guilmartin, Major Rick Wrona, Jr., Thom Sherlock, Brian

Fishman, Clint Watts, Will McCants, Lianne Kennedy Boudali, Bill Braniff, Erich Marquardt, and, of course, my good friend Ruth Margolies Beitler.

Throughout this professional journey, a great many colleagues and friends at other institutions have also been vital to developing my understanding of terrorism, and I must take the opportunity here to thank Alex Schmid, Jennifer Giroux, Matthew Levitt, Erica Chenoweth, David Kilcullen, Peter Neumann, Vera Eccarius-Kelly, Annette Idler, Max Abrahms, Gary Ackerman, Victor Asal, Arie Perliger, Ami Pedahzur, Vanda Felbab-Brown, Gabriel Weiman, Magnus Ranstorp, Paul Pillar, John Hogan, Joshua Sinai, Jessica Stern, JM Berger, and no doubt hundreds more whom I have sadly overlooked at the moment. And certainly this adventure would not have been possible without the generosity, 15 years ago, of people like Vincent Viola, Rob Andy, George Gilmore III, and Ross Perot, whose financial support of the Combating Terrorism Center at West Point was absolutely critical.

The adventure continues today at the Center for Terrorism and Security Studies at the University of Massachusetts Lowell, where I am most grateful to work with great scholars like Arie Perliger and Neil Shortland. Other colleagues in the School of Criminology and Justice Studies have provided support and inspiration, including our chair, Professor Sheldon Zhang. I sincerely appreciate the editing assistance and suggestions provided by Eli Stiefel, Robert Kerins, and Jodi Pomeroy. And of course, Nathan Gonzales of Nortia Press has been tremendously important to the continued improvement and success of this Lectures book project.

Finally, I share my deepest gratitude to my family for their enduring support and encouragement: my father, my four brothers and sister, my wife Alicia and my two amazing children Chloe and Jackson, all of whom have provided years of encouragement and hope. And as I explained in the acknowledgments to the first edition of this book (published in 2012), these lectures are dedicated to my mother, Jeri Lynn Mallard, who died of cancer when I was 14 years old (she was 37). All of her children remain inspired by her commitment to family, education, serving her community, and improving the world around us. I also dedicate the book to Frank Crotty, who recently died of cancer. He was a devoted husband, father and grandfather, a military veteran, a leader of Boston longshoremen, and an avid reader of books whom I was proud to call my father-in-law.

PROLOGUE TO THE THIRD EDITION

If you have seen other books on terrorism, you might be asking yourself, "Okay, what's unique about this one?" Here's my 10-second response: This book is meant to simulate the experience of a semester-long university course on terrorism. Each chapter represents a 45- to 60-minute lecture.

That's it, in a nutshell. If the study of terrorism is in fact something of interest to you, my intent has been to make this collection of lectures informative, engaging, and accessible to a general readership.*

The lectures have also been helpful to some friends and colleagues who teach their own courses on terrorism. Each chapter provides a short list of questions for discussion that are meant to encourage classroom interaction and are also sometimes useful for short paper assignments or midterm exam questions. And the final lecture in this series offers several questions about the future of terrorism, which could also be used for course assignments (final exam questions, research papers, etc.). There might even be some useful nuggets in here for researchers and scholars of terrorism studies, policymakers, congressional staffers, military and intelligence officers, newspaper editors, and Hollywood scriptwriters.

UPDATES TO THE 3RD EDITION

Much has happened in the world of terrorism and counterterrorism since the first edition of this lecture series was published in 2012. The Islamic State came to the

---

*If you are interested strictly in the topic of *combating* terrorism, please note that a separate volume of my lectures on counterterrorism strategies and tactics will be published at a later date.

forefront of the global Salafi-jihadist landscape, launching attacks and capturing territory in Iraq and Syria—where they announced their so-called caliphate—as well as inspiring (and in some cases directing) terror attacks in France, Belgium, Germany, the U.K., and other European countries. Then, particularly through the latter half of 2017, the group was forced out of its territory and lost much of its resource base and ideological attraction to foreign fighters. In the United States, terror attacks in Boston, San Bernardino, Calif., and Orlando, Fla. were motivated by the same jihadist ideological objectives. Meanwhile, longstanding groups like the FARC in Colombia and ETA in Spain have declared permanent ceasefires and engaged in demobilization and political processes. And in early 2017 the Palestinian terror group Hamas issued a new charter in which they had deleted their historical demands for the destruction of Israel, and toward the end of that year they negotiated a peace deal with the Palestinian Authority and relinquished control of the Gaza Strip.

As a result of these and other events, this new edition of the textbook contains a variety of updates from the previous editions. To begin with, the lectures on al-Qaeda have been replaced with much a more expansive discussion of the global Salafi-jihadist movement (in Lecture 12) that encompasses Islamic State, al-Qaeda and their networks of affiliates groups. This was necessary to account for how the movement has evolved significantly over the last 10 years. Likewise, the former lecture on terrorist groups as learning organizations has been replaced by a new and more robust lecture on terrorist group decision-making (Lecture 13). The increase in violence by right-wing extremists, particularly following the election of President Trump, inspired some revision and expansion of the lecture on that topic (Lecture 10). New material on assessing the threat of a nuclear terrorist attack has been added to Lecture 18. And of course, the final chapter on the future of terrorism and counterterrorism has been significantly revised to account for recent events.

The organization of the lectures has also been revised to reflect feedback from professors around the country who use this textbook in their courses and offered suggestions for how the sequence of lectures could better align with the organization of their syllabi. Within each of the lectures, a host of updates and revisions have been made to account for recent events, as well as to reflect insights gained from newly published research in the study of terrorist radicalization, decision-making, and the ways that terrorists are using social media and other technologies to advance their ideological agendas. The lists of recommended resources for further study, provided at the end of each chapter, have also been updated accordingly.

AUTHOR'S BIO

Now that you've read some explanation about this book, I suppose another question you may have is something like, "Well then, who is this guy?" I'm a tenured full professor in the School of Criminology and Justice Studies at the University of Massachusetts Lowell. I also serve as a senior fellow at the Joint Special Operations University, where I hold a security clearance and work on research and other initiatives. I previously spent nine years on the faculty of the United States Military Academy (2001–2010). During six of those years, I served as Director of Terrorism Studies within the Combating Terrorism Center at West Point, originally led by Colonel (now Brigadier General, retired) Russell Howard, a U.S. Special Forces officer and Head of the Social Sciences Department. Retired four-star General Wayne Downing, formerly a Commander-in-Chief of U.S. Special Operations Command (SOCOM) and a Special Advisor to the President for Counterterrorism, served as our Distinguished Chair until his sudden and tragic passing in July 2007. During my last few years there, the Center was led by Colonel Mike Meese, Head of the Social Sciences Department, and retired four-star General John Abizaid served as our Distinguished Chair. If you're not familiar with the Center, please take a look at the website (https://www.ctc.usma.edu). It truly is a terrific institution.

While a good deal of time was spent teaching courses on international relations, terrorism, counterterrorism, information warfare, weapons of mass destruction, and so forth, I was also able to publish nine books and many articles that have hopefully been useful to colleagues and professionals in the field. Other highlights of those years include being invited to give testimony at a U.S. Senate subcommittee hearing on countering violent extremism; giving keynote addresses and speeches at events for senior NATO officers, FBI field office supervisors, and the Department of the Army; and lecturing at the University of St. Andrews, University of Haifa, and Harvard University, among other institutions. At one point, I found myself on a stage in Zurich, Switzerland giving a speech at an international security conference alongside John Brennan, who later became President Obama's chief Advisor for Counterterrorism, and then CIA Director. And I'll never forget meeting with then-Rear Admiral Bill McRaven during a visit to Special Operations Command–Africa.

As part of a multi-year collaboration between the Combating Terrorism Center at West Point and the FBI Deputy Director for Counterterrorism, I developed a new textbook on terrorism that was subsequently adopted for their New Agent Training program in Quantico, and then I traveled to various parts of the United States giving talks at Joint Terrorism Task Force seminars. I also accompanied groups of West Point cadets on visits to the White House, National Counterterrorism Center, State Department, and Directorate of National Intelligence. Overall, when I look back at nearly a decade on the faculty at West Point, it certainly was a wild and fantastic adventure, one that I will always cherish fondly.

Within the past few years, I've been privileged to collaborate with world-renowned scholars in the Center for Terrorism and Security Studies at the University of Massachusetts Lowell. Professor Emeritus Alex Schmid and I serve as co-editors of the internationally acclaimed scholarly journal *Perspectives on Terrorism*, with over 8,000 subscribers worldwide and many more thousands reading the open source issues on our website. I've had opportunities to give lectures at the National Intelligence University, Joint Special Operations University, and various events for senior U.S. military and NATO officers. In 2010, I was able to spend time in Nigeria to conduct research on Boko Haram, and visited Senegal in 2011 to study the political and security challenges facing that country. In 2013, I spent some time in Uganda to study counterterrorism lessons that can be drawn from the recent cooperation between U.S. Special Operations Forces and regional militaries in tracking down Joseph Kony and his murderous followers in the Lord's Resistance Army. And each spring semester since 2011, I've taught (as a visiting professor) a graduate course on terrorism and counterterrorism at Tufts University's Fletcher School of Law and Diplomacy.

In sum, I've been studying, writing, and teaching about terrorism and counterterrorism for the bulk of my professional career. And yet, I still consider myself a student of this field. There is so much to learn, so many things to understand about the complex phenomenon we call terrorism and the ways in which we can confront it more successfully. For my part, I plan to keep working in this field for many years to come. Hopefully, this book will encourage and inspire some of you to do the same.

James J.F. Forest
Dover, N.H.
February, 2018

I

Definitions and Historical Frameworks

1

An Introduction to Terrorism

Welcome to the first lecture in the series on terrorism. We begin with a look at the definition of terrorism. Mainstream media, Hollywood movies, and some politicians often portray terrorists as crazy dudes blowing stuff up. However, that's not entirely accurate. In truth, terrorism is a complex phenomenon that has been studied and debated for several decades. Further, there are many competing definitions of the term *terrorism*, not only among scholars but also among policymakers and government agencies. For example, according to the U.S. Department of State, the term "terrorism" means "premeditated, politically motivated violence perpetrated against non-combatant targets by sub-national groups or clandestine agents, usually intended to influence an audience."[1] Meanwhile, the Department of Justice defines terrorism as "the unlawful use of force or violence against persons or property to intimidate or coerce a Government, the civilian population, or any segment thereof, in furtherance of political or social objectives."[2] The distinction that the Department of State makes in referring to "politically motivated violence" is an important one, as it is a key reason why terrorism is considered different from other kinds of violent acts.

The political motivations behind acts of terrorism vary across a broad spectrum. Many terrorist groups have pursued goals that are common among the broader landscape of political insurgency or revolution, including sociopolitical control or regime change. Some have sought to establish a geopolitically separate identity (often referred to as nationalism or ethnonational self-determination), while others have tried to use terrorism to bring about the cessation of animal testing, deforestation, or abortion clinic services. Some terrorists pursue religiously oriented goals like imposing **Shari'a** (Islamic law) on a population or subjugating members of another faith, but these goals are still related to politics and power.[3] The challenge of finding a common definition of terrorism has been illustrated most prominently by decades of debate at the United Nations. For instance, while the United States and Western European nations usually endorse Israel's definition of Palestinian suicide bombers as terrorists, many Arab nations in the Middle East support the Palestinians' cause and argue that they are "freedom fighters" (another term used within the genre of political violence) or tend to use some other more benign label.

We have seen similar debates on a national or local level as well. Many Catholics in Northern Ireland refused to call the Provisional Irish Republican Army (Provisional IRA) terrorists, while many Protestants in Northern Ireland refused to call the Ulster Defence Association (UDA) or Ulster Volunteer Force (UVF) terrorists, when each of these groups were clearly responsible for significant terrorist violence for nearly half a century. The definitional debate has led some to suggest that terrorism should be considered a matter of perception, promoting the old adage that "one man's terrorist is another man's freedom fighter." However, I personally believe that freedom fighters or insurgents can certainly attempt to achieve their political objectives without resorting to terrorism.

Essentially, those of us who study terrorism have a variety of definitions to choose from. According to the eminent political scientist David Rapoport, "Terror is violence with distinctive properties used for political purposes both by private parties and states. That violence is unregulated by publicly accepted norms to contain violence, the rules of war, and the rules of punishment. Private groups using terror most often disregard the rules of war, while state terror generally disregards legally codified rules of punishment, i.e., those enabling us to distinguish guilt from innocence. But both states and non-state groups can ignore either set of rules."[4] Louise Richardson, another scholar whom I admire, explains that terrorist organizations have a political objective that they seek to obtain through violence or the threat of violence, and that the use of this violence is not really meant to defeat the enemy but to send a message through violent acts of symbolic significance that gain maximum attention to a cause.[5]

Professor Cindy Combs refers to terrorism as "a synthesis of war and theatre: a dramatization of violence which is perpetrated on innocent victims and played before an audience in the hope of creating a mode of fear without apology or remorse for political purposes."[6] And Bruce Hoffman, one of the most internationally respected scholars in this field, defines terrorism as "the deliberate creation and exploitation of fear through violence or the threat of violence in the pursuit of political change . . . [it is] designed to have far-reaching psychological effects beyond the immediate victim(s) or object of the terrorist attack . . . [and] to create power where there is none or to consolidate power where there is very little."[7] Hoffman also notes that certain aspects of various terrorism definitions are fundamental. For example, most definitions of terrorism include some political dimension (as demonstrated by many of the authors I have just mentioned). Most terrorists desire political change, but some terrorist groups are motivated by a desire to prevent political change and preserve the status quo. (We'll talk more about those kinds of groups in Lecture 10.) Further, states can also terrorize their citizens, and when this happens it's usually the case that political change is not desired.

Fundamental to most descriptions and definitions of terrorism is the notion that those who engage in it do not abide by conventional norms of warfare—rather, they intentionally target innocents (including off-duty military, law enforcement, or other government officials), and they seek to cause psychological trauma as much as (if not more than) death and damage. And of course, there are also criminal dimensions to terrorism as well. Terrorists kill, maim, and destroy, and it would be difficult to find a court of law anywhere in the civilized world that does not view these as crimes, regardless of motives or ultimate goals. Further, terrorists have also routinely engaged in money laundering, theft, fraud, extortion, smuggling (including drugs, weapons, and humans), bank robbery, and many other kinds of criminal activity.

Alex Schmid, another internationally respected senior scholar in this field, notes that criminal and terrorist organizations have much in common: both are rational actors, they produce victims, they use similar tactics such as kidnapping and assassination, they operate secretly, and both are pursued as criminals by the authorities of the state governments in which they operate.[8] However, in most definitions of terrorism, a common theme is that *motives matter*. For example, organizational crime expert Phil Williams distinguishes terrorist and criminal organizations by their motives: at the heart of terrorist organizations is the desire to bring about (or prevent) political change, while criminal organizations focus on profit generation and maximization.[9] Further, terrorist attacks should be seen as a sum total of activities that include fundraising, recruitment, training, development of special skills, and preparation for an attack—all of which can stretch over several months or even years. Criminal organizations focus much of their energies on protecting themselves from peer competitors or government and law enforcement agencies, and they pursue strategies to manage, avoid, control, or mitigate risk—but of course, many terrorist groups do this as well.[10] For the most part, the one aspect that distinguishes terrorists from other criminals is the political nature of the violence they inflict. Many see terrorism as the use or threat of violence to bring about change, and most often the kind of change terrorists seek is political in one way or another.

You can also see clear distinctions between terrorists and criminals in how they view money. As researcher Loretta Napoleani notes, criminal organizations run their operations like private corporations, with the accumulation of profit as the ultimate goal. In contrast, terrorist organizations are more interested in money disbursements than money laundering; instead of accumulation and profit maximization, money is to be distributed within the network of cells to support operations.[11] Overall, while terrorism is often considered a form of political violence, it is also seen by law enforcement professionals as a unique form of violent crime—unique primarily because of the motives behind it. However, a growing number of authors have also begun to suggest that the distinctions between organized crime and terrorism may be fading. For example, professor emeritus Walter Laqueur has argued that, 50 years ago, a clear dividing line existed between terrorism and organized crime, but that "more recently this line has become blurred, and in some cases a symbiosis between terrorism and organized crime has occurred that did not exist before."[12] Other scholars have described the phenomenon as a nexus, a confluence, a continuum or some other kind of paradigm involving fluid, constantly changing relationships among members of terrorist and criminal networks.[13] We'll discuss more about these evolving changes in the world of terrorism later in this lecture series.

In the late 1980s, Schmid and several of his European colleagues conducted a study involving hundreds of publications about terrorism, and found a number of common themes, shown in Table 1.1.

Based on this research, they offered a definition that attempts to capture most of what the scholarly community seems to agree on in its use of the term:

> Terrorism is an anxiety-inspiring method of repeated violent action, employed by (semi-) clandestine individual, group or state actors, for idiosyncratic, criminal or political reasons, whereby—in contrast to assassination—the direct targets of violence are not the main targets. The immediate human victims of violence are generally chosen randomly (targets of opportunity) or selectively

TABLE 1.1: Frequency of definitional elements in the study of terrorism

Concept/theme	How often it was part of definition (%)	Concept/theme	How often it was part of definition (%)
Violence, force	83.5	Arbitrariness; impersonal, random character	21
Political	65	Civilians, noncombatants, neutrals, outsiders as victims	17.5
Fear, terror emphasized	51	Intimidation	17
Threat	47	Innocence of victims emphasized	15.5
Psychological effects and anticipated reactions	41.5	Group, movement, organization as perpetrator	14
Victim-target differentiation	37.5	Symbolic aspect, demonstration to others	13.5
Purposive, planned, systematic, organized action	32	Incalculability, unpredictability, unexpectedness of occurrence of violence	9
Method of combat, strategy, tactic	30.5	Clandestine, covert nature	9
Extranormality, in breach of accepted rules, without humanitarian constraints	30	Repetitiveness; serial or campaign character of violence	7
Coercion, extortion, induction of compliance	28	Criminal	6
Public aspect	21.5	Demands made on third parties	4

Source: Alex P. Schmid, Albert J. Jongman, et al., *Political Terrorism: A New Guide to Actors, Authors, Concepts, Data Bases, Theories, and Literature* (Amsterdam: Transaction Books, 1988): 5–6.

(representative or symbolic targets) from a target population, and serve as message generators. Threat- and violence-based communication processes between terrorist (organization), (imperiled) victims, and main targets are used to manipulate the main target (audience(s)), turning it into a target of terror, a target of demands, or a target of attention, depending on whether intimidation, coercion, or propaganda is primarily sought.[14]

To me, this is a nice way of comprehensively representing the vast scholarship in the study of terrorism. Unfortunately, it is a bit too long and complicated to deliver in a standard classroom lecture. So, in my introductory lectures on terrorism, I typically draw on some version of the following as a working definition:

> **Terrorism is a combination of strategies and violent tactics in which the victims (e.g., ordinary citizens) are a sub-element of a broader target (e.g., a government). These strategies and tactics are used by individuals or groups in pursuit of some type of objectives—typically of a political, social, criminal, economic and/or religious nature—and they perceive terrorism to be the most effective way to *obtain the power* needed to achieve those objectives.**

Essentially, this definition reflects my own thinking that terrorism is to some degree a product of a basic unequal distribution of power on local, national, or global levels. This admittedly simplistic view of terrorism is underscored by a much broader and more important basic issue: the choice to engage in terrorism is driven by a belief that the present is inadequate, and thus something dramatic (using violent tactics) must be done to ensure a better future.

Thus, from political revolutionaries to religious militants, the results are similar in terms of their adoption of politically violent tactics as a means to achieve their objectives. Dissatisfaction with the status quo has led to terrorist group formation in Ireland, Italy, Egypt, Germany, Sri Lanka, Japan, Indonesia, the Philippines, the United States, and many other nations. Moreover, terrorism has proven effective in bringing about change, from the perspective of some observers. For example, supporters of Hizballah believe that terrorism drove the powerful United States (and later Israel) out of Lebanon, and Islamists believe that terrorist attacks convinced the French to pull out of Algeria. To understand terrorism requires, at some level, an ability to consider how terrorists view themselves and how they rationalize their behavior.

In many cases, individuals who carry out acts of terrorism are consumed by hatred toward others, and display a willingness and ability to kill without remorse or regard for those who may die from their terrorist acts.

A good deal of this animosity—particularly in the developing world—may stem from a perception that they have been victimized by corrupt governments, backed by powerful nations and multinational corporations, that have little concern for their lives, needs, or suffering. This results in widespread perceptions of helplessness (again, a lack of power) and

TO THE POINT

Terrorism has criminal, political and communicative dimensions.

hate, which can lay the groundwork for terrorist recruitment. However, it can also be said that hatred in the soul of the terrorist is a symptom of something deeper, a central dissatisfaction with one's place in this world vis-à-vis others.

The unequal distribution of power feeds a perception of "us versus them," a perception found in almost all ideologies associated with politically violent groups and movements. From William Potter Gale's rabid white supremacy radio shows in the United States to the firebrand imams in the mosques of Riyadh or Finsbury Park, London, the hardships and challenges "we" face can be framed in terms of what "they" are, or (more likely) what "they" have done to "us." From this perspective, "we" desire a redistribution of power in order to have more control over our destiny, and one could argue that many terrorist groups use violence as the way to bring this about.

A cursory look at the stated objectives of some of the world's more notorious terrorist groups exemplifies this view. Ethnic separatist groups like the Liberation Tigers of Tamil Eelam (LTTE, in Sri Lanka), the Abu Sayyaf Group (ASG, in the Philippines), and the Euzkadi ta Askatasuna (Basque Homeland and Freedom, or ETA, in Spain) all want the power to form their own recognized, sovereign entity, carved out of an existing nation-state. The Provisional IRA and its various dissident offshoots have tried to use terrorism to force the six counties of Northern Ireland to leave the U.K. and reunite with the rest of the Republic of Ireland. Groups engaged in the Middle East conflict against Israel—like the al-Aqsa Martyrs Brigade, Hamas, the Palestinian Islamic Jihad, and the People's Front for the Liberation of Palestine—want the power to establish an independent Palestinian state. Other groups have wanted the power to establish an Islamist government where they live, including Ansar al-Islam (in Iraq), the Armed Islamic Group (in Algeria), al-Gama'a al-Islamiyya (in Egypt), the Islamic

Movement of Uzbekistan (in Central Asia), and Jemmah Islamiyyah (in Southeast Asia). Terrorists like these groups seek the power to change the status quo and to forge a future that they do not believe will come about naturally. They have convinced themselves that acts of terrorism are necessary to achieve their objectives.

The pursuit of power to control resources can be seen in many terrorist campaigns. In seeking the power to decide what to do with a country's natural endowments—including land, oil, diamonds, water, etc.—some have resorted to terrorism as a tactic for compelling others into reluctant agreement with their preferred agenda. We've seen this kind of violence most recently in the Niger Delta region of Nigeria. Land is another important finite resource and source of conflict; indeed, a relatively tiny strip of land plays a key role in the deadly Middle East conflict. Both Palestinians and Jews focus on the "occupation" of "our land" by "the other." Zionist groups complain about the "evil forces who have become stronger in our Holy Land,"[15] while Palestinians focus on a history of Israeli forces entering villages and driving entire populations out into what became the refugee settlements in Gaza, the West Bank, Lebanon, Egypt, Jordan, and elsewhere. The powerful combination of a conflict over territory and an "us versus them" narrative framing that conflict remains the primary motivation for terrorism in this region.

Further, throughout its history, terrorism has also been used (by both Muslims and Jewish extremists) to disrupt the Middle East peace process. This is often referred to as a "spoiler" strategy of terrorism. For example, on November 4, 1995, Israel's Prime Minister Yitzhak Rabin was assassinated by Yigal Amir, a Jewish ultra-Orthodox student. Investigators found that Amir was convinced his attack was a necessary way of exacting God's retribution for Rabin's plan to evacuate a small settler enclave in Hebron as part of the Oslo Accords Rabin had signed with Yassir Arafat in 1993. As a result of the attack, the implementation of the accords was slowed and eventually abandoned, fueling a resurgence of violence on both sides of the conflict. A similar kind of "spoiler" terrorist attack occurred on August 15, 1998, when a car bomb killed 29 people in Omagh, Northern Ireland. The group responsible for the attack, the so-called Real Irish Republican Army (RIRA), was attempting to blow up the local courthouse and disrupt the peace process that had begun with the signing of the Good Friday Agreement earlier that year.

In sum, terrorism can be seen as a combination of strategies and tactics used in the pursuit of power to achieve some form of political, social, criminal, economic, religious, or other objective. At a most basic level, those with a comparatively greater position of power over others and over their own future typically have little incentive to use terrorism to achieve their goals. When one has power, one's goals can be achieved through other means. But the relatively powerless—engaged in a struggle with the powerful over resources, political and economic decisions, and the shape of their future—may resort to terrorism as a primary way to influence the evolution of history.

From this perspective, it is intuitive to suggest that only through the global spread of democracy—in which all groups, large and small, have equal opportunity to influence the course of future events—will we ever find a way to bring about the decline of terrorism. However, democracies require compromise, and it is here that the argument hits a stumbling block: in true democ-

Figure 1.1: The World Trade Center towers in New York City being struck by hijacked aircraft on September 11, 2001, attacks. Source: Flickr user Robert (TheMachineShop)

racies, small groups—particularly those with relatively unpopular social, political, or religious agendas—are often unable to achieve their objectives, and a willingness to compromise may not be among their core values in the first place.

This is a particularly worrisome factor in today's era of sacred terror, where terrorism is being used as a tactic for achieving an ideologically absolutist agenda without regard for the niceties of diplomatic negotiation or democratic compromise. For example, since the 1980s the United States has suffered numerous terrorist attacks by the Army of God, a loose underground network of Christian extremists committed to attacking abortion clinics and doctors. Members of this network are convinced that God wants them to use violence "in defense of the unborn child," and in this sense they are not much different from the jihadists of al-Qaeda who are convinced God wants them to use violence "in defense of the *umma* [global Muslim community]." In both cases, a negotiated settlement to their grievances seems virtually impossible. We'll examine this critical challenge of modern terrorism at several points throughout this lecture series.

THE STUDY OF TERRORISM

Obviously, the study of terrorism can get very complicated and confusing, especially because there are so many different kinds of terrorist groups, and gaining a solid understanding of each one requires studying its political goals, leaders, and sources of financial support, as well as the specific contexts from which it emerged. In short, there is no easy way to simplify the study of terrorism. In my courses on terrorism, as reflected in this book of lectures, most of my lessons focus on either attributes of the groups, or attributes of the environment in which they operate.[16] I also begin each semester with a review of key terms that one finds prominently in the terrorism studies literature. A handful of these are highlighted in bold type throughout this book. A glossary and additional online materials are available at: **www.TerrorismLectures.com.**

Attributes of Terrorist Organizations

When describing a typical terrorist organization, I usually begin with a look at what seems to motivate all terrorists: a **vision**. Terrorism is most often fueled by an individual's or group's vision of the future, a future which they believe cannot be achieved without resorting to violence. Further, as I mentioned a moment ago, individuals who embrace this kind of vision do not believe they have the **power** to bring about change or a vision of the future *without* resorting to violence. In some instances, terrorism is used in an attempt to gain the power to impact the policies of a government, or to decide the fate of a certain piece of land.

When a terrorist group describes its grievances and a strategy through which they can be addressed, we generally refer to this as the group's **ideology**. These terrorist group ideologies typically call for the use of various forms of violent action in the pursuit of objectives like establishing a utopian political system, religious governance, or an independent geopolitical entity based on ethnic identity. There are four primary types of terrorist ideologies that represent the majority of terrorist groups that have existed over the past century: ethnonationalist/separatist, left-wing, right-wing, and religious.[17]

Ethnonationalist terrorist groups usually have clear territorial objectives, like the liberation of a particular region of a country from a government that they view as oppressive and illegitimate. Groups in this category may draw their support from those who share their ethnic/racial background, even if they live elsewhere. Examples include the Tamil Tigers in Sri Lanka, the ETA in Spain, the PKK in Turkey, the Irish Republican Army, Chechens in Russia, and various Kashmir separatist groups. We'll focus on groups like these in Lecture 8.

Left-wing terrorists are usually driven by liberal or idealist political concepts that are anti-authoritarian, revolutionary, and sometimes anti-materialist. Groups in this category have typically targeted elites (business, government, etc.) who symbolize authority. Some examples include the Red Brigades of Italy, the Red Army Faction in Germany (also known as the Baader-Meinhof Group), and Sendero Luminoso (Shining Path) in Peru. We'll focus on groups like these in Lecture 9.

Next, there are the **right-wing** terrorists, whose violence is usually aimed against individuals of a particular race or ethnicity, and may be in reaction to perceived threats to the status quo. Examples include various white supremacist groups as well as certain groups that mix a religious (sometimes anti-Semitic) dimension with racial supremacy. We'll focus on groups like these in Lecture 10.

Finally, the largest proportion of active terrorist groups today adhere to some kind of **religious-oriented** ideology. Among the ideological categories that describe modern terrorism, religious ideologies are unique for many reasons. First, they provide a long-term view of history and the future, meaning that adherents come to believe they are taking part in an epic battle of good versus evil. Piety and persistence in the faith will give you the strength to overcome anything, and will lead to rewards in this life and the next (including for your family). Religious ideologies also draw on a common reliance on individuals with special intellectual gifts for interpreting sacred texts (imams, clergy, rabbis, etc.)—individuals who provide meaning for those seeking enlightenment, or who are pursuing an understanding of "what God wants from me." This, in turn, means extremist religious leaders have a particular opportunity to exploit the need of some people for religious guidance. Doing the bidding of a higher power demands sacrifice but also means fewer limits on violence. It's easier to kill if you think you're doing God's will—violence is seen as necessary in order to save oneself, one's family, or even the world from the forces of evil. Examples of religiously oriented terrorist groups are found among Shia and Sunni Islamist extremists, Jewish/Zionist extremists, and some Christian extremist groups in the United States and Europe. We'll focus on groups like these in Lectures 11 and 12.

Of course, there are several other types of terrorist groups as well, like anarchists, violent environmentalists (including the Earth Liberation Front), and animal rights extremists (including the Animal Liberation Front). And it should be remembered that several groups have drawn on ideological combinations (for example, a combination of right-wing and religious ideologies, or of left-wing and ethnonationalist ideologies). But the important point to make here is that a terrorist group's ideological orientation determines the kinds of members and funding they can attract, their strategic and tactical decisions, and of course the kinds of things they hope to achieve through their use of violence. For example, Army of God members attack abortion clinics and doctors, animal rights extremists attack research laboratories, and Palestinian groups attack Israeli targets. Table 1.2 offers a brief glimpse at the most active terrorist groups in the world today, many of which will be described in greater detail throughout this book.

Typically, a terrorist group's ideology will try to convince you that you have a **duty** to do something in support of its vision of the future—from providing financial or material support, to the most extreme **self-sacrifice** of so-called **martyrdom** (note that the term "martyrs" has been used by Catholics in Ireland, Buddhists in Sri Lanka, and the anti-abortion movement in the United States, as well as by Islamist extremists in the Middle East and elsewhere). Terrorism is seen by these groups as a **strategy** to achieve the objectives described in their ideology, while terrorist-related **tactics** can include a fairly broad range of violence, from suicide bombings or even the use of weapons of mass destruction (WMD), to kidnappings and beheadings, to flying passenger airplanes into tall buildings.

The ways in which the terrorist group mobilizes people and convinces them to support its strategy and tactics is often referred to as **radicalization**. Often, according to Stanford University psychologist Albert Bandura, this radicalization will involve a form of **moral disengagement**, a multistep psychological process that members of terrorist groups often go through.[18] First, the new recruit must acquire an ability to sanctify violence as honorable and righteous. He or she must also learn to minimize the consequences of violence, including the murder of others. This disregard for consequences makes it easier for a new terrorist recruit to hurt or kill innocent civilians in pursuit of the larger political objective. And finally, Bandura notes that people find violence easier if they don't consider their victims as human beings. We'll focus more on the psychological aspects of terrorist radicalization in Lectures 3 and 14.

Of course, it's not enough to develop a desire to be a terrorist—you also have to develop the skill to pull that trigger, manufacture that bomb, and so forth. We'll talk some more about this particular type of terrorist learning in Lecture 13, but an important thing to keep in mind here is that many terrorist organizations have shown the attributes of **learning organizations**—that is, they scan the environment, look for vulnerabilities in their enemies, examine successful terrorist practices of other groups, and incorporate this new knowledge into their own operations. Understanding this helps us avoid underestimating the capabilities of terrorists.

Terrorism is also considered by military and security specialists as a form of **asymmetric warfare** (AW) or **unconventional warfare** (UW) involving nonuniformed combatants. Earlier in this lecture, I described terrorism as a distinct form of **political violence** (as distinguished from criminally oriented violence) involving attacks in which the killing of civilians is not really the primary objective. That is, when a car bomb explodes in Baghdad or Kabul, the primary objective is not only or primarily just to kill a group of people. Instead, the terrorist group seeks to influence public opinion (including confidence in the government's ability to provide security); it wants to communicate a sense of power to supporters and to enemies, and often it wants to motivate new recruits or supporters to join its cause. From this perspective, terrorist attacks have also been described as **communicative acts**—in other words, the violent attacks are meant to communicate certain messages to various audiences, including enemies, supporters, potential supporters and constituents, and so forth.

Many terrorist groups try to portray themselves as a **vanguard**, a group of dedicated elite fighters heroically leading the way in liberating an oppressed people toward a better future. The terrorists' ideologies typically argue that they alone recognize the **"truth"** and because of this knowledge they are motivated to carry out violent terrorist actions. In some cases, like the white supremacist movement in the United States during the 1980s, and more recently the global Salafi-jihadist movement, the ideology is intended to promote a **"leaderless resistance"** campaign of terrorism, through which violent acts are carried out in support of the overall vision and goals, but without any formal group structure. As we'll discuss in Lecture 10, white supremacists in the United States developed this concept loosely, and violent Islamists have expanded it to promote a virtual "leaderless jihad" in which individuals can contribute to the cause by any means available to them, including orchestrating their own terrorist attacks on behalf of the global

TABLE 1.2: Partial list of the world's most active terrorist groups

Group	Brief Description
Abu Sayyaf Group (ASG)	Violent Islamist group founded in the early 1990s in southern Philippines; responsible for kidnappings and bombings
Al-Aqsa Martyrs Brigade (AAMS)	Palestinian nationalist group founded in the early 2000s; responsible for several suicide bombings against Israelis
Al-Qaeda (AQ)	Global jihadist terrorists with a "base" in the Afghanistan-Pakistan border region; group wants to re-establish an Islamic caliphate through the use of terrorism on a global scale
Al-Qaeda in the Arabian Peninsula (AQAP)	Local affiliate of global AQ jihadist movement in Yemen; linked to several recent terrorist plots against the United States
Al-Qaeda in the Islamic Maghreb (formerly GSPC)	Local affiliate of global AQ jihadist movement in Algeria and North Africa; responsible for several recent kidnappings
Al-Shabaab	Violent Islamist group in Somalia founded in the late 2000s; has used suicide bombings against many civilian targets
Aum Shinrikyo (AUM)	Japanese cult responsible for 1995 sarin nerve agent attack on the Tokyo subway
Basque Homeland and Freedom (ETA)	Ethnonationalist group in northern Spain and southern France, founded in the late 1950s; linked to bombings and assassinations over several decades; declared permanent ceasefire in 2011
Continuity Irish Republican Army (CIRA)	Ethnonationalist group founded in mid-1980s in Northern Ireland; dissident Republican group with few members
Hamas (Islamic Resistance Movement)	Violent Islamist and ethnonationalist group founded in the late 1980s in the Palestinian territories; responsible for many suicide bombings and rocket attacks; elected to power in Gaza Strip
Hizballah (Party of God)	Shiite Islamist group founded in Lebanon in the early 1980s; responsible for many suicide bombings; has members in senior positions throughout the government; fought war with Israel in 2006; also engaged in the Syrian conflict
Islamic State (IS)	Sunni militant group active in Syria and Iraq; also known as ISIS or ISIL; leader al-Baghdadi declared an Islamic caliphate and attracted thousands of foreign fighters to "defend" this territory; also inspired "DIY" terrorist attacks in Europe, Asia, and the U.S.
Jaish-e-Mohammed (JEM) (Army of Mohammed)	Violent Islamist and ethnonationalist group formed in Pakistan in the early 2000s; wants to unite Kashmir with Pakistan; also attacks foreign troops in Afghanistan
Jemaah Islamiyyah organization (JI)	Violent Islamist group founded in Indonesia during the mid-1990s; responsible for several major bombings; wants to establish an Islamic state in Southeast Asia

Group	Brief Description
Kahane Chai (Kach)	Zionist and racist terrorist group in Israel founded in the early 1990s; advocates killing or expelling all Arabs from the Palestinian Territories
Kongra-Gel (KGK, formerly Kurdistan Workers' Party, PKK, KADEK)	Ethnonationalist Kurdish group founded in the early 2000s with fighters in southern Turkey as well as parts of Iraq, Syria, and Iran; wants to establish a Kurdish state
Lashkar-e-Taiba (LT) (Army of the Righteous)	Violent Islamist and ethnonationalist group founded in the 1990s; wants to unite Kashmir with Pakistan; responsible for several terrorist attacks in India
Liberation Tigers of Tamil Eelam (LTTE)	Ethnonationalist Tamil group founded in Sri Lanka during the mid-1960s; pioneered suicide bombing tactics throughout the 1990s; militarily defeated in 2009
National Liberation Army (ELN)	Left-wing Marxist revolutionary group in Colombia; founded in the mid-1960s; very active in kidnapping and extortions
Popular Front for the Liberation of Palestine (PFLP)	Left-wing Marxist revolutionary group in the Palestinian Territories; founded in the late 1960s
Real IRA (RIRA)	Ethnonationalist group in Northern Ireland; dissident Republican group with few members; founded in the late 1990s; responsible for the 1998 Omagh bombing
Revolutionary Armed Forces of Colombia (FARC)	Originally Marxist revolutionary group founded in Colombia during the mid-1960s; signed a peace agreement with the government in 2016
Shining Path (Sendero Luminoso, SL)	Left-wing Marxist revolutionary group in Peru founded during the late 1960s; mostly destroyed with the capture of leader Abimael Guzmán in 1992, but several attacks in recent years have been blamed on the group
Tehrik-i-Taliban Pakistan (TTP)	Also known as the "Pakistani Taliban," founded in the late 2000s; promotes attacks against Pakistan and NATO-led forces in Afghanistan; took credit for 2010 attempted terrorist attack in Times Square in New York City

Sources: Bureau of Counterterrorism, U.S. State Department, "Designated Foreign Terrorist Organizations," https://www.state.gov/j/ct/rls/other/des/123085.htm (accessed May 15, 2017); and the National Counterterrorism Center, "Terrorist Groups" https://www.dni.gov/nctc/groups.html (accessed May 15, 2017).

jihadist movement with no direct ties to any formal terrorist group leaders or affiliated cells. We will examine this version of leaderless resistance more in Lectures 12 and 15.

Finally, when describing terrorism in general, I sometimes use the term **psychological warfare**, which according to the U.S. Department of Defense involves actions that are meant to influence the emotions, motives, objective reasoning, and (ultimately) the behavior of foreign governments, organizations, groups, and individuals. From the perspective of terrorists or insurgents engaged in asymmetric warfare against a government, a major target of these operations will be the population's support of its government. Thus, terrorism requires an ability to influence beliefs, a focus of efforts that I call **influence warfare**.

Attributes of the Terrorist Groups' Operating Environments

While the study of terrorism is focused quite a lot on the groups themselves, there is also an important area of research which looks at the environments in which these groups emerge and sustain themselves. For many years now, my own research in this area has examined the nature of ideological resonance, a term which describes the degree to which members of a particular population find a terrorist group's ideology appealing. A resonating ideology can influence an individual's willingness to embrace terrorism as a reasonable course of action, and is essential for the success of any terrorist group or movement; if their vision of the future appeals to nobody, there will be no radicalization, no financial support or recruitment, and the movement will die on the vine.

To understand why a terrorist group's ideology resonates, we have to examine the kind of political, social, economic, religious, or other insecurities and **grievances** that a local population may have and that are used by the terrorist group to rationalize the use of violent acts. We will cover these topics in depth in Lectures 3 through 7, but to give just a summary here, an ideology may resonate among a particular community due to a broad range of political issues like incompetent, authoritarian, or corrupt governments, as well as economic issues like widespread poverty or unemployment. In many instances, the political and socioeconomic grievances that lead to terrorism are tied to a government's **legitimacy**, or lack thereof. As Ted Robert Gurr has noted, the legitimacy of a government can be severely undermined by a range of things, like widespread injustice or a major gap between the aspirations of a population and the opportunities for them to achieve those aspirations.[19]

Political repression is clearly an important structural element beneath the unequal distribution of power I described earlier. When a government exhibits outright hostility and commits open violence against members of its citizenry, this represents a form of the powerful subjugating the relatively powerless. Many corrupt governments around the world seek to maintain and increase their power over others (and over resources) by any means necessary, while the powerless see the corruption and look for ways to combat it—even through violent acts of terrorism. In essence, when a government fails to uphold a fair and honest social contract between the state and its citizens, people become angry and may often seek the power to force change; this, in turn, has led to a variety of revolutionary and terrorist movements throughout history.

Some of the literature in the field of terrorism studies has used terms like **root causes** to describe these and other kinds of grievances, but in my view the overall root cause of terrorism is most often an individual's decision to pull that trigger, hijack that plane, detonate that bomb, and so forth. Decisions like these are influenced by a wide range of contexts and perspectives that must be appreciated in order to truly understand terrorism. For example, poverty and unemployment don't "cause" terrorism, but they can certainly influence a person's decisions about the legitimacy of a terrorist movement's ideology and actions. Actually, most of the research on so-called root causes really just seeks to find meaningful relationships between certain historical, cultural, economic, and sociopolitical characteristics of the larger society and the occurrence of terrorism. These characteristics could help create an **enabling environment** for a terrorist group to capitalize on what Harvard University psychologist John Mack describes as "a reservoir of misery, hurt, helplessness and rage from which the foot soldiers of terrorism can be recruited."[20]

Other so-called "root causes" are actually **facilitators** of terrorism and can include things like easy access to weapons, financial support, and safe haven. Weak or **failed states** can also facilitate terrorism, particularly in places where the government's authority is routinely challenged and undermined by a variety of violent nonstate actors.[21] These are countries in which a weak central government is unable to provide adequate **human security** to all segments of its population, creating an environment that can serve as a conduit for radicalization and terrorism.[22] In weak states, the absence of rule of law or peaceful ways to resolve conflict can lead those seeking power to use violent means to achieve their objectives. In many weak states, where security can be readily purchased by the highest bidder, the powerful do what they want, while the powerless are made to do their bidding.

The challenge of state weakness is now explicitly recognized in U.S. national security circles as a strategic problem almost equal in importance to state competitors. As the 2002 *National Security Strategy of the United States* notes, "America is now threatened less by conquering states than we are by failing ones."[23] The 2015 *National Security Strategy* echoes this by emphasizing the "security consequences associated with weak or failing states."[24] And most recently, the 2017 *National Security Strategy* points to the concern that "Transnational threat organizations, such as jihadist terrorists and organized crime, often operate freely from fragile states."[25] It is certainly no coincidence that a significant number of terrorist plots and attacks against the United States and its allies have been linked to places like Yemen, Somalia, and Afghanistan. These are also the same kind of environments in which we find a strong presence of organized criminal networks, which I'll talk more about in Lecture 6.

Finally, the ability for a society to resist and deflect the terrorist group's efforts to coerce their behavior and beliefs depends largely on its **resilience** in the face of violent attacks or the continual threats thereof. The more resilient a society proves to be, the less likely any terrorist group will achieve its core goals of coercing that society through fear and the threat of violence. In other words, a society that refuses to panic or over-react to terrorism is unlikely to give in to the demands of the terrorists. While the complex topic of countering terrorism will be addressed in a different volume of lectures (forthcoming), it is important to mention this resilience issue here because it is one of the fundamental challenges that a terrorist group faces when trying to achieve its objectives.

SUMMARY

To sum up this introductory lecture, defining terrorism is clearly not a simple, straightforward task. As we delve deeper into the contested terrain of terrorism studies, you will be encouraged to formulate your own personal definition and description of terrorism. Further, the study of terrorism has become more complicated than in decades past. Because of the global nature of transportation, financial, and communication networks, and media, terrorists can now wage campaigns on a global scale, particularly if they effectively exploit new communications technologies like the Internet. During the 1980s and '90s, terrorist group recruiters would use CDs and DVDs as part of their indoctrination efforts. However, they still relied largely on conventional media to get national or international news coverage of the attacks they conducted. The Internet changed all that, through the ease of distributing videos—even of nearly real-time events—worldwide, as well as the widespread use of social media and discussion boards to create virtual communities of ideologically aligned "true believers." Further, the Internet has enabled a whole new kind of information gathering by the terrorists, particularly in open societies—they can monitor changes in government security procedures (including information on what airport screeners might be looking for), gather details of transit systems or important government buildings, and get information on how the public is responding to terrorist attacks or the government's response. We'll take a closer look at the relationship between terrorism and the Internet in Lecture 7.

However, amid the many changes we have seen over the years, a fundamental element of modern terrorism is really not all that new: taking instruments from daily life—the backpack, the car, the shoe, the cellphone—and turning them into weapons. Their overall goal here is to damage the trust necessary for an open society to function effectively. We find ourselves looking suspiciously at someone wearing a backpack on a subway train; we have to remove our shoes at airport checkpoints; we can buy cellphones in a convenience store that can be used as a bomb detonator. And while the typical Hollywood portrayal of a terrorist is a wide-eyed, crazy-haired male between the age of 18 and 35, the reality is much different: terrorist groups have been increasingly using women and even children to carry out their lethal attacks. There is no real "profile" of a terrorist. As we'll discuss in Lectures 7 and 14, potentially anyone can be radicalized, indoctrinated, and taught why and how to murder others in pursuit of some broader vision. This is a key challenge for confronting terrorism in today's world.

Overall, there is clearly much to study in the world of terrorism, including the characteristics of terrorist groups and those who join them, which is what we'll look at in the next couple of lectures and in Part III of this volume. We also have to look beyond violent actions and goals, to include the role of perceptions and beliefs that sustain terrorists' ideological resonance, as we'll discuss at various points throughout this book. But first, in the next lecture, we'll take a brief journey through the history of modern terrorism.

QUESTIONS FOR DISCUSSION

- What are the most central elements to any definition of terrorism?
- Why are there so many different definitions of terrorism?
- Why is there not even a common definition across all U.S. organizations?
- How are strategies of terrorism different from tactics of terrorism?
- What is the relationship between "root causes" of terrorism and facilitators of terrorism?
- How is the nature of terrorist violence different from other kinds of political or criminal violence?

RECOMMENDED READING

Abrahms, Max. "What Terrorists Really Want." *International Security* 32, no. 4 (Spring 2008): 78–105.

Ahmad, Eqbal. "Terrorism: Theirs & Ours." In *Terrorism and Counterterrorism*. Edited by Russell Howard and Bruce Hoffman. New York: McGraw-Hill, 2011.

Combs, Cindy C. *Terrorism in the Twenty-First Century*. New Jersey: Prentice Hall, 2003.

Crenshaw, Martha. 2017. "The Strategic Logic of Terrorism." In *Conflict After the Cold War: Arguments on Causes of War and Peace*. Edited by Richard K. Betts. New York: Routledge: 448–61. http://bit.ly/2xbjkTo.

Crenshaw, Martha and Gary LaFree. "Pinning Down and Elusive Adversary: What Is a Terrorist Organization?" *Countering Terrorism: No Simple Solutions*. Brookings Institution Press, 2017: 99–130.

Crenshaw, Martha. *Explaining Terrorism: Causes, Processes and Consequences*. London: Routledge, 2010.

Crenshaw, Martha. "The Logic of Terrorism: Terrorist Behavior as a Product of Strategic Choice." In *Terrorism and Counterterrorism*. Edited by Russell Howard and Bruce Hoffman. New York: McGraw-Hill, 2011.

Eidelson, Roy and Judy Eidelson. "Dangerous Ideas: Five beliefs that propel groups toward conflict." *American Psychologist* 58 (2003).

Fanon, Frantz. *The Wretched of the Earth*. Translated by Richard Philcox. New York: Grove Press, 1963.

Forest, James J. F. "Introduction to the Root Causes of Terrorism." In *The Making of a Terrorist*. Vol. 3. Edited by James J. F. Forest. Westport, CT: Praeger, 2005.

Hoffman, Bruce. *Inside Terrorism*. New York: Columbia University Press, 2006.

Howard, Russell and Bruce Hoffman, eds. *Terrorism and Counterterrorism: Understanding the New Security Environment*. 4th ed. McGraw-Hill, 2011.

Horgan, John and Kurt Braddock, eds. *Terrorism Studies: A Reader*. London: Routledge, 2011.

Kydd, Andrew H. and Barbara F. Walter. "The Strategies of Terrorism," *International Security* 31, no. 1 (Summer 2006): 49–80.

Moghadam, Assaf. *The Roots of Terrorism*. New York: Chelsea House, 2006.

Moghadam, Assaf, Ronit Berger, and Polina Beliakova. "Say Terrorist, Think Insurgent: Labeling and Analyzing Contemporary Terrorist Actors." *Perspectives on Terrorism* 8, no. 5 (2014).

Richards, Anthony. "Conceptualizing Terrorism." *Studies in Conflict & Terrorism* 37, no. 3 (2014): 213–36.

Richardson, Louise. *What Terrorists Want*. New York: Random House, 2007.

Schmid, Alex P. "Frameworks for Conceptualizing Terrorism." *Terrorism and Political Violence* 16, no. 2 (2004).

Schmid, Alex P. "Revised Academic Definitions of Terrorism." In *Handbook of Terrorism Research*. London, Routledge (2011): 86–87.

Silke, Andrew. *Research on Terrorism: Trends, Achievements and Failures*. London: Routledge, 2004.

Stern, Jessica. "A Protean Enemy." *Foreign Affairs* 82, no. 4 (July/August 2003).

Tilley, Charles. *The Politics of Collective Violence*. Cambridge University Press, 2003.

Weinberg, Leonard, Ami Pedahzur, and Sivan Hirsch-Hoefler. "The Challenges of Conceptualizing Terrorism." *Terrorism and Political Violence* 16, no. 4 (2004).

Weinberg, Leonard and William L. Eubank. "Twenty-First Century Insurgencies: The Use of Terrorism as a Strategy." *Countering Terrorism and Insurgency in the 21st Century*. Vol. 1. Edited by James J. F. Forest. Westport, CT: Praeger, 2007.

Weinberg, Leonard, Ami Pedahzur, and Sivan Hirsh-Hoefler. "The Challenges of Conceptualizing Terrorism." *Terrorism and Political Violence* 16, no. 4 (2004).

WEBSITES

National Consortium for the Study of Terrorism and Responses to Terrorism
http://www.start.umd.edu/

National Counterterrorism Center
https://www.nctc.gov/

National Institute of Justice, Research on Radicalization and Terrorism
https://nij.gov/topics/crime/terrorism/pages/welcome.aspx

Perspectives on Terrorism
http://www.terrorismanalysts.com/pt

RAND Corporation, research on terrorism and homeland security
https://www.rand.org/pubs/online/terrorism-and-homeland-security.html

Sentinel—a journal by the Combating Terrorism Center at West Point
https://www.ctc.usma.edu/publications/sentinel

St. Andrews U., Handa Center for the Study of Terrorism and Political Violence
https://www.st-andrews.ac.uk/~cstpv/

START Global Terrorism Database
http://www.start.umd.edu/gtd/

UML Center for Terrorism and Security Studies
http://www.uml.edu/research/ctss

NOTES

1. 22 U.S.C. § 2656f(d). Cited in *United States Department Patterns of Global Terrorism, 1999* (Washington, DC: Dept. of State Publication, April 2000): viii.

2. See paragraph (l) of 28 C.F.R. § 0.85, available at https://www.law.cornell.edu/cfr/text/28/0.85.

3. However, Charles Tilly also asserts that terror denotes a conflict strategy that may pursue a "distinct extra-political goal." See Charles Tilly, "Violence, Terror, and Politics as Usual," *Boston Review* 27, no. 3–4 (2002).

4. David C. Rapoport, "Before the Bombs There Were the Mobs: American Experiences with Terror," *Terrorism and Political Violence* 20, no. 2 (2008): footnote 12.

5. Louise Richardson, *What Terrorists Want* (New York: Random House, 2007): 4–5.

6. Cindy C. Combs, *Terrorism in the Twenty-First Century* (New Jersey: Prentice Hall, 2003).

7. Bruce Hoffman, *Inside Terrorism* (New York: Columbia University Press, 2006): 40–41.

8. Alex P. Schmid, "The Links between Transnational Organized Crime and Terrorist Crimes," *Transnational Organized Crime* 2, no. 2 (1996): 66–67.

9. Phil Williams, "Strategy for a New World: Combating Terrorism and Transnational Organized Crime," in *Strategy in the Contemporary World*, ed. John Baylis, et al. (Oxford University Press, 2007): 195–96.

10. Ibid., 196.

11. Loretta Napoleoni, "The New Economy of Terror: How Terrorism is Financed," *Forum on Crime and Society* 4, nos. 1 and 2 (2004): 31–33.

12. Walter Laqueur, *The New Terrorism* (Oxford University Press, 1999): 211.

13. Tamara Makarenko, "The Ties that Bind: Uncovering the Relationship between Organized Crime and Terrorism," in *Global Organized Crime: Trends and Developments*, ed. Dina Siegel, Henk Van De Bunt, and Damian Zaitch (Dordrecht: Kluwer, 2003): 159–70; R. T. Naylor, *Wages of Crime: Black Markets, Illegal Finance and the Underworld of Economy* (Ithaca, NY: Cornell University Press, 2002): 44–87; Chris Dishman, "Terrorism, Crime and Transformation," *Studies of Conflict and Terrorism* 24, no. 1 (2001): 43–58; Thomas M. Sanderson, "Transnational Terror and

Organized Crime: Blurring the Lines," *SAIS Review* 24, no. 1 (2004): 49–61; John T. Picarelli, "The Turbulent Nexus" (2006); Rachel Ehrenfeld, *Funding Evil: How Terrorism is Financed, and How to Stop It* (Chicago: Bonus Books, 2003); Louise Shelley and John Picarelli "The Diversity of the Crime-Terror Interaction," *International Annals of Criminology* 43 (2005): 51–81; Louise Shelley and John Picarelli, "Organized Crime and Terrorism," in *Terrorism Financing and State Responses: A Comparative Perspective*, ed. Jeanne Giraldo and Harold Trinkunas (Stanford: Stanford University Press, 2007): 39–55.

14. Alex P. Schmid, Albert J. Jongman, et al., *Political Terrorism: A New Guide to Actors, Authors, Concepts, Data Bases, Theories, and Literature* (Amsterdam: Transaction Books, 1988): 5–6.

15. See Allan C. Brownfeld, "Religious Zionism: A Growing Impediment To Middle East Peace," *Washington Report on Middle East Affairs* 21, no. 9 (2002): 71.

16. I also teach courses on counterterrorism. Lectures from those courses are forthcoming.

17. For descriptions of these and other terrorist ideological categories, along with profiles of groups that are typically categorized within each, see the Terrorist Organization Profiles website at http://goo.gl/416or.

18. See Albert Bandura, "Training for Terrorism through Selective Moral Disengagement," in *The Making of a Terrorist*, vol. 2, ed. James J. F. Forest (Westport, CT: Praeger, 2005): 34–50.

19. Ted Robert Gurr, *Why Men Rebel* (Princeton, NJ: Princeton University Press, 1970).

20. John E. Mack, "Deeper Causes: Exploring the Role of Consciousness in Terrorism," *Ions Noetic Sciences Review* (2003): 13.

21. See James J. F. Forest and Matthew V. Sousa, *Oil and Terrorism in the New Gulf* (Lanham, MD: Lexington, 2006), particularly Chapters 3, 4 and 9.

22. For more on the relationship between human security and terrorism, please see Cindy R. Jebb and Madelfia A. Abb, "Human Security and Good Governance: A Living Systems Approach to Understanding and Combating Terrorism," in *The Making of a Terrorist*, vol. 3, ed. Forest.

23. The White House, "Overview of America's International Strategy," *The National Security Strategy of the United States of America* (September 2002), http://georgewbush-whitehouse.archives.gov/nsc/nss/2002/.

24. The White House, *The National Security Strategy of the United States of America* (February 2015), http://nssarchive.us/national-security-strategy-2015/.

25. The White House, *The National Security Strategy of the United States of America* (December 2017), https://www.whitehouse.gov/wp-content/uploads/2017/12/NSS-Final-12-18-2017-0905.pdf.

2

Surfing the Historical "Waves" of Terrorism

In this lecture, we will briefly explore some early historical examples and then discuss David Rapoport's widely popular categorization of the "four waves" of terrorism over the past 130 years, before taking a brief look at some common elements of modern terrorism. To begin with, it is important to remember that the phenomenon of terrorism has been with us for a very long time. During the first century A.D., Jewish Zealots (sometimes called Zealots-Sicarii) murdered Romans in broad daylight in Jerusalem. During the eleventh and twelfth centuries, a Shiite Muslim sect in Persia known as the Hashashin were widely feared for their ability to attack their enemies either covertly or in broad daylight, usually using a small blade like a dagger. And throughout the Indian subcontinent beginning in the thirteenth century, members of a religious cult known as Thuggee (or Thugs), strangled and robbed travelers in a ritual sacrifice that they believed pleased their Hindu goddess Kali.[1]

Other early historical examples include a form of state terrorism developed by the revolutionary French Republic during the time of Robespierre, whose "lists" of potential enemies of the state and revolutionary tribunals were responsible for many people meeting the guillotine. Here, the goal was to rule the masses by fear and terror—in fact, the word "terrorism" is considered by many to have originated from this period. Of course, it is interesting to note that eventually, Robespierre was seen to be keeping too many such "lists" and powerful people who were afraid of appearing on one of them decided to arrange his own meeting with the guillotine.

Another form of state terrorism was seen more recently in Iraq, when during the 1990s Saddam Hussein used chemical weapons to subdue an uprising among Kurdish villages in the north. The overall objective of these attacks was not simply to kill Kurds, but rather, to terrorize all the other Kurdish villages and prevent them from objecting to Hussein's rule. As an aside, events like these reflect how states can certainly *terrorize*—that is, use the strategy and tactics of terrorism—and yet we do not refer to them as *terrorists*, which is a term that conventionally applies only to nonstate actors.

Turning to the history of the United States, early examples of terrorism can be seen in the actions of the "Sons of Liberty"—provoked by the Stamp Act, they organized mobs to tar and feather colonists loyal to the king, forcing many to flee the country and settle in Canada. And more recently, during the nineteenth and twentieth centuries, the Ku Klux Klan built a fearsome reputation for its violent atrocities, and forced the federal government to end Reconstruction efforts in the South.[2]

FOUR WAVES: A BRIEF HISTORY OF TERRORISM

Let's turn now to the eminent political scientist David Rapoport, who has organized a popular historical analysis of terrorism. His research describes how modern terrorism can be conceptualized through the framework of four successive overlapping "waves": the "anarchist" wave began in the 1880s and was basically completed by the 1920s; the "anti-colonial" wave succeeded it and lasted until the 1960s; a "New Left" wave (the rise of left-wing revolutionary Communist/Marxist groups) then began and was virtually over by 2000; and the "religious" wave began in 1979 (inspired in part by the Islamic revolution in Iran) and continues through today.[3] Each completed wave lasted approximately a generation, or about 40 years. However, no credible scholars today believe the current wave of religious terrorism will end any time soon. We'll discuss this further in Lectures 11 and 12.

Let's take a few moments and surf these waves. As we do, I'd like you to focus on a few themes: (1) different ideologies or doctrines, (2) changes in technologies used for weapons and for communication/propaganda, and (3) changes in how terrorists receive funding and support. Finally, please keep in mind that a few groups, like the

Irish Republican Army and its splinter groups, have transcended the timelines associated with these waves.

First we have the **anarchists**, who were mostly active from the 1880s through the 1920s. The overall objective of their violent attacks was to provoke governments to the point where a reaction (or often, an oppressive overreaction) led to a popular revolt. One of the earliest examples of anarchist violence comes from Russia, where in 1861 Czar Alexander II decreed all serfs (one-third of Russia's population) to be free, and promised funds so they could purchase land. Unfortunately, he was unable to provide those funds. Raised expectations among the masses weren't met, and this led to widespread anger, disappointment, unrest, violence, and assassinations.

Anarchists, in general, believe that formal governments of any kind are harmful and unnecessary, and that all human interaction should be organized by voluntary associations. This is the era during which an influential Russian anarchist named Pyotr Kropotkin gave us one of the most lasting depictions of terrorist attacks as "propaganda by the deed"—the idea that the attention-grabbing actions of the anarchists would boost the popularity of the movement's political ideas. In his books and articles, he urged people to engage in so-called "revolutionary action" in order to inspire the masses. He believed that when the government responded to these actions with violence, it would lead more individuals to join the revolution. Another influential anarchist during the mid-1880s—Johann Most—published *The Science of Revolutionary Warfare*, a handbook providing detailed instructions for individuals to engage in the kinds of actions Kropotkin felt would benefit the anarchist movement.[4]

Anarchists were responsible for the assassination of Spanish Prime Minister Antonio Cánovas del Castillo in 1897, and the assassination of U.S. President William McKinley in 1901, among several other such high profile attacks. In the United States, a series of bombings, riots, and strikes in 1919 led the government to round up and deport hundreds of anarchists and other radical extremists. Anti-American speech had been made illegal a year earlier, through the Sedition Act of 1918, which basically made it illegal to give speeches that were highly critical of the government. The use of undercover informants and other measures were taken to address the security situation, in many cases violating the kinds of civil liberties that we largely take for granted today. It's important that we look back on that era, almost 100 years ago, and remind ourselves about these kinds of reactions to the threat of terrorism.

The technology that these anarchist groups had available to them during this period was relatively primitive by today's standards, but the telegraph, daily newspapers, and railroads were instrumental for their communication and transportation needs. In terms of financing, most anarchists relied on basic criminal activity, like bank robberies and extortion. Because of the nature of their ideologies, it was obviously difficult to get any sort of state sponsorship. The weapons used during this time were mostly guns and knives, but those that could afford it used dynamite (invented in 1866 by Alfred Nobel—you may have heard of his Peace Prize). The handbook published by Most in 1885, mentioned above, placed considerable emphasis on the use of dynamite as "a formidable weapon against every kind of paramilitary, policeman or detective who suppresses the cry for justice."[5] In fact, as David Rapoport has noted, the invention of dynamite made modern terrorism possible.[6]

Here's a trivia question I like to ask each semester: Where and when do you think the first vehicle-borne improvised explosive device (or "car bomb") terrorist attack occurred? Each year the most common answers include Hamas, Hizballah, and the Middle East. But you'd probably be surprised to learn that actually, the first major attack of this sort took place in New York City in September 1920. Okay, so it was a horse-drawn wagon instead of a car, but the concept is still the same. In this attack, an Italian anarchist named Mario Buda parked his wagon—packed with dynamite and iron slugs—at the corner of Wall and Broad streets (directly across from J.P. Morgan & Co.), and then disappeared into the lunchtime crowd. The bomb exploded at precisely noon in a fireball of shrapnel, killing nearly 40 people and wounding more than 150.[7] His motivation was revenge against the government and elites for the recent arrest of several fellow anarchists, and he was quite disappointed to learn that his primary target—J. P. Morgan himself—was not in the office when the bomb went off.

I also like to ask students to guess when and where the second car bomb terrorist attack occurred. As before, the common answers focus mainly on Islamist extremists, and people are surprised to hear that actually it was a Jewish extremist group that in January 1947 drove a truckload of explosives into a British police station in Haifa (now Israel), killing four and injuring 140. In this instance, members of the militant group Lehi (also known as the Stern Gang, a fascist-like splinter group led by Avraham Stern that broke away from the right-wing Zionist paramilitary group Irgun) were trying to drive the British out of the region. (They would soon use truck and car bombs to kill Palestinians as well, as part of their extremist agenda.)

This leads us to the second "wave" in David Rapoport's historical framework: the **anti-colonial wave**, which took place roughly from the 1920s through the 1960s. Throughout Latin America and Asia, groups in this era used terrorist violence against a

Figure 2.1: Wall Street bombing of 1920.

colonial power. Their ideologies were typically focused on gaining the power to decide their own form of government—the same kind of motivation that led to attacks by the Stern Gang I mentioned a moment ago in what was then Palestine.

One of the most poignant literary contributions of this era is found in the writings of Frantz Fanon, a French psychiatrist whose 1961 book, *The Wretched of the Earth*, argues that Western powers had dehumanized non-Western people by destroying their cultures and replacing them with Western values. As a result, colonized masses suffered a perpetual identity crisis and were forced to deny their heritage. The only course of action possible, then, was guerrilla warfare revolution. *In other words, he argued, achieving freedom is an inherently violent process.* To Fanon, violence had a specific purpose: to terrorize Western-ers and their followers into submission. Urban terror was intended to create mayhem, and all terrorism was to be excessively brutal in order to communicate a sense of determina-tion and provoke fear. The violence was also meant to help psychologically liberate people from oppressive colonialism: "At the level of individuals, violence is a cleansing force. It frees the native from his inferiority complex and from his despair and inaction."[8]

During the early 1950s, Fanon moved to Algeria and eventually joined the National Liberation Front (FLN), a group of self-proclaimed freedom fighters who wanted liberation from French colonial rule. In 1956, the group's leader—Abane Ramdane— launched a campaign of terrorist attacks in the nation's capital, Algiers. His overall strategic intent was to attract attention, polarize Algerian society, disrupt the lives of the tens of thousands of French settlers in the city, provoke the French colonial government to overreact with force, and eventually undermine its claim to legitimacy as a benign colonial power.[9]

Terrorist attacks in cafes and marketplaces did provoke a brutal French reaction, involving disappearances, torture, and executions. And while the French army won the so-called Battle of Algiers in 1957 (about which there is a compelling movie that I have shown students in my class), the populations of both Algeria and France were appalled at the way victory was achieved, resulting in massive public debates about the moral legitimacy of French control over Algeria. Less than five years later, France's President Charles de Gaulle announced Algeria would be granted its independence. Fanon's writings on using violence as a strategy to bring about change drew significantly on his experiences with FLN during this period, and were influential for many terrorist groups throughout the latter half of the twentieth century.

The strategy of using terrorism to provoke a government overreaction is thus something we see in both the anarchist wave and the anti-colonial wave. However, compared to the anarchists, there were fewer assassinations during the period of anti-colonial terrorism, with groups opting instead to attack primarily police, military, and colonial government targets. The changes in technology during this period included faster means of communication, transportation, and money transfers. And financial support for these groups often came from diaspora members, people from the colony who had moved to more developed Western countries and sent money back home to support the struggle.

A few ethnonationalist groups were also launched during this period, including the Irish Republican Army. After a lengthy anti-colonial war against the British, the Anglo-Irish Treaty of 1921 divided Ireland into two separate states, the pro-U.K. (and predominately Protestant) Northern Ireland, and the independent (and mainly Catholic) Republic of Ireland. A civil war began shortly thereafter in the Republic of Ireland between pro-treaty and anti-treaty factions, which was won by the former. Meanwhile, those Catholics who remained in Northern Ireland became increasingly disenchanted with Protestant Home Rule, and over time the conditions became ripe for a militant pro-Catholic movement to emerge. More on this group, and on ethnonationalist terrorism in general, will be covered in Lecture 8.

During the early 1960s, according to Rapoport, a **New Left wave** (also sometimes called a leftist anti-Western sentiment wave) of terrorism emerged. To understand why, we first need to look at the historical context. We're talking about the latter half of the twentieth century, so one of the main factors influencing this era is the Cold War, and particularly the Soviet Union's commitment to the spread of communism. In fact, the Soviets provided covert support to a number of Marxist and left-wing terrorist groups during these years. This time period also saw the rise of several decolonization conflicts, including the French in Southeast Asia and Algeria, the Americans in Southeast Asia, and the British in East Africa.

From the 1940s to the early 60s, successful revolutionary movements were led by Mao Zedong in China, Ho Chi Minh in Vietnam, and Fidel Castro in Cuba. Mao Zedong was particularly influential during this time period because of the way he orchestrated the revolution in China. He articulated the concept of a "People's War," in which inferior forces overcome superior ones. He articulated the need to unite the oppressed classes, to forge an alliance between peasants and the working class, who then go on to lead the revolution. His approach was to some degree focused on creating the conditions for a revolution, and he was convinced of the need to first build up support among the rural masses in the countryside, a process which could take several years. Nonetheless, his thoughts on revolutionary warfare and political organization, generally referred to as Maoism, have been instrumental to many insurgent movements that followed, especially Sendero Luminoso in Peru, and several groups in India and Nepal.

There were also several Latin American and African civil wars during this time period, along with various political movements in the 1960s that spawned extreme left-wing activist groups, some of whom turned to violence. The late 1950s into the early 1960s were also the years of prominence for one of the most influential revolutionaries of the century: Ernesto "Che" Guevara. Like Mao, Guevara was also a revolutionary Marxist. He was born and raised in Argentina, but as a young medical student he began to travel throughout Latin America. During these travels, he became convinced that the region's economic problems were caused by capitalism, neocolonialism and imperialism, with the only remedy being world revolution. Che became involved in several revolutionary movements throughout Latin America, and helped Fidel Castro in his insurgency against the Batista regime in Cuba, after which he published some of his "lessons learned." However, in contrast to Mao's concept of a "People's War," Che articulated what he called the "Foco theory of revolution," in which a vanguard of small, fast-moving paramilitary groups provide a focus for popular discontent against a sitting regime, and thereby lead a general insurrection. He argued that popular forces can win a war against an army; that immediate action is necessary (that is, it is not necessary to wait until all conditions for making revolution exist; the insurrection can create them); and that the countryside is the basic area for armed fighting (which means attacks must be mobilized and launched from rural locations).

Guevara became a leftist celebrity during the early 1960s, traveling to a variety of countries and giving speeches about defeating imperialism. He argued that the superpowers—both the United States and the Soviet Union—were exploiting the less developed countries in the Southern Hemisphere, particularly in Africa and Latin America. While he also spent several years helping Castro build a functioning communist government in Cuba, crafting economic and fiscal policies as well as serving as an instructor to the military, his views toward the Soviet Union became problematic for Castro, since Cuba's economic survival became increasingly dependent on the Soviets. In early 1965, Che left Cuba and led a small group of fighters to join a Marxist guerrilla movement in Congo, but within a year he had relocated to Bolivia, where he established a guerrilla force known as the National Liberation Army of Bolivia. He was captured and executed by Bolivian forces in October 1967.

While the rural guerrilla warfare theories of Mao and Guevara were embraced by terrorist movements around the world, another Latin American contributed significantly to the development of *urban* guerrilla warfare. Brazilian revolutionary Carlos Marighella authored several influential texts including the *Liberation of Brazil* and the *Mini-Manual of the Urban Guerilla*, which are actually practical guides for terrorism. He argued that *the basis of revolution is violence*, and that all violence could be urban-based and controlled by a small group of urban guerrillas. Thus, he gave careful attention to how one can most effectively use violence to achieve political objectives. Unlike Mao and Che, however, he argued that violence should move from the countryside to the city, and he designed a method for organizing a campaign of terror using separate cells—a method that modern terrorist groups across the political spectrum have used.

Marighella's urban model involved two phases: (1) conducting violent attacks, and (2) giving that violence meaning through propaganda and other forms of communication. He argued that a terror campaign must be accompanied by a mass movement of revolutionary sympathizers, who provide peripheral support for terrorists, and that a campaign of revolutionary terrorism in an urban setting can be used to destabilize government power. In essence, a terrorist campaign would force the government to reveal its inherently repressive nature, thereby alienating the public. At this stage, the goal of terrorism is to provoke government repression, which would eventually undermine its own perceived legitimacy among the population.

Several terrorist groups during this New Left wave period embraced the revolutionary ideologies of Fanon, Guevara, Mao, and Marighella. Examples include the Italian Red Brigades, the Popular Front for the Liberation of Palestine, 17 November in Greece, the Red Army Faction (also known as the Baader-Meinhof Group) in Germany, the Japanese Red Army, and Sendero Luminoso in Peru. Most of these revolutionary groups were domestic and Marxist in orientation, and almost all of them promoted armed violence against the capitalist state. We will discuss more on these and other left-wing terrorist groups in Lecture 9.

As Brian Jenkins has noted, there were nearly 10,000 incidents of terrorism during the 1970s. Of these, almost 1,500 occurred within the United States, making it by far the worst period of terrorism in our nation's history (for comparison, he notes, there were slightly more than 200 acts of terrorism in the U.S. between 2002 and 2013).[10] One left-wing group of particular note during this time period was the Weather Underground, which was responsible for terrorist attacks against police, the U.S. Senate, the Pentagon, the U.S. State Department, and major banks. Warnings were usually issued in advance of bombings to avoid human casualties. Like many other left-wing groups, its goal was to provoke communist revolution through violence. Leaders of the group read the books by Fanon and Marighella mentioned above, and believed (just like the anarchists and the anti-colonial revolutionaries) that violent attacks would provoke the government to reveal its truly evil nature, and eventually inspire a popular uprising. And yet, like the other groups in this ideological category, the Weather Underground failed to achieve any of its core objectives (something we'll address further in Lecture 13 on terrorist group decision-making).

Meanwhile, this time period was also marked by increasing violence between Israel and the Palestinians, featuring groups like the Palestinian Liberation Organization (PLO), the Popular Front for the Liberation of Palestine (PFLP), the Popular Front for the Liberation of Palestine-General Command (PFLP-GC), and the Democratic Front for the Liberation of Palestine (DFLP). These and other groups launched a campaign of terrorist attacks, including kidnappings, shootings, bombings, and hijackings. They viewed terrorism as a means to achieve several objectives: to boost recruitment and moral support among Palestinian refugees; to attract financial support from Iraq, Syria,

Libya, and the Soviet Union (among others); and to draw international attention to the Palestinian cause. Their leaders frequently described terrorism as a necessary means to liberate Palestinians by making lives unbearable for Israelis. Over time, however, the failure of these secular terrorist groups to achieve meaningful improvements for the lives of Palestinians led to the rise of more extreme and lethal religious terrorist groups like Hamas and Palestinian Islamic Jihad.

A civil war in Lebanon, combined with Israeli forces invading and attacking Palestinian refugee camps in Lebanon, led to the rise of another religious terrorist group during the early 1980s. Hizballah (also known as Hezbollah or HizbAllah, the Party of God) is a Shiite militant group that pioneered and popularized the use of suicide bombings during this time period, which we'll discuss more in Lecture 16. Their attacks against the U.S. Embassy in Beirut, and against the U.S. Marine barracks, were responsible for the United States removing its troops from the multinational forces that had been sent there on a U.N.-brokered attempt at bringing an end to that country's bloody conflict.

Changes in technology were also coming fast and furious during these years, including cellphones, digital timers, radar guns, and other types of devices that could be used as trigger switches for explosives. Most importantly, a rapidly expanding television media created new opportunities for terrorists to broadcast their grievances to broader, global audiences. The most dramatic example of this occurred at the 1972 Olympics in Munich, Germany. On September 5, a group of nine Palestinians (members of the PLO-affiliated group Black September) stormed the Olympic athletes compound and took 11 members of the Israeli team hostage. After nearly 24 hours of failed negotiations (during which the group demanded the release of incarcerated Palestinians and other terrorists), the German government provided helicopter transport for the terrorists and hostages to an airport, where they would ostensibly board a flight to an undisclosed Arab country. At the airport, the police attempted a rescue attempt that failed, resulting in the deaths of all Israeli hostages and most of the Palestinian terrorists. Throughout the day's events, hundreds of media services from around the world—in Munich to cover the Olympics—provided a global audience to the unfolding drama. The Palestinians finally had the international attention they had craved for nearly a decade.

Elsewhere in the world of terrorism, apartheid and racial violence in South Africa led to the rise of the African National Congress. The long-running conflict in Northern Ireland significantly worsened during the 1970s. Kidnappings of elites in Europe, and a proliferation of commercial aviation hijackings and bombings in the Middle East and Europe contributed to a widespread sense of insecurity and fear of terrorism. And two watershed events during this period—the Soviet invasion of Afghanistan, and the Islamic revolution in Iran, both of which took place in 1979—set the groundwork for what became the next (and current) wave in the history of terrorism, the rise of the **religiously oriented terrorist groups**.

As we will discuss at length in Lectures 11 and 12, religious terrorists are different in several ways from their counterparts in other, secular terrorist groups. For example, a devout person may be convinced that they are acting on God's behalf when carrying out their terrorist act, especially if they believe violence is necessary to protect or defend others, like the *umma* (the global Muslim community), or an unborn child (e.g., the Army of God's justification for attacking abortion clinics and doctors). This belief that they are following the will of their God can lead individuals to rationalize for themselves any number of atrocities. Further, religious ideologies typically provide a long-

> ## TO THE POINT
>
> Religious terrorists portray their violent acts as required to serve the will of their God.

term view of history and the future, and often promise rewards in the afterlife (perhaps even eternal salvation for you and your family). True believers come to see themselves as participants in an epic battle of good versus evil, one in which they will eventually win because God is on their side.

In addition to these metaphysical dimensions, religious ideologies can imbue followers with a belief in their own revealed truth from God, and are often theologically supremacist—meaning that all believers assume superiority over nonbelievers, who are not privy to the truth of the religion. In a similar vein, as J. P. Larsson notes, these ideologies tend to be exclusivist—believers are a chosen people, or their territory is a holy land.[11] They are usually absolutist as well. In other words, it is not possible to be a half-hearted believer: you are either completely committed or you are not. Further, only the true believers are guaranteed salvation and victory, whereas the enemies and the unbelievers (as well as those who have taken no stance whatsoever) are condemned to some sort of eternal punishment or damnation, as well as death. Terms like "infidel," "apostate" and "godless" are used to dehumanize these enemies and unbelievers, helping justify the violent acts that victimize them. Overall, religious ideologies help foster polarizing values in terms of right and wrong, good and evil, light and dark. This can lead to a complete alienation from the norms of social and political interaction.[12]

In terms of motivating terrorist attacks, the most influential religious ideology of our age is known as Salafi-jihadism, which Lecture 12 will examine in-depth. The roots of this ideology are centuries old, but in the modern era, few extremists have been more important than an Egyptian schoolteacher, Hassan al-Banna. In 1928, al-Banna founded the Muslim Brotherhood, primarily as a response to what he saw as threats from both outside and within the Muslim world. In his writings, he encouraged Muslims around the world to engage in violent struggle against infidel rulers in Muslim lands, and to do anything possible to resist and reject the growing influence of Western culture. The Muslim Brotherhood grew into a powerful political force in countries throughout the Middle East, from Morocco to Syria and the Palestinian Territories.

In addition to the many terrorist groups linked to the Muslim Brotherhood (including Hamas and the Palestinian Islamic Jihad), ideological entrepreneurs within the movement promoted new ideas that influenced the modern evolution of Islamist extremism. For example, Sayyid Qutb, a civil servant in Cairo, published several books that criticized Western society and described a loss of direction in the Muslim world because people were not following true Islam. Muhammad Faraj's "The Neglected Duty" built on Qutb's ideas and argued that Muslim rulers who were un-Islamic must be overthrown. Ideas like these led to the 1954 attempted assassination of Egyptian President Gamal Abdel Nasser, a bloody insurgency by the Syrian Muslim Brotherhood in the early 1970s, and the 1981 assassination of Egyptian President Anwar Sadat. In 1979, these ideas also inspired a group of extremists in Saudi Arabia to attack the Grand Mosque in Mecca and demand the resignation of the ruling Saud family.

Meanwhile, following the Soviet Union's invasion of Afghanistan in 1979, Islamist extremists from the Middle East, North Africa, and Southeast Asia raised a call for jihad to expel an "infidel invader" from a Muslim country. A charismatic Palestinian cleric named Abdullah Azzam (who was heavily influenced by al-Banna's writing about using force to defend Islam and the global Muslim community) traveled widely to promote Muslim participation in the Afghan jihad. One of those he inspired to do so was a young Saudi dissident named Osama bin Laden. Bin Ladin used his connections and personal wealth to help bring funds to the jihad and support Azzam's work. After the Soviets withdrew from Afghanistan in 1989, he helped establish "al-Qaeda" (Arabic for "the base") to serve as a central hub of support for launching a jihad against apostate regimes and other perceived enemies of the Muslim world (and eventually, their Western supporters like the United States).

Throughout the 1980s and the 1990s, Afghanistan served as a hub of training for thousands of aspiring young jihadists, many of whom went on to participate in violent conflicts in locations such as Kashmir, Kosovo, Uzbekistan, Bangladesh, the Philippines, Algeria, Bosnia, and Chechnya (among others). In essence, al-Qaeda launched a new era of Islamist terrorism. The core principles of the Muslim Brotherhood—using violence to achieve an Islamist political agenda—remain at the center of the global Salafi-jihadist ideology, but while Muslim Brotherhood-affiliated groups have focused mainly on local or national objectives, al-Qaeda and its various affiliate groups have regional and even global ambitions, beginning with the re-establishment of a transnational caliphate and eventually altering the global system of political and economic relations in ways that give primacy to Salafist interpretations of Islam. Al-Qaeda's efforts also led to the establishment of the Islamic State, which we will discuss in later lectures.

Beyond Islamist extremism, other examples of religious terrorism range across a wide spectrum, from religious cults (like Aum Shinrikyo in Japan) to Christian anti-abortion groups (like the Army of God), and Jewish extremists (like Kahane Chai). Even insurgencies and ethnic separatist groups like the Chechens are using religious-oriented ideologies to justify violence. We will focus much more on religious terrorism in Lectures 11 and 12.

In addition to ideological dimensions, it is important to note how changes in technology during the last few decades have led to entirely new forms of terrorism. For example, we have seen an increasing sophistication of improvised explosive devices (IEDs), particularly in Iraq and Afghanistan. There has been an increase in the use of suicide bombers worldwide, as we'll discuss in Lecture 16. Interestingly, when you take a look at some of the most prominent terrorist attacks over the past century (see Table 2.1), the increasing prominence of suicide bombings is striking.

We are, of course, progressively worried about new and emerging weapons of mass destruction (or disruption), like chemical, biological, radiological, and nuclear weapons, which we'll examine in Lectures 17 and 18. And then there's the Internet, which has made it easier to learn how to make bombs and acquire other types of useful knowledge for carrying out terrorist attacks. And of course, the Internet has also made it much easier for terrorist groups to communicate globally, both among themselves and with various audiences of supporters, potential supporters, and enemies. We'll talk much more about the role of the media and the Internet in modern terrorism during Lectures 7 and 14.

TABLE 2.1: 50 Major Terrorist Attacks in the Past 100 Years That Everyone Should Know About

Date	Incident	Date	Incident
9/16/20	New York: Bombing of Wall Street	9/1/2004–9/3/2004	Beslan, Russia: Hostages, bombing and shootings at a school
7/22/46	Israel: Bombing of King David Hotel	11/15/03–11/20/03	Istanbul, Turkey: Multiple bombings
9/5/72–9/6/72	Munich Olympics siege, hostage taking, mass shooting	2/27/04	Manila bombing of SuperFerry 14
12/29/75	New York: Bombing at LaGuardia Airport	3/11/04	Madrid, Spain: Coordinated bombings of commuter railway trains
8/19/78	Abadan, Iran: Mass killing by intentional fire at Cinema Rex	8/24/04	Russia, simultaneous bombings of 2 passenger airlines
11/20/79–012/5/79	Mecca, Saudi Arabia: Siege of the Grand Mosque	7/7/05	London, UK: Coordinated suicide bombings of public transportation
4/18/83	Beirut, Lebanon: Bombing of US Embassy	10/29/05	New Delhi, India: bombings and shootings of civilians
10/23/83	Beirut, Lebanon: Simultaneous Bombings of US Marine Barracks and French Paratrooper Barracks	7/11/06	Mumbai train bombings
8/29/84–10/10/84	The Dalles, Oregon: Salmonella attacks by Rajneeshee cult members	11/23/06	Sadr City (Iraq) multiple bombings
6/14/85–6/30/85	Hijacking of TWA 847; hostage taking	3/6/07	Al Hillah (Iraq) suicide bombing
6/23/85	Air India Flight 182 bombing	8/14/07	Kahtaniya and Jazeera (Iraq): Coordinate suicide car bombings
10/7/85–10/10/85	Achille Lauro: hostage taking aboard cruise ship	10/18/07	Karachi, Pakistan coordinated bombings
4/2/86	TWA 840: bombing	11/26/08–11/29/08	Mumbai, India: Coordinated attacks against multiple civilian targets
12/21/88	Pan Am 103 bombing over Lockerbie, Scotland	11/5/09	Ft. Hood, Texas: Multiple shootings
2/26/93	New York: Truck bombing of World Trade Center	3/29/10	Moscow, Russia: Metro suicide bombings
3/12/93	Bombay (Mumbai) coordinated bombings	7/22/11	Oslo, Norway: Bombings and shootings of civilians
3/20/95	Tokyo: Subway attack with sarin nerve agent	4/15/13	Boston, MA: Coordinated bombings at Boston Marathon

4/19/95	Oklahoma City: Truck bombing of Murrah Federal Building		5/5/14– 5/6/14	Gamboru and Ngala (Nigeria): Mass shootings and kidnappings
7/27/96	Atlanta: Bombing of Olympics, Centennial Park		10/31/15	Egypt, bombing of Russia MetroJet flight 9268
8/7/98	Nairobi, Kenya and Dar es Salaam, Tanzania: Coordinated truck bombings of U.S. Embassies		11/13/15	Paris: Multiple suicide bombings and mass shootings
10/12/00	Aden, Yemen; USS Cole bombing		12/2/15	San Bernadino, CA: Mass casualty shootings
8/10/01	Angola: Mass shooting of train passengers		3/22/16	Brussels: Bombings at airport and metro station
9/11/01	New York and Washington, DC: Planes used as suicide bombs against buildings; thousands killed		6/12/16	Orlando, FL: Mass casualty shootings
10/12/02	Bali, Indonesia: bombing of two nightclubs		7/3/16	Baghdad (Iraq) multiple bombings

Homework assignment: Details for each of these attacks can be easily found online via Google search.

SUMMARY

So, to wrap up this lecture, Rapoport has nicely organized about 130 years' worth of terrorism into an easily digestible form. My own variation of his approach is to ride the waves with various kinds of conceptual surfboards—ideological, technological, financial, etc.—in order to see different thematic developments that carry forward from one wave to another. Other professors will inevitably teach the history of terrorism much differently—in fact, not everyone agrees fully with Rapoport's framework, and there are some terrorist groups that do not fit neatly into any one wave. For instance, as I noted earlier, several ethnonationalist groups are neither anti-colonial nor New Left wave, though some have had elements of one or both of these ideological motivations, and many of them have transcended the waves more than being consumed by them. For example, the Basque separatist group ETA was founded in 1959 by nationalist students as a response to repression under the Franco regime, and was active until 2011. The Liberation Tigers of Tamil Eelam (also known as LTTE or Tamil Tigers), was founded in 1976 in response to persecution of Tamils by the Sinhalese government, and was active until 2009. And the Provisional Irish Republican

Army, founded as a splinter group from the IRA during the early 1970s, was active until the late 1990s, and spawned several dissident groups—including the Real IRA and the Continuity IRA—that remain actively engaged in terrorist activities in Northern Ireland today.

Also, how do the waves account for the environmentalists and animal rights activists who have been responsible for hundreds of attacks since the 1980s?[13] Some may argue that their ideological pedigree stems from the New Left wave revolutionary theories, particularly Che Guevarra's thoughts on the need for a vanguard to lead a revolution on behalf of others. Meanwhile, other observers have suggested that when the decline of the Soviet Union undermined the resonance of the communist ideology, some members of left-wing movements chose to embrace a more specific topic, like environmental or animal rights causes.

Overall, however, Rapoport's framework offers a nice way to cover a lot of history fairly quickly. There are other scholars as well, of course, whose work I also recommend for learning about the history of terrorism. For example, Brian Jenkins has written about how terrorism has become bloodier—more civilians are killed these days by terrorist attacks than in years past—and terrorists have also developed new financial resources, and are less dependent on state sponsors like Iran, Syria, or Libya.[14] We are seeing new models of terrorist organizations, including "leaderless resistance" and "franchises" among others, as we'll examine later in this lecture series. We are seeing both an increasing number of attacks and an increasing lethality of attacks, and in several cases these attacks have not been orchestrated by formally established terrorist groups but by individuals inspired by some form of extremist ideology, as we'll examine in Lecture 15.

Understanding the contemporary history of terrorism provides us with an important perspective about the terrorist threats we face today. Despite the ways in which some politicians and media outlets portray terrorism, this is not a phenomenon that began on September 11, 2001. Countries and societies have struggled to combat the scourge of terrorism for centuries. While the ideological orientations of terrorism have shifted and evolved over time, the study of history reveals common patterns among the underlying radicalization processes that lead a person to embrace a terrorist ideology, and the relevant impacts of socioeconomic and political conditions that give these ideologies resonance. These patterns will be the focus of the next several lectures of this book.

QUESTIONS FOR DISCUSSION

- What technological innovations have we seen among terrorists over the last 100 years?
- Is there really a "new" and an "old" terrorism, and if so, what is the difference?
- Is there really a difference between politically and religiously motivated terrorism? Is the increasing level of violence and willingness to use violence a result of a shift from political motivations to religious motivations?
- What are some different ways of studying the history of terrorism?
- How have terrorist tactics evolved over the past century, and what does this evolution suggest about the future of terrorism?
- What should contemporary military and political leaders learn from this history of terrorism?
- Do you see this history playing a role in contemporary counterterrorism campaigns? If so, where and how?

RECOMMENDED READING

Ahmad, Eqbal. "Terrorism: Theirs & Ours." In *Terrorism and Counterterrorism*. Edited by Russell Howard and Bruce Hoffman. New York: McGraw-Hill, 2011.

Arquilla, John, David Ronfeldt, and Michele Zanini. "Networks, Netwar and Information Age Terrorism." In *Networks and Netwars*. Edited by John Arquilla and David Ronfeldt. Santa Monica, CA: Rand Corporation, 2001.

Crenshaw, Martha. "The Debate over 'New' vs. 'Old' Terrorism." In *Terrorism and Counterterrorism*. Edited by Russell Howard and Bruce Hoffman. New York: McGraw-Hill, 2011.

Cronin, Audrey Kurth. "Behind the Curve: Globalization and International Terrorism." In *Terrorism and Counterterrorism*. Edited by Russell Howard and Bruce Hoffman. New York: McGraw-Hill, 2011.

Frantz Fanon. *The Wretched of the Earth*. Jackson, TN: Grove Press, 2005 reprint. Originally published 1961.

Hoffman, Bruce. "The Internationalization of Terrorism." *Inside Terrorism*. New York: Columbia University Press, 2006: 63–79.

Homer Dixon, Thomas. "The Rise of Complex Terrorism." *Foreign Policy* (January/February 2002).

Jenkins, Brian Michael. "The New Age of Terrorism." In *Weapons of Mass Destruction and Terrorism*. Edited by James J. F. Forest and Russell Howard. New York: McGraw-Hill, 2012.

Larsson, J. P. "The Role of Religious Ideology in Modern Terrorist Recruitment." In *The Making of a Terrorist*. Vol. 1. Edited by James J. F. Forest. Westport, CT: Praeger, 2005.

Neumann, Peter R. *Radicalized: New Jihadists and the Threat to the West.* London: I.B. Tauris, 2017.

Parker, Tom and Nick Sitter. "The Four Horsemen of Terrorism: It's Not Waves, It's Strains." *Terrorism and Political Violence* 28, no. 2 (2016): 197–216.

Rapoport, David C. "Before the Bombs, There Were Mobs: American Experiences with Terror." *Terrorism and Political Violence* 20, no. 2 (2008).

Rapoport, David C. "The Four Waves of Terrorism." In *Attacking Terrorism: Elements of a Grand Strategy.* Edited by Audrey Kurth Cronin and James M. Ludes. Washington, DC: Georgetown University Press, 2004.

Reeve, Simon. *One Day in September: The Story of the 1972 Munich Olympics Massacre.* London: Faber and Faber, 2000.

NOTES

1. David C. Rapoport, "Fear and Trembling: Terrorism in Three Religious Traditions," *American Political Science Review* 78, no. 3 (1984).

2. For a detailed analysis, see David C. Rapoport, "Before the Bombs, There Were Mobs: American Experiences with Terror," *Terrorism and Political Violence* 20, no. 2 (2008): 167–94.

3. David C. Rapoport, "The Four Waves of Terrorism," in *Attacking Terrorism: Elements of a Grand Strategy*, ed. Audrey Kurth Cronin and James M. Ludes (Washington, DC: Georgetown University Press, 2004).

4. Johann Most, *The Science of Revolutionary Warfare: A Little Handbook of Instruction in the Use and Preparation of Nitroglycerine, Dynamite, Gun-Cotton, Fulminating Mercury, Bombs, Fuses, Poisons, Etc., Etc.* (Cornville, AZ: Desert Publications, 1978) (originally published New York, 1885).

5. Ibid., 1978, p. 56.

6. Rapoport, "Before the Bombs."

7. Beverly Gage, *The Day Wall Street Exploded: A Story of America in its First Age of Terror* (New York: Oxford University Press, 2009).

8. Frantz Fanon, *The Wretched of the Earth.* Jackson, TN: Grove Press, 2005 reprint: 72 (Originally published 1961).

9. This description of events in Algeria is adapted from Peter R. Neumann, *Radicalized: New Jihadists and the Threat to the West* (London: I.B. Tauris, 2017): 18–20.

10. Brian Michael Jenkins, "The 1970s and the birth of contemporary terrorism," *The Hill* (July 30, 2015), http://bit.ly/2tclLDM.

11. J. P. Larsson, "The Role of Religious Ideology in Modern Terrorist Recruitment," in *The Making of a Terrorist*, vol. 1, ed. James J. F. Forest (Westport, CT: Praeger, 2005).

12. Ibid.

13. For a detailed analysis, see Jennifer Varriale Carson, Gary LaFree, and Laura Dugan, "Terrorist and Non-Terrorist Criminal Attacks by Radical Environmental and Animal Rights Groups in the United States, 1970-2007," *Terrorism and Political Violence* 24, no. 2 (2012).

14. Brian Michael Jenkins, "The New Age of Terrorism," in *Weapons of Mass Destruction and Terrorism*, ed. James J. F. Forest and Russell Howard (New York: McGraw-Hill, 2012): 29–37.

3

Grievances and Opportunities

Terrorism is a highly contextual phenomenon. Indeed, the old maxim that "all politics is local" usually holds true for political violence as well. We sometimes hear a lot of talk about terrorism as if it were a monolithic, easily understood term, but as we already noted in Lecture 1, it is certainly not. Just as there are many different kinds of terrorism, there are many different contexts in which terrorism occurs. Within each context, we find a variety of grievances that motivate a terrorist group and its supporters, along with circumstances and influences that facilitate terrorist activities.

In this lecture, I'll examine two primary themes in the research on these contexts: preconditions ("things that are") and triggers ("things that happen").[1] My thinking about these themes is informed by the research of terrorism scholars like Jeffrey Ian Ross, Assaf Moghadam, and, most notably, Martha Crenshaw.[2] Of course, a lot of attention has been focused on the impact of political conditions, like oppressive or corrupt governments, and socioeconomic conditions, like poverty and ethnic discrimination, in explaining why terrorism emerges within a certain context.[3] Lectures 4 through 6 will examine specific details of economic, financial, criminal, and political dimensions of terrorism, but I'll mention some of them in this lecture as well to provide an overall framework that helps us understand the radicalization process.

PRECONDITIONS: GRIEVANCES AND FACILITATORS

To begin, a major topic in the study of terrorism involves the conditions that generate or give legitimacy to a core set of grievances articulated in a terrorist group's ideology. Generally, these are seen as structural reasons for why a terrorist group's ideology resonates in a particular community and can include a broad range of political issues like incompetent, authoritarian, or corrupt governments as well as economic issues like widespread poverty, unemployment, or an overall lack of political or socioeconomic opportunities. When a government fails to adhere to the conventional social contract between its political leadership and the governed, its citizens typically become disenchanted and seek the power to force change. This, in turn, has contributed to a variety of revolutionary movements and terrorist groups throughout history. In essence, a terrorist group's recruitment efforts draw on what Harvard University psychologist John Mack described as "a reservoir of misery, hurt, helplessness and rage from which the foot soldiers of terrorism can be recruited."[4]

TO THE POINT

When a government's legitimacy declines, political violence is more likely.

In his research, Ross identified seven kinds of "structural" grievances that are the most important contributors to political violence—ethnic, racial, legal, political, religious, social, and economic.[5] Later in this lecture series, we will take a close look at terrorist groups motivated by ethnic grievances (Lecture 8), racial grievances (Lecture 10), and religious grievances (Lectures 11 and 12). But there are also a whole lot of legal, political, social, and economic grievances (including poverty, exploitation, expropriation, indebtedness, and unemployment) that contribute to the emergence of terrorist groups across all of these ideological categories. In Lecture 5, we will examine more closely the relationship between terrorism and poverty or other economic dimensions.

According to a variety of scholarly books and articles, the grievances that have motivated terrorists over the past several decades are often tied to a government's legitimacy, or lack thereof. As Ted Robert Gurr noted in his 1970 book, *Why Men Rebel*, a government's legitimacy can be severely undermined by a range of factors, like widespread injustice or a major gap between the aspirations of a population and the opportunities for its members to achieve those aspirations.[6]

Many researchers have identified government repression and a lack of democracy, civil liberties, and the rule of law as preconditions for many forms of domestic terrorism. We know of several countries in which opposition political parties have been outlawed, political dissidents and opposition candidates have been jailed on security charges just before elections, torture has been used to extract confessions, political prisoners have died while in custody, and suspects have been arrested and held without charge. When a government exhibits outright hostility and commits open violence against members of its citizenry, this represents an example of the powerful subjugating the relatively powerless, a situation that often generates support for those who call for the use of terrorism in responding to a government that has lost its legitimacy.

Authoritarian governments are among those most likely to lose legitimacy in the eyes of the people they rule. As Lydia Khalil observed, authoritarian governments usually succumb to the accumulation of power for power's sake.[7] They also routinely stifle civil liberties in order to maintain their hold on power and keep society in check. Further, more often than not, authoritarian governments are also corrupt governments. Resources, privileges, and advantages are reserved for a select group of the people or ruling elite. Corruption prevents the fair distribution of social services and adds another layer to the resentment caused by the lack of political participation. The rest of society lacks a voice and is ignored. This corruption further erodes the government's legitimacy in the eyes of its citizens and often gives credence to those who argue that political violence is necessary to bring about significant change.

Corrupt governments seek to maintain and increase their power over others (and over resources) by any means necessary while the powerless see the corruption and are rightfully incensed by it. Some may launch public protests or look for ways to directly confront a corrupt government—including through violent acts of terrorism if they believe that to be their only form of recourse. A quick look at countries that have high levels of corruption reinforces this point (see Table 3.1). According to Transparency International's 2017 Corruptions Perceptions Index,[8] we see countries like Somalia, Afghanistan, Syria, Sudan, and Libya among the top 10 worst countries on the list. It is no coincidence that these are also countries where we have seen significant levels of terrorism and political violence for many years. High levels of corruption can fuel widespread grievances against a government and can also serve as a facilitator of criminal and terrorist activity, as we will discuss in Lectures 4 through 6.

At the start of this lecture, I noted that terrorism is a highly contextual phenomenon and that most often it is the local context that matters most. But sometimes the

TABLE 3.1: Fifty countries with the highest perceived levels of corruption

Somalia	Democratic Republic of Congo	Lebanon
South Sudan	Cambodia	Kenya
Syria	Zimbabwe	Guatemala
Afghanistan	Uzbekistan	Bangladesh
Yemen	Haiti	Russia
Sudan	Burundi	Paraguay
Libya	Central Africa Republic	Papau New Guinea
North Korea	Madagascar	Mexico
Guinea-Bissau	Mozambique	Lao PDR
Equatorial Guinea	Cameroon	Kyrgyzstan
Venezuela	Uganda	Honduras
Iraq	Nicaragua	Dominican Republic
Turkmenistan	Nigeria	Ukraine
Angola	Guinea	Sierra Leone
Eritrea	Comoros	Myanmar
Chad	Mauritania	Iran
Tajikistan		
Republic of Congo		

Source: "2017 Corruption Perceptions Index," Transparency International, https://www.transparency.org/research/cpi/overview.

things that impact a local context are forces from beyond a country's borders such as a spillover effect of terrorism in a neighboring state or being the target of terrorists whose bases are just across the border (e.g., India and Pakistan, Colombia and Ecuador, Turkey and northern Iraq). Also, as research by Paul Pillar demonstrates, the foreign policies of one nation like the United States can contribute to the motivations of terrorists in other countries such as Lebanon, Iraq, or Afghanistan.[9]

In some parts of the world, there is also a good deal of animosity—particularly in the developing world—toward globalization. This animosity often stems from a perception that certain people have been victimized by corrupt governments, backed by powerful nations and multinational corporations, that have little concern for their lives, needs, or suffering.[10] Political theorist Benjamin Barber argues that in some cases terrorism can be seen as the collision between two forces: one, an integrative modernization and aggressive economic and cultural globalization, and, two, a kind of tribalism and reactionary fundamentalism.[11] In essence, violence is seen as necessary to preserve the status quo, to protect things like tribal customs, traditional power structures, and so forth. Some of this violent reaction to the forces of globalization is reflected in the Salafi-jihadist ideology, as we will discuss in Lecture 12.

Beyond grievances, the preconditions for terrorism can also include a range of **facilitators**, loosely defined as the structural or temporary conditions at the community or regional level that provide individuals and organizations with ample opportunities to engage in terrorist activity. Examples include significant access to weapons and explosives, a general sense of lawlessness, freedom of movement (across borders, through ungoverned territories, etc.), availability of funding and safe haven, state sponsorship, and a weak government or incompetent security apparatus. Countries with a robust **shadow economy** (economic activities that are underground, covert, or illegal) can provide an infrastructure for terrorist organizations to operate in, whereby financing becomes easier and detecting it becomes more difficult.[12]

According to Vanda Felbab-Brown, terrorist groups derive three sets of gains from their involvement with the illicit economy: increased *physical capabilities* (money and weapons), increased *freedom of action* (the ability to optimize tactics and strategies), and increased *political capital* (legitimacy, a relationship with the local population, the willingness of the local population to withhold intelligence on the terrorist organization from the government, and the willingness of the local population to provide intelligence about government units to the terrorist organization).[13] In essence, as long as a global drug trade exists—in which there is high consumer demand and lucrative rewards for production and trafficking—terrorist groups will continue to profit from this trade and can be expected to commit violent acts in order to protect these profits. We will examine the intersections of crime and terrorism further in Lecture 6.

Weak or failed states can also facilitate terrorism, particularly in places where a government's authority is routinely challenged and undermined by a variety of violent nonstate actors.[14] These are countries in which a weak central government is unable to provide adequate human security to all segments of its population.[15] The challenge of state weakness is now explicitly recognized in U.S. national security circles as a strategic problem almost equal in importance to state competitors. As noted earlier, several U.S. security strategy documents emphasize the security challenges of weak or failed states. We will look at this issue more closely in Lecture 4, but here I should just point out that a significant number of terrorist plots and attacks against the United States and its allies over the past decade have been linked to places like Yemen, Somalia, Syria, and Afghanistan—all of them classified as weak or failed states.

Political instability can also provide an environment that benefits a terrorist group.[16] Research by Erica Chenoweth found that politically unstable regimes—regardless of regime type—are more likely than stable regimes to provide hospitable environments for terrorist organizations to develop. The essential argument she made is that the "permissive conditions" of politically unstable regimes inhibit domestic institutional mechanisms that could potentially prevent terrorist organizations from taking root in particular countries.[17]

> **TO THE POINT**
>
> The choices a government makes can contribute to terrorism.

Certain kinds of natural resource constraints, physical geography, and cultural conditions can also contribute to the kinds of political instability that provide opportunities for terrorist groups to thrive. For example, urban population growth in numerous locations across the Lagos-Cairo-Karachi-Jakarta arc of megacities—where jobs and educational opportunities are increasingly unavailable—can result in greater levels of discontent, crime, and urban instability that terrorist groups can capitalize upon.[18] When these local factors are combined with powerful clan or tribal networks, it becomes very difficult for a government to foster national loyalty or peaceful coexistence In a population, which then contributes to an enabling environment for a terrorist group's ideology to resonate.

And, of course, a terrorist group's opportunities to act are greatly enhanced by the availability of small arms and light weapons.[19] In Yemen, in the North-West Frontier Province of Pakistan, and in the Caucasus Mountains, the proliferation of small arms has allowed many groups to challenge the primacy of the state and to create conditions of instability, which can enable criminal and terrorist group operations. In such places, traffickers in drugs, humans, and weapons cohabit with warlords, militia leaders and political opportunists in an environment that precludes good governance and judicial oversight.[20]

Aside from local contexts, there are elements of the global environment that can also lead to opportunities for facilitating terrorist activity. For example, globally dispersed diaspora communities such as the Tamils in Canada, Somalis in the United States, and Pakistanis in Denmark and the U.K. have provided funding to militants back home.

The global connections of the Internet provide a wealth of new opportunities for terrorist groups to influence and draw support from a global audience.[21] Al-Qaeda and the Islamic State have been notable innovators of online terrorist-oriented activity, from soliciting and moving funds to the dissemination of propaganda videos and military instruction manuals in multiple languages. As we'll examine in Lectures 7 and 14, terrorists use thousands of websites as virtual training camps, providing an online forum for indoctrination, inspiration, training, and operational instruction. They can also capture information about the users who browse their websites, which can be useful for the early stages of recruitment.[22] Indeed, leaders of the global Salafi-jihadist movement (including senior members of al-Qaeda and the Islamic State) view those at the center of their information strategy—the website designers, bloggers, and video editors—as vital to their efforts.

To sum up, researchers in the field of terrorism studies have collectively assembled a broad and colorful landscape of the many structural issues that must be addressed by governments seeking to reduce the risk of terrorism. Further, a local population's *perceptions* about these issues must also be addressed, as oftentimes politically violent groups will seek to convince others that things are far worse than they truly are and that they cannot make a positive impact on their environment without resorting to violent means. We'll take a closer look at this issue of influencing perceptions, as well as the underlying economic and political dimensions of terrorism, in many of the lectures in this book.

POTENTIAL TRIGGERS FOR TERRORIST ACTIVITY

Beyond preconditions, another major theme in the research on terrorism involves the study of environmental triggers, described as specific actions, policies, and events that enhance the perceived need for action within a particular environment. Environmental triggers are very dynamic and time-relevant, and terrorist organizations often seize upon them in their attempts to enhance the resonance of their violent ideologies.

A trigger for action can be any number of things: a change in government policy like the suspension of civil liberties, a banning of political parties, or the introduction of new censorship or draconian antiterrorist laws; an erosion in the security environment like a military invasion or a massive influx of refugees, or a natural disaster that diverts the government's attention away from monitoring the group; a widely publicized incident of police brutality or invasive surveillance; and even a coup, an assassination, or another

sudden regime change.[23] In some instances, a trigger may occur in an entirely different country. For example, the invasion and subsequent occupation of Iraq by U.S.-led
coalition forces has been linked to major terrorist attacks in Madrid (2004) and London
(2005), as well as in Iraq itself. Obviously, the presence of U.S. and NATO troops in
Afghanistan has triggered a variety of terrorist attacks over the last decade as well.

It is also important to note that a trigger does not necessarily need to be a relatively
quick or contained event. For example, research by Paul Ehrlich and Jack Liu suggests
that persistent demographic and socioeconomic factors can facilitate transnational
terrorism and make it easier to recruit terrorists.[24] Specifically, they described how
increased birth rates and the age composition of populations in developing countries
affects resource consumption, prices, government revenues and expenditures, demand
for jobs, and labor wages. In essence, these demographic and socioeconomic conditions in certain countries could lead to the emergence of more terrorism and terrorists
for many decades to come. Similarly, the National Intelligence Council's 2025 Project
report notes that pending "youth bulges" in many Arab states could contribute to a rise
in political violence and civil conflict.[25]

A trigger could also be an event that leads to new opportunities for terrorism. For
example, a sudden regime change may create an anarchic environment in which groups
find greater freedom to obtain weapons or conduct criminal and violent activity. Terrorist groups will usually seize any opportunity to capitalize on events from which they
could benefit strategically, tactically, or operationally. It is important to note that any
potential triggers are far more likely to enhance a terrorist organization's ideological resonance when the structural conditions described earlier are already a source of grievances.

This brings us to one of the most visible and easily identifiable kinds of trigger: a
government's decision to sponsor terrorism. Clearly, a government can choose whether
to provide support to a terrorist group; most countries choose not to. But there are
several countries that have been linked to sponsorship of terrorism like Afghanistan,
Eritrea, Iran, Sudan, Syria, and the former Soviet Union. In one of the most authorita-
tive studies of this issue, Daniel Byman defined state sponsorship as "a government's
intentional assistance to a terrorist group to help it use violence, bolster its political activities, or sustain [its] organization."[26] His research identifies six areas in which
states provide support to terrorists: (1) training and operations; (2) money, arms, and
logistics; (3) diplomatic backing; (4) organizational assistance; (5) ideological direction; and, (6) perhaps most important, sanctuary.[27] These are all things that can help
facilitate terrorist activities by a suitably motivated group.

Byman argued that terrorist groups that receive significant amounts of state support are far more difficult to counter and destroy than those that do not.[28] It is, however, important to note that there are several types of state sponsorship of terrorism: "strong supporters" are states with both the desire and the capacity to support terrorist groups; "weak supporters" have the desire but not the capacity to offer significant support; "lukewarm supporters" offer rhetorical but little actual tangible support; and "antagonistic supporters" actually seek to control or even weaken the terrorist groups they appear to be supporting. Then there are the "passive supporters," which Byman described as states that "deliberately turn a blind eye to the activities of terrorists in their countries but do not provide direct assistance."[29]

A state's tolerance of (or passivity toward) a terrorist group's activities, Byman argued, is often as important to their success as any deliberate assistance they receive. Open and active state sponsorship of terrorism is rare, and it has decreased since the end of the Cold War. Yet this lack of open support does not necessarily diminish the important role that states play in fostering or hindering terrorism. At times, the greatest contribution a state can make to a terrorist's cause is by not policing a border, turning a blind eye to fundraising, or even tolerating terrorist efforts to build their organizations, conduct operations, and survive. Passive support for terrorism can contribute to a terrorist group's success in several ways. It often allows a group to raise money, acquire arms, plan operations, and enjoy a respite from the counterattacks of the government it opposes. Passive support may also involve spreading an ideology that assists a terrorist group in its efforts to recruit new members.[30]

Perhaps one of the most prominent examples of state sponsorship in recent history has been Afghanistan under the Taliban regime. According to Rohan Gunaratna and Arabinda Acharya, the training camps established by al-Qaeda and its associates during the 1990s were essential for developing a broad array of Islamic militant groups and for providing indoctrination and training for foot soldiers, go-betweens, planners, document forgers, communications specialists, scouts, technicians, bombers, and even hijackers. According to some estimates, thousands of militant Muslims from more than 50 countries passed through the camps, spending from two weeks to more than six months learning the general and specific skills that modern terrorism requires.[31] Learning materials (manuals, notebooks, lesson plans, and reference books) recovered from guerrilla training schools in Afghanistan indicate that there were two tiers of courses, one for standardized, basic guerilla skills like cleaning and firing a rifle, using a rocket-propelled grenade launcher, reading maps, and dealing with explosives. Recruits deemed to have special skills were given additional training in either advanced infantry techniques or in specific tactics of terrorism. (For more on this, see Lecture 13). Military experts who reviewed these captured materials agreed that there was a high level of training on everything except in some of the more advanced terrorism skills, and that much of the instructions provided in these manuals had been borrowed from similar training materials used by the military in the United States and the former Soviet Union.[32] Thus, Afghanistan under Taliban rule played a key role in creating the global terrorist threat now faced by the West.

Essentially, the choices that a government makes can contribute to the emergence of terrorism. If only the Taliban in Afghanistan had made different choices about a particular Saudi dissident and his band of merry murderers, maybe even deciding not to give safe haven for Osama bin Laden to run his training camps and plan attacks, one could argue that 9/11 might never have happened.

Of course, terrorism is often a response to government decisions beyond state sponsorship. For example, in the United States, the government's decisions about the conduct of the Vietnam War led to the rise of student political activist movements that spawned the terrorist group known as the Weather Underground, which we'll discuss in Lecture 9. The decision by Western European countries to establish colonies in Asia and Africa eventually led to the rise of anti-colonial terrorism in those places. In Sri Lanka, the government's decision to discriminate against Tamils, banning their language and cultural symbols, led to the rise of ethnonationalist terrorism groups, most notably the Tamil Tigers. Similar situations are seen in the case of Spain, with regard to the Basque separatist group ETA, and in Turkey, whose bans against Kurdish language and culture gave rise to terrorist groups like the PKK. We'll look more closely at these and other examples of ethnonationalist terrorism in Lecture 8.

Really, when we think about it, any number of triggers could lie behind the emergence of terrorism. In some cases, people may take up terrorism in response to a major court ruling, as we have seen in the U.S. case of *Roe v. Wade* (1973), which sparked a violent anti-abortion movement. Members of the so-called Army of God have bombed clinics and murdered doctors and nurses, among other acts of terrorism—all as part of their attempt to coerce the public (and the government) to reverse this legal decision. In April 1995, the attack by Timothy McVeigh against the Murrah Federal Building in Oklahoma City was triggered by what he and his fellow right-wing extremists saw as an increasingly intrusive federal government, demonstrated by events earlier in the decade at Ruby Ridge, Idaho, and Waco, Texas. (For more on these incidents, please see Lecture 10.)

Political elections can also become a trigger for terrorism. For example, the 1991 elections in Algeria were canceled by the military when it became apparent that the Islamic Salvation Front was most likely to win a majority of the seats in parliament. In response to the government's crackdown on the country's Islamist movement, several terrorist groups were launched, including the Armed Islamic Group (GIA) and the Salafist Group for Preaching and Combat (GSPC), which in 2007 declared its loyalty to Osama bin Laden and changed its name to al-Qaeda in the Islamic Maghreb (AQIM).

Meanwhile, civil wars in Lebanon, Colombia, and Afghanistan set the stage for the emergence of groups like Hizballah, FARC, and the Taliban, respectively. Syria offers the most recent example of this connection, with street protests in early 2011 gradually evolving into a full-scale civil war involving a wide array of militant groups, some of which have embraced the strategy and tactics of terrorism. Groups fighting against the brutal regime of Bashar al-Assad—including the Free Syrian Army, the al-Qaeda affili-ate Hayat Tahrir al-Sham (formerly Al-Nusra Front), the Islamic State, the Democratic Federation of North Syria, the Kurdish Front—range in size and capabilities, but are collectively responsible for thousands of violent attacks. These attacks, combined with the Syrian government's military attacks against rebel-held territory, have resulted in hundreds of thousands of deaths and millions of Syrian civilians fleeing the country. There is little doubt that the impact of the events in Syria will be felt throughout the region for many years to come.

A peace process could also be a trigger for new kinds of terrorism. For example, throughout the past four decades, terrorism has been used by both Muslim and Jewish extremists to disrupt the Middle East peace process. Those conducting the terrorist acts are not the decision makers in this process, but instead are the relatively powerless, seeking ways to shape the course of future events that concern them, especially when these events deal with a bit of highly coveted land. In perhaps the most poignant and tragic example of this, Orthodox Jewish student Yigal Amir assassinated Israeli Prime Minister Yitzhak Rabin because of his government's plan to evacuate a small settler enclave in Hebron as part of the Oslo Peace Accords that Rabin had signed with Yassir Arafat in 1993.[33]

Meanwhile, a peace accord (known as the Good Friday Agreement) in Northern Ireland was signed by all parties on April 10, 1998, effectively putting an end to several decades of violent atrocities between Catholic Republicans and Protestant Loyalists. Or at least, that's what most people thought. But just a few months later, on August 15, 1998, a car bomb packed with 500 pounds of explosives detonated in the popular

Figure 3.1: The al-Zaatari refugee camp in Jordan is currently home to 160,000 Syrian refugees

shopping district of Omagh, a small town in County Tyrone, Northern Ireland (about 70 miles west of Belfast).[34] The entire front wall of S. D. Kells clothes shop was blasted into the building, and the roof collapsed onto the top floor. At the Pine Emporium, a furniture shop, the blast was such that furniture could later be seen sticking out the windows at the back of the building. A water main under the road was exposed by the blast, and this began pouring gallons of water over the wreckage, washing bodies down the hill. In all, 28 people were killed by the blast, and hundreds more were injured. The group responsible for this—the worst single terrorist attack in Northern Ireland's history—was a Republican dissident group calling itself the Real IRA, whose members denounced the Good Friday Agreement and called for a continuation of the struggle to unite the northern counties with the rest of Ireland.

SUMMARY

To sum up, there are a wide variety of preconditions and triggers that collectively provide a context in which terrorism is more likely. These conditions and triggers are used by terrorists to justify the need for violence in pursuit of some form of political, social, economic, or other changes. Without such conditions, it would be much more difficult to shape people's perceptions or to influence the course of future events. Further, terrorist organizations thrive in an environment where they can find weapons and safe haven, communicate, transport humans and materiel, and attract financial or other forms of support. As a result, structural conditions influence a terrorist group's strategic choices and rationales for violence.

Naturally, an exhaustive account of the full body of research on these things far exceeds the scope of this lecture. There are excellent books out there on virtually all the topics mentioned here, some of which are listed among the recommendations provided below. But the most important point to remember is that terrorism is a very contextual phenomenon. Political violence—or conflict of any kind—does not occur in a vacuum. Thus, understanding terrorism requires a solid appreciation for a particular context in which a terrorist group operates.

In the next lecture, we will examine how terrorist groups capitalize on these conditions in their efforts to try and convince people to support the use of violence in pursuit of change. Naturally, an individual's decision to engage in (or provide support for) terrorist activity is a product of personal motivations (including revenge, psychological attributes, belief systems, personal grievances, and so forth) as much as it is a result of the kind of preconditions and triggers described here. Further, an individual's decision is naturally influenced by his or her family, friends, religious or community leaders, and many others. Organizational characteristics, such as leadership, reputation, and history, also influence an individual's willingness to embrace or reject terrorism as a course of action. As a result, terrorism as a whole can be seen as the product of complex and dynamic interactions between individuals and organizations within certain kinds of contexts—interactions that can motivate or facilitate terrorist radicalization.

QUESTIONS FOR DISCUSSION

- What are the main elements of the relationship between governance and terrorism?
- What role do economics, psychology, or sociology play in motivating terrorist groups?
- What kinds of economic conditions appear to motivate terrorism, and are these the same or different from the kinds of economic conditions that appear to facilitate terrorism?
- At what point can anger and frustration in a democratic system become impetus for acts of violence? And why does this seem to happen in some democracies but not others?

RECOMMENDED READING

Abrahms, Max. "What Terrorists Really Want." *International Security* 32, no. 4 (Spring 2008): 78–105.

Chenoweth, Erica. "Instability and Opportunity: The Origins of Terrorism in Weak and Failed States." In *The Making of a Terrorist: Recruitment, Training and Root Causes.* Vol. 3. Edited by James J. F. Forest. Westport, CT: Praeger, 2005.

Blomberg, Brock et al. "Economic Conditions and Terrorism." *European Journal of Political Economy* 20 (2004).

Eidelson, Roy and Judy Eidelson. "Dangerous Ideas: Five beliefs that propel groups toward conflict." *American Psychologist* 58 (2003).

Felbab-Brown, Vanda. "The Intersection of Terrorism and the Drug Trade." In *The Making of a Terrorist.* Vol. 3. Edited by James J. F. Forest. Westport, CT: Praeger, 2005.

Forest, James J. F. "Terrorism as a Product of Choices and Perceptions." In *Terrorism and Counterterrorism.* Edited by Russell Howard and Bruce Hoffman. New York: McGraw-Hill, 2011.

Howard, Russell D. and Colleen M. Traughber. "The Nexus of Extremism and Trafficking: Scourge of the World or So Much Hype." In *Terrorism and Counterterrorism.* Edited by Russell Howard and Bruce Hoffman. New York: McGraw-Hill, 2011.

Larsson, J. P. "Organized Criminal Networks and Terrorism." In *Countering Terrorism and Insurgency in the 21st Century.* Vol. 2. Edited by James J. F. Forest. Westport, CT: Praeger, 2007.

Lia, Brynjar and Katja H. W. Skjølberg. "Facts and Fiction in Theories of Terrorism—An Expanded and Updated Review of the Literature on Causes of Terrorism." Paper presented at Statsvitenskaplig Fagkonferanse, Trondheim, Norway, January 3–5, 2007.

Naghshpour, Shahdad, Joseph J. St. Marie and Samuel S. Stanton, Jr. "The Shadow Economy and Terrorist Infrastructure." In *Countering Terrorism and Insurgency in the 21st Century.* Vol. 2. Edited by James J. F. Forest. Westport, CT: Praeger, 2007.

Patrick, Stewart. "Failed States: The Brutal Truth." *Foreign Policy* (July/August 2011).

Takeyh, Ray and Nikolas K. Gvosdev. "Do Terrorist Networks Need a Home?" In *Terrorism and Counterterrorism.* Edited by Russell Howard and Bruce Hoffman. New York: McGraw-Hill, 2011.

Wahlert, Matthew H. "The Failed State." In *Countering Terrorism and Insurgency in the 21st Century.* Vol. 2. Edited by James J. F. Forest. Westport, CT: Praeger, 2007.

WEBSITES

Corruption Index, Transparency International
http://www.transparency.org

Fragile States Index
http://fundforpeace.org/fsi/

United Nations Office of Drugs and Crime
http://www.unodc.org

"Descriptions and Case Studies of Money Laundering," U.S. Department of Treasury
http://www.ustreas.gov/offices/enforcement/money_laundering.shtml

NOTES

1. For more detailed analysis of these preconditions and triggers, see James J. F. Forest, "Terrorism as a Product of Choices and Perceptions," in *Terrorism and Counterterrorism*, eds. Russell Howard and Bruce Hoffman (New York: McGraw-Hill, 2011).

2. Jeffrey Ian Ross, "Structural Causes of Oppositional Political Terrorism," *Journal of Peace Research* 30, no. 3 (1993); Assaf Moghadam, *The Roots of Terrorism* (New York: Chelsea House, 2006); and Martha Crenshaw, "The Causes of Terrorism," *Comparative Politics* (July 1981).

3. For example, see Mohammed Hafez, "Political Repression and Violent Rebellion in the Muslim World," in *The Making of a Terrorist: Recruitment, Training, and Root Causes*, vol. 3, ed. James J. F. Forest (Westport, CT: Praeger, 2005); Lydia Khalil, "Authoritarian and Corrupt Governments," in *Countering Terrorism and Insurgency in the 21st Century*, vol. 2, ed. James J. F. Forest (Westport, CT: Praeger, 2007); Ted Robert Gurr, *Why Men Rebel* (Princeton University Press, 1970); and Alan B. Krueger and Jitka Malečková, "Education, Poverty and Terrorism: Is There a Causal Connection?" *Journal of Economic Perspectives* 17, no. 4 (2003.

4. John E. Mack, "Deeper Causes: Exploring the Role of Consciousness in Terrorism," *Ions Noetic Sciences Review* (June-August 2003): 13.

5. See Jeffrey Ian Ross, "Structural Causes of Oppositional Political Terrorism," *Journal of Peace Research* 30, no. 3 (1993): 325. According to Michael Leiter, the most common catalysts that lead to terrorist radicalization include blocked social mobility, political repression, and relative socio-economic deprivation. See *Senate Homeland Security and Governmental Affairs Comm. Hearing on Roots of Violent Extremism and Efforts to Counter It* (July 10, 2008) (statement of Michael Leiter). Shawn Teresa Flanigan has suggested that a great deal of political violence originates from a sense of social and political exclusion and in situations where the minority grievances are not sufficiently met. Shawn Teresa Flanigan, "Charity as Resistance: Connections between Charity, Contentious Politics, and Terror," *Studies in Conflict and Terrorism* 29, no. 7 (2006): 644.

6. Gurr, *Why Men Rebel*.

7. Khalil, "Authoritarian and Corrupt Governments." in *Countering Terrorism and Insurgency in the 21st Century*, vol. 2, ed. James J. F. Forest (Westport, CT: Praeger, 2007)

8. "2017 Corruption Perceptions Index," Transparency International, https://www.transparency .org/research/cpi/overview.

9. Paul Pillar, "The Democratic Deficit: The Need for Liberal Democratization," in *Countering Terrorism and Insurgency in the 21st Century*, vol. 2; and Paul Pillar, "Superpower Foreign Policies: A Source for Global Resentment," in *The Making of a Terrorist*, vol. 3.

10. See, for example, Benjamin R. Barber, "Terrorism, Interdependence and Democracy," in *The Making of a Terrorist*, vol. 3; and Michael Mousseau, "Terrorism and Export Economies: The Dark Side of Free Trade," in *The Making of a Terrorist*, vol. 3.

11. Benjamin R. Barber, "Terrorism, Interdependence and Democracy," in *The Making of a Terrorist*, vol. 3.

12. Shahdad Naghshpour, Joseph J. St. Marie and Samuel S. Stanton, Jr., "The Shadow Economy and Terrorist Infrastructure," in *Countering Terrorism and Insurgency in the 21st Century*, vol. 2.

13. Vanda Felbab-Brown, "The Intersection of Terrorism and the Drug Trade," in *The Making of a Terrorist*, vol. 3.

14. See James J F. Forest and Matthew V. Sousa, *Oil and Terrorism in the New Gulf* (Lanham, MD: Lexington, 2006), particularly Chapters 3, 4, and 9.

15. For more on the relationship between human security and terrorism, see Cindy R. Jebb and Madelfia A. Abb, "Human Security and Good Governance: A Living Systems Approach to Understanding and Combating Terrorism," in *The Making of a Terrorist*, vol. 3.

16. For more on this, see Erica Chenoweth, "Instability and Opportunity: The Origins of Terrorism in Weak and Failed States," in *The Making of a Terrorist*, vol. 3. Also, Kydd and Walter speculate that "democracies may be more constrained in their ability to retaliate than authoritarian regimes." Andrew H. Kydd and Barbara F. Walter, "The Strategies of Terrorism," *International Security* 31, no. 1 (2006): 61.

17. Erica Chenoweth, "Instability and Opportunity: The Origins of Terrorism in Weak and Failed States," in *The Making of a Terrorist*, vol. 3. Also see Roland Paris, *At War's End* (New York: Cambridge University Press, 2004).

18. P. H. Liotta and James F. Miskel, "Digging Deep: Environment and Geography as Root Influences for Terrorism," in *The Making of a Terrorist*, vol. 3.

19. Peter W. Singer, "Corporate Warriors: The Rise of the Privatized Military Industry and its Ramifications for International Security," *International Security* 26, no. 3 (2001/2002): 196. Also, an excellent example is found in "African Struggle over Smuggled Weapons," *Jane's Intelligence Review* (November 23, 1999).

20. Christopher Carr, "Combating the International Proliferation of Small Arms and Light Weapons," in *Countering Terrorism and Insurgency in the 21st Century*, vol. 2.

21. James J. F. Forest, "Influence Warfare and Modern Terrorism," *Georgetown Journal of International Affairs* 10, no. 1 (2009). Also, see *Testimony presented to the House Permanent Select Comm. on Intelligence* (May 4, 2006) (testimony of Bruce Hoffman on "The Use of the Internet By Islamic Extremists"): 18. http://rand.org/pubs/testimonies/CT262-1.

22. Gabriel Weimann, "Terrorist Dot Com: Using the Internet for Terrorist Recruitment and Mobilization," in *The Making of a Terrorist*, vol. 1.

23. Examples of triggering events include the films of Theo Van Gogh, which precipitated a violent response among Islamist radicals and eventually led to Van Gogh's murder; the publication of cartoons portraying Prophet Muhammad, producing a wave of violent protests and actions worldwide; and Israel's military actions against Lebanese and Palestinian militants, which have mobilized protests among Muslims as far away as Indonesia.

24. Paul R. Ehrlich and Jianguo Liu, "Socioeconomic and Demographic Roots of Terrorism," in *The Making of a Terrorist*, vol. 3.

25. Directorate of National Intelligence, Global Trends 2025: A Transformed World (Report of the National Intelligence Council's 2025 Project, November 2008): 43. http://www.dni.gov/nic /NIC_2025_project.html. Also, see Colleen McCue and Kathryn Haahr, "The Impact of Global Youth Bulges on Islamist Radicalization and Violence," *CTC Sentinel* 1, no. 1 (October 2008): 12–14.

26. Daniel Byman, *Deadly Connections: States that Sponsor Terrorism* (Cambridge University Press, 2005).

27. Ibid.

28. Ibid.

29. Ibid.

30. Daniel L. Byman, "Confronting Passive Sponsors of Terrorism," Saban Center for Middle East Policy, Analysis Paper no. 4 (Washington, DC: Brookings Institution, February 2005).

31. Rohan Gunaratna and Arabinda Acharya, "The Al Qaeda Training Camps of Afghanistan and Beyond," in *The Making of a Terrorist*, vol. 2.

32. C. J. Chivers and David Rohde, "Turning Out Guerrillas and Terrorists to Wage a Holy War: The Jihad Files—Training the Troops," *New York Times* (March 18, 2002): A1.

33. See the chapter by Allan C. Brownfeld in *The Making of a Terrorist*, vol. 1.

34. A vivid, detailed account of this event is available at: http://goo.gl/9MBQg. Also see the *BBC News* website at http://news.bbc.co.uk.

II

Terrorism's Facilitators

4

Politics and Governance

The first lecture of this book identified a central element of terrorism as the pursuit of power to bring about political change, or, in the case of some right-wing groups, the power to prevent change and preserve the status quo. Several other lectures in this series have highlighted how terrorism is typically seen as a form of political violence. Thus, it will come as no surprise that there is a great deal of research in this field focused on the relationship between political conditions and terrorism. Much of this research examines either the kinds of political grievances that motivate terrorist groups or the kinds of political contexts that enable terrorists to operate. This lecture highlights several of the main themes in this area of research and then addresses a unique type of enabling environment, which I've called the **zone of competing governance**.

As you might guess, a country's political system and government have historically played a significant role in the motivating ideologies of terrorist groups. A terrorist's life is not an easy one. Nobody joins a terrorist movement in order to get rich; people do it because they are motivated by something they want in the future, and that future typically has some political dimensions. As the saying goes, "all politics is local," and the same typically holds true for political violence. Relatively few people have launched a terrorist campaign in one country because of political conditions in an entirely different country. Left-wing terrorists have typically wanted regime change (e.g., to replace a capitalist democracy with a Marxist regime). Meanwhile, other terrorist groups may want their government to make certain kinds of policy changes, but they have no interest in wholesale regime change. For example, some violent Christian extremist groups such as the Army of God want to make any kind of abortion illegal, while environmentalist groups like the Earth Liberation Front want government policy to be more eco-friendly, and animal rights groups want the government to ban the use of animals in laboratory tests. Often, the government is portrayed as not doing what is needed, or not doing anything at all, and thus the extremists must take up violent means to try and coerce the government to change its policies or behavior. And ethnonationalists are an entirely different kind of terrorist group, whose political objective is the establishment of an independent homeland for a distinct ethnic group.

But in all these kinds of terrorism, the legitimacy of a government plays an important role in whether or not a terrorist group's ideology resonates with members of a particular community. The research literature on conflict and security clearly supports the notion that as legitimacy of a political regime declines, its citizens are more likely to rebel.[1] A recent example of this can be seen in northeast Nigeria. Alex Thurston has observed that places in which state legitimacy is at its weakest are also where we have seen an increasingly violent terrorist campaign by the Muslim extremist group Boko Haram.[2] In my own research on Nigeria in 2011, I interviewed scores of people who told me they no longer believed in their country's political, economic, or legal institutions.[3] The most common and salient grievances include corruption among political and economic elites, economic disparity, barriers to social and educational opportunity, energy poverty, environmental destruction, human insecurity, and injustice. If these kinds of grievances remain unresolved, it does not bode well for the future of the Nigerian government—a country which, by the way, has already endured an exceptionally high number of military coups and a civil war since its independence in 1960.

Another common theme in the literature here focuses on the importance of oppressive or authoritarian governance and its relationship to terrorism. These are countries in which the leaders always seem to grab and hold on to power for decades. In particular, oppression of a particular minority has fueled terrorist campaigns, as we have seen in the case of the Tamils in Sri Lanka, the Kurds in Turkey, and the Chechens in Russia. Meanwhile, Egypt in the Hosni Mubarak era and Libya under Muammar Qadhafi have been frequently cited as examples in which oppressive leaders routinely stifled civil liberties in order to maintain their hold on power and keep society in check. It is instructive that both of these regimes were eventually removed from power. The so-called Arab Spring has also been linked to regime change in Tunisia and the ongoing civil war in Syria. In each of these cases, a country's population has rejected the legitimacy of its government to rule over it, resulting in protests and political violence, including terrorism

In the Middle East, violence has often been a product of institutional exclusion and indiscriminate state repression, particularly following an extended period of Islamic mobilization. Research by Mohammed Hafez found that if a democratic process were to grant Islamists substantive access to state institutions, the opposition would be channeled toward conventional political participation and shun violence.[4] This may be what we saw in places like Tunisia, Libya, and Egypt immediately following the Arab Spring revolts of 2011. On the other hand, if the state denies Islamists access and if the state applies repression indiscriminately—punishing both moderate and radical proponents of political opposition—Islamists are more likely to resort to militancy, as we have seen in places like Syria.

As Lydia Khalil has illustrated in her research, more often than not, authoritarian governments are also corrupt governments.[5] Resources, privileges, and advantages are reserved for a select group of people or ruling elite. Corruption encumbers the fair distribution of social services and adds another layer to the resentment caused by the lack of political participation. The rest of society, because it has no voice, is ignored or placated. This corruption further erodes the government's legitimacy in the eyes of its citizens. And, as noted in Lecture 3, the question of legitimacy is a key aspect in many kinds of political violence. When a state loses the mantle of legitimacy, it allows other nonstate actors to claim that space, including terrorists.

AT A GLANCE

Government Legitimacy?

Nigeria: Decades of neglecting the (mostly Muslim) northern provinces has created an environment for the terrorist group Boko Haram to recruit and operate effectively. The military's indiscriminate use of force has only made things worse.

Somalia: After two decades of military dictatorship, the government of Mohamed Siad Barre collapsed in 1991, and a diverse mix of clans and militia groups has been fighting for power ever since. Recently, the Islamist group al-Shabaab has been responsible for the highest number of indiscriminate attacks against civilians.

Syria: Through its brutal attacks on its own citizens, plus a legacy of cronyism and corruption, the regime of Bashar al-Assad lost its legitimacy. Assad now holds on to power solely through the use of force, while confronting dozens of militant groups (including some linked to al-Qaeda), most prominent the so-called Islamic State.

Meanwhile, other researchers have examined various politically-related enablers of terrorism. One prominent area of this research has focused on the nature of state sponsorship. States that have been linked to sponsorship of terrorism include Afghanistan, Eritrea, Iran, Sudan, Syria, and the former Soviet Union. In fact, terrorism researcher Daniel Byman notes that during the 1970s and 80s, "almost every important terrorist group had some ties to at least one supportive state."[6] State support comes in both active and passive forms, and includes access to money, weapons, freedom of movement, documents, protection, infrastructure, tolerance, and training.[7] In recent years, the most well-known example was the Taliban providing safe haven to al-Qaeda throughout the late 1990s and into 2001 until the United States responded to the 9/11 attacks and invaded Afghanistan. One of the greatest challenges to the international community today is preventing the rise of new Talibans or other regimes that see supporting terrorism as ideologically vital. This is one of the reasons why there's been so much concern recently about Somalia, North Africa, and of course the Afghanistan-Pakistan border region.

Iran is another problematic case of state sponsorship. In 1979, after Iran took 66 Americans hostage, most Western European countries joined the United States and imposed a range of economic penalties on the clerical regime. Today, Iran is considered one of the most active sponsors of terrorism, in large part because of the weapons, training, and funding it has provided to the Lebanese Shiite militia group Hizballah as well as to Hamas and other Palestinian terrorist groups, including Palestinian Islamic Jihad (PIJ) and the Popular Front for the Liberation of Palestine-General Command (PFLP-GC). One of the many covert ways that Iran provides its support to terrorists is through front organizations like **Jihad al-Binna**, which calls itself an Islamic "charity" fund and claims to seek money from international development organizations for social welfare programs in the Middle East. This organization uses a variety of proxy names to mask its relationship with Hizballah, even though it raised millions for Hizballah to reconstruct southern Lebanon after the 2006 war between Israel and Hizballah. This so-called charity was designated as a financer of terrorism by the U.S. Treasury in February 2007, and is estimated to have a budget over $500 million. Most of its money has come from Iran. More recently, Iran has also provided various kinds of support to Shiite militia groups in Iraq and Syria as part of an effort to fight the Islamic State and bolster the Assad regime in Syria, as well as gain more influence over the Iraqi government.

In addition to Iran, other countries designated by the United States as state sponsors of terrorism include Sudan and Syria. Iraq, Cuba, Libya and North Korea were also on this list until recently. For example, government agents of Libya were responsible for the 1988 downing of Pan Am Flight 103 over Lockerbie, Scotland, killing 259 passengers and crew in one of the worst terrorist attacks of the twentieth century. Countries designated by the United States as state sponsors of terrorism face a number of economic sanctions, restrictions (bans on technologies and U.S. foreign assistance), and U.S. opposition to support from international financial institutions like the World Bank and the International Monetary Fund. However, as Dan Byman notes, despite diplomatic protests, economic sanctions, and even military pressure, states like Iran and Syria have supported terrorist groups for decades.[8] Their persistence in the face of pressure suggests that cutting the deadly connection between states and terrorist groups is difficult at best and impossible at worst.

Of course, Saudi Arabia and other oil-rich countries have also provided billions of dollars to Hamas and other Palestinian groups for many years, and Pakistan has supported various Kashmir separatist groups. State sponsorship goes beyond actively arming and training terrorist groups. For some groups, *state inaction* is often vital. Governments that do not crack down on terrorist fundraising, recruitment, training and transit are important assets for modern terrorist groups. To further complicate things, some countries have the political will to crack down on terrorists but not the capacity—their police, military or intelligence forces are too small, lack equipment and expertise, and are generally overstretched already. But while there are dozens of countries that could be considered to some degree as passive sponsors of terrorism, the active state sponsors of terrorist groups are the ones that receive the most attention among U.S. policymakers and scholars.

This, in turn, leads us to another important topic: state weakness. In many cases, researchers have asserted that terrorist groups find safe haven in weak, failed, and collapsed states. Experts have described weak states as lacking "the capacity and/or will to perform core functions of statehood effectively."[9] The Bush administration highlighted this issue in the *National Security Strategy of 2002* and the *National Security Strategy of 2006*, each of which specifically

> **TO THE POINT**
>
> Terrorist groups find safe haven in weak, failed, and collapsed states.

pointed to the importance of addressing both failed and failing states as a component of America's overall counterterrorism effort. This theme is also prominent in the 2010 and 2015 *National Security Strategy* documents released by the Obama administration, and is mentioned as well in the most recent *National Security Strategy* released in December 2017 by the Trump administration.

Matt Wahlert's research found a variety of factors that contribute to the usefulness of failed states as bases for terror groups.[10] First, failed states lack any semblance of law enforcement. In addition, a failed state also offers a population of ready-made recruits by offering them basic amenities (food, security, etc.) that the state is unable to provide. And the levels of poverty and corruption typically associated with failed states makes the viability of bribes more compelling—again, allowing terrorist or criminal organizations the freedom to behave in any manner they wish.

For many scholars and policymakers, the most troubling dimension of weak states is the absence of a central government presence in a particular region of a country—typically described as an "ungoverned space" or "lawless area." For example, the National Intelligence Council has described "failed or failing states" as having "expanses of territory and populations devoid of effective government control."[11] Similarly, the U.S. Government Accountability Office (GAO), in its 2007 report *Forces that Will Shape America's Future*, defines "failed or failing states" as "nations where governments effectively do not control their territory."[12] A more recent report by the American Security Project describes how "the challenge of ungoverned spaces remains a core issue in the management of the threat posed by transnational terrorism. A lack of government capacity allows terrorist groups to find sanctuary."[13]

The overall consensus here appears to be that dire threats to U.S. national security may be originating from places where a central state authority is absent, mainly because it is either unable or unwilling to govern that territory. One geopolitical territory of particular concern is a nation's borders. A state's inability to control its borders is seen as a contributing factor to terrorist groups, particularly in places like the Afghanistan-Pakistan border region, the Sahel region of northern Africa, and various parts of Latin America.

And in a similar area of research related to state weakness, Erica Chenoweth has found that the political stability of a nation's government is a significant factor affecting the origins of terrorism.[14] Her analysis indicates that politically unstable regimes are more likely than stable regimes to provide hospitable environments for terrorist organizations to develop. Essentially, her argument is that the "permissive conditions" of politically unstable regimes inhibit domestic institutional mechanisms that could potentially prevent terrorist organizations from taking root in particular countries.

Therefore, the international community should seek to provide multilateral, legitimate support to transitioning states in order to provide the institutional framework by which such a state can develop.[15]

Policy recommendations that stem from this attention to ungoverned spaces and unstable governments normally focus on strengthening the capabilities of a central government to extend its writ to all parts of a country, and building up its legitimacy. As a result, a flow of equipment, training, and funding has been provided by the United States and others to weak states in order to shore up their military, police, and border security capabilities—the idea being that increased firepower (and to a minor degree, the provision of services) will directly lead to reduced security threats from the state's ungoverned spaces. The central argument here is that their security helps us be more secure at home.

However, when we examine specific attributes of these ungoverned spaces and their propensities to offer safe haven to terrorists, we find that a more refined and nuanced perspective is necessary. If an area is described as "ungoverned," one may assume that nobody is providing any services for the common good, like security or law and order. Such a "no man's land"—where there is truly nobody in charge, nobody providing the slightest sense of order—is relatively rare such as the most remote parts of African jungles and deserts, distant ocean passages, and huge tracts of frozen land in northern Canada, Greenland, northern Russia, and Antarctica. These are actually very unstable and insecure places that offer relatively few benefits to terrorists or criminals other than isolation from prying eyes. There is no infrastructure to use for establishing viable training facilities and operational headquarters; transportation to, from, or through these kinds of places can be difficult, dangerous, and expensive; the climate and terrain may render these places inhospitable or even uninhabitable; and, as a result of this confluence of factors, attracting new recruits or financial support becomes increasingly difficult.

As Angel Rabasa notes, "if the territory is so undeveloped that terrorists cannot communicate, move funds, or travel from remote locations to urban areas, it will be difficult for them to organize and execute attacks. . . . As a result, completely ungoverned territories lacking even those basic assets would hold little appeal for a terrorist group that, like any organized entity, requires at least a semblance of structure to operate."[16]

Instead, terrorists benefit much more from places that are actually not "ungoverned" at all but instead have some kind of political and social rules and order that keep people from just arbitrarily killing each other at random. Such an area can be called a "zone of competing governance"—in essence, a place governed by entities other than the forces of an established nation-state.[17] Within these zones, a diverse array of forces seen by locals as having legitimacy or power to govern may include tribal leaders, warlords, clan patriarchs, or sometimes even mafia dons or leaders of terrorist or insurgent groups. In essence, the importance of these regions lies not in the *absence of governance* but, rather, the *manner in which they are governed.*[18]

ZONES OF COMPETING GOVERNANCE

There are many factors that contribute to the existence of these zones. In some cases, a state's capacity or will to provide critical services (like security, health, education, economic assistance, etc.) is limited, and its lack of presence in a zone creates an enabling opportunity for other forms of governance. In other cases, inhabitants of a zone of competing governance may reject the state's claim of legitimate authority, and direct their loyalties instead toward informal power structures within ethnic groups, clans, or tribal systems.[19]

Within zones of competing governance, those who have power play by a different set of rules than the formal governments of nation-states. Trust is established not by a legal system or formal contract between a leader and those governed but by informal systems of traditional customs and codes. Here we may find a functioning security and intelligence apparatus, some forms of commerce and transportation, even a local customs-based mediation system for resolving disputes—none of which are controlled or perhaps even sanctioned by the nation-state. The important point is that, unlike the image that comes to mind when using the term "ungoverned areas," there is actually some sense of order here, although the nation-state is not considered the primary authority maintaining that order.

Essentially, terrorist networks invariably require some form of safe haven in which to carry out their illicit activities (like providing terrorist training or smuggling weapons). In some cases, these groups may establish a stronghold in a place of relative isolation, far from the prying eyes of a state's security services. Thus, it is more often the case that both criminal and terrorist networks thrive under the protection of local power structures (these can sometimes involve both state and nonstate actors) in places where they can move and operate invisibly. In fact, invisibility within a secure territory that has a functioning infrastructure may be the most important kind of safe haven a clandestine network can have. Rather than exist in a chaotic, unstable "ungoverned space," these groups are much more likely to prefer places where someone other than the state is providing security and other basic services, and where their activities can be conducted with relative openness and impunity. In essence, zones of competing governance can provide order and infrastructure, things absent in truly ungoverned territories.

There are generally two kinds of zones—rural and urban—in which these nonstate forms of governance take place. A rural zone of competing governance will typically be located in rough terrain at a fair distance from any major presence of the nation-state government. From dense jungles to arid deserts, the isolation afforded by these places allows maximum freedom and flexibility for organized nonstate actors. This kind of geographic terrain may also be of particular interest to terrorists and criminals if it offers a bounded territory that can be defended by locals from outsiders or government forces. Prominent examples of rural zones of competing governance in recent years include

- several eastern portions of the Democratic Republic of Congo, where people identify more with clans or ethnic groups than with the state, and especially in several eastern provinces where civil war remnant factions and armed groups from neighboring countries control territories and considerable resources;[20]
- portions of the island of Mindanao in the Philippines, where Muslim inhabitants commonly known as Moros or Bangamoro (the Moro nation) have contested the authority of the Manila government and its religious and cultural influence since the Spanish colonial period;[21]
- dense jungle areas of eastern Peru, particularly the Huallaga Valley, where Shining Path (Sendero Luminoso) at one point had established a network of revolutionary governments and training camps, and has recently seen a resurgence;
- southern and northern regions of Colombia until recently controlled by the Revolutionary Armed Forces of Colombia (Fuerzas Armadas Revolucionarias de Colombia, or FARC), or in some cases by paramilitary groups like the United Self-Defense Forces of Colombia (Autodefensas Unidas de Colombia, or AUC); and
- several regions of Yemen, often described by scholars and the media as "lawless" and desperately poor, although locally based informal governance systems are common.

Many zones of competing governance transcend the border regions of multiple states, such as

- the tri-border area of South America (where Argentina, Paraguay, and Brazil meet), whose overcrowded cities are hubs of arms and drug smuggling, extortion, counterfeiting, and other illicit network activities;
- the vast Sahel region in Africa, south of the Sahara Desert, where tribes like the Tuareg and Berabiche cooperate with elements of al-Qaeda in the Islamic Maghreb (AQIM) when doing this generates revenue, but could (if they wanted to) easily eliminate AQIM's safe havens in Mali, Mauritania, and Niger, either alone or with the help of their government's security services;[22]
- the Pashtun tribal border regions of Afghanistan and Pakistan; the Kurdish regions of southern Turkey and northern Iraq; and the Iraq-Syria border.[23]

In contrast to these geographically large rural areas, urban zones of competing governance may exist within parts of a city—like Karachi, where Taliban militants from the tribal areas come to take refuge among the hundreds of thousands of Afghan and Pakistani refugees in the *kacha abadi* (slums) such as Quid Abad, Sohrab Goth, and Kiamaree.[24] Hybrid zones of competing governance (both rural and urban) also exist, encompassing several cities in a particular region, like southern Lebanon—the primary control and power base for the radical Shiite militia Hizballah. Other examples of hybrids include parts of the Black Sea Region, particularly in Abkhazia, South Ossetia, and Nagorno-Karabakh.[25]

Much of Iraq in the immediate post–Saddam Hussein era provided temporary examples of zones of competing governance, where warlords, tribal leaders, clan leaders, and others claimed control of sizable territories. As the central government of Iraq tried to strengthen its capacity to provide public goods like security, a primary challenge has been to work with and through these groups to establish and maintain physical security while also reducing the sphere of influence established by other armed groups. But unfortunately the sectarian agenda of the Iraqi government's leaders eventually alienated large portions of the Sunni population. Thus, when the Islamic State stormed into Mosul in 2014, the Shiite-dominated military fled, leaving behind a largely Sunni population that initially saw the jihadist group as liberators. Similarly, the civil war that erupted in Syria provided a prime opportunity for the Islamic State to significantly expand the territorial control of its so-called Islamic caliphate. At one point, the group controlled territory larger in size than the U.K.

Not all zones of competing governance exist within weak states or aspiring independent nations; witness the powerful mafia presence in places like Italy, Russia, and Ukraine—where it is widely acknowledged that the most powerful (and widely feared) forces in certain places are not of the government—or some particularly troublesome *banlieues* of Paris, where the police often fear to tread. Several zones of competing governance are home to prominent armed groups that provide the backbone for separatist movements, as in Chechnya, the Basque region of northern Spain, and Mindanao.

Turkey is not considered a weak state by most observers, despite their ongoing economic struggles and a coup attempt in 2016. However, in the Kurdish regions, the perceived legitimacy of the government is quite low. For decades, as Vera Eccarius-Kelly observes,[26] the Kurdish people have felt they were deliberately kept poor and backward, with the government limiting services to Kurdish villages and failing to provide jobs, proper roads, electricity, schools, or hospitals. Feeling marginalized and excluded by the dominant sectors of society, a fair amount of anger and resentment—particularly among young Kurds—is directed toward the Turkish state and the Turkish population. Places like these, where people have suffered so much and developed so much animosity against the state, can provide opportunities for nonstate actors to gain influence by supplying vital services where needed.

Some of these nonstate actors can be significantly large, like the estimated 200,000 Tuaregs in northern Mali who have considerable territorial disagreements with the Malian government and have at times collaborated with transnational terrorist groups like AQIM. Another large and powerful entity of this type is Hizballah, which has tremendous influence in the areas of commerce, housing, politics, education, religion, and social activities of southern Lebanon—indeed, nothing meaningful can be accomplished in southern Lebanon without Hizballah's awareness (and tacit approval). For some time, Hizballah members have not only been "above the law," they have "been the law." With an annual budget estimated at over $250 million, the group runs a network of schools, charities, and clinics, along with its own satellite television and radio stations. In essence, southern Lebanese know and recognize the power held and exercised by Hizballah; for some, this power is viewed as legitimate, and, for others, it is not. But it is certainly noteworthy that in the May 2018 parliamentary elections in Lebanon, Hizballah and its Shiite allies won a majority of seats, a milestone achievement given the longstanding commitment of the organization's leaders toward improving perceptions of its legitimacy.[27]

In Afghanistan, there is limited knowledge of how many Pashtun tribes populate the border region with Pakistan, but there is ample literature on the traditional lifestyle and rules of conduct (like *Pashtunwali*) of these tribes. Law and order in these tribal areas has traditionally been maintained by *Arbakai*, militias that operate within a limited geographic area and carry out at least three common functions: (1) enforce the decisions of the Jirga, an assembly of tribal leaders; (2) maintain law and order; and (3) protect and defend borders and boundaries of the tribe or community.[28] While Afghanistan is clearly a weak state, "strengthening" the state is unlikely to change the power and influence of these tribal governance structures, in part because of low perceptions of legitimacy toward the nation-state. For example, numerous reports from the region describe how Afghans are forced to pay bribes to police and government officials. Among Pashtuns, this produces a stronger affinity toward tribal governance structures, for whom honor and integrity are such vital parts of life. Thus, addressing the problem of state weakness here is perhaps less important than tackling endemic corruption among representatives of the state.

Figure 4.1: Map of Lebanon highlighting districts with strong Hizballah influence. Source: Orthuberra, WikiMedia.

In other cases, corruption and bribery help provide revenue streams that sustain the power and influence of informal governing systems. Along the Turkey-Iraq border, for example, local representatives of Kurdish sociopolitical networks collect so-called transfer taxes or customs fees from truckers, weapons smugglers, and drug traffickers who pay as they pass through territory under Kurdish control. Leaders of these

Kurdish networks benefit from the tax payments and employ standard patronage systems to assure loyalty.[29] Networked men get jobs, and their loyalty to this system helps to sustain their families while ensuring the continued sociopolitical power of these Kurdish leaders.

In sum, there are myriad examples that illustrate how zones of competing governance are markedly different from truly "ungoverned" spaces. Here we find some semblance of order and security provided by entities who are often suspicious of outsiders and who draw on local disenchantment (or even hostility) toward a corrupt, ineffectual, or completely absent nation-state regime. These zones of competing governance compound pre-existing challenges of border and transportation security, facilitate smuggling routes for trafficking of any type of contraband, and potentially provide safe haven for terrorists.[30] They are not, however, demographic blank slates; they are home to complex societies, some of which lend themselves to terrorist penetration while others do not.

SUMMARY

To conclude, let's return to the macro level from which we started this lecture. There are clearly a number of important political dimensions to explore in the study of terrorism, and many of them fall into one of two categories: grievances that motivate terrorist groups, or contexts that enable terrorist groups to operate. Political grievances could include things like oppression, corruption, ineptitude, and so forth, while geopolitical facilitators can include areas in which the state has less power or perceived legitimacy than local tribes and other nonstate entities. Understanding terrorism, and finding ways to combat it successfully, obviously requires significant attention to these kinds of political dimensions.

In the next several lectures, we will examine more closely the major kinds of political grievances reflected in terrorist group ideologies, beginning with the ethnonationalist/separatist category of terrorists, and followed by discussions of left-wing and right-wing terrorists. Even religious terrorists—from Hamas and al-Qaeda to the Lord's Resistance Army—are pursuing primarily political goals, as we will examine in Lectures 12 through 14. As we discussed in Lecture 1, a central aspect of terrorism is the pursuit of power to make (or prevent) change, and terrorists use violence as a means to acquire that power. This is why the study of terrorism requires a solid appreciation for a community's political grievances, goals, and aspirations for the future.

QUESTIONS FOR DISCUSSION

- How does terrorism compare to other forms of political violence (like civil wars, insurgencies, or rebellions)?
- If oppressive and authoritarian regimes are believed to influence terrorist group recruitment, why have we seen so many terrorist attacks in liberal democracies, including the U.S., Belgium, France, and the U.K.?
- In what ways do religious ideologies of terrorism have political dimensions?
- What are your impressions of this "zones of competing governance" concept?

RECOMMENDED READING

Abadie, Alberto. "Poverty, Political Freedom, and the Roots of Terrorism." *American Economic Review* 96 (2006).

Abrahms, Max. "What Terrorists Really Want." *International Security* 32, no. 4 (Spring 2008): 78–105.

Bellin, Eva. "The Robustness of Authoritarianism in the Middle East." *Comparative Politics* 36 (2004).

Byman, Daniel. "Combating State Sponsors of Terrorism." In *Countering Terrorism and Insurgency in the 21st Century.* Vol. 2. Edited by James J. F. Forest. Westport, CT: Praeger, 2007.

Chenoweth, Erica. "Instability and Opportunity: The Origins of Terrorism in Weak and Failed States." In *The Making of a Terrorist.* Vol. 2. Edited by James J. F. Forest. Westport, CT: Praeger, 2005.

DeVore, Marc R. "Exploring the Iran-Hezbollah Relationship: A Case Study of How State Sponsorship Affects Terrorist Group Decision-Making." *Perspectives on Terrorism* 6 no. 4 (August 2012): 85–107.

Forest, James J. F. "Zones of Competing Governance." *Journal of Threat Convergence* 1(1).

Gurr, Ted Robert. *Why Men Rebel.* Princeton University Press, 1970.

Hafez, Mohammed. "Political Repression and Violent Rebellion in the Muslim World." In *The Making of a Terrorist.* Vol. 2. Edited by James J. F. Forest. Westport, CT: Praeger, 2005.

Horgan, John and John Morrison. "Here to Stay? The Rising Threat of Violent Dissident Republicanism in Northern Ireland." *Terrorism and Political Violence* 23, no. 4 (2011): 642–69.

Jebb, Cindy R. and Madelfia A. Abb. "Human Security and Good Governance: A Living Systems Approach to Understanding and Combating Terrorism." In *The Making of a Terrorist.* Vol. 3. Edited by James J. F. Forest. Westport, CT: Praeger, 2005.

Kassem, Maye. *Egyptian Politics: The Dynamics of Authoritarian Rule*. Boulder, CO: Lynne Rienner, 2004.

Khalil, Lydia. "Authoritarian and Corrupt Governments." In *Countering Terrorism and Insurgency in the 21st Century*. Vol. 2. Edited by James J. F. Forest. Westport, CT: Praeger, 2007.

Kydd, Andrew and Barbara Walter. "The Strategies of Terrorism." *International Security* 31, no. 1 (Summer 2006): 49–80.

Marks, Edward. "The War on Terrorism: The Critical Role of Governments." *American Diplomacy* 9, no. 4 (2004).

McCauley, Clark and Sophia Moskalenko. "Mechanisms of Political Radicalization: Pathways Toward Terrorism." *Terrorism and Political Violence* 20, no. 3 (2008): 415–33.

Rabasa, Angel. "Ungoverned Territories." *Testimony presented before the House Oversight and Government Reform Committee, Subcommittee on National Security and Foreign Affairs*. Santa Monica, CA: The RAND Corporation (February 14, 2008).

Rice, Susan E. and Stewart Patrick. "Index of State Weakness in the Developing World." Brookings Institution (2008).

Tan, Andrew. *The Politics of Terrorism*. London: Routledge, 2006.

Wahlert, Matt. "The Failed State." In *Countering Terrorism and Insurgency in the 21st Century*. Vol. 2. Edited by James J. F. Forest. Westport, CT: Praeger, 2007.

Wood, Graeme. "What ISIS Really Wants." *The Atlantic*. (March 2015). http://www.theatlantic.com/features/archive/2015/02/what-isis-really-wants/384980/.

Zartman, I. William, ed. *Collapsed States: The Disintegration and Restoration of Legitimate Authority*. Boulder, CO: Lynne Rienner Publishers, 1995.

WEBSITES

National Intelligence Council, Global Trends
https://www.dni.gov/index.php/global-trends-home/

Transparency International
http://www.transparency.org/

NOTES

1. See Tedd Robert Gurr, *Why Men Rebel* (Princeton, NJ: Princeton University Press, 1970) and Jurgen Habermas, *Legitimation Crisis* (Boston: Beacon Press, 1975).

2. Alex Thurston, "Threat of Militancy in Nigeria," *Commentary for Carnegie Endowment for International Peace* (September 1, 2011), http://carnegieendowment.org/2011/09/01/threat-of-militancy-in-nigeria/4yk8.

3. See James J. F. Forest, *Countering the Terrorist Threat of Boko Haram in Nigeria* (Tampa, FL: Joint Special Operations University Press, 2012).

4. Mohammed Hafez, "Political Repression and Violent Rebellion in the Muslim World," in *The Making of a Terrorist*, vol. 2, ed. James J. F. Forest (Westport, CT: Praeger, 2005): 74–91.5. Lydia Khalil, "Authoritarian and Corrupt Governments," in *Countering Terrorism and Insurgency in the 21st Century*, vol. 2, ed. James J. F. Forest (Westport, CT: Praeger, 2007): 76–92.

6. Daniel Byman, *Deadly Connections: States that Sponsor Terrorism* (New York: Cambridge University Press, 2005): 1.

7. Jonathan C. Byrom and James Walker. "Afghanistan's Transformation to a Narco-Terrorist State: An Economic Perspective," in *Countering Terrorism and Insurgency in the 21st Century*, vol. 2: 198.

8. Daniel Byman, "Combating State Sponsors of Terrorism," in *Countering Terrorism and Insurgency in the 21st Century*, vol. 2, 25–41.

9. Susan E. Rice and Stewart Patrick, "Index of State Weakness in the Developing World," Brookings Institution (2008): 5.

10. Matt Wahlert, "The Failed State," in *Countering Terrorism and Insurgency in the 21st Century*, vol. 2, 93–108.

11. National Intelligence Council, *Mapping the Global Future: Report of the National Intelligence Council's 2020 Project* (2004), http://www.foia.cia.gov/2020/2020.pdf. Cited in Liana Sun Wyler, "Weak and Failing States: Evolving Security Threats and U.S. Policy," CRS Report for Congress (August 28, 2008): 25.

12. U.S. Government Accountability Office, "Forces that Will Shape America's Future: Themes from GAO's Strategic Plan, 2007–2012" (2007), https://www.gao.gov/assets/210/203135.pdf.

13. American Security Project, "Are We Winning? Measuring the Progress in the Struggle Against al Qaeda and Associated Movements" (Washington, DC: American Security Project, 2009): 14.

14. Erica Chenoweth, "Instability and Opportunity: The Origins of Terrorism in Weak and Failed States," in *The Making of a Terrorist*, vol. 2: 17–30.

15. Roland Paris, *At War's End* (New York: Cambridge University Press, 2004).

16. Ibid, 6.

17. An earlier version of this discussion was published in the *Journal of Threat Convergence* 1, no. 1 (2010): 10–21.

18. For more on this, see *Testimony presented before the House Oversight and Government Reform Comm., Subcomm. on National Security and Foreign Affairs* (Testimony of Angel Rabasa on "Ungoverned Territories") (Santa Monica, CA: The RAND Corporation, February 14, 2008): 6.

19. Ibid, 4.

20. Specific examples in the DRC abound, from the Banyamulenge community on the High Plateau of South Kivu to the Burundian Hutu insurgency movement FDD (Forces pour la Défense de la Démocratie), the Mai Mai, Interhamwe, and Rwandan RCG (Rally for Congolese Democracy)/Goma forces.

21. Angel Rabasa, "Ungoverned Territories," 4.

22. *Testimony presented before the Senate Foreign Relations Comm., Subcomm. on African Affairs* (Testimony of Lianne Kennedy-Boudali on "Examining U.S. Counterterrorism Priorities and Strategy Across Africa's Sahel Region") (November 17, 2009): 4.

23. For example, see Andrea Plebani, "Ninawa Province: Al-Qaida's Remaining Stronghold," *CTC Sentinel* 3, no. 1 (2010): 20.

24. Imtiaz Ali, "Karachi Becoming a Taliban Safe Haven?" *CTC Sentinel* 3, no. 1 (2010): 15. Also, for a brief account of Karachi as an "ungoverned urban space," see American Security Project "Are We Winning?," 15.

25. Patricia Taft and David Poplack, *The Sum of its Conflicted Parts: Threat Convergence Risks in the Black Sea Region* (Washington, DC: Fund for Peace, January 2008): 8–10.

26. Vera Eccarius-Kelly, *The Militant Kurds: A Dual Strategy for Freedom* (Westport, CT: Praeger Security International, 2010).

27. For example, Nasrallah called upon his followers to heed traffic signs and pay their electric and water bills, reflecting a need for Hizballah members to be seen as good citizens in order to improve the proportion of the population in southern Lebanon that views them as a legitimate source of governance. See Associated Press, "Hezbollah tries to break out of militant mold" (February 18, 2010), http://www.ap.org.

28. The traditional institution of Arbakai exists in a variety of regions but sometimes under different names; for example, in the Federally Administered Tribal Area (FATA) region of Pakistan, it is called *Salwishti* or *Shalgoodn*, and in Kandahar, it is known as *Paltanai*. For more information, see Mohammed Osman Tariq, "Tribal Security System (Arbakai) in Southeastern Afghanistan," Crisis States Research Center (London, December 2008).

29. Eccarius-Kelly, *The Militant Kurds*.

30. Taft and Poplack, *The Sum of its Conflicted Parts*, 9. See the discussion on Abkhazia, South Ossetia, and Nagorno-Karabakh.

5

Economic Contexts

In this lecture, we focus on several ways in which economics can have some connection to an outbreak of terrorist violence. Sometimes it can be easy to confuse economic dimensions of terrorism with financial aspects of terrorism. Both involve money, clearly, but there are important differences between the two, so we'll cover them in separate lectures. In Lecture 6, we'll address the financial sources of terrorism, covering issues like charities, kidnapping for ransom, and money laundering. But in this lecture, we'll focus on three primary ways that terrorism intersects with economic issues. First, economic conditions—and widely held grievances related to those conditions—can be used as motivations for terrorist violence. Second, certain kinds of economic conditions can facilitate terrorist violence. And finally, there are, of course, important ways in which terrorist violence can have a devastating economic impact, as we saw in the aftermath of the 9/11 attacks.

ECONOMIC CONDITIONS AS GRIEVANCES

First, let's look at the relationship between political violence and economic grievances. People have been examining this relationship for a long time. Plato and Aristotle argued that economic factors play a key role in the outbreak of violence. More recently, Marxists have described war as a mechanism for maintaining inequalities in a struggle for control of raw materials and markets. To them, violence is an inevitable outcome of capitalism. By extension, then, it makes sense that the Marxist left-wing revolutionary terrorists have tended to rationalize their acts of violence in terms of responding to structural economic grievances. But what about other kinds of terrorist groups? It depends largely on the contexts within which these economic grievances are seen.

One of the most fundamental contextual issues here involves aspirations, hopes, and expectations for a better life that are met with limited opportunities. From structural problems like unemployment or underemployment, to endemic cronyism and corruption, there are unfortunately a whole variety of factors in certain countries that can prevent an individual from achieving higher socioeconomic status by merit alone. In countries with authoritarian or repressive regimes that overly control their economy, where there is a severe lack of transparency in private and public sector finance, and where the majority of resources are owned or controlled by a very small elite, ordinary citizens come to feel that they have limited or no power to enact change.

Expectations are a particularly important consideration in oil-rich countries, where discontented activists rightly ask why illiteracy is so high, why the roads are so bad, why so many people are impoverished, why unemployment is so high, and so on, when there is so much money flowing to the country's government. This is a particularly apt description for the kind of economy-related grievances that have motivated the terrorist violence in Nigeria over the past three decades.[1] Here, in concert with massive corruption, there is high unemployment and unequal provision of basic services (like clean drinking water and electricity). According to one report, Nigeria has the worst income disparities in all of West Africa, with only one percent of the elites controlling 80% of the accrued oil wealth, almost 70% of which is held in foreign banks.[2] Meanwhile, an overwhelming majority of Nigerians live below the United Nations–designated poverty threshold, with no access to jobs or a decent education, and a minimum wage in some parts of the country at $50 per month or less.[3] Further, the economic pain in Nigeria is certainly not shared equally. Some of it is due to the aforementioned corruption, which has produced a small English-speaking elite who prominently display their massive wealth through their cars, houses, clothing, and elaborate parties. They are concentrated in just a few places, mainly Lagos, Onitsha, and Abuja. But much of the economic inequality is also structural and geographically concentrated. Incomes in the primarily Muslim north are 50% lower than in the south, for example.[4]

Unfortunately, what has been called the "curse of oil" also plays a role here. This term is used to describe the situation in which a country's economic welfare becomes mostly or even completely dependent on global oil prices. For example, in Iraq, home to several terrorist insurgencies over the last decade, it is no coincidence that 99% of the government's budget comes from the oil industry. Before Nigeria discovered oil in the late 1950s, it had a largely agrarian economy and exported more food than it imported. After the oil wells started pumping, though, local indigenous economic activities were allowed to atrophy, as oil extraction became the country's primary source of revenue. Over time, massive oil revenues generated from the Niger Delta have disincentivized initiative at the local or personal level for many Nigerians. As an industry that employs very few Nigerians, the oil industry in essence replaced its most important resource—its people—with one that is dependent on global market prices to bring in revenue. Making things worse, the government did not invest in economic development beyond the Niger Delta's oil infrastructure.

With no income taxes or social security, the economic system results in ordinary Nigerians having less interest in fulfilling their obligations in a participatory democracy—like holding their government officials accountable. Further, being Africa's largest oil producer and exporter means that many Nigerians have expectations that things should be better, but instead things have gotten worse. Despite billions spent over the last decade, Nigeria's roads are in disrepair, its water, energy, health, and education systems are in crisis, and basic necessities like jobs or credit from banks are in short supply. These economic conditions have created an environment in which terrorist groups in both the south (like the Movement for the Emancipation of the Niger Delta) and the north (like the militant groups Hisba and Boko Haram) can mobilize a population of angry, unemployed youth to take up violence against a government they see as corrupt and illegitimate.[5]

Similar kinds of economic conditions are seen in other major oil producing countries, like Saudi Arabia, Libya, Iraq, Angola, and Kuwait—places where the oil industry provides over 90% of the funding, but the oil wealth has led to unmet aspirations and eventual frustrations among the country's citizens. Really, anywhere we see these kinds of economic conditions—with the combination of bad governance, centralization of power and wealth, political intrigue, crumbling (or nonexistent) infrastructure, regional disparities (especially north versus south), and so forth—we see a toxic brew of grievances, dejection, and frustration. It is in these places that revolutionaries and extremists the world over have found fertile ground for recruiting and launching violent movements.

Another structural economic challenge that we see in countries like Nigeria is a direct result of sociodemographic pressures that are sometimes called a "youth bulge."

As noted in Lecture 3, research by Paul Ehrlich and Jack Liu suggests that persistent demographic and socioeconomic factors can facilitate transnational terrorism and make it easier to recruit terrorists.[6] Specifically, they describe how increased birth rates and the age composition of populations in developing countries affect resource consumption, prices, government revenues and expenditures, demand for jobs, and labor wages. In essence, these demographic and socioeconomic conditions could lead to the emergence of more terrorism and terrorists for many decades to come. Similarly, the National Intelligence Council's 2025 Project report notes that pending "youth bulges" in many Arab states could contribute to a rise in political violence and civil conflict.[7]

This is particularly salient with regard to Nigeria: nearly half the population is under the age of nineteen. These problems are also found in countries throughout the Middle East and Asia, and could lead to the emergence of more terrorism and terrorists for many decades to come. For example, it has been widely reported that over half the populations of Saudi Arabia and other countries in the Persian Gulf are under age 30. When a society's collective grievances—and concurrent demands for change—are combined with limited economic opportunities and relatively low levels of power to enact change, this creates opportunities in which terrorists and other violent armed groups can exploit disgruntled masses and try to mobilize them to join their cause.

You will note that I have not been focusing exclusively or even primarily on poverty in this lecture on economic dimensions of terrorism. Despite some claims to the contrary, poverty is not by itself a root cause of terrorism. If it were, we would certainly have a heck of a lot more terrorism around the world, from the Appalachian Mountains in the United States, to the far corners of sub-Saharan Africa and northeast Siberia. Poverty can be seen as a *contributing factor* to the resonance of a terrorist ideology, but even here the links are tenuous.[8]

Of course, it is important to separate the economic dimensions of a group's ideology from the socioeconomic backgrounds of the group's members. For example, research has shown that members of the major left-wing revolutionary groups of the past half-century tended to be at least middle class and fairly well-educated. Even when the group was focused on rural political revolt, like Sendero Luminoso in Peru, the leaders were from more privileged socioeconomic backgrounds than the peasant masses they sought to mobilize. However, it is also true that the ideologies of many such groups focused attention on economic inequalities, poverty, and the sufferings of poor people as reasons for needing political change.

A similar case is seen in how al-Qaeda's leaders have highlighted economic grievances in their anti-Western ideology. For example, they claim that for several decades the West has been stealing oil from the Muslim world, in part by manipulating global energy markets and keeping the price of oil at artificially low prices. Al-Qaeda also criticizes the West for supporting corrupt, secular regimes in the Middle East, which prevents economic advancement in the Muslim world. Some of al-Qaeda's statements have emphasized how the West negatively impacts poorer, underdeveloped countries by subsidizing domestic producers of certain goods, particularly in agriculture and textiles. And they complain that by imposing economic sanctions on countries like Iran, Syria, and (until 2003) Iraq, the West is severely hurting millions of ordinary Muslim families. Islamic State's ideology highlights similar grievances against the West, and argues that the caliphate it attempted to establish in Iraq and Syria was the first step toward building a new, more powerful future for Muslims worldwide. In short, the ideology of the global Salafi-jihadist movement combines a range of economic and political grievances in its efforts to inspire new recruits and supporters throughout the Muslim world.

So, to sum up this part of the lecture, economic issues have had a prominent place in the motivating grievances and ideologies of many terrorist groups. The economic grievances contained in the Salafi-jihadist ideology are primarily global in orientation, but the more common economic grievances are locally oriented, like high unemployment, corruption among extremely wealthy political and social elites, bad economic policies, and so forth. In countries where price inflation is rampant, people can become frustrated in their quest to secure food or shelter for themselves and their families. And a major source of frustration related to structural economic contexts involves ethnic favoritism—that is, countries in which entire segments of the population are perennially disadvantaged because of their ethnic background. As we'll discuss in Lecture 8, this has most prominently been the case among the Tamils in Sri Lanka, Kurds in Turkey, and the Muslim Uighurs in the western Chinese province of Xinjiang.

ECONOMIC CONDITIONS AS FACILITATORS

A second dimension of the relationship between economics and terrorism is seen in various forms of facilitators, both at the local and global levels. For example, a "shadow economy" can provide an infrastructure for terrorist organizations to operate in, whereby financing becomes easier and detecting it becomes more difficult.[9] A shadow economy is loosely defined as economic activities that are unregulated and untaxed by a country's government, activities which are mainly underground, covert, or illegal.[10] They can include both monetary and nonmonetary asset exchanges, including the sale of goods and services, and can provide numerous opportunities for violent nonstate actors to expand their operational capabilities. In Nigeria, for example a shadow economy empowers criminal and terrorist networks and undermines the legitimate economy as well as the authority of the state. A vibrant drug trade is intensifying corruption and a basic weakening of law enforcement and rule of law. The desire to control the massive flows of drug trafficking has led to several turf battles, particularly among Niger Delta militants[11]—very similar in some ways to the kind of turf war violence that we've been seeing in northern Mexico over the past several years.

Meanwhile, those involved in trafficking are sometimes viewed locally as powerful and effective at getting things done, and as having significant resources. This translates for many locals into a belief that organized crime networks have good leadership, and they take care of their own and those who assist them—a belief that, in turn, helps the trafficking networks attract new recruits and secure local support or acquiescence. Similarly, there have been several instances in which militants in the Niger Delta have provided social services, electricity, funding for students to pay for exams, micro-credit for local businesses, hospital supplies, subsidies for teacher's pay, and so forth. These things, in turn, further erode an already fragile perception of legitimacy toward the Nigerian state.

Essentially, in a country where access to resources is constrained by policy and economic deficiencies, a shadow economy can potentially fuel terrorist activity.[12] Impoverished communities tend to be vulnerable to exploitation by criminal networks, militias, etc.—some of whom provide social and economic programs that fill needs unmet by the local government. Examples of this include the Shiite militia group Hizballah in Lebanon, and the Islamist group Hamas in the Palestinian Territories, both of whom combine an agenda of political violence with social welfare programs for the needy. And as we'll examine more closely in the next lecture, a shadow economy is a prime facilitator of trafficking in weapons, drugs, sex slaves, counterfeit goods and many other forms of profit-generating activities that provide criminal networks with the means to bribe local law enforcement, border security and other officials. In essence, this kind of environment facilitates a vicious cycle, in which corruption and a shadow economy facilitate criminality, the profits from criminality feed the corruption, and the corrupted authorities turn a blind eye to the shadow economy.

The problems of weak governments are made worse by the increasing availability of small arms and light weapons, particularly in places where civil wars and insurgencies have taken place. As Christopher Carr has noted, these weapons can create an architecture of insecurity which fosters the very circumstances that protect and sustain the culture of terrorism.[13] In some parts of the world, it is easier to acquire Kalishnikov rifles—a weapon of choice for many armed groups over the last half-century—than to feed your family. One recent UN report estimated that there are 1.4 weapons for every man, woman and child on the African continent. In Yemen, in the Northwest Frontier Province of Pakistan, in the slums of urban Jamaica and in the Caucasus Mountains, the proliferation of small arms has allowed armed groups to challenge the primacy of the state and to create conditions of instability which provide aid and comfort to criminals and terrorists.[14]

Afghanistan is a classic example of this problem. Its long history of warfare has created alternate systems of profit, power, and protection.[15] In 1979, the Soviet Union invaded Afghanistan and fought unsuccessfully for 10 years to gain control of the country. During this war, the arms and opium traders mutually supported each other, as mujahideen commanders received support from outside countries and generated revenue internally from the opium trade. In 1989, following the defeat of the Soviets, the amount of foreign aid to Afghanistan declined significantly, creating stronger incentives for the Afghan warlords to dramatically increase production of opium to 2,200 metric tons per year to offset the loss in external support.[16] This dependence on opium continued during the Taliban's rule, except in 2001, when the Afghan leadership outlawed opium production (according to some reports, with the intention of increasing profits by reducing supply).

Just as Afghanistan's geography, absence of rule of law, and war economy give it a comparative advantage in the production of opium, its labor force also contributes to the efficient production of the poppy plant.[17] First, Afghanistan already has a labor force skilled in the conversion of poppy plants into raw opium. The precise art of lancing poppies requires an experienced workforce. As Jonathan Goodhand has noted, this skilled labor "can have a major impact on production. During the 1990s, a vast pool of competent workers emerged, giving Afghanistan a comparative labor advantage relative to other potential producers."[18] In essence, Afghanistan came to possess a rare combination of skilled and inexpensive unskilled workers, land, and a weak government to make the labor-intensive harvesting of poppy profitable.[19] This, in turn, has allowed terrorist groups like the Haqqani Network and the Taliban to fund their violence through the extortion of farmers and drug traffickers, or in some cases even becoming directly involved in the lucrative business of poppy cultivation and trafficking.

Meanwhile, after the fall of the Gaddafi regime, Libya emerged as a new hub of weapons trafficking in weapons, oil and illegal migrants. Some reports indicate that tons of weapons were stolen from Libyan arms depots and made their way to al-Qaeda in the Islamic Maghreb among several other terrorist networks in West Africa. The chaos that has taken hold in that country, with different armed factions fighting each other for power and territory, is now cited as a central reason why Islamic State has established a growing presence there. Surely the country's oil reserves are also an attraction to that jihadist network (much like it did in Iraq). As the remnants of Islamic State are forced out of their remaining strongholds in Syria and Iraq, it becomes more likely that Libya might offer a new, hospitable environment for them to establish some new kind of "caliphate" in order to continue their brutal pursuit of the global jihadist agenda (which we'll examine later in this book).

Throughout the world, trafficking in drugs, humans, diamonds and so forth has generated new revenue streams for terrorist groups. But the important point here is that certain economic conditions make this kind of criminal activity more viable. Terrorist groups in South America, like FARC and Sendero Luminoso, are able to take advantage of a terrain and climate that is hospitable to both growing coca and hiding from the Colombian or Peruvian authorities. In the mountains of southern Turkey, the PKK operates in a strategically vital corridor for the drug trade from Asia to Europe. Nigeria has become a prime transit hub for smuggling large amounts of cocaine and marijuana from South America to markets in Europe and North America, in part because of the expansion of nonstop commercial flights. According to reports by the United Nations Office on Drugs and Crime (UNODC), in 2006–07, over 30% of all cocaine traffickers arrested in France were Nigerian.[20] More recently, UNODC has published an annual "World Drug Report" describing in detail the directional flows of drug trafficking (especially cocaine, heroin, methamphetamines, and cannabis), noting that West Africa features prominently here.

In short, various economic conditions can enable and facilitate terrorist-related activity. Most often, these conditions are local, but there are some global dimensions to this as well. For example, the forces of economic globalization have reduced barriers to transportation, shipping, and asset transfers. As a result, terrorist groups can exploit global trade vulnerabilities with relative ease. Further, while a country may generally benefit from strengthening its economic connections with other countries, terrorist and criminal networks are able to take advantage of this increased access to global infra-structure, allowing them to use a country as a transit hub for trafficking illicit goods from external source (supply) countries to external destination (demand) countries. In this way, globalization can actually amplify the capabilities of a terrorist network.

Another dimension is global energy dependence, which has facilitated funding streams for violent groups. Several recent books and reports have described how wealthy oil sheikhs—usually with their government's approval—provided support to mujahidin fighters in Afghanistan during the 1980s and beyond, and many of the same sources have also provided support to Palestinian groups like Hamas or the al-Aqsa Martyrs Brigade, as well as to al-Qaeda, Islamic State, and various other militant groups operating in Syria, Iraq, Yemen, Libya, and elsewhere. Meanwhile, after Islamic State captured oil fields near Mosul, it began selling oil to buyers in Syria, Turkey, and elsewhere—essentially capitalizing on the global need for this vital energy resource. Energy dependence also creates important vulnerabilities; terrorist attacks on energy installations could have major ramifications, and this leads us to the third topic I want to cover: the economic impacts of terrorism.

ECONOMIC IMPACTS

A third dimension of the relationship between economics and terrorism is found in the impact of terrorist attacks themselves, which cause disruptions in commerce, transportation, tourism, and financial markets. In several countries, insurance premiums increased dramatically following one or more significant terrorist attacks. And if the government chooses to step in and subsidize the costs of insurance, this discourages the initiative for businesses to responsibly protect themselves, while the public has to pay the price. Other economically related impacts of terrorist attacks often include a severe tightening of border controls, which can constrain trade and increase costs, along with increases in public spending on security and military operations, which are inherently expensive.

Let's take a few moments to look at some data on the economic impact of the 9/11 terrorist attacks, to get a sense of this relationship. To begin with, there really is a lot of disagreement about the true economic impact, with estimates of jobs lost, cleanup and repair costs, and other factors ranging across a fairly broad spectrum. What reliable data we have indicates that the financial sector in New York City was the hardest hit, accounting for 40% of the World Trade Center casualties.[21] The New York Stock

Exchange and the New York Mercantile Exchange were both closed for several days. The aviation sector was also hit hard. Planes were grounded for at least a week, and millions of Americans were afraid to fly, leading to a 20% drop in passengers, over 100,000 jobs lost, and bankruptcy for several airlines.[22] According to estimates in the insurance sector, the attacks caused a loss of life and property estimated at $40–$50 billion.[23] Other industries were also badly affected, such as hotels, tourism, automobile rentals, travel agents, and civilian aircraft manufacturing. Hotels reported higher vacancy rates and employment in the sector as a whole fell by 58,000 (about 3%) in October and November 2001.[24] Overall, in New York City alone, nearly 18,000 businesses were dislocated, disrupted, or destroyed by the attacks.[25] And of course, most tragically, over 300 firefighters and nearly 100 police officers were killed while trying to evacuate the World Trade Center before it collapsed.

Taking a longer-term view of the economic impact of 9/11 shows that New York City lost a significant amount of office space and close to 200,000 jobs were destroyed or relocated to other cities.[26] However, there were also some positive responses that reduced the overall severity of the 9/11 attack's economic impacts. For example, the Federal Reserve cut interest rates aggressively. Special financing incentives offered by U.S. car companies led to record motor vehicle sales for October 2001. The securities market was only closed for four days, opening again after the telecommunications network in lower Manhattan became operational. And the New York Stock Exchange reopened on September 17; within nineteen trading days, the S&P 500 index had bounced back to its pre-September 11 level.[27]

So, in the end, the events of 9/11 clearly did have a significant impact on all businesses, government offices, and other organizations located in and around the World Trade Center complex (as well as, of course, the Pentagon in Washington, D.C.). Many thousands of dead, injured, missing, physically displaced and traumatized employees led directly to losses of data, information, and institutional knowledge in both the private and public sectors. But nationwide, the economic impact of 9/11 over the long term has been most significant in the billions of dollars spent on new homeland security initiatives, military deployments, etc. Just consider how much money has already been spent in creating and consolidating the Transportation Security Administration or the Department of Homeland Security. Then add a few more zeroes to account for all the hundreds of billions we've spent on military deployments to Afghanistan, Iraq, and other countries (including those to which the CIA, U.S. Special Operations

Forces, and other operatives have been sent covertly). According to a March 2011 report, nearly 10 years after the attacks, Congress had approved a total of $1.283 trillion for "military operations, base security, reconstruction, foreign aid, embassy costs, and veterans' health care for the three operations [Afghanistan, Iraq and the Global War on Terror] initiated since 9/11."[28]

From this perspective, as we'll explore further in Lecture 13, it becomes obvious why al-Qaeda's leaders have consistently encouraged attacks against economic targets in the United States and other Western nations. Al-Qaeda's manuals, as well as several statements by Osama bin Laden, Ayman al-Zawahiri, and others, have described a primary strategic objective of "bleeding" the United States economically and militarily by directly causing inordinate economic losses and forcing the United States to spend excessive amounts of money to protect its vast infrastructure. They argue that the United States derives its considerable military power and political influence from its superior economy. Thus, they believe that disrupting the American economy will in turn defeat the United States as an opponent and end its military hegemony and presence overseas.

Impeding Western economies is therefore a cornerstone of the jihadists' targeting strategy. In one example, Abu Bakr Naji—a prominent jihadist ideologue—justifies attacks on petroleum facilities, making it clear that such attacks are designed to have a negative impact on the economies of al-Qaeda's "enemies."[29] Consequently, jihadist cells and individual "lone wolves" inspired by this ideology are encouraged to attack targets with high economic value so as to inflict serious economic losses on the United States. For the past several years, al-Qaeda ideologues have pointed to the 9/11 attacks against the World Trade Center (a global financial center) as a prime example. In fact, an assessment of al-Qaeda's targeting rationale reveals that the network's most likely targets will be facilities of high economic value in the United States and Europe.[30] Although the network's literature does not specify the precise sectors it intends to target, such facilities would most likely include financial districts and buildings, airports and planes, train and bus stations, ports and ships, subways, shopping malls, hotels, resorts, tourist attractions, sports arenas, entertainment centers, and embassies. As well, an attack on a critical component of a country's transportation infrastructure—like one of the major bridges across the Mississippi River—would impact such things as power distribution, food and water supply chains, waste management, the domestic retail sector and so forth.

SUMMARY

To wrap up this discussion, it's important to recognize that the relationship between economics and terrorism is far more complicated than many have suggested—for example, those who have argued we should combat terrorism by eradicating poverty are woefully simplifying the many reasons why people choose to engage in terrorist activity. Research has found no strong link between poverty and the propensity to generate terrorists, and as you know from our previous lectures, there have been plenty of examples of terrorism in rich nations, as well as terrorists who were certainly not poor.[31]

Let me repeat a theme that I have been emphasizing at various points throughout this lecture series: *context* is essential to our understanding of terrorism. In regard to the focus of this lecture, there are actually three major dimensions of the relationship between economics and terrorism: motivations, facilitators, and impacts. Economic conditions—like poverty—do not by themselves produce terrorism, but they can contribute to a context in which terrorism thrives. This is particularly true in countries with significant levels of blocked social mobility, political repression, and relative socioeconomic deprivation. Here, groups can motivate people to join or support a group by tapping into pre-existing feelings of frustration and helplessness. Various local and global economic conditions can also help facilitate the activities of terrorist organizations. And economic targets (like oil pipelines, financial centers, Western hotels, etc.) can be a prominent type of target for terrorist attacks, largely because these kinds of attacks can have significant economic impacts. With these conditions as our backdrop, we will turn now in the next lecture to discuss the financial and criminal aspects of terrorism.

QUESTIONS FOR DISCUSSION

- What kinds of economic conditions seem most likely to motivate terrorism?
- Are these the same or different from the kinds of economic conditions that appear to facilitate terrorism?
- Where in the world today do we find economic conditions that we may assume would contribute to terrorism?
- In many of those places, however, there is no terrorist activity. Why not?

RECOMMENDED READING

Blanche, Ed. "Oil Industry Increasingly Vulnerable to Terrorist Attack." *Middle East* 347 (2004).

Blomberg, S. Brock, Gregory D. Hess, and Akila Weerapana. "Economic conditions and terrorism." *European Journal of Political Economy* 20, no. 2 (2004).

Byrom, Jonathan C. and James Walker. "Afghanistan's Transformation to a Narco-Terrorist State: An Economic Perspective." In *Countering Terrorism and Insurgency in the 21st Century*. Vol. 2. Edited by James J. F. Forest. Westport, CT: Praeger, 2007.

Carr, Christopher. "Combating the International Proliferation of Small Arms and Light Weapons." In *Countering Terrorism and Insurgency in the 21st Century*. Vol. 2. Edited by James J. F. Forest. Westport, CT: Praeger, 2007.

Felbab-Brown, Vanda and James J. F. Forest. "Political Violence and Illicit Economies of West Africa." *Terrorism and Political Violence* 24, no. 5 (2012): 787–806.

Forest, James. J. F. and Matthew V. Sousa. *Oil and Terrorism in the New Gulf: Framing U.S. Energy and Security Policies for the Gulf of Guinea*. New York: Lexington Press, 2006.

Goodhand, Jonathan. "Frontiers and Wars: the Opium Economy in Afghanistan." *Journal of Agrarian Change* 5, no. 2 (2005).

Hawramy, Fazel, Shalaw Mohammed, and Luke Harding. "Inside Islamic State's Oil Empire: How captured oilfields fuel ISIS insurgency." *The Guardian*, November 19, 2014. https://www.theguardian.com/world/2014/nov/19/-sp-islamic-state-oil-empire-iraq-isis.

Kimmel, Michael S. "Globalization and its Mal(e)contents: The Gendered Moral and Political Economy of Terrorism." *International Sociology* 18, no. 3 (2003).

Krueger, Alan B. and Jitka Maleckova. "The Economics and The Education of Suicide Bombers: Does Poverty Cause Terrorism?" *New Republic* (June 24, 2002).

Li, Quan and Drew Schaub. "Economic globalization and transnational terrorism: A pooled time-series analysis." *Journal of Conflict Resolution* 48, no. 2 (2004).

Lizardo, Omar A. "The Effect of Economic and Cultural Globalization on Anti-U.S. Transnational Terrorism 1971-2000." Research Paper, University of Arizona, June 16, 2004. http://goo.gl/EsiGa.

Naghshpour, Shahdad, Joseph J. St. Marie, and Samuel S. Stanton, Jr. "The Shadow Economy and Terrorist Infrastructure." In *Countering Terrorism and Insurgency in the 21st Century*. Vol. 2. Edited by James J. F. Forest. Westport, CT: Praeger, 2007.

Naji, Abu Bakr. *The Management of Savagery: The Most Critical Stage through which the Umma Will Pass*. Translated by William McCants (2006).

Piazza, James. "Rooted in Poverty? Terrorism, Poor Economic Development, and Social Cleavages." *Terrorism and Political Violence* 18, no. 1 (2006).

Quiggin, Thomas. "Cutting the Cord: Economic Jihad, Canadian Oil, and U.S. Homeland Security." In *Homeland Security: Protecting America's Targets*. Edited by James J. F. Forest. Westport, CT: Praeger, 2006.

United Nations Office on Drugs and Crime. *Transnational Trafficking and the Rule of Law in West Africa: A Threat Assessment*. Vienna: UNODC, July 2009.

WEBSITES

National Intelligence Council, Global Trends
https://www.dni.gov/index.php/global-trends-home/

Transparency International
http://www.transparency.org/

United Nations Organization on Drugs and Crime
http://www.unodc.org/

NOTES

1. For a detailed analysis, see James J. F. Forest, *Countering the Terror Threat of Boko Haram in Nigeria* (Tampa, FL: JSOU Press, 2012).

2. Abdel-Fatau Musah, *West Africa: Governance and Security in a Changing Region* (International Peace Institute, February 2009): 7.

3. Ibid.

4. James J. F. Forest, *Countering the Terror Threat of Boko Haram.*

5. Ibid.

6. Paul R. Ehrlich and Jianguo Liu, "Socioeconomic and Demographic Roots of Terrorism," in *The Making of a Terrorist*, vol. 3, ed. James J. F. Forest (Westport, CT: Praeger, 2005).

7. Directorate of National Intelligence, *Global Trends 2025: A Transformed World* (Report of the National Intelligence Council's 2025 Project, November 2008: 43, http://www.dni.gov/nic /NIC_2025_project.html. Also, see Colleen McCue and Kathryn Haahr, "The Impact of Global Youth Bulges on Islamist Radicalization and Violence," *CTC Sentinel* 1, no. 1 (2008): 12–14.

8. In fact, a recent study by Jim Piazza found that, contrary to popular opinion, there was no significant relationship between terrorism and any basic measures of economic development. Rather, dimensions such as a country's population, ethnoreligious diversity, increased state repression, and, most significantly, the structure of party politics, were found to be significant predictors of terrorism. He concluded that "social cleavage theory" is better equipped to explain terrorism than are theories that link terrorism to poor economic development. Piazza, "Rooted in Poverty? Terrorism, Poor Economic Development, and Social Cleavages," *Terrorism and Political Violence* 18, no. 1 (2006).

9. Shahdad Naghshpour, Joseph J. St. Marie, and Samuel S. Stanton, Jr., "The Shadow Economy and Terrorist Infrastructure," in *Countering Terrorism and Insurgency in the 21st Century*, ed. James J. F. Forest (Westport, CT: Praeger, 2007).

10. Ibid.

11. Abimbola O. Adesoji, "Between Maitatsine and Boko Haram: Islamic Fundamentalism and the Response of the Nigerian State," *Africa Today* 5, no. 4 (Summer 2011): 113.

12. Naghshpour, St. Marie, and Stanton, "The Shadow Economy and Terrorist Infrastructure."

13. Christopher Carr, "Combating the International Proliferation of Small Arms and Light Weapons," in *Countering Terrorism and Insurgency in the 21st Century*, vol. 2, ed. Forest, pp. 127–41.

14. Ibid.

15. Jonathan C. Byrom and James Walker. "Afghanistan's Transformation to a Narco-Terrorist State: An Economic Perspective," in *Countering Terrorism and Insurgency in the 21st Century*, vol. 2, ed. Forest, p. 204.

16. Jonathan Goodhand, "Frontiers and Wars: the Opium Economy in Afghanistan," *Journal of Agrarian Change* 5, no. 2 (2005): 198.

17. Byrom and Walker, "Afghanistan's Transformation," 205.

18. Goodhand, "Frontiers and Wars," 205.

19. Byrom and Walker, 205.

20. United Nations Office on Drugs and Crime, *Transnational Trafficking and the Rule of Law in West Africa: A Threat Assessment* (Vienna: UNODC, July 2009). See also the UNODC website on drug trafficking in Nigeria, http://www.unodc.org/nigeria/en/drug-prevention.html.

21. New York City Partnership and Chamber of Commerce, *Working Together to Accelerate New York's Recovery: Economic Impact Analysis of the September 11th Attack on New York City* (2001): 21.

22. J. Alfred Broaddus, "Attack at the Economic Heart of America: What 9/11 Taught the United States about its Economic Security" (remarks at the Homeland Security Conference, Lexington, VA, October 29, 2003).

23. Insurance Information Institute (New York: October 21, 2002). Cited in Gail Makinen, "The Economic Effects of 9/11: A Retrospective Assessment," Congressional Research Service Report #RL31617 (Washington, DC: September 27, 2002): 2.

24. Robert Looney, "Economic Costs to the United States Stemming From the 9/11 Attacks," *Strategic Insight* (August 5, 2002).

25. Makinen, "The Economic Effects of 9/11: A Retrospective Assessment."

26. Looney, "Economic Costs to the United States."

27. Chen and Siems, "The Effects of Terrorism."

28. Amy Belasco, "The Cost of Iraq, Afghanistan, and other Global War on Terror Operations since 9/11," Congressional Research Service (March 29, 2011), http://www.fas.org/sgp/crs/natsec/RL33110.pdf.

29. Abu Bakr Naji, *The Management of Savagery: The Most Critical Stage through which the Umma Will Pass*, translated by William McCants (2006), retrieved June 4, 2006 from the website of the Combating Terrorism Center at West Point, http://www.ctc.usma.edu/naji.asp.

30. James J. F. Forest and Sammy Salama, "Jihadist Tactics and Targeting," in *Jihadists and Weapons of Mass Destruction: A Growing Threat*, ed. Gary Ackerman and Jeremy Tamsett (Washington, DC: CRC Press, 2009): 81–97.

31. Alen B. Krueger and D. D. Laitin, "Faulty Terror Report Card," *Washington Post*, May 17, 2004, editorial. Also see Piazza, "Rooted in Poverty?"

6

Financing

It's fairly obvious that terrorists need money. Thus, unless they are independently wealthy or have a job (which is difficult when they're living underground and trying to avoid being tracked by authorities), they're basically relying on the support of others to provide for their food and shelter. This is why, when you start looking at various terrorist-related websites around the Internet, you see all sorts of appeals for people to donate to the cause. But while it's fairly easy to say that terrorists need money, there are disagreements about just how much money they need. For example, some have argued that terrorist attacks themselves cost very little money to carry out, pointing as evidence to the trivial cost of a suicide belt or similar device. Even major, headline-grabbing terrorist attacks are quite cheap when compared to how much it costs for a military attack that produces the same amount of destruction. For example, a Predator drone costs roughly $4 million, and a single Hellfire missile costs over $100,000. In comparison, according to some estimates, the 9/11 attacks in New York and Washington, D.C. cost around $500,000; the 2002 bombing of two nightclubs in Bali, Indonesia cost about $50,000; the 2004 attacks against several commuter trains in Madrid cost between $10,000 and $15,000; and the 2005 attacks on London's mass transit system cost about $2,000.

However, Congressional testimony by Stuart Levey, a former undersecretary of Treasury for Terrorism and Financial Intelligence, argues a different perspective.[1]

In the first place, the cost of financing terrorist activity cannot be measured by the cost of a destructive act. The daily maintenance of terrorist networks like al-Qaeda is expensive—even if a particular attack does not cost much to carry out. Indeed, as the 9/11 Commission pointed out in their report, groups like al-Qaeda must spend money for many purposes—to recruit and train members, provide them with travel funds, plan operations, and bribe corrupt officials, for example. In essence, these reports have argued, it takes a fairly large amount of cash to run a terrorist group over a long period of time.

Others have also argued that the total costs of terrorist attacks are often misunderstood and underestimated. Some specific costs of terrorist operations can include living expenses for the operatives as they prepare for their attack. The day-to-day living expenses are not trivial even if the terrorists live a very frugal lifestyle. Of course, the costs will also vary depending on the location of the targets and the proximity of the terrorists to these targets. For example, the costs of operations in the United States or Western Europe will obviously be much greater than operations in countries such as Tanzania, Kenya, or Yemen.

A terrorist group may also have to cover the costs involved in special training and the development of expertise that is critical to the successful completion of a mission. While terrorist training camps can help develop basic skills in weaponry and attack strategies, there is often a need for specialized knowledge that can only be gained from more formal and expensive sources—like proficiency in chemistry, biology, truck driving, or, as in the case of 9/11, flight training. The group also has to purchase weapons or explosive materials that will be used in an attack. The September 11 hijackers were relatively unusual in that they were so lightly armed—they had smuggled box cutters and small utility knives on board their airplanes. Ordinarily, acquiring explosives or weapons for terrorism can get quite expensive.

In the case of the March 2004 terror attacks in Madrid, the terrorist cell actually traded drugs for explosives. One of the key members of this terrorist cell was a 30 year-old named Jamal Ahmidan. Born in Morocco, Ahmidan had gotten involved in petty crime during his teen years, and wound up in prison, where he became radicalized by an extreme jihadist ideology known as Takfir wal-Hijra.[2] After his release from prison, Ahmidan entered Spain illegally and became a drug dealer in the Madrid area. He also joined a small cell of Takfiris, upon whose behalf he acquired weapons and ammunition through his contacts in the Spanish criminal world, sometimes trading drugs for weapons. In early 2004, a large amount of explosives were stolen by criminals from a mine in Asturias in northern Spain. Using his contacts, Ahmidan acquired these explosives, exchanging them for drugs and a considerable amount of money. These explosives were then used in a coordinated attack against commuter trains that left 191 people dead and over 1,000 wounded on March 11 of that year.[3]

A terrorist group may also need to cover the costs of travel related to a specific plan. These can include meetings among the conspirators, meetings with senior people in the network, or meetings with members of the network providing some kind of support services. Many recent planned or actual attacks by terrorist networks operating in the United States and Western Europe have involved considerable travel prior to the event itself. The 9/11 Commission found significant travel related to the preparations for that attack, involving places like Malaysia, the Philippines, Pakistan, Germany, and Spain.

So, where do terrorists get the money they need to cover these and other costs? As we discussed in Lecture 5, there are several economic contexts that provide a variety of legal and illegal funding opportunities for terrorist organizations. We've already discussed state sponsorship of terrorism in Lecture 4, including Iran's support for Hizballah and Hamas, so we'll focus in this lecture on nonstate sources of terrorist finance, such as support from diaspora members, charities, and criminal activity like trafficking and money laundering.

First, let's look at the role of diaspora members, who are individuals from one country who have migrated to another—often a wealthier, industrialized Western country—and send money back home to friends and family. Examples of terrorist groups who have taken advantage of a diaspora as a source of funding include: the Tamil Tigers in Sri Lanka, who used various extortion rackets to get funding from large Tamil communities in Canada and elsewhere; Kashmir separatist groups, who both legally and illegally raise funds from Pakistani communities in the U.K., Denmark, and elsewhere in Western Europe; North African terrorist groups, like al-Qaeda in the Islamic Maghreb, which gets money from members of the Algerian communities in France and Moroccan communities in Spain; the Kurdish militia group PKK in Turkey, which raises funds in Kurdish communities in Germany and elsewhere in Western Europe;[4] and of course, the IRA and Provisional IRA, which raised money from millions of Irish-Americans in the United States to support the Republican cause.[5] In addition to a nationwide organization called the "Irish Freedom Committee," certain communities in the Eastern United States were particularly important sources of IRA funding. For example, Irish pubs in the Northeast often kept donation jars on the counter labeled "For the Children," "For the Families," or "For the Lads." In these and

other cases, the challenges of combating terrorist financing involve both the host country where the conflict is taking place, as well as the residence countries of these diaspora
communities. If these countries aren't on good speaking terms, or have limited desire
to work together to address the problem, you can expect little will be done to address
the financing of terrorism here.

Terrorist groups have also frequently employed legal activities to raise funds,
including general solicitations for contributions (in person and online) from anyone
who might be attracted to their ideology and goals, operating seemingly legitimate
businesses and skimming off the profits to support terrorist activities, and creating
charitable organizations, one of the largest sources of funding for terrorist groups
worldwide. Keep in mind that there are hundreds of thousands of charities that exist
throughout the world, from small local ones to global enterprises. If we add up the
tremendous amount of money that they raise altogether, diverting just a small fraction
of that diverted to terrorist-related causes would be quite significant.

For years, beginning in the 1980s, charity funds throughout the Middle East were
used to support the Arab fighters against the Soviets in Afghanistan. A 2002 report
by the Council on Foreign Relations concluded that individuals and charities based
in Saudi Arabia were the most important source of funds for al-Qaeda. A number of
charities—like the Holy Land Foundation and the International Benevolent Fund—
have repeatedly faced legal actions in the United States and Europe for providing funding to Hamas and other Palestinian groups that engage in terrorism.

Some of the major problems with investigating and combating terrorist funding
from charitable organizations include the fact that many are formed in other countries.
Several charities are supported by the government or legitimate businesses, particularly in authoritarian regimes where wealth is often owned and controlled by relatively
few people. The lack of transparency in many countries' financial systems also con-
strains countries' ability to track potential terrorist funds. Charitable organizations
that knowingly support terrorism tend to hide their true purpose from all but their
most trusted supporters. Further, many of the most clandestine charitable networks
supporting terrorism are notoriously difficult to infiltrate. And of course, money from
legitimate charities has also been diverted to fund terrorist groups without the intention or knowledge of donors or even fund administrators.

Finally, we have what is likely the biggest problem of all when it comes to terrorist
financing: criminal activity. Terrorist groups have always engaged in an array of crimes
to help fund their political violence. Examples include trafficking in drugs, weapons,

humans, diamonds, precious metals, etc.; armed robbery (including piracy); extortion and protection rackets (as with the Tamil Tigers and the Ulster Volunteer Force); oil bunkering (stealing oil to sell on the black market, as seen in the Niger Delta region of Nigeria); fraud and embezzlement (including establishing phony companies); cigarette smuggling (like the case of the Hizballah operatives in the United States who bought truckloads of cigarettes in North Carolina, sold them in Michigan where the prices are much higher, and then sent profits to Hizballah's leaders in Lebanon[6]); the production and distribution of counterfeit DVDs, CDs, software, etc. (especially in the Tri-Border Area, where the borders of Argentina, Brazil, and Paraguay intersect[7]); counterfeiting documents and currency; ID theft and credit card theft (which we are increasingly seeing occur through the Internet); and money laundering.

Kidnapping for profit has also been a significantly lucrative form of criminal activity for certain terrorist groups. For example, on September 28, 1977, Japan Airlines Flight 472 en route from Paris to Tokyo was hijacked by the Japanese Red Army (JRA) after stopping for fuel in Mumbai, India. The terrorists ordered the plane to land in Dhaka, Bangladesh, where they took the passengers and crew hostage, demanding $6 million and the release of nine imprisoned JRA members. On October 1, then-Prime Minister Fukuda announced that the Japanese government would accept the hijackers' demands and pay the ransom, on the principle that "human life is more important than the world."[8]

There are many other examples of financially lucrative kidnappings by terrorist groups during the 1970s, particularly in Argentina. For example, in 1973, Victor Samuelson, a U.S. citizen working as the general manager of the Esso Oil Refinery, was kidnapped in Buenos Aires by the Ejército Revolucionario del Pueblo (ERP), and a ransom of $14.2 million was paid for his release.[9] An even larger ransom was paid when the two sons of Juan Born, co-owner of Argentina's largest private company, were kidnapped by Montoneros guerrillas in Buenos Aires on September 19, 1974. The younger of the brothers, 39-year-old Juan Born, Jr., was released in April, 1975 after an undisclosed ransom was paid, but then the group demanded a $60 million ransom for the other son, Jorge, who was released on June 20 after this ransom was paid.[10]

Several prominent kidnappings for profit also occurred in Europe during this same time period. For example, in 1973, the Basque separatist group ETA kidnapped Felipe Huarte Beaumont, the president of a local administrative council, and was paid $700,000 for his release.[11] In 1974, the Armed Proletarian Nuclei (NAP) in Italy kidnapped local industrialist Giuseppe Moccia and released him after receiving a ransom of $1.5 million. In 1977, wealthy Spanish industrialist Javier de Ybarra y Bergé was kidnapped by ETA and released for a ransom of $5.1 million.[12]

Most recently, religiously oriented terrorist groups in North Africa, the Middle East, and Southeast Asia have become increasingly active in the world of profit-motivated kidnapping. Foreigners kidnapped in Iraq have garnered particularly large ransom payments, as observed in a May 2006 report published by *The Times* in London that describes ransom payments made by France ($25 million), Italy ($11 million), and Germany ($8–10 million).[13] Meanwhile, in February 2003, the Salafist Group for Preaching and Combat (GSPC, a Muslim extremist group in Algeria) kidnapped 32 European tourists traveling in the Sahara, and was paid a ransom for their release that is estimated by at least one report to be $5–10 million.[14] In 2008, shortly after changing their name to al-Qaeda in the Islamic Maghreb (AQIM), members of this group abducted two Austrian tourists in Tunisia and took them to Mali, then went to Niger where they kidnapped two Canadian diplomats and four European tourists in 2010. All but one of the tourists, a Briton, were subsequently released, with ransoms worth several million dollars allegedly paid.[15]

Of all the kinds of activity I have mentioned, however, most observers agree that the largest criminal-oriented source of terrorist financing comes from the illicit drug trade. No other illicit activity is as profitable as the global drug trade.[16] By some estimates it generates between $300 billion and $500 billion annually,[17] so it certainly makes sense that terrorist groups would want a piece of that action. Examples of this are plenty: a few years ago, federal agents broke up a methamphetamine ring in a dozen U.S. cities that funneled proceeds to Hizballah; in Colombia, the FARC (and other paramilitaries) have increasingly relied on the cocaine trade to finance their operations; and Afghanistan's poppy fields, which the United Nations says are responsible for over 90% of the world opium supply, provide funding sources for the Taliban and al-Qaeda. By some estimates, half of all the world's major terrorist groups are involved to some degree in the global drug trade.[18]

Of course, when we examine the issue of how crime and terrorism intersect, we have to acknowledge that sometimes it's hard to tell the criminals apart from the terrorists. In fact, as Alex Schmid notes, criminal and terrorist organizations have much in common: both are rational actors, they produce victims, they use similar tactics such as kidnapping and assassination, they operate secretly, and both are criminalized by the ruling regime and stand in opposition to the state.[19] However, by portraying their criminality with a cloak of ideological justification, politically violent actors demonstrate how purpose matters—as David Rapoport observed, the act of robbing a bank or engaging in drug trafficking can be to enrich oneself as a person or to get money for an organization that sees itself as creating a better society.[20] Further, as Schmid notes, terrorism and crime are distinguished not only by different purposes (e.g., political motivation versus a greater share of illicit markets), but also by their violence (e.g., terrorists tend to be less discriminate than criminals), and by their communication strategies (e.g., terrorists claim responsibility for violent acts and use the media to propagate their cause, while criminals avoid the media).[21]

Studies of crime and terror often grapple with the central debate over definitions: What separates a terrorist group from a criminal organization, a liberation movement, or some other entity? We described various aspects of the definition of terrorism in Lecture 1, but just to recap here the U.S. Department of State views "terrorism" as "premeditated, politically motivated violence perpetrated against non-combatant targets by sub-national groups or clandestine agents, usually *intended* to influence an audience."[22] Bruce Hoffman defines terrorism as "the deliberate creation and exploitation of fear through violence or the threat of violence *in the pursuit of political change* . . . [it is] designed to have far-reaching psychological effects beyond the immediate victim(s) or object of the terrorist attack . . . [and] to create power where there is none or to consolidate power where there is very little."[23] In these and other definitions of terrorism, which we examined in the first lecture of this series, a common theme is that *motives matter*.

Phil Williams also distinguishes terrorist and criminal organizations by their motives: at the heart of terrorist organizations is the desire to bring about political change, while criminal organizations focus on profit generation and maximization.[24] Further, he notes, terrorist attacks should be seen as a sum total of activities that include fundraising, recruitment, training, development of special skills, and preparation for an attack—activities that can stretch over several months or even years. Criminal organizations focus much of their energies on protecting themselves from peer competitors or government and law enforcement agencies, and pursue strategies to manage, avoid, control, or mitigate risk—but of course, many terrorist groups do this as well.[25] Loretta Napoleoni draws clear distinctions between terrorists and criminals in how they view money. Criminal organizations run their operations like private corporations, with the accumulation of profit as the ultimate goal. In contrast, terrorist organizations are more interested in money disbursements than money laundering; instead of accumulation, money is to be distributed within the network of cells to support operations.[26]

Thus, the scholarly literature is rich with thoughtful arguments for how terrorists should be viewed as different from ordinary criminals. However, a growing number of authors have begun to suggest that the distinctions between the two may be fading. For example, Walter Laqueur has argued that 50 years ago a clear dividing line existed between terrorism and organized crime, but that "more recently this line has become blurred, and in some cases a symbiosis between terrorism and organized crime has occurred that did not exist before."[27] Other scholars such as Tamara Makarenko, Thomas Sanderson, Chris Dishman, R. T. Naylor, Rachel Ehrenfeld, Louise Shelley, and John Picarelli have described the phenomenon as a nexus, a confluence, a continuum, or some other kind of paradigm involving fluid, constantly changing relationships among members of terrorist and criminal networks.[28]

According to Makarenko, the end of the Cold War and subsequent decline of state sponsorship for terrorism forced groups to seek new revenue sources, and most often this led them to engage in various kinds of organized crime activities.[29] Some groups—like the FARC in Colombia and the Abu Sayyaf Group in the Philippines—eventually moved away from their original commitment to political violence and more toward increasing levels of purely criminal activity. In the case of the FARC, these Marxist guerrillas in Colombia initially banned drug trafficking,[30] then began to tax and protect the drug trade, and eventually became so deeply involved in it that they were seen by many as more of a peer competitor with Colombian drug cartels than as an ideologically motivated group seeking political change. Now that FARC has declared an end to its armed struggle and turned over its weapons—following the 2016 peace accords with Colombia—it remains to be seen how the group's involvement in the drug trade will change. But is important to note that in mid-2017, the remnants of the group announced the formation of a new political party, whose leader Rodrigo Londono (a.k.a. "Timochenko") briefly ran for the presidency in 2018. If history is any guide, the pursuit of political power tends to constrain a group's active criminal engagements because of its concern about bolstering perceived legitimacy in the eyes of the broader public. We'll have to see if that holds true in the case of FARC's future.

Meanwhile, a different trajectory can be seen regarding the Abu Sayyaf Group in the Philippines, where there are indications that profit derived from criminal activity (especially kidnapping for profit) has supplanted sociopolitical ideology as the organization's *raison d'être*. For example, in the past few years, the group has kidnapped dozens of German tourists, Malaysian sailors, Filipino civilians, Indonesian fishermen, and many others, each time demanding large monetary ransoms. Not once have any demands been made regarding government policy concessions nor have any recent statements from the group articulated a political ideology; its only communications have been demands for money, or in a few instances, videos of the group murdering a hostage when a ransom was not paid. From this perspective it would seem that the group is more interested in criminality today than in achieving the political or religious goals it originally articulated in its jihadist-oriented ideology.

In these and other examples, the blurred lines between criminals and terrorists have become almost nonexistent. There is an increasingly robust body of research examining these activities, and particularly what some refer to as the "nexus" of organized crime and terrorism. This research mainly focuses on one or more of the following topics: (1) people (including the perpetrators of crime or terrorism, and their motives); (2) places (political and socioeconomic contexts that seem to enable or facilitate crime and terrorism); (3) things that form the crux of crime-terror linkages (e.g., trafficking in drugs, weapons, humans, and so forth, as well as money laundering, document forgery, kidnapping, extortion, and moving counterfeit goods); (4) impacts of these linkages (including victims, or the economic and political consequences); and (5) responses (who is doing what, or should do what, to deal with various kinds of linkages between crime and terrorism).

Within each of these categories, we find a wealth of case studies and analyses of regional or global patterns of group behavior. For example, in the category of "things," there is research on what Napoleoni refers to as a "new economy of terror," in which sources of revenue include remittance from diaspora members, charities, profits diverted from legal and illegal businesses, kidnapping, piracy, and many other kinds of criminal activity I described earlier.[31] A central activity within this economy of terror is money laundering, which is associated with all kinds of criminal activity, terrorist-related or otherwise, and is particularly important for anyone involved in the global drug trade. In essence, money laundering is a process by which the proceeds derived from a criminal activity are disguised in an effort to conceal their illicit origins and to legitimize their future use. How does it work? Laundering schemes fall within the three phases of the "money laundering cycle": placement of illegal funds (cash) into the financial system; layering (structuring) transactions to disguise the source of the funds; and integration (reinvestment) of the funds into legitimate businesses.[32] The methods for money laundering are as varied as people's imaginations. We are naturally creative beings, and unfortunately too many people have come up with too many ways to beat the system of monitoring that is meant to track and interdict criminal and terrorist finances. Many terrorist organizations attempt to operate legitimate businesses, which generate their own profits and can also be used as a front for money laundering. Links to terrorism have been found with businesses involved in agriculture, construction, livestock, fish, and leather—really, all kinds of commodities and services. Not only do business transactions help launder money, but shipments of goods associated with these transactions can be used to conceal shipments of drugs, weapons, and other kinds of contraband.

Money laundering is really quite hard to investigate for several reasons. First, the criminal organizations have become quite adaptive and creative in their schemes, laundering billions of dollars annually. Some organizations even cooperate with each other in finding and utilizing new ways to beat the system. Offshore accounts—especially in countries with special banking regulations, like the Cayman Islands or Switzerland—can help organizations break or hide audit trails. The most sophisticated organizations are undoubtedly able to coerce (some with bribes, others with threats of violence) some of the finest lawyers, accountants, bankers, and other officials who are in a position to facilitate an easier funding flow. And, as we'll examine in Lecture 13, many of these groups exhibit the attributes of a learning organization, and are thus keen to embrace and utilize new technologies and systems. When it comes to money laundering, the terrorist groups are proving to be extremely versatile and creative. They are reverting to more fundamental methods of transferring money, such as enlisting informal value transfer systems, engaging in bulk cash smuggling, or simply transferring "value" anonymously via e-cash (or e-gold) on the Internet.[33]

In addition to examining how terrorists engage in criminal activity, we also need to develop a solid understanding of where we see these kinds of criminal activities occur— i.e., the research category of "place" that I mentioned earlier. Contextual factors that influence a terrorist or criminal organization's activities include access to weapons, illicit economies, and safe haven—as I described in Lectures 3 and 5, these are often referred to as "enablers." Studies of these enablers are often driven by the desire to understand where and when criminal or terrorist activities (including collaboration) are most likely, and why. According to this area of research, there are specific locations throughout the world within which greater criminality, terrorism, and crime-terror collaboration have been facilitated in the past or are likely to be facilitated in the future. For example, the presence of organized crime may attract terrorists into a particular location, where they offer themselves as protectors of the population against the deficiencies of the government and the predatory behavior of criminal groups, and in return they expect support for their ideological agenda.[34] Research has also pointed to greater amounts of crime in places with high levels of poverty and economic desperation, and in countries with limited or no transparency in public or private finance, which is often the case where authoritarian regimes are in charge.

Scholars have also drawn links between terrorism, crime, and local conditions like government oppression or corruption, foreign occupation, poverty, discrimination, real or perceived injustice, and a lack of political or socioeconomic opportunities. Numerous books, journal articles, and reports—including the Fund for Peace's annual Failed State Index[35]—highlight the importance of a central government's weakness as a potential enabler for criminal and terrorist activity. In-depth case studies of the crime-terror nexus have also been published on the Black Sea region, Chechnya and the northern Caucasus, the Afghanistan-Pakistan border region, the Horn of Africa, the Tri-Border area of Latin America, and many other regions.[36]

Trends in globalization have also contributed to the capabilities and opportunities of terrorist and criminal networks to operate and collaborate. According to Yuri Fedotov, the executive director of the United Nations Office of Drugs and Crime, "Thanks to advances in technology, communication, finance and transport, loose networks of terrorists and organized criminal groups that operate internationally can easily link with each other. By pooling their resources and expertise, they can significantly increase their capacity to do harm."[37] It is also quite likely that successful counterterrorism strategies can lead to greater levels of collaboration between terrorists and criminals; a constrained operating environment may compel an organization to pursue any and all options to achieve its objectives. Overall, the literature is rich with examples of how contextual attributes can enable (or constrain) terrorist and criminal activities.

SUMMARY

To wrap up this lecture on terrorism finance and criminality, let's recap the main themes: terrorists need money, and they get that money from a variety of sources, including diaspora communities, charity funds, and most important, criminal activity. In terms of the latter, nothing beats the amount of profits you can get from drug trafficking; thus many of the wealthiest terror groups today have their fingers in the global drug trade, particularly opium, cocaine, and marijuana. According to one report published shortly after 9/11, about half of the 28 organizations identified as terrorists by the U.S. State Department were funded by the sales of illegal drugs.[38] And if the researchers I've mentioned are right, which I think they are, the more sophisticated terrorist groups are in various stages of a transformation into a hybrid terror-crime networked organization that will pose increasingly difficult challenges for law enforcement and security professionals throughout the international community.

Responding to this dimension of a terrorist threat requires specific knowledge and skills that are not usually found among military, diplomatic, or even law enforcement professionals. In the United States, the mission of the Treasury Department—and particularly the Office of Terrorism and Financial Intelligence—includes "safeguarding the financial system against illicit use and combating rogue nations, terrorist facilitators, weapons of mass destruction proliferators, money launderers, drug kingpins, and other national security threats."[39] There are also multinational entities involved in this effort to combat terrorist financing, including INTERPOL (the international police organization, with 192 member countries), and the Financial Action Task Force (an international policy-making and standard-setting body dedicated to combating money laundering). And of course, the worldwide banking industry has a very important role to play in these efforts. Overall, when we consider the broad and diverse landscape of terrorism financing and criminal activity, it becomes quite clear that combating terrorism effectively requires collaboration at multiple levels. Despite what some politicians and media pundits might suggest, there are no simple, easy solutions to the challenges posed by a terrorist network.

QUESTIONS FOR DISCUSSION

- What are the major challenges to combating how contemporary terrorists fund their operations? Where do we start, and who should be in charge?
- How do organized crime networks and terrorist groups overcome their natural distrust of each other enough to collaborate effectively?
- What local contexts in a country seem to facilitate greater crime-terror collaboration?

RECOMMENDED READING

Byrom, Jonathan C. and James Walker. "Afghanistan's Transformation to a Narco-Terrorist State: An Economic Perspective." In *Countering Terrorism and Insurgency in the 21st Century*. Vol. 2. Edited by James J. F. Forest. Westport, CT: Praeger, 2007.

Clarke, Ryan and Stuart Lee. "The PIRA, D-Company, and the Crime-Terror Nexus." *Terrorism and Political Violence* 20, no. 2 (2008).

Dishman, Chris. "The Leaderless Nexus: When Crime and Terror Converge." *Studies in Conflict and Terrorism* 28, no. 3 (2005).

Grabosky, Peter and Michael Stohl. *Crime and Terrorism*. London: Sage, 2010.

Forest, James J. F. "Criminals and Terrorists." *Terrorism and Political Violence* 24, no. 2 (2012).

Forest, James J. F. "Global Trends in Kidnapping by Terrorist Groups." *Global Change, Peace and Security* 24, no. 3 (2012): 311–30.

Forest, James J. F., ed. *Intersections of Crime and Terror*. London: Routledge, 2013.

Freeman, Michael. "The Sources of Terrorist Financing: Theory and Typology." *Studies in Conflict and Terrorism* 34, no. 6 (2011): 461–75.

Freeman, Michael and Moyara Ruehsen. "Terrorism Financing Methods: An Overview." *Perspectives on Terrorism* 7, no. 4 (2013).

Holmes, Leslie, ed. *Terrorism, Organised Crime and Corruption: Networks and Linkages*. Cheltenham, UK: Edward Edgar Publishing, 2007.

Horgan, John and Max Taylor. "Playing the 'Green Card'—Financing the Provisional IRA." *Terrorism and Political Violence* 11, no. 2 (1999).

Horgan, John and Max Taylor. "Playing the 'Green Card'—Financing the Provisional IRA: Part 2." *Terrorism and Political Violence* 15, no. 2 (2003).

Hudson, Rex. *Terrorist and Organized Crime Groups in the Tri-Border Area of South America*. Federal Research Division. Washington, DC: Library of Congress, 2003.

Larsson, J. P. "Organized Criminal Networks and Terrorism." In *Countering Terrorism and Insurgency in the 21st Century*. Edited by James J. F. Forest. Westport, CT: Praeger, 2007.

Levitt, Matthew. "Hezbollah's Organized Criminal Enterprises in Europe," *Perspectives on Terrorism* 7, no. 4 (2013): 27–40.

Levitt, Matthew and Michael Jacobson. *The Money Trail: Finding, Following and Freezing Terrorist Finances*. Policy Focus no. 89. Washington Institute for Near East Policy (November 2008): 7–14, 48–68.

Makarenko, Tamara. "The Crime-Terror Continuum: Tracing the Interplay Between Transnational Organized Crime and Terrorism." *Global Crime* 6, no. 1 (2004).

Napoleoni, Loretta. *Terror Incorporated: Tracing the Dollars Behind the Terror Networks*. New York: Seven Stories Press, 2005.

Picarelli, John T. "Osama bin Corleone? Vito the Jackal? Framing Threat Convergence Through an Examination of Transnational Organized Crime and International Terrorism." *Terrorism and Political Violence* 24, no. 2 (2012).

Picarelli, John T. "The Turbulent Nexus of Transnational Organized Crime and Terrorism." *Global Crime* 7, no. 1 (2006).

Schmid, Alex. "The Links Between Transnational Organized Crime and Terrorist Crimes." *Transnational Organized Crime* 2, no. 4 (1996).

Shelley, Louise I. and Sharon A. Melzer. "The Nexus of Organized Crime and Terrorism: Two Case Studies in Cigarette Smuggling." *International Journal of Comparative and Applied Criminal Justice* 32, no. 1 (2008).

Shelley, Louise and John T. Picarelli. *Methods and Motives: Exploring Links Between Transnational Organized Crime and International Terrorism*. Washington, DC: National Institute of Justice, 2005.

Smith, Paul J. "Terrorism Finance: Global Responses to the Money Trail." In *Countering Terrorism and Insurgency in the 21st Century*. Vol. 2. Edited by James J. F. Forest. Westport, CT: Praeger, 2007.

Zimmermann, Doron and William Rosenau, eds. *The Radicalization of Diasporas and Terrorism*. Zurich: Swiss Federal Institute of Technology, 2009.

WEBSITES

International Convention for the Suppression of the Financing of Terrorism (1999)
http://www.un.org/law/cod/finterr.htm

United Nations Interregional Crime and Justice Research Institute
http://www.unicri.it

United Nations Office on Drugs and Crime
http://www.unodc.org

U.S. Department of Treasury, Terrorism and Illicit Finance
http://www.treasury.gov/resource-center/terrorist-illicit-finance/Pages/default.aspx

NOTES

1. *Testimony before the Senate Comm. on Banking, and Urban Affairs* (September 29, 2004) (testimony of Stuart A. Levey, Under Secretary of Terrorism and Financial Intelligence U.S. Department of the Treasury), http://goo.gl/61pJ2.

2. See Lecture 11 for an explanation of this ideology.

3. For a complete account of this incident, see Rogelio Alonso, "The Madrid Attacks on March 11: An Analysis of the Jihadist Threat in Spain and Main Counterterrorist Measures," in *Countering Terrorism and Insurgency in the 21st Century*, vol. 3, ed. James J. F. Forest (Westport, CT: Praeger, 2007).

4. For an excellent account of this, see Vera Eccarius-Kelly, *The Militant Kurds: A Dual Strategy for Freedom* (Westport, CT: Praeger, 2010); and Vera Eccarius-Kelly, "Surreptitious Lifelines: A Comparative Analysis of the FARC and the PKK," *Terrorism and Political Violence* 24, no. 2 (2012).

5. John Horgan and Max Taylor, "Playing the Green Card—Financing the Provisional IRA," *Terrorism and Political Violence* 11, no. 2 (1999); and John Horgan and Max Taylor, "Playing the 'Green Card'—Financing the Provisional IRA: Part 2," *Terrorism and Political Violence* 15, no. 2 (2003).

6. Louise I. Shelley and Sharon A. Melzer, "The Nexus of Organized Crime and Terrorism: Two Case Studies in Cigarette Smuggling," *International Journal of Comparative and Applied Criminal Justice* 32, no. 1 (2008).

7. Rex Hudson, *Terrorist and Organized Crime Groups in the Tri-Border Area (TBA) of South America*, Federal Research Division (Washington, DC: Library of Congress, 2003).

8. Guillaume de Syon, "Aviation Security," in *Homeland Security: Protecting America's Targets*, vol. 3, ed. by James J. F. Forest (Westport, CT: Praeger, 2006): 270.

9. Michael Newton, *The Encyclopedia of Kidnappings* (New York: Facts on File, Inc., 2002): 261. Also see Edward F. Mickolus, "Chronology of Transnational Terrorist Attacks upon American Business People, 1968-1976," *Studies in Conflict and Terrorism* 1, no. 2 (1978).

10. Michael Newton, *The Encyclopedia of Kidnappings* (New York: Facts on File, Inc., 2002): 32. Also see Mickolus, "Chronology of Transnational Terrorist Attacks."

11. See "ETA: The 'Mother' of Separatist Terrorism," *Executive Intelligence Review* (November 17, 1995), http://goo.gl/dgZHd; and "Las Victimas," *Terrorismo en España*, http://goo.gl/2Nf6r.

12. See the Global Terrorism Database incident summary at http://goo.gl/FmB4B.

13. Daniel McGrory, "How $45m Secretly Bought Freedom of Foreign Hostages," *Times* (London), May 22, 2006, http://goo.gl/319GM.

14. Andrew Hansen and Lauren Vriens, "Backgrounder: Al-Qaida in the Islamic Maghreb," *Council on Foreign Relations* (July 21, 2009), http://goo.gl/ysVg1.

15. Mark Galeotti, "Spirited Away: The Rise of Global Kidnapping Trends," *Jane's Intelligence Review* (April 27, 2010).

16. Thomas M. Sanderson, "Transnational Terror and Organized Crime: Blurring the Lines," *SAIS Review* 24, no. 7 (2004): 49–61.

17. Loretta Napoleoni, *Terror Incorporated: Tracing the Dollars Behind the Terror Networks* (New York: Seven Stories Press, 2005): 205.

18. Jonathan C. Byrom and James Walker, "Afghanistan's Transformation to a Narco-Terrorist State: An Economic Perspective," in *Countering Terrorism*, vol. 2, ed. Forest.

19. Alex P. Schmid, "The Links between Transnational Organized Crime and Terrorist Crimes," *Transnational Organized Crime* 2, no. 2 (1996): 66–77.

20. Personal correspondence with David Rapoport, September 6, 2011.

21. Schmid, 67–68.

22. 22 U.S.C. § 2656f(d). Cited in *United States Department Patterns of Global Terrorism, 1999* (Washington, DC: Department of State Publications, 2000): viii. Emphasis added.

23. Bruce Hoffman, *Inside Terrorism* (New York: Columbia University Press, 2006): 40–41. Emphasis added.

24. Phil Williams, "Strategy for a New World: Combating Terrorism and Transnational Organized Crime," in *Strategy in the Contemporary World*, ed. John Baylis, et al. (Oxford University Press, 2007): 195–96.

25. Ibid., 196.

26. Loretta Napoleoni, "The New Economy of Terror: How Terrorism is Financed," *Forum on Crime and Society* 4, nos. 1 and 2 (2004): 31–33.

27. Walter Laqueur, *The New Terrorism* (Oxford University Press, 1999): 211.

28. Tamara Makarenko, "The Ties the Bind: Uncovering the Relationship between Organized Crime and Terrorism," in *Global Organized Crime: Trends and Developments*, ed. Dina Siegel, Henk Van De Bunt, and Damian Zaitch (Dordrecht: Kluwer, 2003): 159–70; R. T. Naylor, *Wages of Crime: Black Markets, Illegal Finance and the Underworld of Economy* (Ithaca, NY: Cornell University Press, 2002): 44–87; Chris Dishman, "Terrorism, Crime and Transformation," *Studies of Conflict and Terrorism* 24, no. 1 (2001): 43–58; Thomas M. Sanderson, "Transnational Terror and Organized Crime: Blurring the Lines," *SAIS Review* 24, no. 1 (2004): 49–61; John T. Picarelli, "The Turbulent Nexus" (2006); Rachel Ehrenfeld, *Funding Evil: How Terrorism is Financed, and How to Stop it* (Chicago: Bonus Books, 2003); Louise Shelley and John Picarelli, "The Diversity of the Crime-Terror Interaction," *International Annals of Criminology* 43 (2005): 51–81; Louise Shelley and John Picarelli "Organized Crime and Terrorism," in *Terrorism Financing and State Responses: A Comparative Perspective*, ed. Jeanne Giraldo and Harold Trinkunas (Stanford, CA: Stanford University Press, 2007): 39–55.

29. Tamara Makarenko, "The Crime-Terror Continuum: Tracing the Interplay between Transnational Organized Crime and Terrorism," *Global Crime* 6, no. 1 (February 2004): 129.

30. Vanda Felbab-Brown, "The Intersection of Terrorism and the drug trade," in *The Making of a Terrorist: Recruitment, Training, and Root Causes*, vol. 3, ed. James J. F. Forest (Westport, CT: Praeger Security International, 2006): 176.

31. Napoleoni, "The New Economy of Terror," 31–33.

32. For more on money laundering, see the U.S. Department of Treasury, "Descriptions and Case Studies of Money Laundering," http://goo.gl/JyWjC.

33. Paul J. Smith, "Terrorism Finance: Global Responses to the Money Trail," in *Countering Terrorism and Insurgency in the 21st Century*, vol. 2, ed. Forest, pp. 142–58.

34. Vanda Felbab-Brown and James J. F. Forest, "Political Violence and the Illicit Economies of West Africa," *Terrorism and Political Violence* 24, no. 5 (2012): 787-806.

35. The Failed State Index compiles a variety of social, economic, and political indicators and is produced annually by the Fund for Peace and published in *Foreign Policy* magazine. For more information, see http://global.fundforpeace.org/index.php.

36. For example, see Louise Shelley and John Picarelli, "Methods and motives: Exploring links between transnational organized crime and international terrorism," *Trends in Organized Crime* 9, no. 2 (December 2005): 52–67; and case studies published by the Center for the Study of Threat Convergence at the Fund for Peace, available at http://global.fundforpeace.org/index.php.

37. "Growing Links Between Crime and Terrorism the Focus of UN Forum," *UN Press Service*, March 16, 2011.

38. Frank Ahrens, "New Pitch in Anti-Drug Ads: Anti-Terrorism," *Washington Post*, February 4, 2002, http://goo.gl/J6Vm6.

39. Mission of the U.S. Treasury Department, Office of Terrorism and Financial Intelligence, available https://www.treasury.gov/about/organizational-structure/offices/Pages/Office-of-Terrorism-and-Financial-Intelligence.aspx

7

Communication

In most definitions of terrorism, there is some mention of communication. Violence is meant to send a message, produce a psychological impact, coerce others through fear, radicalize potential supporters and recruits, and so forth. In this lecture, we focus on two very powerful arenas in which "influencers" communicate and try to spread their violent ideologies to a broad audience: the media and the Internet. These are important facilitators and enablers of what I have called **influence warfare**,[1] and they play a critical role in a terrorist group's ability to advance its cause.

Of course, the mission of "influencing" goes beyond radicalization to include several other objectives, as I will explain. But first, to understand the importance of communications and the media for terrorism, we have to look at some underlying principles of asymmetric warfare, beginning with the teachings of Sun Tzu, who argued that the overall objective should be to break down an enemy's will to fight a conventional war. In other words, instead of focusing entirely on kinetic weapons and actions (bombs, guns, etc.) to try and destroy an enemy physically, success can come from efforts to collapse the enemy internally.

Some of this type of activity is called "psychological operations" by the U.S. Department of Defense, a term loosely defined as actions that are meant to influence emotions, motives, objective reasoning, and, ultimately, the behavior of foreign governments, organizations, groups, and individuals.[2] From the perspective of terrorists or insurgents engaged in asymmetric warfare against a government, a major target of psychological operations will be the population's support of its government and its counterterrorism or counterinsurgency efforts.

Skillful practitioners of psychological operations, or PSYOP, must become adept at manipulating domestic and world opinion, particularly when it comes to impacting a country's commitment to send combat forces into a battlefield—for example, like Iraq or Afghanistan. Thus, in this type of warfare, television news may become a more powerful operational weapon than armored divisions. Through audio and video statements from terrorist leaders, as well as statements from hostages or captive soldiers, a group like the Taliban or the Islamic State engages in what is known as "propaganda with a purpose," which can have several objectives like encouraging the spread of doubts among members of a population, building doctrinal confidence among supporters, and attracting greater numbers of supporters and sympathizers.

TO THE POINT

Terrorists seek to influence several different audiences.

To be effective, this kind of propaganda has to reach many audiences. During the first waves of terrorism described in Lecture 2, most terrorist groups published and circulated their own leaflets, pamphlets, magazines, newspapers, and so forth. They actively sought—and sometimes gained—significant coverage in the mainstream press as well. Then, as I'll describe later in this lecture, television came to offer an entirely new and more powerful means of connecting a terrorist group with multiple audiences. Hizballah, the Shiite terrorist group in Lebanon, actually has its own satellite television station called al-Manar—the "Beacon" or "Lighthouse" in Arabic—which it uses as a weapon in its fight against Israel and its allies.[3] But most other groups provide their materials to a number of media outlets, as well as the Internet, in multiple formats. In order to resonate among their target audiences, the terrorists' messages will incorporate key cultural elements like language, music, and images that impact the emotions of audience members and can lead to changes in their behavior.

Over the last half-century, terrorist groups have formulated various PSYOP strategies that use the media to communicate with several key audiences. In fact, terrorism itself can be considered a form of psychological warfare since it is intended to create a mood of fear in a certain audience. Through the media and, increasingly, the Internet, terrorists can spread disinformation, convey threats to their enemies, or display horrible images of recent actions, such as the beheading of a victim or the explosive destruction of a subway—all of which are part of their psychological warfare efforts.

Through their violent attacks, terrorist groups seek to influence at least three primary audiences. First, their attacks are meant to produce terror and pain among members of the victimized locals and the broader population of observers in the target country or region, or throughout the world. In fact, the target audience is the broader population watching, listening, and fearing that these kinds of attacks will be repeated and that it might fall victim to the next one.

Second, the terrorists are communicating to sympathizers, individuals who believe in the group's ideology but have not actively joined the cause. One important aspect of this type of communication is that the group's attacks are meant to convey a sense of greater commitment and capacity than other terrorist groups who are competing for support among the same population of potential sympathizers, including potential funders in other parts of the world.

Third, they are communicating to themselves—that is, members of the terrorist organization in other parts of the country or the world, whose morale is boosted after a successful attack by their comrades.

To communicate to all these audiences, terrorists capitalize on **media amplification**—that is, the media play an important role in conveying images, perhaps even dramatic film footage and news coverage, in ways that benefit the group's communication strategies. Some scholars like Cindy Combs have described terrorism as "a synthesis of war and theatre: a dramatization of violence which is perpetrated on innocent victims and played before an audience in the hope of creating a mode of fear without apology or remorse for political purposes."[4] In order for terrorism to be effective, the terrorists need to be able to communicate their actions and threats to their audience as quickly and dramatically as possible, and they take advantage of the media to achieve this aim.

Statistically, terrorist incidents worldwide are insignificant—both in terms of the number of dead and injured, and in terms of the number of incidents reported annually—compared to the number injured or killed in wars, famines, natural disasters, or even auto accidents. But massive media coverage of each terrorist attack reaches a vast audience, creating an impact far beyond that which the incident, in the absence of this media, could be expected to generate. Without intensive media coverage, the thinking goes, few would know of the terrorists' actions and motivations.

The relationship between the media and terrorism has evolved over time. In the earlier decades of television, governments could have some influence over what was broadcast over the airwaves, and terrorists had limited opportunity to showcase their attacks and ideological demands. But over time, as Combs has noted, the relationship often became a symbiotic one between terrorists seeking to communicate to and gain influence over various audiences, and news organizations seeking dramatic stories to increase their readership and ratings. In essence, the goals of the media and the goals of the terrorist groups converge, with news coverage of a particular incident benefiting both to some degree or another.

From this point of view, it makes sense that terrorists would begin staging events that were intended to draw attention, via global media coverage, much more than to merely kill people. Beginning in the late 1960s, kidnappings—and especially airplane hijackings—became a particularly media-friendly type of terrorism. For example, on July 22, 1968, an El Al flight departing from Rome and headed for Tel Aviv, Israel, was hijacked by members of the Popular Front for the Liberation of Palestine (PFLP). They diverted the plane to Algiers and subsequently held seven crew members and five Israeli passengers hostage for 40 days until Israel agreed to release a number of terrorists from their prisons. In September 1970, the PFLP also hijacked three passenger planes and took them to an airfield in Jordan; after the planes were emptied, the hijackers blew them up, and the exploding planes were featured on news programs worldwide. George Habash, the founder of PFLP, told the German magazine *Der Stern* in 1970 that, "When we hijack a plane it has more effect than if we kill a hundred Israelis in battle . . . For decades, world public opinion has been neither for nor against the Palestinians. It simply ignored us. At least the world is talking about us now."[5]

The watershed event during this era occurred in 1972, when a PLO cell called Black September attacked a team of Israeli athletes during the Summer Olympics in Munich, Germany. Two of the athletes were killed in the initial assault, and 11 were taken hostage. The group then demanded the release of 236 Palestinians held in Israeli jails, along with safe passage for themselves. The terrorists and hostages were eventually provided with transportation to a local airport, under the guise that they would board a plane and fly free, but West German police sharpshooters hidden at the airport had other plans. In the resulting firefight on the airport tarmac, all the hostages were killed (several by a hand grenade thrown at them by one of the terrorists), along with all but three of the kidnappers and a policeman. Because there were so many TV cameras and reporters already in Munich to cover the Olympics, this entire incident unfolded in front of an international TV audience, thus garnering more attention for the plight of the Palestinians than ever before. As Abu Iyad, a co-founder of the militant group Fatah, later observed: "World opinion was forced to take note of the Palestinian drama, and the Palestinian people imposed their presence on an international gathering that had sought to exclude them."[6]

Then there was the June 1985 hijacking of TWA Flight 847 by Lebanese Shiite militia members. After forcing the plane to land and refuel in several locations, the hijackers eventually stopped in Beirut, where one of the passengers, U.S. Navy diver Robert Stethem, was brutally tortured and then shot, his body dumped on the tarmac. Hours later, passengers were taken in small groups to locations throughout the city. Over the next 16 days of the hostage crisis, the kidnappers demanded that Israel release 766 Arab prisoners and held several press conferences that were featured on all the major U.S. television networks in part because the hostages, most of them Americans, were featured and allowed to speak directly to the television cameras.[7] The crisis was finally resolved through diplomatic negotiations involving Syria, Israel, and the United States.

Just a few months later, in October 1985, a global audience was again captivated by terrorist drama when members of the Palestine Liberation Front (PLF) hijacked the *Achille Lauro*, a cruise ship owned by the Italian government.[8] The hijackers ordered the captain to sail toward Syria and radioed their demands for the release of 50 Palestinian prisoners in Israel. Ultimately, though, the hijackers abandoned their attack and fled in a small boat, but not before murdering one of the passengers, a wheelchair-bound American named Leon Klinghoffer, and dumping his body overboard. Throughout the 1970s and '80s, a variety of other dramatic kidnappings were perpetrated by Palestinian and left-wing groups, including the Red Army Faction (a.k.a. Baader-Meinhof Group) in Germany and the Red Brigades in Italy. Details of these incidents are provided in Lecture 9.

More recently, the most notorious kidnapping incidents to gain massive media attention have been orchestrated by Chechen separatists. For example, in June 1995, Chechen leader Shamil Basayev seized control of a hospital in the town of Budyonnovsk, Russia, taking almost 1,000 hostages and demanding that then-President Boris Yeltsin withdraw troops from Chechnya.[9] Subsequent attempts by Russian forces to retake the hospital resulted in hundreds of casualties and injuries among the hostages but failed to resolve the crisis, which eventually resulted in a temporary ceasefire between Russia and Chechen rebels. In October 2002, Chechen rebels stormed the Dubrovka Theater in Moscow, taking over 800 hostages and demanding the withdrawal of Russian forces from Chechnya.[10] After a three-day standoff, Russian forces attempted to end the siege by first pumping a highly potent version of fentanyl (used as an anesthetic) into the building, and then storming the building and shooting the terrorists. Tragically, 129 of the hostages were killed, almost all of them by the gas.[11]

And in September 2004, a group of Chechen terrorists took more than 1,200 hostages at a school in the North Ossetian town of Beslan, Russia, demanding an end to the war in Chechnya and withdrawal of Russian troops; the release of 31 terrorists held in Russian jails; and the government's formal recognition of Chechen independence. Here, too, the incident ended in tragedy when the detonation of explosive devices in the school triggered a chaotic rescue operation in which 31 terrorists and 331 victims were killed, 176 of them children.[12]

More recently, the Islamic State (or IS) has demonstrated how terrorists often believe heightened levels of brutality are necessary in order to capture media attention. For several years, the group has been notorious for its public executions of captured Iraqi and Syrian officials, soldiers, and citizens. In one instance, it placed a captured Jordanian pilot in a cage and burned him alive. People accused of homosexuality were thrown from the tops of buildings.

But early on, the IS group recognized that a prime way to attract Western media coverage was to stage dramatic beheadings of Westerners (often journalists, like James Foley and Steven Sotloff). If the victim of an IS killing is an attractive young woman, like Kayla Mueller (an American former NGO worker), it attracts even more media attention. Similarly, the IS group found that filming a child carrying out a public execution also attracted news coverage. And destroying famous landmarks, like the ancient city of Palmyra or the famous Al-Nuri Mosque in Mosul, resulted in front page news headlines.

These dramatic accounts exemplify the kind of incidents that make for prime-time news coverage and enable the terrorist group to attract global attention. This attention then provides a platform for the terrorist group's efforts to disseminate its ideology and attract followers. As al-Qaeda leader Ayman al-Zawahiri noted, the media are very important to a terrorist organization. In a 2005 letter to Abu Musab al-Zarqawi, who at the time was the leader of the al-Qaeda terrorist cell in Iraq, Zawahiri wrote, "We are in a battle, and more than half of this battle is taking place in the battlefield of the media. We are in a race for hearts and minds of our umma [the global community of Muslims] . . . We must get our message across to the masses . . . This is an independent battle that we must launch side by side with the military battle."[13] Without doubt, the media have played a critical role in getting the terrorists' messages to global audiences. However, over the past two decades, terrorists have found another, far more powerful means through which they can disseminate their ideology to a global audience: the Internet.

TERRORISM AND THE INTERNET

Generally speaking, the Internet has become a more important conduit for influencers to communicate with their intended audiences. Of course, the news media still play an important role, which is why for several years militant groups in Iraq would plan their attacks in ways that would ensure coverage by the U.S. evening news.[14] Today, the Internet allows terrorist groups to tailor their messages to different audiences, incorporate multiple forms of information (images, video, sound, music and animation, for example), and, most important, bypass the role of editorial gatekeeper found in mainstream media outlets. The importance of this transformation is reflected in a 2002 observation by Abu al-Quraishi, a prominent al-Qaeda member, on one of its online bulletin boards: "Anyone who knows the media will discover that the mujahidin have been able to move from the defensive to the offensive in the field of psychological warfare. Unlike previous decades, when it was possible to play completely with the news, the leap in communication technology has made it impossible for anyone to monopolize information."[15]

Al-Qaeda has been a pioneer in this arena since its early years in the 1990s, establishing a media branch—called as-Sahab ("the Clouds")—and developing a sophisticated system of studios, video distribution channels, and websites. This media branch spends a good deal of time trying to articulate and convince others about the validity of their doctrine, strategy, and, in some cases, tactics. Many attacks, especially in Iraq and Afghanistan, are filmed and uploaded to the Internet complete with ideological spin even before local military commanders of coalition forces can give a full report on the incident. Some research even indicates that certain attacks—like roadside bombings and sniper attacks—are planned in ways that will maximize camera angles and produce the most dramatic film footage, well before the bombs or snipers are even deployed. In terms of suicide bombers, or terrorist fighters killed in battles with coalition forces, their so-called martyrdom videos are used to boost morale among members and supporters and to create fear among others; audio and video recordings are often released strategically during significant events like religious holidays. Anniversaries of major attacks like 9/11, and other dates of special significance (July Fourth, New Year's Eve, etc.) are exploited for propaganda value, but are not necessarily tied to planned or imminent attacks.

While al-Qaeda was an early innovator, the Islamic State has become more prominent in terms of terrorists utilizing the Internet in new and groundbreaking ways. For instance, it uses every social media platform to disseminate propaganda and attract new recruits, particularly Twitter and Facebook. The IS invests heavily in the creation of new content—such as videos with dramatic images and background music, popular magazines like *Dabiq* and *Rumiyah*, and motivational sermons from jihadist leaders—and has built a robust system for flooding the Internet with this content. The IS uses Telegram, WhatsApp, Instagram, and even Snapchat to forge personal connections and boost morale among followers of its global jihadist agenda. More than any other group today, the IS has demonstrated the many ways that the Internet can be useful for terrorist networks. The group can use websites, online magazines, discussion forums, and other means of communication to motivate and teach others to carry out attacks in support of its ideological goals; it can utilize encrypted communication platforms to support operational communications between cells and leaders; and it can use a variety of social media platforms to foster a sense of shared purpose and community for like-minded individuals worldwide. In these ways, the Internet has enabled a new and troubling dimension to the challenge of combating terrorism.

MOTIVATING AND INSPIRING

The Internet offers terrorist groups an ability to do many things, like spread propaganda that is focused on recruitment, radicalization, and indoctrination of new members, as well as communicate to sympathizers, boost morale among ideological believers, and threaten their enemies. An especially prominent example of these efforts is found in the 2009 al-Qaeda publication, *44 Ways to Serve and Participate in Jihad*. In this widely circulated manual, published in several different languages including English, Anwar al-Awlaki provided guidance to the potential new al-Qaeda recruit, updating a previous publication called *39 Ways to Support Jihad*, published in 2006 by Muhammad bin Ahmad al-Salim, who used the pen name Abu Bakr Naji. It reflects a rather Marxist view of human endeavor, in terms of encouraging participation "from each according to your ability"—anything you can do to help advance the cause of al-Qaeda, do it. For example, supporters of al-Qaeda are encouraged to praise al-Qaeda fighters, both alive and dead. Through artwork, photos, and other imagery—as well as audio and video recordings—individuals who fight in the name of al-Qaeda, or have conducted suicide bombings, for example, are depicted as heroic, courageous, selfless, and as having other attributes that are revered in most societies. Young men, and increasingly women, searching for a sense of importance or significance in their lives are attracted to such things and hope that their own actions will be similarly praised and memorialized. As well, terms like "duty" and "honor" are frequently incorporated into these kinds of propaganda in order to evoke certain emotions that may lead to mobilization and radicalization of new recruits.

> **TO THE POINT**
>
> The Internet allows terrorists to bypass the editorial gatekeepers in traditional media.

With the loss of its territory in Iraq and Syria, the Islamic State has also begun to promote a similar message: anything you can do to help advance the cause of the global jihad, do it. We will focus on this "do it yourself" mode of terrorism in Lecture 15, but for now, it's worth noting that most of the prominent jihadist-related terrorist attacks in recent years—Paris, Brussels, Nice, Stockholm, Boston, Orlando, London, Istanbul, New York, San Bernardino, etc.—have been of this kind. In each case, individuals with little or no formal training in weapons or terrorist tactics were motivated to prepare and carry out an attack against a civilian target like a nightclub or an outdoor public gathering (often not far from where they lived). This is in marked contrast with the more traditional, centralized mode of terrorist operations in which a small leadership cadre would plan, train, and direct others to attack a specific target of strategic or symbolic importance. When individual attacks are carried out successfully, they demonstrate a certain perverse kind of power for others, inspiring them to consider following in the footsteps of the attackers in hopes of making some kind of personal impact on the course of history. This can be particularly impactful for someone looking for a sense of importance or significance in the world. Further, while execution videos and dramatic terrorist attacks may garner the Islamic State the most media attention, in truth, a large amount of the material the group posts online addresses issues of religious devotion, Islamic governance, and attempts to morally justify the horrific crimes it commits as necessary to achieve the Salafi-jihadist vision of a better future for all Muslims.

Overall, webmasters, bloggers, and others play an important role in motivating people to join the global jihadist movement. Several years ago, Abu Yahya al-Libi—considered by several analysts as a key player in al-Qaeda's central leadership—praised what he called the "mujahideen on the information frontline" (in other words, the website designers, bloggers, video editors and others, who support the vast online presence of al-Qaeda). He said, "May Allah bless you lions of the front, for by Allah, the fruits of your combined efforts—sound, video, and text—are more severe for the infidels and their lackeys than the falling of rockets and missiles on their heads."[16] According to al-Awlaki's guide, anyone incapable of joining the fight against infidels directly must encourage others to join instead, and many have embraced this role. Over the last decade, we have seen a proliferation of online extremist activity, with throngs of al-Qaeda and Islamic State supporters posting new websites, blog content, and You-Tube videos, forwarding links to other online resources via email distribution lists, and generally promoting the cause to a global audience.

And we have seen various English-language publications circulated online, including the popular *Inspire* magazine, produced by a cell of jihadists in Yemen with support from Anwar al-Awlaki. With lots of photos and colloquial English, this publication was clearly meant for a mass American and European audience. Instead of long, dry Arabic-language interpretations of the Quran, which we usually see in videos from Ayman al-Zawahiri, for example, this was meant to be sort of a *People* magazine for jihadists. The first issue of *Inspire* offered a colorful section of provocative talking points meant to provide readers with simple questions that they can use for their own self-radicalization process as well as in their debates with non-jihadi types. As al-Qaeda expert Jarret Brachman notes, this kind of "boiling-down" of complex political issues to these bite-sized talking points is critical for making an ideology more accessible to the masses. The magazine also offered readers tips on how to use encrypted forms of communication and guidance on what to expect when you attend an al-Qaeda training camp, with discussion on "what not to bring with you" and the "the importance of the jihadi buddy system."[17]

According to federal authorities, *Inspire* contributed to the motivations of Tamerlan and Dzhokhar Tsarnaev, whose terrorist attack against the 2013 Boston Marathon killed three people and injured over 250 more. The article "How to make a bomb in your mom's kitchen" provided detailed instructions for the pressure cooker improvised explosive device used in their attack. Other articles have provided information about obtaining forged documents and taking advantage of lax regulations at gun shows in the United States, among other practical advice for terrorist tradecraft. Even though the original creators and editors of *Inspire*—Samir Khan and Anwar al-Awlaki—were killed in late September 2011, other members of al-Qaeda in the Arabian Peninsula (AQAP) in Yemen picked up the mantle and continued publishing issues.

As noted earlier, the Islamic State has also invested in online magazines of its own. For several years, *Dabiq* (see Figure 7.1) was the group's premier publication, the intent of which was to spread the jihadists' ideological message and provide tactical and operational guidance to followers. The magazine was published online in Arabic, English, German, and French. Each issue was released on multiple websites and discussion forums, and readers would then duplicate the PDF files and repost them to scores of other sites throughout the Internet, including anonymous file sharing services. *Rumiyah* is another popular magazine, first published by the IS group in September 2016 and made available in multiple languages, including English, Arabic, French, German, and Russian. Articles in this magazine range from justifications for

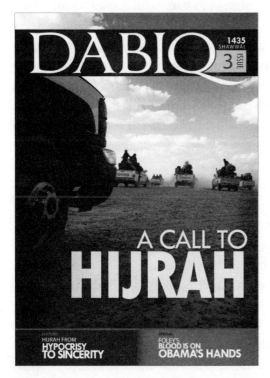
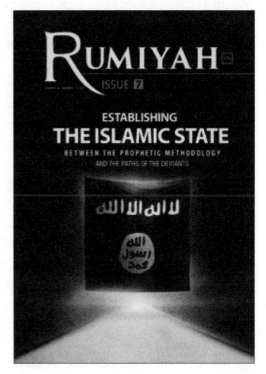

Figure 7.1: Recent issues of Islamic State magazines

attacking non-Muslims to guidance on how to obtain weapons and how to carry out knife attacks against groups of people.

Obviously, digital publications like these will likely remain available forever in the open source virtual library we call the Internet, helping to radicalize future generations of jihadist supporters. As noted earlier in this lecture series, terrorism is largely understood as a type of violent behavior that is influenced by ideas and contexts. Thus, one cannot underemphasize the important role that these kinds of popular jihadist publications have played in attracting new followers to the movement and in helping to foster a belief among the jihadists that they are part of a powerful, global movement that is slowly but surely moving toward the establishment of an Islamist caliphate, the imposition of Shari'ah law, and a brighter future for the Muslim world.

TEACHING

Terrorists are also using the Internet to provide online training in strategies and tactics. Instruction manuals and videos are available on a variety of topics, from where to acquire (or how to make) explosives and other weapons, to assembling and firing a surface-to-air missile against an airline (a tactic we have recently seen in Kenya, Iraq, and Afghanistan),[18] to guidance for conducting an ambush, taking hostages, or smuggling weapons and contraband across a country's borders. Manuals by the Irish Republican Army or the Red Army Faction (Baader-Meinhof gang) in Germany can still be found on various websites today as can the *Mini-Manual of the Urban Guerilla* described in Lecture 2. More on the topic of terrorist group tactical resources and operational decision-making is provided in Lecture 13.

For the past two decades, the majority of online instructional materials for terrorism have been related to the global jihadist movement. For example, a 26-minute video posted to the al-Qaeda affiliated forum "al-Ansar" lays out in precise detail how to construct a suicide bomber's explosive belt and includes tips on how to estimate the impact of an explosion, how best to arrange the shrapnel for maximum destruction, how to strap the belt onto the bomber's body, and even how to avoid the migraine headache that can come from exposure to the recommended explosive chemicals.[19]

Sympathizers of the movement are also encouraged to provide Muslims with the information and expertise they need to fight their enemies. Readers of the *41 Ways* manual are told, "No one can conceal his expertise. He must make available what he knows." The manual offers a few specific examples of the kinds of expertise that would be useful, from providing tactical advice (for bomb making or computer hacking) to advising sleeper cells on how to adapt to their local surroundings (for example, dressing appropriately, establishing friendly relationships with locals, etc.)

In 2003, several issues of the online al-Qaeda publication *In the Shadow of the Lances* carried a series of articles by Saif al-Adel (believed to be a high-ranking member of al-Qaeda's military operations) that offered Iraqi insurgents tactical lessons learned from the battle against U.S. forces in Afghanistan.[20] His observations and advice included organizing the fighters into small units, building "covered trenches with more than one entrance inside the yards of homes to avoid bombardment or blockage of the entrance by falling rocks" and to "have alternatives to advanced technology," including couriers.[21] Through these kinds of online publications, the Islamic State, al-Qaeda, and other terrorist groups have provided both motivational and operational support for the insurgencies in Syria, Iraq, Afghanistan, and elsewhere.

As noted earlier, the Islamic State's online magazines *Dabiq* and *Rumiyah* have played a prominent role in promoting certain kinds of operational tactics. For example, articles in these magazines have offered guidance on manufacturing homemade explosives, acquiring weapons and forged documents, traveling covertly to Syria or Iraq, using encrypted communications software, and conducting target surveillance. One article in particular provides detailed instructions for using a rented vehicle (see Figure 7.2) to plow into crowds of pedestrians on busy streets, a mode of attack that we have seen in France, Sweden, Germany, the U.K., and the U.S. in the past few years.

In addition to these kinds of written materials available online, one can also find animated videos demonstrating how to assemble a sniper rifle or explaining how a grenade works. And beyond tactical and operational advice, some well-known jihadi thinkers, like Abu Musab al-Suri, have provided strategic guidance for members of the al-Qaeda movement. In 2000, he gained prominence through a 20-hour video recording lecture series, released online, in which he argued that "individual terrorism" needed to replace the hierarchical, more traditional approach to terrorism that al-Qaeda had embraced thus far.[22] He envisioned a "mass participation jihadist movement" in which individuals would attack targets worldwide "where it hurts the enemy and costs him the most," and "where it awakens Muslims and revives the spirit of jihad and resistance."[23] Also, in December 2004, al-Suri published a 1,600-page book, *The Call for Global Islamic Resistance*, which became one of the most influential and widely circulated documents on jihadist web forums to date. More on al-Suri, and on "do it yourself" terrorism generally, is provided in Lecture 15.

Figure 7.2: Islamic State guidance on using a truck for a terrorist attack.

OPERATIONAL CAPABILITIES

Beyond the dissemination of information, the Internet also offers several new operational capabilities that terrorists did not have before. For example, communicating with cells and leaders in real time over vast distances is now much easier and quite inexpensive. Some terrorist groups like al-Qaeda have even adopted a strategic use of free email accounts like on Yahoo and Hotmail. In several cases, they will use these accounts as virtual drop boxes, where one member will write a message and leave it in the draft folder of the account, and then another member will log in to that account, read the message in the draft folder, and then delete it. Because the message was not actually sent from one email account to another, it becomes very difficult for anyone to track or monitor these kinds of communications.

Meanwhile, Telegram has become a platform of choice for the Islamic State because of several unique features. While users of this service can communicate in open "channels" that anyone can join, there are also private messaging and secret chat functions, the latter of which is protected by a sophisticated form of end-to-end encryption that makes it virtually impossible for intelligence or law enforcement agencies to monitor the information being shared by one user to another. Jihadists have also learned to use coded messages in social media accounts on Twitter and Facebook, among others.

The Internet is also used for fundraising—for example, a number of terrorist-related websites solicit donations from visitors. On some, you can make a donation by using a credit card, PayPal, and so forth. And of course, with the abundance of information available online today, terrorist groups can gather surveillance intelligence on any number of potential targets. A few years ago, a computer was captured from an al-Qaeda supporter that had engineering and structural features of a dam in the United States. These materials had been downloaded from the Internet and enabled al-Qaeda planners and engineers to simulate catastrophic failures. And finally, terrorists can use the Internet to identify and exploit online vulnerabilities, from hacking, fraud, and data theft at the individual level, to infiltrating a local power grid or other utility system and causing problems with vital community services.

VIRTUAL COMMUNITIES AND SOCIAL MEDIA

Clearly, the Internet has become increasingly vital to sustaining a terrorist movement. Social media platforms like Facebook, Twitter, Instagram, Telegram, and several others are of particular importance to terrorists and militant groups worldwide. For example, fighters in Syria use social media accounts to foster a sense of camaraderie, celebrate martyrs as heroes, report real-time battlefield events, encourage recruitment, and regularly communicate to friends, family, and foes. During its 2013 attack against the Westgate Mall in Kenya, al-Shabaab used multiple Twitter accounts like the one shown below (see Figure 7.3) to claim responsibility.

As noted earlier, leaders of the global jihadist movement have demonstrated a belief that the Internet provides the best means to influence the Muslim nation (the *umma*) today. Indeed, both al-Qaeda and the Islamic State are heavily reliant on the Internet in their efforts worldwide to convince the Arab and Muslim youth—the largest, most educated, and tech-savvy segment of Muslim societies—that the jihadists' vision of the future, and the movement's grievances against the West, are valid and worth fighting

Figure 7.3: Example of an al-Shabaab Twitter feed.
Source: Will Oremus, "The Militant Group Behind the Kenya Mall Attack is Live-Tweeting the Massacre," Slate.com (September 21, 213).

for. Today, there are literally thousands of social media accounts, discussion forums, interactive websites, and blogs that offer video clips, photos, audio recordings, books, articles, and other items meant to indoctrinate these target audiences, encourage feelings of pride, a sense of belonging, and a new identity, and to intimidate Western audiences. One of the important things to note here is that these are increasingly posted online not only in Arabic, but in English, Urdu, Pashtun, French, German, and many other languages. In doing so, the intent is to foster a global virtual community of individuals who share a vision for an imagined future they want to build.

The Taliban's Twitter account has often been used in similar ways to take credit for (some would say brag about) successful attacks against U.S. and Afghan military forces. Meanwhile, terrorists have used a variety of social media platforms as a way to develop virtual communities of shared purpose, in which a member's identity is closely tied to their belief in a particular ideology. These kinds of social media are particularly useful for terrorist movements employing a leaderless resistance model, like the environmental extremists, anti-abortion attackers, and global Salafi-jihadists. For example, a Facebook account claiming to be located in Toronto used the social networking site as a platform to promote English-language jihadi propaganda encouraging lone wolf attacks in the West.[25] As we'll examine more closely in Lecture 10, the right-wing extremist movement in the United States has been heavily involved in the use of online media to disseminate its propaganda for decades. One of its most popular websites (Stormfront.org) serves as a place to find others who share racial hatred and anti-government views, a place that forges a sense of belonging and perceived legitimacy for those views (even when those same views, if expressed in person in a public forum, would surely generate condemnation).

There are other dark sides of social media to consider as well. In the immediate aftermath of the 2013 Boston Marathon bombings, a variety of conspiracy theories and other forms of misinformation were rapidly spread online through Twitter, Reddit, Facebook, and other means. People were told about tragic deaths of several young children, which were untrue. A Twitter account named @_BostonMarathon was launched, and, posing as the organizers of the race, the account owner tweeted: "For every retweet we receive we will donate $1 to the #BostonMarathon victims #PrayForBoston" (Twitter disabled the account soon afterward). Meanwhile, several media outfits, in a race to be the first to report "news," provided irresponsible speculation both on camera and online, exacerbating an already confusing situation. This, in turn, prompted an even greater flurry of social media activity that had no positive impact on the eventual outcome of the investigation or the manhunt for the Tsarnaev brothers. Any would-be terrorist watching these events unfold surely learned an important lesson about the misperceptions and chaos that can be caused in an information-rich liberal democracy following an attack.

More recently, research on the uses of the Internet by terrorists have identified the widespread proliferation of so-called "bots," automated accounts that are set up for the sole purpose of repeating and reposting certain kinds of information provided by other accounts. The purpose behind this is to give viewers the impression that hundreds or thousands of Internet users are supporters of the ideological messages posted, for example, by an Islamic State propaganda creator. This also helps establish online "echo chambers" of individual users whose ideological views are reinforced by other like-minded users, providing them with a sense of community and legitimacy that encourages them to continue supporting the terrorists' cause even in the face of major operational setbacks.

In essence, the rapid growth of connectivity through social media has become a mixed blessing. Members of the global village are connected to one another in unprecedented ways, allowing us to form new virtual communities, share ideas and insights, and—one would hope—learn new ways of addressing complex problems with greater sophistication. But when these kinds of technology are used by extremists and terrorist groups for similar reasons, the end result could be a virtual community of increasingly capable and lethal adversaries. Unfortunately, we will undoubtedly see more of this kind of terrorist-related social media activity in the years ahead.

SUMMARY

So, to wrap up this lecture, the media and the Internet have played significant roles in the history of modern terrorism. Both have facilitated community and mutual reinforcement in the radicalization process. The Internet has been a particularly vital asset in the areas of psychological operations, knowledge transfer, and operational capabilities (which we'll address in Lectures 13 and 14). And, as we have seen, both al-Qaeda and the Islamic State have invested considerable time and effort in using the Internet as their primary means of disseminating the global jihadist ideology. In fact, several years ago Ambassador Dell Dailey, at the time U.S. State Department's counterterrorism chief, testified before Congress that "Al-Qaeda and other terrorists' center of gravity lies in the information domain, and it is there that we must engage it."[26]

Leaders of the global jihadist movement have demonstrated a belief that the Internet provides the best means to influence the Muslim nation (the *umma*) today. Both al-Qaeda and the Islamic State have invested countless resources in producing and disseminating various kinds of information through every online means available. They provide this information in multiple languages and in multiple formats. In turn, they demonstrate how the Internet has become a most critical asset to a leaderless resistance model of terrorism. As noted in Lecture 1, white supremacists in the United States developed this concept loosely, but al-Qaeda, the Islamic State, and affiliated groups have expanded it to promote a virtual "leaderless jihad" in which individuals can contribute to the cause by any means available to them, including orchestrating their own terrorist attacks on behalf of the jihadist movement with no direct ties to any formal terror group leaders or cells. We will examine this concept of leaderless resistance more in Lectures 10 through 15.

QUESTIONS FOR DISCUSSION

- Why do some folks consider videos, audio, and images to be more powerful than words?
- How do you evaluate the truth of online materials?
- How do you think your perceptions and/or behavior might be influenced by what you find on the Internet, as opposed to traditional media?

RECOMMENDED READING

Berger, J. M. "The Metronome of Apocalyptic Time: Social Media as Carrier Wave for Millenarian Contagion." *Perspectives on Terrorism* 9, no. 4 (2015).

Berger, J. M. "Extremist Construction of Identity: How Escalating Demands for Legitimacy Shape and Define In-Group and Out-Group Dynamics." ICCT Research Paper (April 21, 2017).

Berger, J. M. "The Turner Legacy: The Stories Origins and Enduring Impact of White Nationalism's Deadly Bible." ICCT Research Paper (September 16, 2016).

Burke, Jason. "The Age of Selfie Jihad: How Evolving Media Technology is Changing Terrorism." *CTC Sentinel* (November/December 2016).

Brachman, Jarret M. "The World's Most Dangerous Jihadi Pundits." *Foreign Policy* (January 2010).

Brachman, Jarret M. "Watching the Watchers." *Foreign Policy* (November 2010).

Brachman, Jarret M. "Going Viral: Al-Qaeda's Use of Online Social Media." In *Terrorism and Counterterrorism*. Edited by Russell Howard and Bruce Hoffman. New York: McGraw-Hill, 2011.

Combs, Cindy C. "The Media as a Showcase for Terrorism." In *Teaching Terror*. Edited by James J. F. Forest. Lanham, MD: Rowman & Littlefield, 2006.

Conway, Maura. "Terror TV? An Exploration of Hizbollah's Al-Manar Television." In *Countering Terrorism and Insurgency in the 21st Century*. Vol. 2. Edited by James J. F. Forest. Westport, CT: Praeger, 2007.

Conway, Maura. "Terrorism and New Media." In *Countering Terrorism and Insurgency in the 21st Century*. Vol. 2. Edited by James J. F. Forest. Westport, CT: Praeger, 2007.

Fisher, Ali. "How Jihadist Networks Maintain a Persistent Online Presence," *Perspectives on Terrorism* 9, no. 3 (2015).

Forest, James J. F. "Influence Warfare and Modern Terrorism." *Georgetown Journal of International Affairs* 10, no. 1 (2009).

Gates, Scott and Sukanya Podder. "Social Media, Recruitment, Allegiance and the Islamic State." *Perspectives on Terrorism* 9, no. 4 (2015).

Hoffman, Bruce. *Inside Terrorism*. 3rd ed. New York: Columbia University Press, 2017: Chapters 6 ("Old Media") and 7 ("New Media").

Lemieux, Anthony, Jarret Brachman, Jason Levitt, and Jay Wood. "Inspire Magazine: A Critical Analysis of its Significance and Potential Impact thorough the Lens of the Information, Motivation and Behavioral Skills Model." *Terrorism and Political Violence* 1, no. 1 (2014): 1–18.

Marsden, Sarah V. "Media Metrics: How Arab and Western Media Construct Success and Failure in the Global War on Terror." *Perspectives on Terrorism* 7, no. 6 (December 2013): 10–26.

Meleagrou-Hitchens, Alexander and Nick Kaderbhai, "Research Perspectives on Online Radicalization," VOX Report, 2017: 4–47.

Nacos, Brigitte L. "Mediated Terror: Teaching Terrorism through Propaganda and Publicity." In *The Making of a Terrorist*. Vol. 2. Edited by James J. F. Forest. Westport, CT: Praeger, 2005.

Neumann, Peter R. *Radicalized: New Jihadists and the Threat to the West*. London: I. B. Tauris, 2017.

O'Rourke, Simon. "Online Recruitment, Radicalization, and Reconnaissance: Challenges for Law Enforcement." In *Influence Warfare*. Edited by James J. F. Forest. Westport, CT: Praeger, 2009.

Ressa, Maria. "The New Battlefield: The Internet and Social Media." *Counterterrorism Exchange* 2, no. 4 (November 2012), https://globalecco.org/ctx-vol.-2-no.-4-article-1.

Weimann, Gabriel. "Virtual Training Camps: Terrorists' Use of the Internet." In *Teaching Terror*. Edited by James J. F. Forest. Lanham, MD: Rowman & Littlefield, 2006.

Weimann, Gabriel. "When Fatwas Clash Online: Terrorist Debates on the Internet." In *Influence Warfare*. Edited by James J. F. Forest. Westport, CT: Praeger, 2009.

Weimann, Gabriel, "Cyber-Fatwas and Terrorism." *Studies in Conflict and Terrorism* 34, no. 10 (2011): 765–781.

Weimann, Gabriel. "www.terror.net: How Modern Terrorism Uses the Internet." In *Terrorism and Counterterrorism*. Edited by Russell Howard and Bruce Hoffman. New York: McGraw-Hill, 2011.

Winn, Aidan Kirby and Vera L. Zakem. "Jihad.com 2.0: The New Social Media and Changing Dynamics of Mass Persuasion." In *Influence Warfare*. Edited by James J. F. Forest. Westport, CT: Praeger, 2009.

Zelin, Aaron. "Picture or It Didn't Happen: A Snapshot of the Islamic State's Official Media Output." *Perspectives on Terrorism* 9, no. 4 (2015).

WEBSITES

IntelWire
http://www.intelwire.com/

International Center for the Study of Radicalization, King's College, London
http://icsr.info/

Program on Extremism, George Washington University
https://extremism.gwu.edu/

Teaching Terror:
http://www.teachingterror.net

NOTES

1. See James J. F. Forest, ed., *Influence Warfare* (Westport, CT: Praeger, 2009); and James J. F. Forest, "Influence Warfare and Modern Terrorism," *Georgetown Journal of International Affairs* 10, no. 1 (2009).

2. See *Psychological Operations: FM 3-05.30/MCRP 3-40.6* (Washington, DC: Headquarters, Department of the Army, 2005).

3. Maura Conway, "Terror TV? An Exploration of Hizbollah's Al-Manar Television," in *Countering Terrorism and Insurgency in the 21st Century*, vol. 2, ed. James J. F. Forest (Westport, CT: Praeger, 2007).

4. Cindy C. Combs, "The Media as a Showcase for Terrorism," in *Teaching Terror*, ed. James J. F. Forest (Lanham, MD: Rowman & Littlefield, 2006): 134–36.

5. Edmund L. Andrews and John Kifner, "George Habash, Palestinian Terrorism Tactician, Dies at 82," *New York Times*, January 27, 2008.

6. Abu Iyad, *My Home, My Land: A Narrative of the Palestinian Struggle* (New York: Times Books, 1981): 111–12.

7. Richard M. Wrona, Jr., "'Beginning of a War': The United States and the Hijacking of TWA Flight 847," in *Countering Terrorism and Insurgency in the 21st Century* (vol. 2).

8. Sean Anderson and Peter Spagnolo, "The Achille Lauro Hijacking," in *Countering Terrorism and Insurgency in the 21st Century*, vol. 3.

9. James S. Robbins, "Insurgent Seizure of an Urban Area: Grozny, 1996," in *Countering Terrorism and Insurgency in the 21st Century*, vol. 1.

10. John B. Dunlop, *The 2002 Dubrovka and 2004 Beslan Hostage Crises* (Amsterdam: Ibidem-Verlag, 2006): 131–54. Also see "Chechen Rebels' Hostage History," *BBC News* (September 1, 2004), http://goo.gl/GzIZj.

11. For complete details of this event, see Adam Dolnik and Keith M. Fitzgerald, *Negotiating Hostage Crises with the New Terrorists* (Westport, CT: Praeger, 2008): 60–92.

12. Adam Dolnik, "The Seige of Beslan's School No. 1," in *Countering Terrorism and Insurgency in the 21st Century*, vol. 3: 176–201; and Timothy Phillips, *Beslan: The Tragedy of School No. 1* (London: Granta, 2008): 210–56.

13. John Hughes, "Winning the war of words in the campaign against terrorism," *Christian Science Monitor*, May 17, 2006.

14. Cori E. Dauber, "The Terrorist Spectacular and the Ladder of Terrorist Success," in *Influence Warfare*: 93–122.

15. Abu-Ubayd al-Qurashi, "The War of the Ether," *Al-Ansar*, November 20, 2002.

16. Abu Yahya al-Libi, "To the Army of Difficulty in Somalia," *al Sahab Media*.

17. For more details about the impact of *Inspire*, see Tony Lemieux, Jarret Brachman, Jason Levitt, and Jay Wood. "Inspire Magazine: A Critical Analysis of its Significance and Potential Impact thorough the Lens of the Information, Motivation and Behavioral Skills Model." *Terrorism and Political Violence* 1, no. 1 (2014): 1–18.

18. For example, see Lisa Myers, "Al Qaeda Web Message Offers Missile Tutorial," MSNBC.com (March 30, 2005): http://goo.gl/wnjOR.

19. Susan B. Glasser and Steve Coll, "The Web as Weapon: Zarqawi Intertwines Acts on Ground in Iraq With Propaganda Campaign on the Internet," *Washington Post* (August 9, 2005): A01.

20. Ben Venzke and Aimee Ibrahim, "Al Qaeda's Advice for Mujahideen in Iraq: Lessons Learned in Afghanistan," *IntelCenter Report* v1.0 (April 14, 2003), http://www.intelcenter.com.

21. Ibid.

22. Paul Cruickshank and Mohannad Hage Ali, "Abu Musab al Suri: Architect of the New Al Qaeda," *Studies in Conflict & Terrorism* 30 (2007): 8.

23. Abu Musab al Suri, jihadist training videos, dated August 2000. Cited in Cruickshank, "Abu Musab al Suri," 9.

24. Will Oremus, "The Militant Group Behind the Kenya Mall Attack is Living-Tweeting the Massacre," *Slate.com* (September 21, 2013).

25. "Alleged Canada Resident Promotes *Inspire*, Lone Wolf Action," *Western Jihadist Forum Digest* (May 23, 2014), https://news.siteintelgroup.com/Table/Western-Jihadist-Forum-Digest/.

26. See James J. F. Forest, "Perception Challenges Faced by Al-Qaeda on the Battlefield of Influence Warfare," *Perspectives on Terrorism* 6, no. 1 (2012).

III

Terrorist Group Ideologies and Strategies

8

Ethnonationalist/
Separatist Terrorism

In the next several lectures of this series, we will take a closer look at each of the largest ideological categories of terrorist groups, beginning with ethnonationalists. The first thing that sets groups in the ethnonationalist category apart from others is the geographic nature of their ideology and strategic objectives. For the most part, these groups are seeking control over a specific territory; in many cases, like the Chechens, Tamils, Kurds, and Basques, they envision carving out a slice of land from an existing country and declaring it an independent state for all those who share a specific ethnic identity.

While nationalists/separatists pursue the goal of an autonomous state, the term "ethnonationalist" is applied to groups whose ideological rationale for that state is based on ethnicity. These groups share a common goal of meaningful autonomy for their ethnic community, reunification of ethnic homelands, or complete separation from the state and the establishment of their own independent statehood. Because of this geographical focus, virtually all of these groups operate within the confines of territorial borders.

Another aspect of ethnonationalists is that in order to be a member of a group like this, you have to have the proper ethnic background. Members of ethnonationalist groups identify with the group's ideology because of the ethnicity they were born into; they live in a region populated with this ethnicity, or their parents have strong ties to it, and thus they have formulated strong opinions about it. Someone like me would not really be allowed to join a group like the Tamil Tigers, the Kurdish separatist group PKK, or the Basque separatist group ETA. This is much different from other categories of terrorism, where all you have to do is demonstrate that you are a "true believer" in the ideology—be it left-wing, right-wing, religious, environmentalist, or whatever—and the group will probably accept you into the fold. Further, as Daniel Byman has illustrated in his research, ethnic terrorism differs considerably from violence committed for ideological, religious, or financial motives; its focus is on "forging a distinct ethnic identity" apart from the state and "fostering ethnic mobilization."[1]

In addition, Bruce Hoffman notes that ethnonationalist "violence has largely been restricted to a specifically defined 'target set'—namely, the members of a specific rival or dominant ethnonationalist group."[2] Insecurities and fear among members of an ethnic community have led them to believe that they are profoundly threatened by "others," and this can contribute to the rise of political violence. Further, research on this kind of terrorist group has highlighted the important dimension of "othering," which is described as a "process of clearly articulating groups and individuals that have a lesser moral or ethical status than members of the terrorist organization and the racial, ethnic, geographic, or language group they purport to represent."[3] This basic tendency to portray the conflict in terms of "us" versus "them" is always based on a variety of grievances shared broadly by members of that particular ethnic minority, including marginalization and discrimination—real or perceived—by the majority population and its government.

In many cases, structural disadvantages within a society give legitimacy to these grievances. Discriminatory government policies could involve restricting access to education, jobs, and land ownership, as well as policies that encourage unbalanced economic growth between urban and rural areas, and disadvantage one segment of a population. In several instances, ethnonationalists have found support among poor rural peasants in parts of a country where government investment has been comparatively low. Human rights abuses and a lack of political representation are also seen in many of these local contexts. These and other grievances are often created or left unresolved by the state, and in many cases, the state is portrayed as unjustly keeping the members of an ethnic group from exercising their rights. Thus, a recurrent theme among many of these groups is the desire to legitimize their actions as representing

Figure 8.1: Members of ETA firing blanks into the air on Day of the Basque Soldier, September, 2006. Photo by Indymedia Barcelona.

the plight of an oppressed people. In this way, they often echo the sentiments of Frantz Fanon, whom I described in Lecture 2. His arguments about the need to use violence in order to liberate an oppressed people are quite common among the ideological statements of ethnonationalist terrorist groups we have seen over the last several decades.

Many nationalist/separatist groups emerged during either the anti-colonial wave or the New Left wave described in Lecture 2, primarily between 1950 and 1990. Some groups began as nonviolent movements, but evolved into terrorist organizations. Several of them initially embraced various aspects of Marxist revolutionary ideologies. In several cases, multiple ethnonationalist groups were formed and competed against each other for recognition by the local population as the legitimate vanguard of the movement. However, the prominence of leftist ideas faded in almost every case, in part because of the overall decline of leftist-oriented terrorism, and in part because a stronger motivating force was found by tying their vision of the future to widely-shared grievances about the oppression of cultural and political freedoms based mainly on ethnic identity.

So let's look now at a small sampling of these groups, and then draw some comparisons among them at the end of the lecture. We begin with some of the most internationally recognized groups like the ETA, LTTE, PKK, and IRA, and then we'll cover some of the lesser-known ethnonationalist groups that also share a lot in common.

ETHNONATIONALIST GROUPS

ETA

One of the most prominent terrorist groups in this category is the Euzkadi ta Askata-suna (**ETA**), which means "Basque Homeland and Freedom" in the Basque language.[4] ETA's ideology calls for an autonomous nation-state for the Basque people, who live primarily in northern Spain and southwestern France. They share a common language (*Euskara*), and a history that dates back to centuries of territorial autonomy. Although Basque nationalism has deep roots, the foundations of ETA are traced to the Franco regime, starting in the late 1930s. During these years, the Spanish state systematically suppressed all Basque cultural expressions, including use of the Basque language. The state also exiled a major political organization, the Basque Nationalist Party (PNV). The government replaced Basque clergy, assassinated political dissidents, and encouraged Spanish-speaking migrant workers to flood the Basque regions of Spain. These were all part of the Spanish government's effort to unite Spain as one country under the same set of regulations, but this was seen by many Basques as oppression of their historic civic, cultural, and economic rights.

Throughout the 1950s, the PNV attempted to raise international condemnation of the way the Spanish government treated Basques, but to no avail. In 1959, a group of students launched a movement called Ekin (to act), which was initially focused on raising political and cultural awareness by spreading propaganda and flying the Basque traditional flag. They were critical of the more passive political efforts of the PNV, and called for more activism in pursuit of Basque autonomy. Many of these students were inspired by national liberation movements in Vietnam, Algeria, and Cuba, as well as by Che Guevara's writings about a revolutionary vanguard and Frantz Fanon's writings about the need for violent action to liberate an oppressed people. These ideas, in time, led the movement's leaders to shift from promoting Basque culture within the Spanish state to fostering an entirely independent, sovereign Basque nation-state. And they began to use violence as a means to achieve this goal, with members of Ekin launching the armed militant group ETA.

Victims of ETA attacks have most often been security forces, government officials, politicians, and other figures of authority. The first known victim of ETA attacks was a police chief, Melitón Manzanas, who was killed in 1968. In December 1973, ETA assassinated Admiral Luis Carrero Blanco, who was killed when an underground bomb was detonated beneath his car. Overall, research indicates that ETA has killed over 800 Spanish government officials, judicia-ries, security service members, and businessmen over a 50-year time span. Because of its cam-paign of terrorism, hundreds of ETA members are imprisoned throughout Spain and France.

TO THE POINT

Geographic territory matters to ethnonationalists more than to terrorists of any other category.

Following the fall of the Franco regime in 1979, the new democratic government in Spain granted significant autonomy to the Basque region, allowing its residents to estab-lish their own parliament and control taxation in the region. However, this did not put an end to ETA's terrorist attacks. In fact, the group was responsible for killing 91 people in 1981 alone. In 1995, the group used a car bomb to attack José María Aznar, who had been an opposition politician during the 1970s. He survived the attack, however, and years later became prime minister of Spain. ETA specialized in targeted bombings and assassinations, but in later years it was also responsible for more indiscriminate public attacks, like in December 2004, when it detonated bombs at five gas stations outside Madrid, and in 2008, when it bombed the Madrid airport, killing two and wounding over 50 and causing millions of dollars in damage.

It should be noted that ETA has not been the only ethnonationalist group of con-cern here. Some, like the Spain-based "Gazteriak" (meaning "Youth" in Euskara) or the Iparretarrak (based in France) are focused on the Basque territory within their respec-tive nation-states. Meanwhile, another group—Gora Euskadi Askatuta—wants a new sovereign state to be established that is comprised of *both* French and Spanish Basque territories.[5] As is common among many ethnonationalist groups, these Basques are animated by a set of beliefs and grievances that need to be addressed.

ETA declared a halt to its terrorist campaign on several occasions (1989, 1996, 1998, 2006, and 2010). But in January 2011, leaders of ETA declared a permanent ceasefire and the creation of a new Basque political party called Sortu.[6] In April 2017, the group announced it would hand over all its weapons and explosives to local authorities, and in May 2018, the group issued a formal announcement that it had disbanded permanently. These and other developments indicate that we may finally be seeing a new commitment among the Basque communities toward engaging in the Spanish political process.

LTTE

Like the Basques, the Tamils in Sri Lanka have also been animated by policies that led to political and socioeconomic disadvantages for an ethnic minority. The Sri Lankan population consists of several different ethnic groups, the largest being the Sinhalese with about 75% of the population (per a census taken in the 1980s). The Tamils form the largest ethnic minority (approximately 12.5% of the population) and live mainly in the northern and eastern regions of the island. The religious and linguistic divide between these two ethnic groups is significant; the Sinhalese are mostly Buddhists and speak Sinhala, whereas the Tamils are defined by their Tamil language and their Hindu religion. During British colonial rule, the minority Tamil population was favored and became the most prosperous, educated, and employed group. However, once Sri Lanka was granted independence, the Buddhist majority Sinhalese took power and began to implement laws that significantly marginalized the Tamils. From the 1950s through the 1970s, periodic outbreaks of communal violence between Sinhalese and Tamil communities exacerbated widespread feelings of insecurity and ethnic hatreds, which in turn fueled a surge in Sinhalese nationalism.

> **TO THE POINT**
>
> There is always some "other" entity blamed for the hardships faced by an ethnic minority.

After Solomon Bandaranaike was elected prime minister in 1956, his government enacted a law to make Sinhala the state's sole official language, and also passed legislation that gave preference to Sinhalese over Tamils for access to government jobs, university admission, and other socioeconomic opportunities. In 1972, the country adopted Buddhism as the official state religion. Responding to these events, several Tamil separatist groups were formed and took up arms against the state. In 1976, a Tamil leader named Velupillai Prabhakaran established a group called the **Liberation Tigers of Tamil Eelam** (LTTE), also known as the Tamil Tigers.[7]

The declared objective of this group was creating an independent state for the minority Tamil population in Sri Lanka. But one of the first actions Prabhakaran took during the 1980s was to eliminate virtually all of the other Tamil groups, which he saw as rivals competing against him for power, recruits, and financial support within the Tamil community. In 1984, he also established a naval wing, called the Sea Tigers, and began incorporating the use of suicide bombings, inspired by the use of this tactic in Lebanon by Hizballah. He also built up an extensive fundraising system, drawing support from members of the Tamil diaspora in India, Europe, and Canada. Taxation and extortion among Tamils also became a prominent source of funding for the group.

Throughout the 1990s, the Tamil Tigers pioneered and perfected the use of the suicide belt, using a combination of military-grade explosives packed with ball bearings.[8] They also developed extensive paramilitary capabilities, including long-range artillery, mortars, anti-aircraft weapons, and armored vehicles. Heavy indoctrination and radicalization were also a key component of the group's evolution. Members of the Tamil Tigers were known for wearing a cyanide capsule around their necks, preferring death if ever captured by Sinhalese forces. One of their most notorious attacks was the murder of former Indian Prime Minister Rajiv Gandhi, who was killed in 1991 by a female suicide bomber. The group also killed Sri Lankan president Ranasinghe Premadasa in 1993. Finally, after a long series of failed peace negotiations, the Sri Lankan military launched an all-out offensive, eventually cornering and killing the leaders of the Tamil Tigers in 2009.

PKK

Another highly prominent ethnonationalist terrorist group is the Kurdistan Workers' Party (in Kurdish, *Partiya Karkeren Kurdistan*, or **PKK**).[9] As with several other groups in this category, the PKK originally promoted a Marxist ideology, but changed its aims to capitalize on widespread grievances about cultural and political rights for Kurdish people. These grievances stem in part from the fact that under modern Turkey's founding leader Atatürk, the Turkish government had banned the Kurdish language from schools and broadcasting as part of an effort to secularize and homogenize Turkish society. Thus, for years Kurds were not allowed to observe their religious and cultural practices in that country. Further, because Kurdish communities are concentrated mainly in southeastern Turkey—the most rural and economically weak region in the country—they have tended to suffer disproportionately during hard economic times. The PKK has blamed the poverty, backwardness, and neglect of this region on Turkish imperialism and ethnic discrimination.

The PKK was founded by a group of students led by Abdullah Ocalan in 1978, who sought to incite popular rebellion among the Kurdish people. They initially attracted many landless peasants, as well as poorly educated and unemployed Kurds, but Turkey's denial of Kurdish ethnic identity and cultural rights also laid the conditions under which more educated and wealthy Kurds came to believe in the ideology and cause of the PKK. Because one of the main supply routes for drugs from Asia to Europe passes through this Kurdish region, the PKK also began taxing drug smugglers. Other funding sources have included illicit and legitimate fundraising operations set up among Kurdish diaspora networks in Europe, where PKK operatives engage in money laundering and smuggling ventures, drug trafficking, and extortion schemes.[10]

The group launched its first attacks in 1984 in the Anatolia region of Turkey. Throughout the 1980s and 1990s, operating out of bases in Syria and northern Iraq, the group engaged in guerrilla attacks against Turkish government facilities and personnel in Anatolia. Their most frequent victims have included policemen, governors, members of the gendarmerie, state officials, and politicians. PKK has also threatened teachers and civilians working on public works projects, and has burned schools, health clinics, and government projects to undermine the state's influence and authority in the region. And the group also targeted civilians who participated in the government's village guard system, as well as any other Kurds who were seen as collaborating with the Turkish government.

Ocalan was captured by Turkish authorities in 1999, and called for his followers to abandon the violent struggle and engage in a political effort for change. However, in recent years, we have seen an increase in the violence in southeastern Turkey, including some attacks launched from bases in the mountains of northern Iraq. Since 2011, thousands of Turkish soldiers and policemen, PKK members, and innocent civilians have been killed or injured in attacks by the PKK or by the government's efforts to defeat the group. There seems to be no willingness at present for these Kurdish militants to end their terrorist campaign and embrace a political process in Turkey.

IRA

Of course, many of you have heard of the **Irish Republican Army** (IRA), one of the longest operating terrorist organizations in Western Europe.[11] It first emerged in 1922 as a nationalist militia committed to a unified and independent Ireland. After a lengthy anti-colonial war waged by the Irish against the British, the Anglo-Irish Treaty of 1921 had divided Ireland into two separate states: six counties in the north became Northern Ireland, and the remaining 26 became the Republic of Ireland. This led to a civil war between pro-treaty and anti-treaty factions. By the end of this war, which the anti-treaty factions lost, the IRA was a group of fighters opposed to the treaty and the partition of Ireland. In 1925, the group added an ethnic component by calling for the revival of the Irish language and culture.

For decades in Northern Ireland, the pro-U.K. Protestant majority increasingly discriminated against the (anti-U.K.) Catholic minority, making it harder for Catholics to have good jobs, education, or political influence. Under Protestant Home Rule in Northern Ireland, Catholics were excluded from entire industries due to traditions of patronage within Protestant-run businesses (shipyards, linen mills, etc.), as well as civil service. They were also excluded from political representation. As a result, during the 1960s a civil rights movement emerged, with marches and protests in places like Belfast. Some of these turned violent, with Protestant mobs attacking Catholic neighborhoods, and then Catholic mobs retaliating with their own attacks. The Protestant-dominated police force, the Royal Ulster Constabulary, violently cracked down on Catholics, but allowed Protestant mobs into Catholic neighborhoods.

Soon things spiraled out of control, and British military forces were eventually called in to help improve the security situation. But then on January 30, 1972, in an event that became known as Bloody Sunday, British soldiers opened fire on a massive civil rights street protest, killing 13 unarmed Catholics. At this time, the IRA splintered into two groups, one that wanted to pursue a political route to resolving the conflict, and another that felt it would be necessary to take up a campaign of violence. This latter group called itself the **Provisional IRA**.

For the next thirty years, the Provisional IRA became notorious for car bombings, assassinations, kidnappings, punishment beatings, extortion, and other related activities, funded by theft, bank robberies, counterfeiting, and racketeering in Ireland as well as overseas donations, including money and weapons from the Irish diaspora in the U.S. If you spent time in Boston, New York, or Philadelphia during those years, and you visited an Irish pub, you might just have seen a little jar on the bar with a sign that read something like "For the Children" or "For the Lads," into which donations were placed. No doubt some of this money did go to proper charities in Ireland and Northern Ireland, but because the money was not tracked or traceable, it was an easy and fairly sizeable source of finances for the IRA and other republican dissident groups.

The Provisional IRA (PIRA) targeted local police, soldiers, judges, prison guards, and other representatives of the government, as well as Protestant civilians and the paramilitary groups they had formed, like the Ulster Volunteer Force and the Ulster Defense Association (groups that, I should mention, engaged in many forms of terrorism on their part). In the early years, the Provisional IRA used snipers, assassinations, and small bombs within Northern Ireland, but over time its operations expanded to the Republic of Ireland and to Great Britain. During the 1970s through the 1990s, the group's attacks ranged from the prime minister's residence to civilian areas such as pubs, shops, subway stations, factories, and shopping centers, though in those cases they often gave advanced warning in order to minimize civilian casualties. The PIRA's largest bombing was in 1993 at London's Canary Wharf financial district, which caused over $1 billion in damage.

The PIRA also became increasingly involved in the political process, mainly through the political party Sinn Fein. This dual-track approach at pursuing its objectives gave us the phrase "the Armalite and the ballot box" (originally attributed to Danny Morrison, Ian McAllister, and Martin McGuinness, among others), in reference to the Armalite rifle which became a popular weapon of choice among the PIRA. In 1998, Sinn Fein and the Provisional IRA signed the Good Friday Agreement, in which they vowed to use only peaceful means to pursue their goal of a united Ireland. However, not everyone agreed with the peace process, and this led to the emergence of splinter groups such as the Real IRA (or RIRA) and the Continuity IRA (CIRA). The largest terrorist attack in Northern Ireland was conducted just a few months later by the Real IRA on August 15, 1998 when a car bomb detonated in the town of Omagh, killing 29 people and injuring more than 200.

While the RIRA and CIRA have been responsible for several small bombings, kidnappings, and murders, they are also known to be increasingly involved in organized criminal activity, including protection rackets and smuggling. Their respective memberships are small but, as recent events have proven, they can still be quite deadly.[12] Bombings and gun attacks by these groups—as well as by individuals unaffiliated with any group, sometimes called "lone wolves"—have particularly targeted police officers and other authorities in Northern Ireland, including while they were in their homes. These so-called "dissident Republicans" are considered by the government to be the country's most severe terrorist threat today.

Other Notable Examples

In addition to these well-known terrorist groups, there are also several others that you may not be familiar with. For example, in Asia we have the **Moro National Liberation Front** (MNLF), which was established in 1969, and sought to bring about the liberation of the Moro homeland located in the southern region of the Philippines.[13] Moro people make up the largest minority group in the country, less than 10% of the population. They differ from the rest of the population in the areas of language, economic occupation, and several cultural characteristics, and they are Muslim in an otherwise heavily Christian country. The MNLF fought during the 1990s for political autonomy and control over land that had once been owned by Moro people. It signed a peace agreement in September 1996, but several splinter groups—including the more religiously oriented Moro Islamic Liberation Front—have continued to launch attacks against government and civilian targets.[14]

Another group, the Free Papua Movement, or **Organisasi Papua Merdeka** (OPM), was formed in the early 1960s in West Papua. Its members seek to establish independence from Indonesia for the indigenous tribes in West Papua. They have engaged in several terrorist attacks, mostly against armed guards at mining and logging operations, and government and military institutions. Their overall grievances include a history of human rights abuses, forced migration, lack of investment in rural development, and other aspects of the Indonesian government's rule over their tribal lands. Then there's a group known as the **East Turkestan Liberation Organization** (ETLO), which is based in China and Kyrgyzstan, and is comprised of ethnic Uighurs, who are Muslims of Turkish descent.[15] In May 2005, the ETLO was blamed for the assassination of the first secretary of the Chinese Embassy in Bishkek, Kyrgyzstan. Many also suspect the ETLO to be an ally of the **East Turkestan Islamic Movement**, an organization based solely in China that is dedicated to establishing an independent Islamic state in Xinjiang province.[16]

Next door in India, there are a number of violent separatist groups based in Kashmir. The conflict over the Kashmir territory began immediately following the end of British rule in India and the creation of two independent states of India and Pakistan. Many Muslims (the majority of the population in India-administered Kashmir) view the Indian military as foreign occupiers and want the territory to be a part of Pakistan. Among the most prominent of the terrorist groups here is the **Lashkar-e-Taiba** (LeT), meaning "Army of the Pure," which began in 1993 with the support of the Pakistani Inter-Services Intelligence (ISI).[17] LeT grew out of the Pakistani Islamist political movement Markaz Dawah wa al-Irshad (MDI) founded in 1989. While the ideology of LeT is religiously oriented, the central emphasis of the group has been on liberating Kashmir. In December 2001, the group drew international attention when it attacked the Indian Parliament building in New Delhi. The U.S. immediately added the group to its "Foreign Terrorist Organizations" list, which led then-president Musharraf to ban the group inside Pakistan. LeT splintered and began using different names—including Jammat ud-Dawa (JUD)—and stopped claiming responsibility for attacks. However, according to evidence gathered by Indian authorities, the group was responsible for the November 2008 attacks in Mumbai, in which 164 people were killed.

India also has a number of separatist groups in the northeast of the country, far away from the conflict in Kashmir. By some estimates, nearly 10,000 people have died from attacks by terrorists and insurgents in the East Indian state of Assam over the last 20 years. One of the main terrorist groups here is the **United Liberation Front of Assam (ULFA)**, which was founded in 1979 and seeks to establish an independent country of Assam, ruled by a socialist government.[18] It began as a student-led resistance group opposed to immigration into the region, but evolved into a terrorist organization by the late 1980s. The group's grievances include high unemployment, corruption, and the lack of development in the Assam region, despite abundant natural wealth and resources. The group has assassinated political opponents, attacked police and other security forces, blown up railroad tracks, and attacked other infrastructure targets in Assam. It has also extorted millions of rupees from local businesses, especially tea corporations, and is said to have several thousand members. In September 2011, the group signed a truce with the Indian government, which was viewed as a positive sign that the violence here might finally be coming to an end. But small-scale gun battles between militants and authorities have continued since then, including several major incidents in 2016.

Then there is also the **National Liberation Front of Tripura** (NLFT), which was formed in 1989 to fight "Indian neocolonialism" and establish an independent country of Tripura.[19] NLFT's ideology is all about confronting the "oppression" of tribal populations by the Indian government. Like many ethnic nationalist groups, land alienation and inequitable control of resources are also central undercurrents here. This group has targeted state officials, local elections, and infrastructure projects. It has also extorted money from local communities, smuggled weapons in from Bangladesh, and abducted local residents for ransom—in fact, this region was a major hotspot for kidnappings during the early 2000s.

A similar group is the **National Socialist Council of Nagaland-Isak-Muviah** (NSCN-IM), considered the largest and most formidable of all the ethnic Naga separatist groups in northeastern India, with 4,500 members.[20] The Nagas are a diverse group of 3 million to 4 million who stem from different tribes and speak different languages, but came together in common cause during the first half of the twentieth century. The Indian government created the state of Nagaland as a full-fledged state of the Indian union in 1963. In 1975, India signed the Shillong Peace Accord, granting the region more autonomy. But the NSCN-IM rejected this as a sellout and vowed to continue the struggle for a fully independent homeland. The group's ideology is both Maoist and Christian. Its funding comes through extortion, bank robbery, and involvement in the global drug trade, especially involving neighboring Myanmar, which is a prime source of opium.

And next door in the state of Manipur is the **United National Liberation Front** (UNLF), one of northeast India's oldest terrorist groups and a sworn enemy of NSCN-IM. The UNLF is an ethnic Meitei group that was founded to achieve independence from India and establish a socialist government.[21] At roughly 1.4 million, Meiteis are about 57% of Manipur's population, and are opposed to the perceived cultural and economic influence of ethnic Nagas.

It should be noted that in late January 2012, in a formal ceremony held at a stadium in Assam, nearly 700 fighters from nine separatist groups laid down their arms—this may be a sign that the Indian government is having some results in its counterterrorism strategy.[22] But by several estimates, there are still at least two dozen more separatist groups that India has to deal with, and as noted earlier there have been several major gun battles throughout the region between militants and Indian Army units.

Meanwhile, in the Middle East there have been various Zionist and other Jewish extremist groups like the Stern Gang and Lehi, groups who mixed religious ideology with ethnically based justification for violence against British peacekeeping forces and then against Palestinians and Arab Israelis.[23] Power and control over a relatively tiny strip of land plays a central role in the violence here. Both Palestinians and Jews focus on the "occupation" of "our land" by the other. Zionists complain about the "evil forces who have become stronger in our Holy Land,"[24] while Palestinians focus on a history of Israeli forces entering villages and driving entire populations out into what became the refugee settlements in Gaza, West Bank, Lebanon, Jordan, and elsewhere. Israeli Prime Minister Yitzhak Rabin was assassinated by Yigal Amir, an Orthodox student, because of Rabin's plan to evacuate a small settler enclave in Hebron as part of the Oslo Peace Accords he signed in 1993.[25]

On the other side of the conflict, we have one of the most well-known terrorist groups of our time, the **Palestine Liberation Organization** (PLO), which was established in 1964 with the goal of forming a Palestinian government in exile, and eventually liberating Palestine from Israel. Many of the earlier leaders of the PLO, including Yassir Arafat, were inspired by a leftist philosophy grounded in the principles of mass struggle, opposition, and revolution.[26] This laid the conceptual groundwork for promoting Palestinian identity as a means to bring about the cohesiveness and shared destiny inherent in the Palestinian cause.[27] The group adopted a strategy of advancing Palestinian nationalism through terrorism—particularly involving the militant factions known as Fatah and the Popular Front for the Liberation of Palestine—and in doing so was able to draw the world's attention to the conflict in the Middle East.

In Africa, too, there have been several ethnonationalist terror groups over the past few decades. In Nigeria, the Movement for the Emancipation of the Niger Delta (MEND) wants to drive all foreign entities (e.g., oil companies and their workers) out of the Niger Delta region and take control of this region.[28] One of the group's core grievances is that the people of the Niger Delta—the Ibo, Ogoni, Ijaw, and other ethnicities—have suffered greatly from oil exploration and extraction activities since the 1960s, and yet the government has not invested in infrastructure, education, health services, or other needs of the people in this region.

Further down the western coast of Africa we find the **Front for the Liberation of the Cabinda Enclave** (FLEC), which was established in the 1960s as a guerrilla movement aimed at securing the independence of Cabinda.[29] It initially fought alongside other nationalist movements against Portuguese colonists until 1975, but when Angola received its independence, Cabinda—being separated from the main geographical boundaries of Angola—wanted its own independence. In fact, up to that point, the Portuguese colonizers had even referred to Cabinda as a separate state from Angola, and during colonial rule it was actually a protectorate (the people of Cabinda share a common colonial language with Angola, but have their own distinct identity, history, and culture). However, Cabinda produces almost 60% of Angola's oil, and oil revenues account for nearly 90% of the nation's annual budget. Angola recently overtook Nigeria as the largest oil exporter in sub-Saharan Africa. For this reason alone, the Angolan government is unwilling to grant Cabinda its independence.

Similar to MEND in the Niger Delta region, a primary grievance in this case is that the central government derives huge revenues from this region, but does not invest adequately in basic infrastructure, and fails to deliver basic services like quality sanitation and drinking water, public health, and education. Over the years, FLEC has targeted primarily Angolan government outposts in Cabinda, and international oil company staff. However, unlike militants in the Niger Delta, FLEC is unable to disrupt the physical production facilities involved in oil extraction because these are located mainly offshore in the Atlantic Ocean. But the group has attacked targets of opportunity on several occasions. Most recently, during the 2010 African Cup of Nations soccer tournament, FLEC attacked a bus traveling through the capital city of Cabinda, killing two members of the Togolese national soccer team.

And finally, some of the world's most notorious ethnically-related terrorist attacks in recent years have been carried out by **Chechen nationalists**. The conflict between the indigenous inhabitants of Chechnya, in the northern Caucasus, and the Russian government can be traced back to the end of World War II, when Soviet authorities forced a massive resettlement of the Chechen population to Central Asia. After the fall of the Soviet Union, Chechnya declared itself an independent state, but Russian troops soon invaded the territory in what became the first Chechen War (1994–1996).[30] This, in turn, led to the establishment of several insurgent and terrorist organizations that represent the desire for Chechen independence, including the Shamil Basayev Gang, the Mosvar Barayev Gang, the Riyad us-Saliheyn Martyrs' Brigade, the Dagestani Shariah Jamaat, and the so-called Special Purpose Islamic Regiment. Because Chechens are predominately Muslim, many of these groups have embraced some aspect of radical Islamist ideology and are sometimes included in discussions of religious terrorism. However, it is clear that the core objective they all pursue, and the main theme of their appeals for recruitment and financial support, is the establishment of an independent geopolitical entity.

Major incidents they have been responsible for include an attack against the Dubrovka Theater in Moscow on October 22, 2002. Members of the Riyad us-Saliheyn Martyrs' Brigade took over 900 people hostage and threatened to kill them unless Russia withdrew its troops from Chechnya and recognized its independence. After three days, Russian troops pumped gas into the theater in an attempt to disable everyone inside. Many believe this was a potent form of fentanyl gas that was probably meant to just put people to sleep, but it actually killed over 120 of the hostages before the Russian Special Forces stormed the theater and shot every member of the terrorist group.[31] Chechen terrorists also attacked a school in Beslan, Russia in September 2004, holding 1,200 people hostage for 52 hours until the detonation of explosives inside the school triggered a chaotic rescue operation in which 31 terrorists and 331 victims were killed, 176 of them children.[32]

One unique variant of Chechen separatists is the so-called Black Widows—female Chechens whose husbands, brothers, or close relatives have been killed by Russian forces in one of the two Chechen wars. These women are responsible for several suicide bombing attacks, including the August 2004 bombings of two commercial airplanes, which killed 90 people; another bombing that month of the Rizhskaya station of Moscow's metro subway system, which killed 10 people; and the March 2010 bombings of two metro trains in Moscow, which killed 40 and injured 160 people.[33] Since 2011, several attacks against trains, buses, and airports in Russia have been attributed to female Chechen terrorists. While not an organized group per se, the Black Widows (a name given to them by the media) are selected, groomed, trained, and equipped for their terrorist attacks by a variety of Chechen militant group leaders. Additional details of these and other attacks are provided in Lecture 16.

SUMMARY

So, to conclude, all of the groups mentioned in this lecture have several things in common: they represent an ethnic minority within a larger population of an established nation-state and operate within the geographic regions where they seek to change the status quo. They typically fight and target the government in response to grievances that they seek to rectify, like political and socioeconomic marginalization. In the case of the LTTE and ETA, the government took away their right to speak their native language. For the PKK, Kurdish literature and cultural symbols were banned by the Turkish government.

Among these examples of ethnonationalist terrorism, one of the most common forms of motivating contexts that we see is a mixture of policies and structures that disadvantage a particular ethnic minority. In many of the cases I have described here, life was harder for members of a particular ethnicity, often due to economic and employment policies of their government. Basques, Tamils, Kurds, and others formed armed groups in response to discrimination and prejudice that were manifested in the way the majority ethnic group treated them. These groups, in turn, have pursued a common goal of self-determination, and have portrayed themselves as a vanguard representing an oppressed people. In two instances (MEND and FLEC), the government's oil extraction activities have contributed to the destruction of the environment in which these ethnic groups primarily live. As a result of such contexts, nationalism runs deep in many of these ethnic communities. For example, there is a great deal of animosity among Chechens toward Russia, among Tamils toward Sri Lanka, among Basques toward Spain and France, and among Kurds toward Turkey. There is always some "other" entity that can be blamed for the difficult struggle that the ethnic minority is facing.

Because ethnic terrorist groups often represent larger political, social, or economic grievances, military or police solutions that do not address these underlying causes will almost certainly fail to remove the terrorist threat. Heavy-handed military responses can even reinforce the perceived need for violence among the aggrieved communities. Essentially, the big challenge that governments face when dealing with ethnonationalist terrorism is that their actions can reinforce a group's ideological resonance. For example, a crackdown on an ethnic terrorist group can foster resentment among others of that same ethnicity, regardless of a person's support for that particular group, and can generate sympathy for the terrorist groups' cause. In some cases, like that of ETA, a campaign of terrorist attacks was *intended* to provoke an overly repressive state response, in order to foster a stronger sense of "us vs. them" among Basque communities, which they could then capitalize on for recruitment and financial support. This should remind you of Carlos Marighella's writings about the urban guerrilla, as we discussed in Lecture 2.

Equally challenging is that even when governments recognize the legitimacy of grievances that many ethnic groups have against the state, they can be reluctant to make concessions that would lead to them being seen as weak or rewarding violence, a perception that could set a precedent for further terrorist and/or separatist groups. This is a complex, multidimensional kind of terrorism, rooted in deep insecurities fueled by policies as well as socioeconomic and political structures in which certain ethnicities are disadvantaged. Thus, the resolution for many of the grievances that animate this kind of terrorist violence is found less in military and law enforcement and more in the development of a healthy, multiethnic nation-state in which power and responsibility is shared equally across all ethnic identities.

QUESTIONS FOR DISCUSSION

- What grievances motivate Kurdish militant groups in Turkey? Did these grievances change over time? Were they addressed by government policies?
- What role have diaspora communities played in the history of ethnonationalist/separatist terrorism?
- What grievances motivated the majority of IRA/PIRA members? Did these grievances change over time? Were they addressed by government policies?
- What kinds of political and/or economic contexts might lead to the emergence of new ethnonationalist terrorist groups today, and in what countries do you see these contexts?

RECOMMENDED READING

Baracskay, Daniel. *The Palestinian Liberation Organization: Terrorism and Prospects for Peace in the Holy Land*. Westport, CT: Praeger, 2011.

Bowman, Robin L. "Moro Insurgents and the Peace Process in the Philippines." In *Countering Terrorism and Insurgency in the 21st Century*. Vol. 3. Edited by James J. F. Forest. Westport, CT: Praeger, 2007.

Brownfeld, Allan C. "Zionism and the Pursuit of West Bank Settlements." In *The Making of a Terrorist*. Vol. 1. Edited by James J. F. Forest. Westport, CT: Praeger, 2005.

Byman, Daniel. "The Logic of Ethnic Terrorism." *Studies in Conflict and Terrorism* 21, no. 2 (1998).

Devotta, Neil. "The Liberation Tigers of Tamil Eelam and the Lost Quest for separatism in Sri Lanka," *Asian Survey* 49, no. 6 (2009).

Eccarius-Kelly, Vera. *The Militant Kurds: A Dual Strategy for Freedom*. Westport, CT: Praeger, 2010.

Eidelson, Roy and Judy Eidelson. "Dangerous Ideas: Five beliefs that propel groups toward conflict." *American Psychologist* 58 (2003).

Horgan, John and John Morrison, "Here to Stay? The Rising Threat of Violent Dissident Republicanism in Northern Ireland." *Terrorism and Political Violence* 23, no. 4 (2011): 642–69.

Jackson, Brian A. "Training for Urban Resistance: The Case of the Provisional Irish Republican Army." In *The Making of a Terrorist*. Vol. 2. Edited by James J. F. Forest. Westport, CT: Praeger, 2005.

Khalil, Lydia. "Turkey and the PKK." In *Countering Terrorism and Insurgency in the 21st Century*. Vol. 3. Edited by James J. F. Forest. Westport, CT: Praeger, 2007.

Marks, Thomas. A. "State Response to Terrorism in Sri Lanka." In *Countering Terrorism and Insurgency in the 21st Century*. Vol. 3. Edited by James J. F. Forest. Westport, CT: Praeger, 2007.

Moloney, Ed. *A Secret History of the IRA*. New York: W. W. Norton & Company, 2003.

Rashke, Diane. *The East Turkestan Islamic Movement: China's Islamic Militants and the Global Terrorist Threat*. Westport, CT: Praeger, 2010.

Sahukar, Behram A. "India's Response to Terrorism in Kashmir." In *Countering Terrorism and Insurgency in the 21st Century*. Vol. 3. Edited by James J. F. Forest. Westport, CT: Praeger, 2007.

Sherlock, Thomas. "The Wars in Chechnya and the Decay of Russian Democratization." In *Countering Terrorism and Insurgency in the 21st Century*. Vol. 3. Edited by James J. F. Forest. Westport, CT: Praeger, 2007.

WEBSITES

Mapping Militant Organizations
http://web.stanford.edu/group/mappingmilitants/cgi-bin/

START Terrorist Group Profiles ("Big, Allied and Dangerous") Database
http://www.start.umd.edu/baad/database

NOTES

1. Daniel Byman, "The Logic of Ethnic Terrorism," *Studies in Conflict and Terrorism* 21, no. 2 (1998): 149–69.

2. Bruce Hoffman, *Inside Terrorism* (New York: Columbia University Press, 2006): 230.

3. Victor Asal and R. Karl Rethemeyer, "The Nature of the Beast: Organizational structures and the lethality of terrorist attacks," *Journal of Politics* 70, no. 2 (2008): 437.

4. A timeline of ETA's terrorist campaign is available on the BBC website at http://www.bbc .co.uk/news/world-europe-11181982. Also, see the ETA group profile at http://goo.gl/qtUwc and Council on Foreign Relations, "Backgrounder: Basque Fatherland and Liberty (ETA)" (November 17, 2008), http://goo.gl/gOeF9.

5. See the profile of Gora Euskadi Askatuta at http://goo.gl/EMOtL.

6. "Basque Terrorism: Dying Spasms," *Economist*, August 7, 2009.

7. See the LTTE group profile at http://goo.gl/lKtRd.

8. Mia Bloom, "What the Tigers Taught Al-Qaeda," *Washington Post*, May 24, 2009.

9. See Greg Bruno, "Inside the Kurdistan Worker's Party," *Council on Foreign Relations* (October 19, 2007, http://goo.gl/q0yKx.

10. Vera Eccarius-Kelly, "Surreptitious Lifelines: A Comparative Analysis of the FARC and the PKK," *Terrorism and Political Violence* 24, no. 2 (2012).

11. For a good book on this, see James Dingley, *The Irish Republican Army* (Westport, CT: Praeger, 2012).

12. John Horgan and John F. Morrison, "Here to Stay? The Rising Threat of Violent Dissident Republicanism in Northern Ireland," *Terrorism and Political Violence* 23, no. 4 (2011).

13. The START profile for the Moro National Liberation Front is available at http://goo.gl /hYu8k.

14. The START profile for the Moro Islamic Liberation Front is available at http://goo.gl /S9gCH.

15. The START profile for the East Turkestan Liberation Organization is available at http:// goo.gl/h4QCb.

16. Diane Rashke, *The East Turkestan Islamic Movement: China's Islamic Militants and the Global Terrorist Threat* (Westport, CT: Praeger, 2010).

17. The START profile for Lashkar-e-Taiba is available at http://goo.gl/Bp3sf.

18. The START profile for the United Liberation Front of Assam is available at http://goo.gl /65E5r.

19. The START profile for the National Liberation Front of Tripura is available at http://goo.gl /d7GbV.

20. The START profile for the National Socialist Council of Nagaland-Isak-Muviah (NSCN-IM) is available at http://goo.gl/pNrGu.

21. The START profile for the United National Liberation Front (UNLF) is available online at: http://goo.gl/SOkdK

22. "Hundreds of India separatists lay down arms in Assam," *BBC News* (January 24, 2012), http://goo.gl/Sux5c.

23. For more on this, see Allan C. Brownfeld, "Zionism and the Pursuit of West Bank Settlements," in *The Making of a Terrorist*, vol. 1, ed. James J. F. Forest (Westport, CT: Praeger, 2005).

24. See Allan C. Brownfeld, "Religious Zionism: A Growing Impediment To Middle East Peace," *Washington Report on Middle East Affairs* 21, no. 9 (December 2002): 71.

25. See Brownfeld, "Zionism and the Pursuit of West Bank Settlements."

26. See Chapter 4 of Daniel Baracskay, *The Palestinian Liberation Organization: Terrorism and Prospects for Peace in the Holy Land* (Westport, CT: Praeger, 2011).

27. Schiff, Ze'ev and Raphael Rothstein, *Fedayeen: Guerrillas Against Israel* (New York: David McKay Company, Inc., 1972).

28. The START profile for the Movement for the Emancipation of the Niger Delta is available at http://goo.gl/bDQm9.

29. The START profile for the Front for the Liberation of the Cabinda Enclave is available at http://goo.gl/pqrJQ.

30. Thomas Sherlock, "The Wars in Chechnya and the Decay of Russian Democratization," in in *Countering Terrorism and Insurgency in the 21st Century*, vol. 3, ed. James J. F. Forest (Westport, CT: Praeger, 2007). Also, see James S. Robbins, "Insurgent Seizure of an Urban Area: Grozny, 1996," in *Countering Terrorism and Insurgency in the 21st Century*, vol. 3, ed. Forest.

31. For a detailed analysis of this incident, see Adam Dolnik and Keith M. Fitzgerald, *Negotiating Hostage Crises with the New Terrorists* (Westport, CT: Praeger, 2008): 60–92.

32. Adam Dolnik, "The Seige of Beslan's School No. 1," in *Countering Terrorism and Insurgency in the 21st Century*, vol. 3, ed. Forest p. 176.

33. See Mia Bloom, *Bombshell: Women and Terrorism* (New York: Penguin, 2011): 1–7.

9

Left-wing Terrorism

Left-wing terrorists are most often described as Marxist, communist, or Maoist revolutionaries because of the kind of ideologies they use to justify their violent actions. Some have been inspired by the utopian ideas of Russian revolutionaries such as Lenin, Mikhail Bakunin, and Leon Trotsky, and claimed to follow pure Marxist-Leninist doctrine, in which a small group of revolutionaries is supposed to inspire massive worker uprisings through attacks on the political structure.[1]

Leaders and supporters of these terrorist groups believed that socialist political parties of their time had become too much a part of a system that sought to maintain the status quo. They believed that the prevailing political system was corrupt and was preventing the emergence of greater human freedoms and equality. Each group incorporated some element of class warfare and socialist revolution into its political ideologies. And, as discussed in Lecture 2, several prominent revolutionary theorists—including Frantz Fanon, Che Guevara, Mao Zedong, and Carlos Marighella—contributed to the rise of what David Rapoport calls the "New Left" wave of terrorism during the 1960s through the 1980s.

In comparison to the ethnonationalist groups examined in the previous lecture, left-wing Marxist revolutionaries are found to have less of an "othering" dimension.

Instead, their ideologies typically frame a utopian and egalitarian future that will benefit *all members of a society*. Most often, these groups argued that the primary obstacle to achieving their utopian vision of the future was a current regime, hence the need to incite the masses to overthrow the government. Instead of an "us" versus "them" struggle, leftists tend to view all members of a general population as potential converts to the cause.[2] Virtually anyone could be a member or a supporter of the cause if they became convinced of the ideology's credibility.

Many of the groups in this left-wing category were proponents of the "provocation" strategy described by Fanon and Marighella, in which acts of terrorism would provoke the police or the armed forces of the state into carrying out indiscriminate attacks that would then antagonize a population and lead to a growing pool of potential recruits.[3] Further, government actions against the groups sometimes intensified the level of terrorist activity, as was seen in Italy after the arrests of several Red Brigades members, and in Germany following the arrests of Red Army Faction leaders. In both cases, the remaining members of the group launched a series of kidnappings in an attempt to force the government to release their comrades in prison (though

Figures 9.1 and 9.2: Red Army Faction insignia and a photo of Ulrike Meinhof as a young journalist, 1964.

neither Italy nor Germany did so). Meanwhile, in the United States, the Weather Underground bombed several police stations and public facilities to protest against "the unlawful incarceration of other revolutionaries," and in 1969 it bombed two police cars to denounce the authority of the police whom it condemned for the killing of two Black Panther members.

The tactics employed by left-wing terrorists were fairly common regardless of the country they operated in. Their attacks included armed robberies, kidnapping (for attention and coercive bargaining as well as for monetary ransom), selective assassination (snipers, letter bombs, etc.), and of course lots of bombings with dynamite or other explosives stolen from mines or construction sites. You'll be hard-pressed to find examples of suicide bombers or interest in weapons of mass destruction among these groups. Left-wing terrorists around the world also attacked fairly similar targets, including symbols of authority and power—for example, police, lawyers, judges, university professors, politicians, union leaders, industrialists, and military or security facilities. In some cases, the anti-capitalist sentiment of these groups motivated attacks against the United States, such as a 1984 mortar attack against the U.S. Embassy in Portugal by the 25 April Movement, a Marxist group that was commemorating the ninth anniversary of a failed coup attempt by the Portuguese Communist Party against the military government.

All of the groups in this category are driven by a sociopolitical vision of the future, focused on greater equality and some form of communist governance. Power relations play a central role in these leftist ideologies. Of course, I should also note that several of the ethnonationalist groups we looked at in the previous lecture—including ETA and the PKK—have also drawn on various flavors of Marxist-communist ideology, combining these utopian ideals with their ethnonationalist/separatist ideology to form a compelling narrative for the use of terrorist violence. In such instances, these narratives found resonance due to the local layers of political, economic, and ethnic struggles found in their areas of influence. More broadly speaking, of course, this is no different from other terrorist groups we've looked at in this lecture series—the experiences of left-wing revolutionaries were shaped by local conditions and political realities. Historically speaking, the most serious outbreaks of left-wing terrorism occurred during the 1960s and 1970s in Western Europe and Latin America, so let's turn now for a closer look at major groups in both of those regions. We begin with Western Europe, where one of the most headline-grabbing groups was known as the Red Army Faction.

LEFT-WING GROUPS

Red Army Faction/Baader-Meinhof

The **Red Army Faction** (RAF) was a West German leftist group founded in 1968 and active for about 30 years. It was called the Baader-Meinhof Group (or sometimes the Baader-Meinhof Gang) in its early days because of its core founding leaders, Andreas Baader and Ulrike Meinhof. By most accounts, membership in the RAF never rose above around 10–20 people, many of them university students, with perhaps a few hundred supporters or sympathizers.[4] Its core ideology, like many other leftist groups of that era, combined a host of grievances about capitalism, corruption among the wealthy and political elite, and other prominent issues. The group was responsible for a spate of bombings and armed assaults against police, U.S. military personnel, and journalists, and also assassinated several important individuals, including Germany's Supreme Court President Gunter von Drenkman in 1974.

> **TO THE POINT**
>
> Left-wing terrorist movements are characterized by a Communist, Maoist, or Marxist ideology. They often target political and social elites in a capitalist society, and demand greater access to wealth and power.

RAF members were also involved in terrorist attacks in Italy, Switzerland, France, and several other countries, and they often collaborated with foreign terrorist groups for training and operational support. Several of their most notorious attacks involved kidnappings and hijackings. For example, in June 1976, two RAF members participated in the hijacking of Air France Flight 139, en route to Paris with 254 passengers. The team of hijackers was led by members of a Palestinian leftist group known as the Popular Front for the Liberation of Palestine (described below), which ordered the plane to land in Libya, where it refueled and then flew to Entebbe, Uganda on the shores of Lake Victoria. The passengers were eventually taken off the plane and moved into an abandoned terminal. The terrorists offered to exchange the hostages in return for the release of imprisoned comrades in West Germany, Israel, and several other countries. Under the cover of darkness, an Israeli special counterterrorism unit carried out a daring raid and rescued the hostages in what became one of the most successful operations of its kind in history.[5]

In another dramatic episode, the RAF kidnapped Hanns-Martin Schleyer, president of the Employers' Association of the Federal Republic of Germany, on September 5, 1977.[6] The group demanded the release of several RAF members being held in Stammheim prison, including founding members Andreas Baader, Gudrun Ensslin, Jan-Carl Rapse and Irmgard Möller, all of whom had been arrested in 1972. For over a month, the West German security services searched in vain for Schleyer. Then on October 13, another group of RAF members hijacked Lufthansa Flight 181 and demanded the release of the same prisoners. A few days later, the elite West German counterterrorist unit GSG9[7] successfully stormed the plane, recovering all the hostages and shooting dead three of the four hijackers. Within hours, authorities at Stammheim announced that they had found the bodies of Baader and Ensslin, the mortally wounded body of Raspe, and the seriously injured body of Möller in their cells. It emerged that Baader and Raspe had shot themselves, Ensslin had hanged herself, and Möller had stabbed herself repeatedly in the chest. The following day, October 19, the RAF revealed that it had murdered the kidnapped Hanns-Martin Schleyer.[8]

After the murder of a German industrialist in 1984, the RAF lost what little support it had left among other left-wing groups as well as the general public. Its vague ideology had never attracted more than a small number of followers, and those that had labored in the group for over a decade became disillusioned; the fall of the USSR later that decade became the final straw, and the RAF declared a permanent ceasefire in April 1998.

Red Brigades (Brigate Rosse)

Next we have the **Red Brigades** (Brigate Rosse, or BR), an Italian Marxist-Leninist terrorist group founded in Milan in 1970 and active until the late 1980s. This was a time of significant social, political, and economic turmoil in Italy, with mass protests by unemployed factory workers and farmers and assassinations of politicians from both the right and left of the spectrum. The members of the Red Brigades were mostly students and low-income or unemployed workers whose initial popularity came from their commitment to targeting "the establishment" and from their demands for political changes that would ostensibly benefit the common man. The number of core members in BR was much larger than that of the RAF, with estimates of up to 1,500 by the end of 1970s.[9] The group incorporated a centralized structure with at least six local "columns" (cells or branches) responsible for their specific areas, with a strategic directorate articulating the group's overall goals and strategies.[10] BR's operations were initially limited to property damage of factories, but in 1974 it was held responsible for the murder of two members of a neo-fascist party, and this led to the arrests of Renato Curcio and Alberto Franceschini, the primary founders of the group. As more radical elements of the group took up the leadership positions, BR began a series of attacks against police and judges, as well as a campaign of kidnappings in which it would demand ransoms and the release of its comrades from prison.

The most notable of these was the March 1978 kidnapping of former prime minister Aldo Moro, the president of the *Democrazia Cristiana* (Christian Democracy) party. The incident took place on a crowded street in Rome, and five of Moro's bodyguards were killed during the attack. The Italian government refused to negotiate with the terrorist group or pay a ransom on Moro's behalf. After Moro had been held hostage for several months, he was killed and his body dumped onto the streets of Rome.[11] While the BR considered this incident to be a victory of sorts, it failed to secure the release of any prisoners, and Italian society viewed the whole event with disgust, which contributed to a significant loss of support.[12]

Italians weren't the only victims of the BR. In December 1981, the group kidnapped U.S. General James Dozier—deputy chief of staff of NATO's Southern European land forces—from his apartment in Verona. However, based upon lessons learned from the Moro abduction, a special unit of the Italian police was able to locate and rescue Dozier after 42 days of captivity. Several BR members were subsequently arrested, and intelligence provided by these individuals led to more than 200 arrests all over Italy.[13] In 1984, BR leaders issued a statement from their prison cells calling for a ceasefire.

Action Directe

Nearby in France, a small leftist group called **Action Directe** (AD) was established in 1979 and remained active for a little under 10 years. Like the BR and RAF, members of AD tended to be young, unemployed, and educated. They called for Marxist-Leninist revolution and attacked elements of the French political structure. Members of AD were responsible for nearly 20 major bombings, including the 1982 attack on the World Bank European headquarters, the 1984 attack on the European Space Agency, and the 1985 attack on the officers' club at the Rhein-Main U.S. Air Force Base. They also carried out several assassinations of prominent individuals, like French General René Audran, killed in 1985, and Georges Besse, the chairman of Renault, who was killed in 1986.

Of course, when Socialist Francois Mitterrand became president in 1981, the group lost much of its ideological justification. A year later, the AD divided into two factions: Action Directe Nationale (ADN) and Action Directe Internationale (ADI). The ADN tried to stick to the original objectives of the AD, which included destroying the French government and establishing a state based on Marxism-Leninism. The group also criticized French intervention in Lebanon, foreign relations with former French colonies in Africa, and U.S.-French relations. Meanwhile, the ADI tried to expand its actions to fight against international imperialism. It conducted assassinations of individuals who represented European-American business and military interests. The ADI also established relationships with other foreign terrorist organizations, beginning with the RAF. Overall, both factions of the AD became more violent after the 1982 split and after the French government banned the group in 1984. In fact, most of the assassinations it was responsible for occurred after 1985. After the assassination of Besse in 1986, the French authorities arrested most leaders of both the ADN and ADI, and the group had ceased operations by the end of 1987.

Weathermen/Weather Underground Organization

Meanwhile, across the Atlantic Ocean, the United States had its own problem with left-wing terrorism. In October 1969, hundreds of young people clad in football helmets and wielding lead pipes marched through an upscale Chicago shopping district, pummeling parked cars and smashing shop windows in their path. Calling themselves the Students for a Democratic Society, these self-proclaimed revolutionaries were often radicalized at college and university campuses throughout the United States, and demanded a variety of changes in government public and foreign policies. They were particularly angry about the Vietnam War. One of the more notorious splinter groups to come from this movement called itself the "Weathermen" but later changed its name to the **Weather Underground Organization** (WUO). This group was responsible for several crimes and terrorist attacks, including robberies, jailbreaks, and nearly two dozen bombings throughout the early and mid-1970s. Targets of their attacks included the New York City police (1970), the National Guard Armory (1970), the Senate side of the U.S. Capitol building (1971), the Pentagon (1972), the U.S. State Department (1975), and major banks. Warnings were usually issued in advance of bombings to avoid human casualties. As Bernardine Dohrn (one of the leaders of the WUO) stated in her May 1970 "Declaration of a State of War," the primary targets of these attacks were considered by the group to be "symbols or institutions of American injustice."[14]

The propaganda issued by the WUO, which called for communist revolution through violence, became quite popular among members and followers of the Students for a Democratic Society and other leftist movements. WUO members regarded themselves as the vanguard of the revolution and viewed the American youth as the rearguard against the U.S. government. However, after the ceasefire of the Vietnam War in 1973, the WUO faced a major ideological difficulty in advancing communist revolution in the United States. By 1978, its leaders had been either arrested or left the organization. I should note that one former leader of the group, Bill Ayers, later became a Distinguished Professor of Education at the University of Illinois at Chicago, and Bernardine Dohrn became a law professor at Northwestern University School of Law. Just goes to show, even a former terrorist can get tenure.

Revolutionary Armed Forces of Colombia (FARC)

Heading south to Latin America, we come to one the largest and longest-active leftist groups of the past half-century: the **Revolutionary Armed Forces of Colombia** (*Fuerzas Armadas Revolucionarias de Colombia*, or FARC). The early foundations for this group can be traced back to *La Violencia*, the 1948–1958 Colombian civil war, which had a severe impact on the poor rural peasants of the country. Policies enacted after the war further exacerbated these conditions; hundreds of thousands of peasants were relocated and their lands were confiscated by the political elite. In the early 1960s, members of the peasant class were recruited by the newly established Colombian Communist Party. In 1964, an armed wing of this party was founded—which became known as FARC—bringing together communist militants and peasant self-defense groups. Its stated objectives included political reform, eliminating government corruption, and demanding more investment in rural social programs.[15] These objectives soon expanded to include overthrowing the democratic government of Colombia and installing a Marxist-Leninist replacement.[16]

Colombia's vast and rugged terrain proved favorable for FARC's ability to develop a financial/criminal network to support its military objectives. During the 1960s and 1970s, the FARC collected revolutionary taxes from landowners and peasants to raise money for supplies, food, and of course, weapons.[17] By the 1980s, FARC units started to profit from the illicit drug trade mainly by imposing taxes or *gramaje* on coca farmers and emerging narco-traffickers. Guerrilla units charged both local peasants and traffickers between 10% and 15% of the value of each shipment; they also earned substantial amounts of money from extortion schemes that targeted oil companies and multinational corporations, and from kidnap-for-ransom operations.[18] During the 1990s, FARC units intensified demands on drug traffickers by requiring payments in exchange for the use of land for cultivation, as well as the construction of labs and landing strips in the jungle. In essence, FARC imposed its authority and enforced rules, behaving like a shadow government in parts of Colombia.

Meanwhile, FARC also developed the ability to manufacture its own military equipment and weapons, including mortars and landmines.[19] Its attacks have included bombings, murders, mortar attacks, hijackings, and guerrilla and conventional military action against Colombian political, military, and economic targets.[20] Prior to 2002, FARC was primarily involved in attacking infrastructure and kidnapping for ransom. However, in 2002 it began to attack cities, including Bogotá, Medellín, and Cali. Both political and military institutions were targeted; the goal appears to have

Figure 9.3: FARC guerrillas in 2006. Notice how many of the fighters in this photo are female.

been an effort to tie down government troops in protecting the cities, forcing them to abdicate control of some rural territories.

While the FARC's messaging and propaganda were still steeped in Marxist principles, its violent activities evolved to focus much more on maintaining control over a large part of Colombia's illegal drug industry.[21] The group actually acquired many of the characteristics of organized crime, with funding through drug trafficking, extortion, kidnapping for ransom, investment in businesses, land assets, taxes on gold mines, vehicle theft, river transport, cigarette smuggling, and oil bunkering.[22] As a result of this transformation into increasing criminality (which some analysts have referred to as the premier case of narco-terrorism), combined with successful government counter-terrorism efforts, membership in the group declined considerably.[23]

After many years of negotiations between FARC and the Colombian government, formal peace talks held in Havana, Cuba beginning in November 2012 produced various agreements on land reform, victims' rights, and efforts to control the illegal drug trade. The peace process was a controversial point of debate during the 2014 presidential elections, in which the incumbent—Juan Manuel Santos—had to defend support for the negotiations against heated opposition before successfully being re-elected for another four-year term in office.[24] In 2016, FARC announced a permanent ceasefire, and in December of that year the Colombian government officially ratified the peace accord. In June 2017, the group provided detailed information for where the United Nations monitoring team could locate its weapons storage bunkers. And in September of that year, FARC's leaders announced the formation of a new political party, as well as its intention to participate in the 2018 Colombian elections. Interestingly, it kept the same acronym, but changed the name to the Common Alternative Revolutionary Force (*Fuerza Alternativa Revolucionaria del Común,* or FARC), and the party's logo is now a red rose.

Sendero Luminoso

A similar case of left-wing terrorism is found just south of the border in Peru, where the Maoist group **Sendero Luminoso** (or Shining Path) was established in 1969 as a militant outgrowth of the Peruvian Communist movement and is still active today. The group's ideology articulates its commitment to a complete restructuring of Peruvian society. It wants to replace existing social, political, and economic institutions with new ones based on communist ideals.[25] In essence, Sendero's goal is the complete overthrow of the Peruvian government and the establishment of a peasant regime based on communist principles.[26]

Members of Sendero Luminoso occupied villages, established revolutionary governments, and trained members in guerrilla strategy and the use of firearms and explosives. Its terrorist tactics included car bombings, kidnappings, and political assassinations. The group's selection of targets evolved over time, initially targeting local authorities such as mayors, governors, and mid-level bureaucrats, and later shifting to wealthy peasants and state agency leaders. From February through July 1992, the group waged continual attacks in Lima, the capital city, employing car bombs to attack the U.S. Embassy, Peruvian political officials, schools, police stations, middle-class neighborhoods, and Lima's banking center. It also bombed major roadways and threatened to kill those who did not do what it wanted. At the height of its power, the group was considered to be one of the most ruthless terrorist groups in the world.

Despite the use of violent tactics, Sendero Luminoso was able to achieve a degree of support in the 1970s and 1980s as a result of the country's economic struggles. During this time, the group focused on recruiting teachers and students, as well as rural peasants whose already precarious economic situation was exacerbated by the poor economy.[27] It raised money by providing protection to other drug traffickers, as well as running its own drug trafficking networks, kidnapping for ransom, and extortion—e.g., imposing "taxes" on businesses and individuals in occupied villages. A large amount of its funding comes from drug trafficking in the Upper Huallaga Valley where it charges traffickers fees for the use of key airstrips in territories under its control.[28]

In 1992, after a lengthy counterinsurgency effort, the Peruvian government was able to find and arrest Abimael Guzmán, the university professor who founded Sendero Luminoso and had maintained tight control of the group.[29] This event led to a dramatic reduction in the group's ranks, capabilities, and activities. However, while the group's new leader, Florindo Eleutorio ("Comrade Artemio") was captured in 2012, Sendero Luminoso appears to be making a comeback. An attack in April 2009 killed 14 soldiers, and another attack in 2016 killed 10 military and civilian personnel on the eve of Peru's presidential election. More significantly, several hundred members of the group have become increasingly involved in the Peruvian cocaine trade, most often extorting protection money from cocaine growers and traffickers in the mountainous central regions of the country. This is similar to the kinds of activity we saw among members of FARC in Colombia. For a few years recently, Peru had even overtaken Colombia as the world's number one exporter of cocaine.

Communist Party of India-Maoist

Now we move west across the Pacific Ocean to Asia, where we find one of the most active left-wing terrorist groups today operating in India. Here, the **Communist Party of India-Maoist** (also known as Naxalites) is a left-wing group established in 2004 that is operating in several northeast states. The organization's goals include inciting a peasant revolution, the abolition of class hierarchies, and expanding Maoist-controlled areas that would serve as territory for a Maoist independent state. The group's long-term goal is the complete overhaul of the Indian government in order to establish a communist society, termed a "New Democratic Revolution" in the traditional language of Mao. This group remains active today; former Prime Minister Manmohan Singh described the organization as India's "greatest internal security challenge."[30] In January 2011, the CPI-M leader Koteshwar Rao announced his prediction that by 2025 India would fall to the Maoist revolution. (Rao was killed by security forces in November of that year.)[31]

Similar to what we saw in Latin America, funding for this leftist group comes from extortion and the imposition of "taxes" on villages and village officials. Estimates of the group's size range from 10,000 fighters[32] to 20,000.[33] The group gets a lot of weapons by raiding police offices. It is strongest in rural parts of the country, especially in the jungle, but has no influence or presence in urban areas. The northeast of India sees frequent CPI-M attacks, as does the "Red Corridor," an area stretching from the northeastern border with Nepal to Karnataka state in the south of India. The CPI-M aims to create a "Compact Revolutionary Zone" along this corridor, gaining control of the land and eventually seceding from India to create an independent communist state. It targets areas where government presence is weak. This group has a reputation for kidnappings, shootings, hit-and-run attacks, and bombings, and has targeted government officials, law enforcement, and schoolteachers. One particularly gruesome aspect of several CPI-M attacks has been the tactic of loading the corpses of victims with mines, so that those who come to retrieve the bodies also die.[34]

As discussed in previous lectures, ideological resonance is an important aspect for the survival of any terrorist group. In this case, the various Maoist groups like CPI-M that are active in eight states across northeast India are able to tap into anti-government sentiment among a largely illiterate and impoverished underclass for whom infrastructure is limited or nonexistent. The government is seen by many as corrupt and protecting a status quo in which the nation's vast wealth is controlled by a tiny fraction of its ultra-wealthy elite. A majority of people in the northeast of the country live in poverty

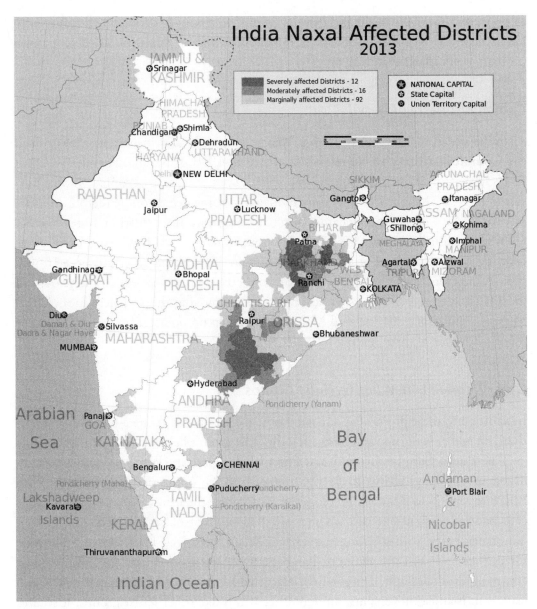

Figure 9.4: "The Red Corridor" in 2013. A relatively underdeveloped region in eastern India that has Naxalite communist militant activity. Image by M. Tracy Hunter.

or poor conditions, especially indigenous groups, which is a contributing factor to why leftists like CPI-M have found increasing support among them for its ideology of a utopian, egalitarian future.

Communist Party of Nepal

A similar situation is seen next door in Nepal, where a Maoist insurgency calling itself the **Communist Party of Nepal** was launched in 1996. It began as a small group of rebels in the jungle but grew quickly to organize a peasant-based "People's War" in pursuit of a "New Democracy," a strategy modeled to some degree on Sendero Luminoso in Peru.[35] Much of its funding came from bank robberies and extortion, but it has also enjoyed much more support among local populations than the Maoists in India. After carrying out hundreds of attacks on government and civilian targets over a 10-year period, the group came to control an estimated 70% of the Nepalese countryside, and in 2007 it achieved its most central objective of removing the Nepalese monarchy.[36] More recently, since 2011 several Maoists have taken up political posts in the government, with four of them serving in Parliament.[37]

Other Notable Left-Wing Terrorist Groups

In addition to these prominent left-wing terrorist groups, there are a handful of others that I should at least mention here, including the groups below.

The **Purbo Banglar Communist Party of Bangladesh** (PBCP) is a group established in 1967 and claims to be fighting against the oppression of peasants.[38] The PBCP follows Mao Zedong's ideology, looking to use the force of the people to eradicate Bangladesh's current parliamentary system in favor of communism. It is also a nationalist party, with a strong stance against any perceived interference by outside forces (like India) in the affairs of Bangladeshis. Assassinations are the PBCP's most common form of assault. The group has targeted local political leaders, the police, and leaders in Islamist movements, among others. And like other leftist groups, it secures a significant amount of funding through "taxes" on rich landowners and contractors.

The **Zapatista Army of National Liberation** (EZLN, often called the Zapatistas) is a group in Mexico whose ideology represents a melding of Marxism and the sociopolitical grievances of indigenous peoples. Although it was founded in 1983, it did not formally declare war on the Mexican government until January 1, 1994, a date that coincided with the coming-into-effect of the North American Free Trade Agreement (NAFTA), which EZLN argues is a system that disproportionately benefits the United States at the expense of Mexicans. Almost all of this group's attacks have occurred in Chiapas, in southeastern Mexico, using bombs and explosives that have primarily targeted utilities, corporations, and government buildings.

Nearby in Nicaragua, the **Sandinista National Liberation Front** (FSLN) is another leftist group, founded in 1961, which also followed a strategy of "prolonged popular war" aimed at mobilizing rural peasants to attain revolutionary victory. However, during the mid-1970s, the group shifted its focus from the rural peasant revolution to a more urban-focused strategy, promoting a Leninist working-class party based on union organization. The FSLN used bank robberies to raise funds, assassinated local officials, and briefly engaged in urban terrorism.

In July 1979, the FSLN succeeded in removing the Somoza family from power. The group led a coalition of students, labor unions, peasants, and economic elites against the regime, and became the new dominant force in the government. In the 1984 national elections, the Sandinistas won the presidency and the majority of seats in the National Assembly. It was defeated by the opposition party in the 1990 and 1996 elections, but the Sandinistas under Daniel Ortega came back to win the 2006 elections and Ortega won reelection in 2011, and remains president to this day (in 2014 the country's National Assembly—dominated by the FSLN—abolished term limits for the presidency, allowing a president to run for an unlimited number of five-year terms).

A similar case of left-wing terrorist violence contributing to political victory was seen nearby in El Salvador, where the **Farabundo Martí National Liberation Front** (FMLN) launched a violent campaign against the Salvadoran regime in 1980.[39] In 1981, a major FMLN offensive failed to achieve popular insurrection or to overthrow the government, and this led to a decade-long bloody civil war against the government of El Salvador.[40] For several years, the group used conventional military combat tactics, and was successful in forcing the Salvadoran military to withdraw from about 25% of the country. However, it also began to use terrorist tactics, such as indiscriminate bombings of public targets, forced recruitment, and economic sabotage, and as a result, it alienated an increasingly large proportion of the local population.[41] In 1989, the FMLN launched a siege of San Salvador, the nation's capital. Though this failed, the renewal of fighting on this scale shattered the belief of the political right-wing that the Salvadoran military could achieve a military victory against the leftist guerrillas. The seeming inevitability of a never-ending conflict encouraged both sides to begin negotiations, and in January 1992 the Chapultepec Peace Accords were signed, which transformed the FMLN into a political party.[42] In 2009, the FMLN's candidate, Mauricio Funes, was elected to the Presidency of El Salvador, and he was succeeded in the 2014 election by another FMLN leader, Salvador Sánchez Cerén.

The **Popular Front for the Liberation of Palestine** (PFLP) is a Marxist-Leninist Palestinian secular nationalist movement founded in 1967. For several years it was a faction within the larger Palestinian Liberation Organization (PLO), but eventually left to pursue its own political agenda through the use of terrorism. The leaders of PFLP are vehemently opposed to the Israeli peace process, and argue that Fatah, the PLO, and the Palestinian Authority sold out the Palestinian people by having negotiated with Israel.[43] Members of this group were responsible for several airplane hijackings, kidnappings, and a major attack against the Munich Airport. Its military wing, the Abu-Ali Mustafa Brigades, has been responsible for several suicide bombings in Israel and has collaborated with various other left-wing terrorist groups, including the Red Army Faction.

Then there's the **Japanese Red Army** (JRA), a leftist revolutionary group founded in the late 1960s that called for overthrowing the Japanese government and monarchy. The group was led by Fusako Shigenobu from 1971 until around 2001. She at one point was considered the most feared female terrorist in the world. Although the JRA remained small, with fewer than 40 members throughout most of its existence, the group trained extensively and acquired significant funding and weapons (in some cases, from Libya and Syria). Most of its attacks occurred outside Japan, like the May 1972 assault on Tel Aviv Lod Airport, in Israel; the August 1975 attack against the U.S. Embassy in Kuala Lumpur, Malaysia; and the September 1977 hijacking of a Japanese airplane traveling from Paris to Tokyo, which it forced to land in Dhaka, Bangladesh, and eventually compelled the Japanese prime minister to release several JRA members from prison and pay a $6 million ransom for the hostages.

And finally, there's the **Irish National Liberation Army** (INLA), which was formed in 1974 as the armed wing of the Irish Republican Socialist Party. This group combined the Irish nationalist ideology pursued by the IRA with a Marxist-oriented class struggle. During the late 1970s and 1980s, INLA was responsible for several bombings, assassinations and armed attacks against British security forces, police, Loyalist paramilitaries, Protestant civilians, and rival Republicans. Its most famous attack was the 1979 assassination of a British Member of Parliament, who was very close to Prime Minister Margaret Thatcher.

SUMMARY

While there are many others, this representative sampling should give you a good sense for what left-wing terrorist groups typically want, and how they try to justify their use of terrorist violence. While the New Left wave of terrorism (described in Lecture 2) may be over, there are still plenty of these kinds of groups around, especially in northeast India. But the good news is that since the end of the Cold War, there has definitely been a global decline in the spread and influence of left-wing Marxist-communist terrorist groups. Many of the groups described here—including the Red Brigades, Baader-Meinhof, Action Directe, Japanese Red Army, and the Weather Underground—clearly failed to achieve their objectives. Others, like the Sandinista National Liberation Front in Nicaragua, the Farabundo Martí National Liberation Front in El Salvador, and the communist insurgents in Nepal, managed to transform themselves into legitimate participants in the official political processes of their countries. Meanwhile, there are still left-wing groups today around the world that use strategies and tactics of terrorism in their attempt to gain power and achieve their objectives, as we have seen recently in Asia, where Maoists have threatened state power in two countries, particularly India and Nepal.

Meanwhile, the two largest left-wing terrorist groups in South America—Sendero Luminoso in Peru and the FARC in Colombia—moved away from their original emphasis on left-wing Marxist ideology and more toward criminal objectives. It is noteworthy that both of these groups are based in adjoining countries with similar geographical and societal makeup, and these things impact their operational capabilities. Further, their criminal activities undermined the resonance of their political ideology, which contributed to decreasing support among their local populations. In the case of the FARC, former leaders and members of the group have been trying to recreate their image by signing a peace treaty and launching a political party.

Generally speaking, these left-wing revolutionary groups have been domestic and either Marxist or Maoist in orientation, and almost all of them promoted armed violence against a democratic capitalist state. Several embraced the revolutionary ideologies of Fanon, Guevara, Mao, and Marighella (see Lecture 2). But although all of these groups were influenced by left-wing ideologies, the ways in which these ideas manifested themselves in the groups' operations were very different. For example, some groups overlooked the rural dimension and focused entirely on urban guerrilla warfare and urban mobilization strategies, while others (like the Maoist revolts in Peru, India, and Nepal) have been primarily rural. Further, those that have been rural in orientation found support among poor peasant farmers, typically the least powerful segment of their society. With little political capital and few financial resources, these rural peasants have also been the least likely to see benefits from their government in terms of public goods and services, creating the conditions in which a leftist utopian ideology could find resonance.

At the same time, a number of these groups were established and led by academics and intellectual elites: Sendero Luminoso, which was founded by Professor Abimael Guzmán at the University of San Cristóbal de Huamanga; the Red Brigades, founded by a couple of students at the University of Trento; the Red Army Faction, founded by a couple of graduate students at the Free University of Berlin; and 17 November, a relatively obscure left-wing terrorist group founded covertly in Greece by a group of students at Athens Polytechnic. But it was also quite often the case that the intellectual elites who controlled the movement got older and lost their ability to connect with increasingly younger student activist audiences. Just as often, these young and impatient leaders (as well as their followers) made mistakes (such as attacking too frequently, killing too many innocent bystanders, and so forth), and the violence that resulted was counterproductive to their cause. In several cases, the leaders of these groups came to have a warped view of reality, becoming too obsessed with their revolutions and exaggerated dichotomy of "us vs. them" and "life vs. death." By dehumanizing the targets of their violence, they inadvertently portrayed themselves as too extremist for the masses to rally behind.

In fact, a key challenge for all terrorist groups—and particularly the left-wing radicals of the last half-century—was to keep from alienating their target audiences, which undermined their political objectives and made popular mobilization virtually impossible. For example, RAF in 1984 encountered massive condemnation after killing a German armaments industry manager. The Weather Underground always issued warnings before bombings to avoid casualties. In France, the AD failed to garner support among the working class because the 1981 election of Socialist Mitterrand provided the working class with political channels to improve their problems without resorting to violence, and this in turn undermined the justification for AD's existence.[44] And in Italy, the Red Brigades lost support when it became seen as too violent and indiscriminate in its attacks.

Thus, what we learn from the study of left-wing terrorists reinforces the point that I've stressed in several previous lectures: context matters, particularly socioeconomic conditions in which benefits (or difficulties) are not shared equally, leading to the resonance for an ideology that expresses an egalitarian, utopian future with better justice and opportunities for a better life. Of course, government actions and improved police tactics certainly contributed to the decline of left-wing terrorism in the United States and Europe. But the decline of the left wave of terrorism can also be attributed to the deficiencies of the motivating ideologies and the inability for most groups to convince the masses that a violent uprising would lead to a brighter future.

QUESTIONS FOR DISCUSSION

- What similarities existed between left-wing groups that were ultimately able to move into positions of power (e.g., the Sandinistas in Nicaragua, and the Community Party in Nepal)? And what might this indicate about the potential future for FARC in Colombia?
- If they truly believed in a more egalitarian system, why were so many left-wing groups organized in a centralized hierarchy?
- What hypocrisies are most glaring in the core narrative of most left-wing terrorist groups?
- What kinds of conditions might lead to the emergence of new left-wing terrorist groups today, and where do you see these conditions?
- Why have left-wing groups in Latin America endured longer than the left-wing groups in Europe?

RECOMMENDED READING

Allison, Michael E. "The Transition from Armed Opposition to Electoral Opposition in Central America." *Latin American Politics and Society* 48, no. 4 (2006).

Burrough, Bryan. *Days of Rage: America's Radical Underground, the FBI and the First Age of Terror* (New York: Penguin, 2015).

Chenoweth, Erica. "Italy and the Red Brigades: The Success of Repentance Policy in Counterterrorism." In *Countering Terrorism and Insurgency in the 21st Century*. Vol. 3. Edited by James J. F. Forest. Westport, CT: Praeger, 2007.

Gonzalez-Perez, Margaret. "Guerrillas in Latin America: Domestic and International Roles." *Journal of Peace Research* 43, no. 2 (2006).

Iriarte, Nicolás Urrutia and Román D. Ortiz. "A Slow Road to Victory: Counterinsurgency and Strategic Innovation in Colombia." In *Countering Terrorism and Insurgency in the 21st Century*. Vol. 3. Edited by James J. F. Forest. Westport, CT: Praeger, 2007.

Marks, Thomas A. "Combating Terrorism in Nepal." In *Countering Terrorism and Insurgency in the 21st Century*. Vol. 3. Edited by James J. F. Forest. Westport, CT: Praeger, 2007.

Miller, Martin A. "The Intellectual Origins of Modern Terrorism in Europe." In *Terrorism in Context*. Edited by Martha Crenshaw. University Park, PA: Pennsylvania State University Press, 1995.

Moghadam, Assaf. "Failure and Disengagement in the Red Army Faction." *Studies in Conflict & Terrorism* 35, no. 2 (2012): 156–81.

Ortiz, Roman D. "The Human Factor in Insurgency: Recruitment and Training in the Revolutionary Armed Forces of Colombia (FARC)." In The Making of a Terrorist. Vol. 2. Edited by James J. F. Forest. Westport, CT: Praeger, 2005.

Palmer, David Scott. "Countering Terrorism in Latin America: The Case of Shining Path in Peru." In *Countering Terrorism and Insurgency in the 21st Century*. Vol. 3. Edited by James J. F. Forest. Westport, CT: Praeger, 2007.

Ross, Jeffrey Ian. "The Primacy of Grievance as a Structural Cause of Oppositional Political Terrorism: Comparing Al-Fatah, FARC and PIRA." In *Faces of Terrorism. Edited by David Canter.* West Sussex: John Wiley & Sons, Ltd., 2009.

Schweitzer, Yoram. "The Case of PFLP and its Offshoots." In *Terrorist Innovations in Weapons of Mass Effect: Preconditions, Causes, and Predictive Indicators*. Edited by Maria J. Rasmussen and Mohammed M. Hafez. Washington, DC: Defense Threat Reduction Agency, 2010.

Smith, Paul J. "The Italian Red Brigades (1969-1984): Political Revolution and Threats to the State." In *Armed Groups: Studies in National Security, Counterterrorism and Counterinsurgency*. Edited by Jeffrey H. Norwitz. Newport, RI: U.S. Naval War College.

Stanski, Keith. "Terrorism, Gender and Ideology: A Case Study of Women Who Join the Revolutionary Armed Forces of Colombia (FARC)." In *The Making of a Terrorist*. Vol. 1. Edited by James J. F. Forest. Westport, CT: Praeger, 2005.

Weinberg, Leonard. "Political and Revolutionary Ideologies." In *The Making of a Terrorist*. Vol. 1. Edited by James J. F. Forest. Westport, CT: Praeger, 2005.

Wright, Joanne. "Countering West Germany's Red Army Faction: What Can We Learn?" In *Countering Terrorism and Insurgency in the 21st Century*. Vol. 3. Edited by James J. F. Forest. Westport, CT: Praeger, 2007.

WEBSITES

Mapping Militant Organizations
http://web.stanford.edu/group/mappingmilitants/cgi-bin/

SDS Documents Archive
http://www.sds-1960s.org/documents.htm

START BAAD Database (terrorist group profiles)
http://www.start.umd.edu/baad/database

U.S. Department of State, Country Reports on Terrorism
https://www.state.gov/j/ct/rls/crt/

NOTES

1. Harvey Kushner, *Encyclopedia of Terrorism* (New York: Sage, 2003): 308.

2. Victor Asal and R. Karl Rethemeyer, "The Nature of the Beast: Organizational structures and the lethality of terrorist attacks," *Journal of Politics* 70, no. 2 (2008): 438.

3. For example, see Leonard Weinberg, "Political and Revolutionary Ideologies," in *The Making of a Terrorist*, vol. 1, ed. James J. F. Forest (Westport, CT: Praeger, 2005): 190.

4. Baader Meinhof Group, START website "Terrorist Group Profile," http://goo.gl/NGz6r.

5. For more on this, see William H. McRaven, *Spec Ops: Case Studies in Special Operations Warfare* (New York: Ballantine Books, 1995): 333–80.

6. Joanne Wright, "Countering West Germany's Red Army Faction: What Can We Learn?" in *Countering Terrorism and Insurgency in the 21st Century*, vol. 3, ed. James J. F. Forest (Westport, CT: Praeger, 2007).

7. The Grenzschutzgruppe 9 (GSG9) had been created largely in response to the events in Munich in 1972, described in Lecture 2. However, it no longer handles terrorist situations outside of Germany and is more akin to the FBI's Hostage Rescue Team (HRT) in the United States.

8. Joanne Wright, "Countering West Germany's Red Army Faction: What Can We Learn?," in *Countering Terrorism and Insurgency in the 21st Century*, vol. 3, ed. James J. F. Forest (Westport, CT: Praeger, 2007).

9. Sean K. Anderson and Stephen Sloan, *Historical Dictionary of Terrorism* (New York: Scarecrow Press, 2002): 576–77; and Paul J. Smith, "The Italian Red Brigades (1969-1984): Political Revolution and Threats to the State," in *Armed Groups: Studies in National Security, Counterterrorism and Counterinsurgency*, ed. Jeffrey H. Norwitz (Newport, RI: U.S. Naval War College): 18.

10. Erica Chenoweth, "Italy and the Red Brigades: The Success of Repentance Policy in Counterterrorism," in *Countering Terrorism and Insurgency in the 21st Century*, vol. 3, ed. Forest, pp. 352–65.

11. Ibid.

12. Alison Jamieson, "Identity and morality in the Italian Red Brigades," *Terrorism and Political Violence* 2, no. 4 (1990): 509.

13. Anderson and Sloan, *Historical Dictionary of Terrorism*, p. 579/

14. See the transcript of her "Declaration" at: http://goo.gl/9kE92.

15. Margaret Gonzalez-Perez, "Guerrillas in Latin America: Domestic and International Roles," *Journal of Peace Research* 43, no. 2 (2006): 321.

16. Jeffrey Ian Ross, "The Primacy of Grievance as a Structural Cause of Oppositional Political Terrorism: Comparing Al-Fatah, FARC and PIRA," in *Faces of Terrorism: Multidisciplinary Perspectives*, ed. David Canter (West Sussex: John Wiley & Sons, Ltd., 2009): 78.

17. Vera Eccarius-Kelly, "Surreptitious Lifelines: A Comparative Analysis of the FARC and the PKK," *Terrorism and Political Violence* 24, no. 3 (2012).

18. Russell Crandall, *Driven by Drugs: U.S. Policy Toward Colombia* (New York: Lynne Rienner, 2002): 90.

19. Roman D. Ortiz, "Renew to Last: Innovation and Strategy of the Revolutionary Armed Forces of Colombia (FARC)," *in Teaching Terror: Strategic and Tactical Learning in the Terrorist World*, ed. James J. F. Forest (Lanham, MD: Rowman & Littlefield, 2006): .205–22; and Roman D. Ortiz, "Insurgent Strategies in the Post-Cold War: The Case of the Revolutionary Armed Forces of Colombia," *Studies in Conflict and Terrorism* 24 (2002): 127–43.

20. Ibid.; and Roman D. Ortiz, "The Human Factor in Insurgency: Recruitment and Training in the Revolutionary Armed Forces of Colombia (FARC)," in *The Making of a Terrorist*, vol. 2, ed. Forest, pp. 263–76.

21. Revolutionary Armed Forces of Colombia (FARC), START website "Terrorist Group Profile" at http://goo.gl/haUwv.

22. Jane's Terrorism and Insurgency Center, "Fuerzas Armadas Revolucionarias de Colombia (FARC)," Jane's Information Group (February 22, 2011).

23. Ibid.

24. "Colombia Vote: Santos Re-elected as President" BBC News (June 15, 2014).

25. Sendero Luminoso (Shining Path), START website "Terrorist Group Profile" at http://goo.gl /1kouF.

26. Gonzalez-Perez, "Guerrillas in Latin America," 320.

27. Cynthia McClintock, *Revolutionary Movements in Latin America* (Washington, DC: United States Institute of Peace, 1988): 14.

28. Cynthia McClintock, "Why Peasants Rebel: The Case of Peru's Sendero Luminoso," *World Politics* 7, no. 1 (1984): 72.

29. Ibid., 64.

30. "Profile: India's Maoist Rebels," *BBC News* (March 4, 2011), www.bbc.co.uk/news/world -south-asia-12640645.

31. "India alert as Maoist Koteshwar 'Kishenji' Rao killed," *BBC News* (November 25, 2011), http://www.bbc.co.uk/news/world-asia-india-15887860.

32. "India's Naxalites: A Spectre Haunting India," *Economist* (August 17, 2006), http://www .economist.com/node/7799247.

33. Communist Party of India—Maoist, START website "Terrorist Group Profile" at http:// www.start.umd.edu/start/data_collections/tops/terrorist_organization_profile.asp?id=4505.

34. "India's Naxalites," Economist.

35. "Who are Nepal's Maoist Rebels?" BBC News (June 6, 2005), http://news.bbc.co.uk/2/hi /3573402.stm.

36. Communist Party of Nepal-Maoist, START website "Terrorist Group Profile" at http://goo .gl/xsyQ1; also see Thomas A. Marks, "Combating Terrorism in Nepal," in *Countering Terrorism and Insurgency in the 21st Century*, vol. 3, ed. Forest, pp. 532–48.

37. "Maoists join Nepal Cabinet, end Stalemate," *Time of India* (March 6, 2011), http://goo .gl/go4vL.

38. "Purbo Banglar Communist Party," South Asia Terrorism Portal (February 9, 2011), http:// goo.gl/DChoZ.

39. McClintock, *Revolutionary Movements in Latin America*, p. 52.

40. Michael E. Allison, "The Transition from Armed Opposition to Electoral Opposition in Central America," *Latin American Politics and Society* 48, no. 4 (2006): 145.

41. McClintock, "Why Peasants Rebel," 77.

42. Michael E. Allison, "The Transition from Armed Opposition to Electoral Opposition in Central America," *Latin American Politics and Society* 48, no. 4 (2006): 145.

43. Popular Front for the Liberation of Palestine (PFLP), START website "Terrorist Group Profile" at http://goo.gl/RjBSg.

44. Isabelle Sommier, "Revolutionary Groups after 1968: Some Lessons Drawn from a Comparative Analysis," *Twentieth Century Communism* 2, no. 1 (2010): 66–91.

10

Right-wing Terrorism

In the previous two lectures, we examined specific attributes and examples of ethnonationalist and left-wing terrorism. Now we will look at right-wing terrorist groups with an eye toward how they are both similar and different from other categories of terrorism. To begin with, we have to acknowledge that there is no single definition that applies to this category; according to one study, there are at least 26 definitions of right-wing extremism, and the most common features mentioned among them—nationalism, racism, xenophobia, anti-democracy, and the desire for a strong and encompassing state—are included in only half of these definitions.[1] Some groups may include anti-leftist, anti-liberal, religious, or paramilitary/militia elements, depending on social, political, and historical context.[2]

Right-wing extremism can be both revolutionary and reactionary; some right-wing adherents may seek a revolution in the relationship between state and citizen, like a reduced government role in our daily lives, or a major policy change, like taking away the legal right for women to have an abortion in the United States. Meanwhile, in several cases, right-wing political parties and terrorist groups emerged in direct response to the kind of left-wing groups described in the previous lecture. Right-wing terrorism has also been commonly associated with racial supremacists, whose violent attacks in liberal democracies are seen as a response to the increasing prevalence of civil rights granted to racial minorities.

This, in turn, can confuse the issue of definitions even further because of disagreement over whether a specific incident is an act of right-wing terrorism or a hate crime. Both are driven by hatreds and denigration of others based on race and ethnicity, hatreds that fuel attacks against an "other" entity that is often perceived as a threat to the status quo. I talked about this kind of "othering" in Lecture 8, but it's worth revisiting here for a moment. In essence, this is a sentiment that is driven by insecurities and fear among members of a community, who believe that they are profoundly threatened by those—often defined by racial and ethnic differences—who are typically seen as having a lower moral or ethical status than the dominant community members.[3] One particularly troubling variant of this is seen in the ideology of Creatorism, followers of which have called for a racial holy war.[4] Formerly called the World Church of the Creator, founded by Ben Klassen in 1973, Creatorists claim that each race must fend for itself, and they publish *The White Man's Bible*, which emphasizes racial purity.[5] Today, you can find a T-shirt or bumper sticker with RAHOWA (which means "RA-cial HO-ly WA-r") in several places throughout the United States and on the Internet.

This basic tendency to portray the threat in terms of "us" versus "them" is further based on a variety of socioeconomic and political grievances shared broadly by members of that particular community. This certainly sounds a bit like the ethnonationalist terrorism we examined in Lecture 8, doesn't it? Indeed, Bruce Hoffman has described how right-wing terrorist groups are fervently nationalist in character and span the globe from the Americas to Europe to East Asia.[6] While a large number of right-wing racist groups are not Anglo-American—for example, groups like Russian National Unity,[7] the Italian New Order, or the neo-Nazi group "Blood and Honor"—this lecture focuses primarily on this phenomenon within the U.S. context.

The modern right-wing extremist movement in the United States encompasses a broad spectrum of groups, far too many to cover in this lecture. I will describe a handful of them in a moment. But from militias to quasi-religious organizations to personal cults, many of these groups have some common elements. Sometimes right-wing groups will portray the government as the source of the threat to the community, a threat which (according to them) requires ordinary citizens to rise up and defend themselves. In the United States, the history of anti-government violence actually goes all the way back to the 1791 Whiskey Rebellion, in which farmers took up arms to oppose the taxation of grains. But the group that most terrorism scholars point to as an early example is the Ku Klux Klan (KKK). Founded shortly after the Civil War by Nathan Bedford Forrest, the KKK was created as an anti-unionist organization that would preserve southern culture and traditions. Hooded Knight Riders of the Klan would terrorize African-Americans to frighten them into political and social submission. And yet, during the 1920s, the Klan also sought political legitimacy, and even in more recent years prominent Klan leaders like David Duke have had some significant political success in the South.

But in general, after World War II, the KKK became fragmented, decentralized, and dominated by hate-filled rhetoric. At the same time as the KKK was declining in prominence, a new form of right-wing extremism appeared during the 1940s, with a radical preacher and former KKK member named Wesley Swift spreading the ideology of Anglo-Israelism. This ideology, which he preached through his Church of Jesus Christ-Christian, basically argues that white Americans are the lost tribes of Israel.[8] His views

> ## TO THE POINT
>
> Right-wing terrorist ideologies are typically a mix of racial supremacy, anti-government (and anti-gun control) views, and sometimes ultra-conservative religious beliefs.

had a distinct aspect of white Christian superiority that appealed to many Americans, and two of his closest adherents went on to form what became prominent right-wing organizations: William Potter Gale established the Christian Defense League as well as Posse Comitatus, a group that became notorious for violent crime, and Richard Butler formed the Aryan Nations (AN), one of the largest white supremacist militias of the last half-century, which I discuss below.

A version of the Anglo-Israelism ideology became popular during this period, and it became known as Christian Identity. It is based on a story of conflict and hate, in which Jews have gained control of the United States, and white Christians must rise up to resist this. Adherents of Christian Identity doctrine believe that the struggle between whites and Jews will continue until whites ultimately achieve victory, and that God is on their side. Christian Identity offers a very conspiratorial view of the world, and resonates among people who feel they are losing economic status because of sinister forces that they must join together to fight. Several versions of the ideology refer to a conspiracy outlined in the *Protocols of the Elders of Zion*, a document written before World War I, claiming that Jews are out to control the world, and that the government is helping them in their effort. Some followers of Christian Identity have also expressed a belief that mainstream Christianity has been corrupted. According to terrorism scholar Marc

Juergensmeyer, Christian Identity activists yearn for a revolution that would undo America's separation of church and state—or rather, because they disdain the organized church, they want to merge "religion and state" in a new society governed by religious law.[9] I should note here that while ethnonationalist and left-wing terrorist groups are typically secular, many right-wing groups' ideologies have strong religious dimensions.

Another common thread we find among right-wing extremist groups is the belief that the federal government and local governments are their enemies, and that God will assist them in their confrontation with evil. Leaders of these groups typically rely on violent passages of Christian scripture quoted out of context to justify their call for violent action. Right-wing extremists tend to embrace patriotism, and they hate gun control laws, which they view as attempts by the government to weaken people's ability to defend themselves.

Two of the most central texts in this ideological world were written by William Pierce under the pseudonym "Andrew Macdonald." Pierce was a leader of the National Alliance, a white supremacist, Christian Identity organization, with its headquarters in rural West Virginia. He also purchased Resistance Records, a recording label for skinhead hate music. But his most famous contribution was a book he wrote called *The Turner Diaries*, which is a novel that describes a race war in the United States that begins after the federal government begins a program to remove all privately owned firearms. It reflects a rabid anti-minority and anti-Semitic view while also offering a how-to manual for conducting fairly low-level but effective terrorist attacks. First published in 1978, the book offered a detailed description of how to build, deliver, and detonate a truck bomb, and the book ends with the protagonist flying a small plane loaded with a nuclear device into the Pentagon. According to terrorism expert J. M. Berger, *The Turner Diaries* is "arguably the most important single work of white nationalist propaganda in the English language" and is linked to dozens of terrorist attacks and hate crimes.[10]

Pierce also wrote the book *Hunter*, which tells the story of a lone wolf who decides to launch a one-person revolution. This idea of a one-person revolution reflects one of the most important concepts to emerge from this genre of political violence: the lead-erless resistance, a concept first developed during the 1960s by Colonel Ulius Amoss as a proposed response to a communist takeover of the United States. Amoss' ideas were later expanded by white supremacist Louis Beam in 1983 as a method to attack the federal government.[11] Beam argued that highly centralized organizations were vulnerable to infiltration and arrest by federal agents, particularly in highly technical societies where the authorities had various means to conduct surveillance.[12] Therefore, he argued, the movement needed to abandon hierarchical arrangements, and instead establish "phantom cells" tied together only by common philosophy and ideology.

The main advantage of leaderless resistance (as Eric Shibuya noted) is that the lack of a coordinated leadership structure makes it virtually impossible for authorities to map the network of an organization.[13] In many cases, members of various cells do not know of each other's existence at all. However, this approach also requires each individual (or small, ad-hoc groups) "to acquire the necessary skills and information as to what is to be done."[14] Clearly, as I described in Lecture 7, the Internet has come to play a major role in facilitating leaderless resistance, as training manuals, videos, and other kinds of resources are now readily available to anyone, anywhere in the world.

One of the more prominent early Christian Identity organizations in the United States was called The Covenant, The Sword, The Arm of the Lord (CSA), and was founded by pastor James Ellison in 1971 in the small community of Elijah in southern Missouri. He set up a 250-acre compound where his followers could conduct paramilitary and survivalist training in preparation for a revolution that would be launched after the collapse of the U.S. government. CSA members were fueled by the typical kinds of anti-Semitic ideology found in other Christian Identity groups and referred to the Zionist Occupied Government as part of a conspiracy that was meant to prevent the spiritual and economic success of white Christians. After a few members of the group were arrested for various kinds of violent crimes, an investigation led to an indictment of Ellison, and on April 19, 1985, a team of 300 FBI agents laid siege to the compound until he surrendered and was arrested.

Then three events early in the 1990s seem to have galvanized the right-wing extremist movement and contributed to its increase in membership. First, on several occasions during the late 1980s and early 1990s, Congress debated an extensive piece of gun control legislation named after White House press secretary James Brady, who was shot during the assassination attempt against President Ronald Reagan. The Brady Bill, which was eventually passed and signed into law by President Clinton in November 1993, became a rallying cry for conservatives who hated federal gun-control legislation and a grievance that connected right-wing extremists with a much broader segment of the population. Then there was the August 1992 Ruby Ridge standoff in a northern remote part of Idaho, in which right-wing leader Randy Weaver and his family were surrounded at home by federal authorities who killed his son and wife before he surrendered. Publicity surrounding this event fueled suspicion in the right-wing movement that the

Figure 10.1: Aftermath of the Oklahoma City bombing of April 1995. Photo credit: U.S. Department of Defense.

government had declared war on anyone who disagreed with government policies.

And the next year, the bungled April 1993 ATF raid on the Branch Davidian compound in Waco, Tex.—which led to the death of dozens of men, women and children—further convinced right-wing extremists that the government was becoming too intrusive in the lives of U.S. citizens. In this case, cult leader David Koresh had the same formula that pervades much of the right-wing militia groups—guns, a survivalist compound, and a belief in a Warrior God—and this helped garner sympathy among the right-wing extremist community.

Then, on April 19, 1995, we saw perhaps the most infamous example of the leaderless resistance model when right-wing extremist Timothy McVeigh bombed the Murrah Federal Building in Oklahoma City, killing 168 and injuring nearly 500. Incidentally, McVeigh was arrested carrying a worn copy and several photocopies of *The Turner Diaries*, and some reports indicated that he used to distribute copies of the book at gun shows throughout Oklahoma, Texas, and Indiana. Also, note the date: April 19. This attack took place on the second anniversary of the Waco siege, the 10th anniversary of the siege on the CSA compound in Missouri, and the 220th anniversary of the start of the American Revolutionary War battles in Concord and Lexington, Massachusetts. It is also the day before Adolf Hitler's birthday.

THE MODERN THREAT OF RIGHT-WING TERRORISM

Groups that adhere to right-wing kinds of terrorist ideologies can be found throughout the United States, and are monitored not only by the government, but also by nonprofit organizations like the Southern Poverty Law Center. According to one of its recent reports, the 1990s saw a surge in membership for right-wing extremist groups. After 9/11, a few of the groups disbanded, and many former members of the movement melted away from large organizations and began to congregate in small groups, which then engaged in more individualistic violence, including hate crimes against specific members of their local community.[15] And yet, for nearly 20 years, law enforcement agencies at local, state, and federal levels have reported a resurgence in right-wing extremist groups and their violent attacks. Some of this resurgence is believed to be a direct response to the election in 2008 of an African-American president and fueled by the use of the Internet in spreading a variety of unfounded conspiracy theories and racial supremacist ideologies. A focus on immigration (both legal and illegal), particularly in the post-9/11 homeland security climate, has led some groups to target day laborers and migrant workers in various parts of the United States. Other observers point to the fact that economic recessions have had the most devastating impact among certain parts of the United States where right-wing groups and ideologies of ethnic and racial hatreds have already established some influence. And among many religiously-oriented right-wing groups, legalized gay marriage has become a popular source of anger and threats of violence.

Then came the 2016 presidential election. Into this troubled economic and political environment stepped one of the most polarizing candidates in U.S. history, Donald Trump. By publicly vilifying Muslims, Mexicans, and many others, the candidate energized and emboldened a variety of far-right extremist groups. Some, like the Ku Klux Klan, publicly endorsed his candidacy. And then, shortly after President Trump's inauguration in 2017, he initiated a series of attempts to ban immigration from many Muslim-majority countries and threatened Congress that he would shut down government services unless it approved a budget that contained funding to build a massive wall along the Mexico–U.S. border. His administration also canceled funding for any initiatives focused on countering right-wing violent extremism and revised the Department of Homeland Security's policies to focus exclusively on Islamist extremism.

During this period, a series of violent attacks inspired by right-wing ideologies captured public attention. For example, 21-year-old white supremacist Dylan Roof carried out a mass shooting at a historic black church in Charleston, S.C. on June 17, 2015.

In Olathe, Kan. on February 22, 2017, Adam Purinton shot two engineers from India while shouting "get out of my country," killing one and severely injuring the other. In May of that year, an African-American student visiting the University of Maryland was stabbed by Sean Urbanski, a member of a group calling itself the "Alt-Reich: Nation", while three men in Portland, Ore. tried to stop white supremacist Jeremy Christian from harassing two women who appeared to be Muslim, and he responded by killing two of them and injuring the third. And on August 12, 2017, following a "Unite the Right" rally in Charlottesville, Va.—described as one of the largest white supremacist gatherings in recent U.S. history—James Fields, Jr. rammed his car into a group of anti-racist protesters, killing a woman and injuring 19 others.

Over the past several years, reports from quality sources provide evidence that right-wing extremists have carried out far more terrorist attacks in the United States than any other type of attackers, including Islamist extremists. According to data compiled by the Combating Terrorism Center at West Point, "Since 2007, there has been a dramatic rise in the number of attacks and violent plots originating in the far-right of American politics."[16] Data produced by the START Center at the University of Maryland shows that from 1990–2017, far-right extremists had killed twice as many people in the U.S. as Islamist extremists.[17] Since 1990, nearly 60 law enforcement officers (i.e., federal, state, local police, correctional officers, and private security guards) have been killed by far-right extremists, compared to only seven by Islamist extremists.[18] Overall, right-wing terrorism in the United States is a significant challenge that needs to be dealt with. A review of some of the more prominent groups and networks in this category demonstrates the scope of the challenge.

Aryan Nations

First, we have the **Aryan Nations**, a right-wing, racist organization dedicated to "the establishment of a white Aryan homeland on the North American continent" based on a supposed right to "racial self-determination" in line with Hitler's Blood-and-Soil ideology. Its ideology combines elements of the Christian Identity movement with neo-Nazi racial supremacy, and its members reject the legitimacy of the U.S. government, claiming it represents a "Judaic-based authority." The Aryan Nations, founded by Richard Girnt Butler in Coeur d'Alene, Idaho, was originally intended to be the political wing of the Church of Jesus Christ-Christian, the Christian Identity-aligned church founded by KKK organizer the Rev. Wesley Swift mentioned earlier. Butler was a former Air Force pilot during World

War II as well as a former aerospace engineer for Lockheed who had invented a method of repairing tubeless tires. He retired at age 55 and used his personal wealth to purchase a 20-acre compound on the shores of Hayden Lake in Idaho, with the goal of focusing full-time on organizing and encouraging the white supremacy movement.[19]

Members of the Aryan Nations were responsible for several acts of terrorism, with its most notable in 1986, when members bombed four separate merchant establishments in Coeur d'Alene. Nobody was injured. In 1999, they gained additional prominence when a former security guard of the compound shot children at a Jewish community center and a U.S. Postal Service delivery agent in Los Angeles. Hayden Lake became a focal point for the entire movement, in part through its annual World Congress of Aryan Nations events. The group brought together a number of formerly disparate and splintered groups: a July 1982 event supposedly included representatives from 13 Ku Klux Klan, neo-Nazi, and other white supremacist groups.[20]

The Aryan Nations also spawned several splinter groups, but in 1999 it largely fell apart when it lost its compound in a court case. In July 1998, security guards at the Hayden Lake compound opened fire at Victoria Keenan and her son after their car stalled and made a loud noise close to the compound gates. After hitting Keenan's car and sending it into a ditch, Aryan Nations members held them at gunpoint before finally releasing them. Under the sponsorship of the Southern Poverty Law Center, the family filed a civil suit, *Keenan v. Aryan Nations*, which ultimately found the group negligent in selecting and supervising the armed guards at its compound. The civil award of $6.3 million in punitive damages bankrupted the group and forced Butler to hand over the compound as well as the trademarked names for the organization and its church. Today, the Aryan Nations is only a shell of what it once was, but its legacy and saga are still a source of motivation for other white supremacists around the United States.

The Order

One of the most infamous splinter groups founded by former members of the Aryan Nations was called **The Order**, and took its name directly from *The Turner Diaries*. Founded by Robert Matthews, the small group sought to increase its ability to fight a future war against a corrupt, Jewish-influenced government by counterfeiting money, robbing banks, and stockpiling weapons. Although The Order only operated from 1982 to 1984, it was responsible for some of the most notorious incidents associated with right-wing terrorism in the United States. For example, in 1984 it carried out an armored car heist and escaped with $3.6 million, money which it later used to purchase weapons and fund other affiliated organizations.[21] Most of its attacks were carried out in Idaho, Washington, and Colorado. One of its members bombed a synagogue in Boise, Idaho,[22] and another member shot and killed a Jewish radio talk show host outside of his home in Denver, Colo.; the gun used in that attack was traced and led to the intelligence that eventually brought down the group. In turn, their capture was seen as a prime example by many in the right-wing movement why a leaderless resistance approach was preferable.

Hammerskin Nation

One of the most prominent groups to embrace the tenets of leaderless resistance is the **Hammerskin Nation**, which the Anti-Defamation League calls "the most respected and feared racist skinhead group."[23] Founded in Texas during the 1980s, its ideology calls for violence against all non-white minorities and adopts a slogan common throughout the white supremacist world: "We must secure the existence of our people and a future for white children." Various kinds of propaganda complain about injustices suffered by the white race at the hands of minorities within the United States and speak of the oppression of whites, who the group claims have become the minority. The organization claims to have chapters in Australia, Germany, Hungary, Italy, and New Zealand.[24] Attacks attributed to Hammerskins are often gang assaults (often with black Americans and Latino immigrants as victims) as well as arson, attacks with knives, and isolated shooting incidents.

One of the more unusual aspects of this organization is its Hammerskin Press, which produces various kinds of literature and a hate music record label that has become highly popular among impressionable young whites in some parts of the United States. The first rock group adopting the Hammerskins moniker, the Confederate Hammerskins, appeared in Dallas in 1988 and was quickly followed by the Eastern Hammerskins, the Northern Hammerskins, and the Arizona Hammerskins. These groups subsequently united under the banner Hammerskins Nation and launched several record labels to promote and make money from their efforts.[25] They have organized a number of rock concerts and focus on the uniting and fundraising power of music in lieu of systematic criminal activity. They also sell T-shirts, bumper stickers, and other items associated with these music groups that carry various connotations of white supremacy and racial violence.[26]

The American Front

A similar racist group in the United States is known as the **American Front**, which advocates violence against all non-whites and calls for the overthrow of the U.S. government and the establishment of an autonomous homeland for whites of European descent.[27] Since its founding by the racist skinhead Robert Heick in 1987, the group has been responsible for attacks against blacks, gays, and Jews in order to draw the nation's attention to race issues. Members of the group also embarked upon a bombing campaign that targeted meeting places of minorities and NAACP officers. While the American Front was originally founded in California, a leadership change in 1993 resulted in the relocation of its headquarters to Harrison, Ark. From there, it began to promote a new leaderless resistance type of ideology, in which any believer in the cause is considered to support the cause and be part of its nationwide organization. However, the group has yet to find a leader capable of unifying the many disparate right-wing factions throughout the United States into a unified racist movement.

Phineas Priesthood

Perhaps the most interesting and confusing of all the right-wing entities in the United States is the **Phineas Priesthood**.[28] In the late 1980s, a former Air Force officer named Richard Kelly Hoskins experienced a religious awakening of sorts and began to author a series of books influenced by the Christian Identity movement. His 1990 book *Vigilantes of Christiandom: The Story of the Phineas Priesthood* is seen as a manifesto among white supremacist groups; he calls on zealots to "administer the judgment" of God, intermingling racist theology into fundamentalist interpretation.[29] The centerpiece of the story is of the Israelite Phineas, who was rewarded with the lifting of a plague—and whose descendants are said to be eternally blessed by God—for killing another Israelite who partook in sexual relations with a non-Israelite.

> Then an Israelite man brought to his family a Midianite woman right before the eyes of Moses and the whole assembly of Israel while they were weeping at the entrance of the Tent of Meeting. When Phineas son of Eleazar, the son of Aaron, the priest, saw this, he left the assembly, took a spear in his hand and followed the Israelite into the tent. He drove the spear through both of them— through the Israelite and into the woman's body. Then the plague against the

Israelites was stopped; but those who died in the plague numbered 24,000. (Numbers 25:6–13 New International Version)

Phineas Priests thus derive their name from a biblical character who slays "heathen Israelites," serving God in doing so. Phineas Priests vehemently oppose racial mixing, fraternization with Jews, and abortion—all of which are condemned as sins against God. However, they are more than just another right-wing racist group that draws inspiration from Christian Identity ideology. Hoskins presented the Phineas Priests as a leaderless movement of vigilante Christian faithful, "selflessly dedicated to tracking down the worst of God's enemies and slaying them without mercy."[30]

In essence, this is a decentralized, diffuse movement with no prophet, no leader, no structure or authority except God. All righteous "Priests" are to act in accordance with the ideology, with the violence placed within the context of a larger apocalyptic battle that will eventually reassert the dominance of righteous white Christians on Earth.

> **TO THE POINT**
>
> Right wing extremists use the Internet extensively as a place to find others who share racial hatred and anti-government views, and to foster a sense of community and ideological legitimacy.

Several individuals have been inspired by the ideology to commit vicious crimes, including Eric Rudolph, who detonated a bomb in July 1996 at the Centennial Olympic Park in Atlanta and then carried out several bombings of abortion clinics and a gay nightclub in 1997; Clayton Lee Waagner, who sent hundreds of fake anthrax letters to abortion clinics; and Paul Evans, who in December 2006 began a terror campaign by mailing explosive devices to abortionists, pornographers, and practitioners of the occult, and then placed a bomb outside an Austin, Tex. clinic that performed abortions.[31] Several websites on the Internet today praise the actions of these individuals and call for others to adopt a similar "lone wolf" strategy in launching future attacks.[32]

Several of these attacks have targeted abortion clinics and doctors, and some of the perpetrators of those attacks have been linked to the Army of God,[33] which we'll discuss in Lecture 11. But the important point here is that we have seen among the category of right-wing terrorism a number of individuals motivated by an ideology to act independently of any formal group or leadership command structure. Anders

FBI TEN MOST WANTED FUGITIVE

MALICIOUSLY DAMAGED, BY MEANS OF AN EXPLOSIVE DEVICE,
BUILDINGS AND PROPERTY AFFECTING INTERSTATE COMMERCE WHICH
RESULTED IN DEATH AND INJURY

ERIC ROBERT RUDOLPH

Date of photograph October 1997   Date of photograph October 1997   Artist rendition July 1998

Aliases: Bob Randolph, Robert Randolph, Bob Rudolph, Eric Rudolph and Eric R. Rudolph.

Figure 10.2: Following his terrorist attack at the Centennial Park during the 1996 Atlanta Olympics, which killed 2 and injured 110, right-wing extremist Eric Rudolph eluded authorities for 6 years. He was also convicted of terrorist attacks against abortion clinics, nightclubs and other targets. Image credit: Federal Bureau of Investigation.

Breivik, the extreme white nationalist who bombed a government building and then killed scores of teenagers at a day camp outside Oslo, Norway (see Lecture 15) is one of the most infamous examples of this phenomenon. His far-right ideology, reflected in his lengthy manifesto published on several websites before his attack, was extremely anti-Muslim and argued that because political leaders in his country had betrayed his race, his acts of mass killing were justified. This "leaderless resistance" model is also the kind of terrorism we are now faced with in the form of jihadists in America, as we will explore in Lectures 12 and 15.

Sovereign Citizens

Finally, no discussion of far-right extremism today would be complete without mentioning the **Sovereign Citizens** movement. Members of this movement reject government authority and have been responsible for attacks against police and government buildings. For example, in 2012, a father and son in Louisiana killed two police officers who had pulled them over for a traffic violation. In 2013, a man carried out an attack at Los Angeles International Airport, killing one Transportation Security Administration officer and wounding two others. In each of these instances, the attackers were described as having rabid anti-government views, and claiming law enforcement had no authority over them. A report produced by the FBI and the Department of Homeland Security examining dozens of violent sovereign citizen-related attacks across the United States since 2010 found that many state and local law enforcement agencies consider Sovereign Citizens to be a great danger to public safety than any other category of ideologically inspired extremists (including al-Qaeda or other Salafi-jihadists).[34] As with some of the other right-wing extremists described in this lecture, the Sovereign Citizens movement is considered an example of the "leaderless resistance" form of violence espoused by Louis Beam.

According to J. M. Berger, the ideology of the Sovereign Citizens movement is very complicated, and many followers of this ideology interpret it in different ways. "So-called sovereign citizens believe in an alternate history of the U.S., replacing reality with a vast conspiracy governed by complex, arcane rules. They believe that if someone understands and properly invokes those rules, that person is exempt from many laws, including the obligation to pay taxes, and that he or she can be empowered to seize private property, enforce legal actions against individuals, and claim money from the government. When faced with arrest for illegal actions that they believe are legal, sovereign citizens can become violent."[35] Unlike most modern terrorist groups or movements, there are no central "leaders" of Sovereign Citizens. Instead, those who are attracted to this subculture typically attend a seminar or two, or visit one of the thousands of websites and online videos on the subject and then simply choose how to act on what they have learned.[36] Discussion forums and social media can help members of the movement connect with each other and share ideas, creating a self-regenerating community of believers. By some estimates, there are between 100,000 and 300,000 Sovereign Citizens spread throughout the United States.[37]

SUMMARY

To sum up this brief review of right-wing terrorism, there are variations in who or what is viewed as the enemy: religion plays a role for some—but not all—groups and movements in this category; gun control is a hot issue for many of these groups, and often their ideologies contain themes of conspiracy and sinister threats to the status quo that people must rise up to defend. We also see a number of groups that share a focus on one preferential racial group, though they may differ in the underlying reasons for the racial ideology. Some have ideological connections to Christian Identity and leverage biblical examples and religious reasoning to justify their beliefs. Central to this ideology is the notion that the race of whites of European descent is supreme and should be given dominion over the Earth. Several groups, like the Aryan Nations, The Order, and Hammerskin Nation, focus on their belief in a global Jewish conspiracy. In many cases, right-wing terrorists are motivated by deep insecurities and fears about the future of their communities. They depict the white race as threatened, oppressed, and dwindling—with a palpable feeling of urgency for action. Groups and individuals must act decisively and immediately, and sometimes these actions may include intimidation, murder, and bombing campaigns. Many right-wing terrorists view themselves as a "revolutionary vanguard"—they want at the very least to be the catalyst of events that will lead to an idealized form of government.[38] And often, the existing government is seen as responsible for the sad state of affairs in which the right-wing group finds itself. Perceiving that federalism, multiculturalism, and racial integration have failed, the groups often seek to assert a white nationalism with little or no centralized government and a land cleansed of ethnic minorities.

Membership and affiliation requirements vary greatly across these groups; admission into The Order was highly regulated, as the group operated with great degrees of secrecy and orchestration. The KKK follows a highly bureaucratic and centralized structure that parallels the U.S. government. For example, Klan leadership has a president, governors, and even country chiefs. On the other hand, according to the mission and ideology of the Phineas Priests and the American Front, all true believers may consider themselves members of the movement and may participate as they see fit in order to bring about the desired societal changes. In particular, Phineas Priests are required to act individually with no provable connection to anyone else. The Hammerskins also characterize themselves as a leaderless resistance movement, and individuals have a great degree of autonomy, but in this case membership is displayed visually, through graphic tattoos, militant attire, and shaved heads to physically demonstrate their beliefs. Further, they have become openly affiliated with like-minded groups internationally, although interaction is limited to conferences and concerts.

Importantly, none of the groups described here have been destroyed via de-radicalization efforts targeting their specific beliefs and ideologies. By comparison, the separatist ideology of ethnonationalists can be weakened in a multiethnic democracy where power is shared more equitably regardless of ethnicity. Many left-wing groups lost ideological resonance and legitimacy when the Soviet Union fell apart and abandoned the Marxist vision for a more egalitarian or utopian future. But proponents of racist right-wing ideologies—particularly those with ties to religion—can be found in every region of the United States, and there is little if anything that is being done to weaken their ideological resonance. Instead, the most violent right-wing groups have largely defeated themselves through counterproductive violence and have been weakened primarily through the efforts of law enforcement to apprehend them. In the realm of influence warfare, as described in Lectures 3 and 7, there is much to do in confronting this category of terrorism in the United States.

QUESTIONS FOR DISCUSSION

- What unique challenges do these right-wing terrorist groups pose for U.S. law enforcement agencies?
- What kinds of political and socioeconomic contexts seem to provide resonance for right-wing extremist ideologies?
- What might the United States learn from studying how other countries have dealt with right-wing terrorism?

RECOMMENDED READING

Aho, James. "Christian Fundamentalism and Militia Movements in the United States." In *The Making of a Terrorist*. Vol. 1. Edited by James J. F. Forest. Westport, CT: Praeger, 2005.

Anti-Defamation League. "Murder and Extremism in the United States in 2016." http://bit.ly/2wMN4n9.

Baracskay, Daniel. "The April 1995 Bombing of the Murrah Federal Building in Oklahoma City." In *Countering Terrorism and Insurgency in the 21st Century*. Vol. 3. Edited by James J. F. Forest. Westport, CT: Praeger, 2007.

Berger, J. M. "Without Prejudice: What Sovereign Citizens Believe." George Washington University Program on Extremism, June 2016. http://bit.ly/2pJFHJG.

Berger, J. M. "The Turner Legacy: The Storied Origins and Enduring Impact of White Nationalism's Deadly Bible. *The International Centre for Counter-Terrorism—The Hague* 7, no. 8 (2016). http://bit.ly/2d00si9.

Berger, J. M. "Extremist Construction of Identity: How Escalating Demands for Legitimacy Shape and Define In-Group and Out-Group Dynamics." *The International Centre for Counter-Terrorism—The Hague* 8, no. 7 (2017). http://bit.ly/2skNemh.

Combs, Cindy C., Elizabeth A. Combs and Lydia Marsh. "Christian Militia Training: Arming the 'Troops' with Scripture, the Law and a Good Gun," In *The Making of a Terrorist*. Vol. 2. Edited by James J. F. Forest. Westport, CT: Praeger, 2005.

Davis, Danny W. *The Phinehas Priesthood: Violent Vanguard of the Christian Identity Movement*. Westport, CT: Praeger, 2010.

Durham, Martin. "The American Far Right and 9/11." *Terrorism and Political Violence* 15, no. 2 (2003).

Guilmartin, Eugenia K. "Rejection of Political Institutions by Right-Wing Extremists in the United States," In *The Making of a Terrorist*. Vol. 3. Edited by James J. F. Forest. Westport, CT: Praeger, 2005.

Hamm, Mark. "Timothy McVeigh and the Oklahoma City Bombing." In *Terrorist Innovations in Weapons of Mass Effect: Preconditions, Causes and Predictive Behaviors*. Edited by Maria J. Rasmussen and Mohammed M. Hafez. Washington, DC: Defense Threat Reduction Agency, 2010.

Kurzman, Charles and David Schanzer. "Law Enforcement Assessment of the Violent Extremism Threat." A Report Sponsored by NIJ. Durham, NC: Triangle Center on Terrorism and Homeland Security, 2015.

Mudde, Cas. "Right-Wing Extremism Analyzed. A Comparative Analysis of the Ideologies of Three Alleged Right-Wing Extremist Parties." *European Journal of Political Research* 27, no. 2 (1995).

National Consortium for the Study of Terrorism and Responses to Terrorism. "Key Concepts to Understand Violent White Supremacy." A START Research Brief (April 2017). http://bit.ly/2vITDWJ.

Perliger, Arie. *Challengers from the Sidelines: Understanding America's Violent Far-Right*. Combating Terrorism Center at West Point (January 15, 2013). http://bit.ly/2wf5lL5.

Shibuya, Eric Y. "The Struggle with Violent Right-Wing Extremist Groups in the United States." In *Countering Terrorism and Insurgency in the 21st Century*. Vol. 3. Edited by James J. F. Forest. Westport, CT: Praeger, 2007.

Simi, Pete, Steven Windisch, and Karyn Sporer. "Recruitment and Radicalization among US Far Right Terrorists." College Park, MD: START, 2016. http://bit.ly/2fZZLoM.

Southern Poverty Law Center. *Terror from the Right: 72 Plots, Conspiracies and Racist Rampages since Oklahoma City* (2005).

Valla, Edward J. and Gregory Comcowich. "Domestic Terrorism: Forgotten, but Not Gone." In *Armed Groups: Studies in National Security*. Edited by Jeffrey Norwitz. Naval War College Press, 2010.

WEBSITES

Mapping Militant Organizations
http://web.stanford.edu/group/mappingmilitants/cgi-bin/

Southern Poverty Law Center
http://www.splcenter.org

START BAAD Database (terrorist group profiles)
http://www.start.umd.edu/baad/database

START Terrorism and Extremist Violence in the United States Database
http://www.start.umd.edu/research-projects/terrorism-and-extremist-violence-united-states-tevus
   -database

United States Extremist Crime Database, 1990–2010
http://www.start.umd.edu/research-projects/united-states-extremist-crime-database-ecdb-1990
   -2010

U.S. Department of State, Country Reports on Terrorism
https://www.state.gov/j/ct/rls/crt/

NOTES

1. Cas Mudde, "Right-Wing Extremism Analyzed. A Comparative Analysis of the Ideologies of Three Alleged Right-Wing Extremist Parties," *European Journal of Political Research* 27, no. 2 (1995): 206.

2. Bruce Hoffman, *Inside Terrorism* (New York, Columbia University Press, 2006): 237.

3. Victor Asal and R. Karl Rethemeyer, "The Nature of the Beast: Organizational structures and the lethality of terrorist attacks," *Journal of Politics* 70, no. 2 (2008): 437.

4. For an excellent explanation of Creatorism, see Brad Whitsel, "Ideological Mutation and Millenial Belief in the American Neo-Nazi Movement," *Studies in Conflict and Terrorism* 24 (2001): 89–106.

5. Jonathan Randall White, *Terrorism and Homeland Security* (Belmont, CA: Wadsworth Publishing, 2008): 376.

6. Hoffman, *Inside Terrorism*, 237.

7. Of particular note, RNU's paramilitary wing is highly sophisticated and organized, with intelligence capabilities, a military cadre, and a youth wing. The youth wing undertakes formal military training, often led by former members of the official Russian army; extreme paramilitary teams within RNU include the "Russian Knights" who are known for stockpiling weapons and explosives in bases scattered across Russia. For more on this, see Cas Mudde, *Racist Extremism in Central and Eastern Europe* (New York: Routledge, 2005).

8. Marc Juergensmeyer, *Terror in the Mind of God: the Global Rise of Religious Violence* (Berkeley: University of California Press, 2003): 33–34.

9. Ibid., 32.

10. J. M. Berger "The Turner Legacy: The Storied Origins and Enduring Impact of White Nationalism's Deadly Bible," The International Centre for Counter-Terrorism—The Hague 7, no. 8 (2016). http://bit.ly/2d00si9.

11. Eric Y. Shibuya, "The Struggle with Violent Right-Wing Extremist Groups in the United States." in *Countering Terrorism and Insurgency in the 21st Century*, vol. 3, ed. James J. F. Forest (Westport, CT: Praeger, 2007): 574–75.

12. Louis Beam, "Leaderless Resistance," *The Seditionist* (February 12, 1992), http://www.louisbeam.com.

13. Shibuya, "The Struggle with Violent Right-Wing Extremist Groups."

14. Beam, "Leaderless Resistance."

15. Southern Poverty Law Center, *Terror from the Right: 72 Plots, Conspiracies and Racist Rampages since Oklahoma City* (2005). See the SPLC website for other reports.

16. Arie Perliger, *Challengers from the Sidelines: Understanding America's Violent Far-Right*, Combating Terrorism at West Point (January 15, 2013), http://bit.ly/2wf5lL5.

17. This excludes two major events, the Oklahoma City bombing and the attacks of 9/11. The report is described in various news sources, including PBS (http://to.pbs.org/2xit4ff) and more fully in academic journal articles like William S. Parkin, Joshua D. Freilich, and Steven M. Chermak, "Ideological Victimization: Homicides Perpetrated by Far-Right Extremists," *Homicide Studies* (April 2014).

18. "Islamist and Far-Right Homicides in the United States," START Infographic (February 2017), http://bit.ly/2liNVZ1.

19. Daniel J. Wakin, "Richard G. Butler, 86, dies; founder of the Aryan Nations," *New York Times*, September 8, 2004.

20. "Aryan Nations," Anti-Defamation League website profile, https://bit.ly/2ru0fHk

21. Southern Poverty Law Center, "Skinhead Rally" Intelligence Report (Spring 2007).

22. The Order, START website "Terrorist Group Profile," http://goo.gl/Ri3Dx.

23. See the ADL website at http://goo.gl/vSkMe.

24. See "Chapters" section of the Hammerskin Nation website, http://www.hammerskins.net/chapters.html.

25. ADL website, https://www.adl.org.

26. See Hammerskin Nation official website: http://www.hammerskins.net; also see the affiliated web discussion forum, very popular among Hammerskin followers, called Stormfront: http://www.stormfront.org/forum/.

27. American Front, START website "Terrorist Group Profile," http://goo.gl/DZfFF.

28. For a detailed analysis of the Phineas Priesthood, see Danny W. Davis, *The Phinehas Priesthood: Violent Vanguard of the Christian Identity Movement* (Westport, CT: Praeger, 2010).

29. Ibid.

30. Jeffrey Kaplan, *The Encyclopedia of White Power: A Sourcebook on the Radical Racist Right* (Lanham, MD: AltaMira Press, 2000): 242–43.

31. For more on these and other individuals linked to the Phineas Priesthood, see Davis, *The Phinehas Priesthood.*

32. "Extremist Chatter Praises Eric Rudolph as 'Hero,'" ADL press release (no longer online).

33. For a detailed analysis of this group, see Jennifer Jefferis, *Armed for Life: The Army of God and Anti-Abortion Terror in the United States* (Westport, CT: Praeger, 2010).

34. Evan Perez and Wes Bruer, "DHS Intelligence Report Warns of Domestic Right-Wing Terror Threat." CNN (Feb. 20, 2015), http://www.cnn.com/2015/02/19/politics/terror-threat-homeland-security/.

35. Berger, J. M. "Without Prejudice: What Sovereign Citizens Believe," George Washington University Program on Extremism (June 2016), http://bit.ly/2pJFHJG.

36. "Sovereign Citizens Movement" overview by the Southern Poverty Law Center, http://bit.ly/29ZImtf.

37. Ibid.

38. Hoffman, *Inside Terrorism*, 238.

11

Religious Terrorism, Part One

The previous three lectures explored key aspects and examples of ethnonationalist, left-wing, and right-wing terrorism. Now, turning to what Rapoport identifies as the fourth wave of terrorism, we look at how religious terrorism differs from secular forms. Religious ideologies can be a powerful motivator for all kinds of human action. As Harvard University psychologist John Mack observed, religion

> deals with spiritual or ultimate human concerns, such as life or death, our highest values and selves, the roots of evil, the existence of God, the nature of divinity and goodness, whether there is some sort of life after the body has died, the idea of the infinite and the eternal, defining the boundaries of reality itself, and the possibility of a human community governed by universal love. Religious assumptions shape our minds from childhood, and for this reason religious systems and institutions have had, and continue to have, extraordinary power to affect the course of human history.[1]

It should come as no surprise, then, to find that religious terrorists are different in several ways from their secular counterparts. For example, a devout person may be convinced they are acting on God's behalf when carrying out a terrorist act especially if they believe violence is necessary to protect or defend others, such as the *umma* (the global Islamic community), or those in utero (e.g., the Army of God's justification for attacking abortion clinics and doctors). Often, leaders of religious terrorist groups will tap into a person's sense of devotion by arguing that the strength of their faith will be rewarded by God and allow them to achieve anything. Most truly religious people have a strong belief in *their own* revealed truth from God and are often theologically supremacist (meaning that true believers assume superiority over nonbelievers, who are not privy to the truth of the religion) and exclusivist (meaning believers are a chosen people or that their territory is a holy land).[2] Further, from their perspective, only true believers are guaranteed salvation and victory, whereas enemies and unbelievers (as well as those who have taken no stance whatsoever) are condemned to some sort of eternal punishment as well as death. Terms like "infidel," "apostate," and "godless" are used to dehumanize these enemies and unbelievers, helping justify the violent acts that victimize them. This is clearly a deeper level of the "othering" discussed in Lecture 8 with regard to ethnonationalist terror groups.[3]

> ## TO THE POINT
>
> True believers assume superiority over nonbelievers; religious terrorists believe God is on their side.

Bruce Hoffman notes that for religious terrorists, "violence is first and foremost a sacramental act or divine duty executed in direct response to some theological demand or imperative. Terrorism thus assumes a transcendental dimension, and its perpetrators often disregard the political, moral, or practical constraints that may affect other terrorists."[4] In one of the most eloquent descriptions to date of religious terrorism, Jessica Stern describes how her interviews with extremist Christians, Jews, and Muslims revealed a sort of "spiritual intoxication," a spiritual high or addiction derived from the fulfillment of God's will (or the individual's interpretation thereof).[5] For these individuals, religion has helped them simplify an otherwise complex life, and becoming part of a radical movement has given them support, a sense of purpose, an outlet in which to express their grievances—which are sometimes related to personal or social humiliation—and find "new identities as martyrs on behalf of a purported spiritual cause."[6] In a unique form of transcendental experience, the religious extremist seems to "enter into a kind of trance, where the world is divided neatly between good and evil, victim and oppressor. Uncertainty and ambiguity, always painful to experience, are banished. There is no room for the other person's point of view. Because they believe their cause is just, and because the population they hope to protect is purportedly so deprived, abused and helpless, they persuade themselves that any action—even a heinous crime—is justified. They believe that God is on their side."[7] Doing the bidding of a higher power demands sacrifice but also means fewer limits on violence, which is seen as necessary in order to save oneself, one's family, or even the world.

Our desire to understand God's will often leads us to seek guidance from individuals with special intellectual gifts for interpreting sacred texts—like priests, imams, rabbis, and so forth—individuals who provide meaning for those seeking enlightenment or are pursuing an understanding of "what God wants from me." This, in turn, means extremist religious leaders have a unique opportunity to exploit the need among many people for religious guidance. Compared to the nonreligious kinds of terrorism covered in previous lectures, this is a very important aspect to think about; religious authorities have a uniquely powerful role in terms of influencing people toward (or away from) acts of violence.

Unfortunately, we have plenty of examples in which these kinds of leaders have provided religious justification for the use of violence. For example, Rabbi Meir Kahane convinced his followers of the need for violence in order to eliminate all Muslims from what he viewed as Jewish holy lands. The Rev. Michael Bray has used his radical interpretation of the Bible to convince members of the Army of God to attack abortion clinics and doctors, and Paul Hill (who murdered a doctor and his bodyguard at a clinic in Florida) was previously an ordained minister. Several radical Muslim clerics like Omar Abdel-Rahman (the blind sheikh, linked to the 1993 bombing of the World Trade Center), Nasir al-Fahd, Abu Qatada, Anwar al-Awlaki, Omar Bakri Muhammad, Anjem Choudary, and Abu Muhammad al-Maqdisi (among others) have provided interpretations of the Quran that are used to justify terrorist violence by Salafi-jihadist groups like al-Qaeda, Islamic State, and their various affiliates.[8]

Around the world, religious ideologies (and leaders) help foster polarizing values in terms of right and wrong, good and evil, light and dark—values that can lead to a complete alienation from the norms of peaceful social and political interaction.[9] They also provide a long-term view of history and the future, meaning that members of religious terrorist groups come to believe they are engaged in an epic battle of good versus evil. Notions like "cosmic war" and "apocalypse" are important motivators for many religious terrorists, who believe their actions will lead to a better world for future generations, as well as (possibly) rewards in the afterlife.

Examples of religious terrorism range across a wide spectrum, from religious cults (like Aum Shinrikyo in Japan) to Christian anti-abortion groups (like the Army of God), Jewish extremists (like Kahane Chai), and Islamist extremists (like Hamas, Hizballah, and al-Qaeda). This category of terrorism also includes adherents of Christian Identity, the Phineas Priesthood, and some of the other groups described in Lecture 10, because these involve combinations of racial supremacy and extremist interpretations of biblical scriptures. Even insurgencies and ethnic separatist groups like the Chechens have begun using religious-oriented ideologies to justify violence.

In short, there really are a frightful number of people out there killing others in the name of their religious beliefs. The most prominent of these in modern times are Salafi-jihadists like al-Qaeda, the Islamic State, and their affiliates, which we will examine in depth in Lecture 12. But in this lecture, I'll review just a small handful of some prominent groups in this unique category of terrorism. And while jihadists get the most headlines in this category, let's begin with a look at some religious terrorist groups that have nothing to do with Islamist extremism.

RELIGIOUS GROUPS

Kahane Chai

Meir Kahane was born in Brooklyn, N.Y. in 1932 and became an Orthodox Jewish rabbi working at a synagogue in Queens by the late 1950s. As a politically active, ultraconservative, and fiery preacher, he gathered a sizable following, and in 1968, he founded a group called the Jewish Defense League (JDL), which protested the Soviet Union's restrictions on Jewish immigration to Israel. The JDL also became known for carrying out vigilante-style attacks on inner-city black and Latino groups as revenge for violence against elderly Jewish people. In 1971, he immigrated to Israel and founded the Kach political party (Hebrew for "thus"). He also began advocating for a restoration of the biblical state of Israel, which would necessitate the expulsion of all non-Jews living in Israel. He argued that an entirely Jewish theocratic "Kingdom of Israel" was needed to create the conditions for the coming of the Jewish Messiah. Kahane's worldview was that all non-Jews were anti-Semitic, and he called for the total separation of Jews and Arabs, proposing a financial compensation plan for Arabs who would leave voluntarily, and forcible expulsion "for those who don't want to leave."[10] Given the growing number of violent attacks by Palestinians against Israelis during this time, his messages found appeal and resonance in various parts of the country.

In 1984, an increasingly popular Kahane was elected to the Knesset. However, his speeches were so racist that others boycotted or rejected him, and in 1985, Israel passed a law specifically barring racist candidates from election, making Kahane ineligible for re-election when his term expired in 1988. The political party Kach was likewise banned. An increasingly angry Kahane began calling for his followers to overthrow the Israeli government, which he felt was too secular and too accommodating to Palestinians and to neighboring Arab governments. In 1990, Kahane was assassinated at one of his speeches in New York, and his son Binyamin transformed Kach into **Kahane Chai** (Hebrew for "Kahane lives"), publicly advocating attacks against Palestinians as well as Arab Israelis. According to Israeli terrorism scholar Ami Pedahzur, citing several credible sources, weapons used by members of this group were supplied by former officers of the Israeli Defence Forces.[11]

In February 1994, Baruch Goldstein—a childhood friend of Meir Kahane and a member of Kahane Chai—shot and killed 29 Muslims who were praying at a mosque in the West Bank before he was overpowered and beaten to death. Afterward, both Kach and Kahane Chai were declared terrorist organizations by the Israeli government and placed on the U.S. Department of State's list of foreign terrorist organizations. In December 2000, Binyamin Kahane and most of his family were killed in a machine gun attack by Palestinians. In August 2005, an Israeli Army soldier named Eden Natan-Zada, who was affiliated with Kahane Chai, deserted his unit and later opened fire on a bus, killing four Arab Israelis and injuring a dozen more. As he tried to reload his weapon, he was overpowered by local bystanders and eventually killed. Kahane Chai continues to operate today, recruiting members and openly criticizing the Israeli government. It is most active in the settlements of Kiryat Arba and Kfar Tapauch, but you can find Jewish settlers and others throughout Israel singing songs in praise of Baruch Goldstein and Rabbi Meir Kahane, and advocating attacks against Arabs.

The Army of God

Here in the United States, one of the more prominent religious extremist networks calls itself the **Army of God**, a leaderless Christian group that targets those its followers believe are violating God's law—in this case, abortion providers. As everyone knows, there are few issues in America as polarizing as abortion: those adamantly opposed to it are quick to condemn anyone involved in it as murderers. Not all anti-abortionists embrace the use of violence, but some have justified their attacks against clinics, doctors, and others as necessary for the defense of the unborn child, and often quote passages from the Bible. Prominent figures in this movement like Michael Bray, Paul Hill, and James Kopp have all argued that "an individual who kills to save a life has not committed murder, but has in fact prevented it."[12] The bombings of abortion clinics in the United States began in the late 1970s and increased through the early 1980s, but then calmed down after President Ronald Reagan publicly condemned these attacks in 1985. But in 1991, a national debate about abortion was sparked by the public demonstrations of Randall Terry and his group Operation Rescue, and contributed to a new rise in violent attacks, most notably the 1993 murder of Dr. David Gunn, the 1993 wounding and 2009 murder of Dr. George Tiller, and the 1994 murder of Dr. John Brittain—all of them abortion providers—by self-proclaimed members of the so-called Army of God.[13]

The Army of God's manual, available on various websites, calls the United States "a nation ruled by a godless civil authority that is dominated by humanism, moral nihilism and new age perversion of the high standards upon which a Godly society must be founded, if it is to endure."[14] Incidentally, the manual also offers detailed instructions on how to build ammonium nitrate bombs and other explosives, as well as how to carry out acid and arson attacks against abortion clinics. By 1995, the number of arsons attacks and bombings against clinics had grown to 180. Federal authorities responded with new efforts to protect clinics and abortion providers, and eventually the frequency of attacks diminished. But they have not gone away entirely. Within the past two decades, attacks against clinics have occurred in Louisiana, Virginia, Minnesota, Florida, and Colorado.[15] We will discuss more about these anti-abortion terrorist attacks in Lecture 15.

Aum Shinrikyo

Then there's **Aum Shinrikyo** ("Supreme Truth"), a Japanese religious cult established in 1984 by Shoko Asahara, who combined yoga and meditation with a belief system integrating elements of esoteric Buddhism, Hinduism, Christianity, and apocalyptic prophesies. He portrayed himself as an enlightened man and convinced his followers that he was on a mission, sanctioned by the Buddha himself, to build a utopian society made of people who had achieved psychological enlightenment. He was able to attract a number of financially well-off members who were coerced into donating all their earthly possessions to the cult. By the mid-1990s, the cult had over 10,000 members in several countries and nearly $1 billion in assets, including with 'secular' businesses across Japan and overseas including a tea plantation, an import-export company, and a sheep ranch in Australia. Several members of Aum were also well-educated, including doctors, scientists, biochemists, and other graduates of Japanese universities who were disillusioned with what they saw as a material society devoid of spirituality, and used their expertise to help develop an industrial chemical facility that was ostensibly one of its businesses, but was also secretly used for developing chemical weapons.[16]

Asahara preached about the end of the world: a war between Japan and the United States, complete with nuclear Armageddon, would lead to a future in which only his true believers would be spared. He also preached the concept of *poa*, originally a Buddhist concept in which members murdered their victims out of love for them. Killers were told they were "offering a benefit to the

Figure 11.1: Paul Jennings Hill, who murdered an abortion clinic doctor and his bodyguard in Pensacola, Florida on July 29, 1994.

victim in a form of improved rebirth."[17] He also ordered the development of various kinds of chemical and biological weapons, including anthrax and the nerve agent sarin, and in several cases ordered his followers to attack people he viewed as threats or enemies. In encouraging his followers to kill, he used the euphemism "transform" in place of "kill" to inject a notion of karma into the act.

In March 1995, Aum Shinrikyo launched an attack on the Tokyo subway using sarin, killing nearly a dozen people and injuring approximately 1,000 others, sending 5,000 to hospitals for checkups. The attackers used a rather crude delivery mechanism for this attack—plastic bags filled with sarin liquid were placed on the floors of subway cars, and members of the group then punctured the bags with the ends of their umbrellas. Their objectives in this attack were both long-term and short-term. The long-term goal was to spark social unrest that would help set things in motion for the apocalypse that Shoko Asahara had envisioned. But the more immediate goal was to disrupt an anticipated effort by law enforcement authorities to arrest members of the group. (They attacked subway lines leading to many government ministries.) This attack was similar to the group's use of sarin the previous year in Matsumoto against judicial officials involved in a legal proceeding against it, an attack that killed seven and injured 34 people. We'll address Aum Shinrikyo and these attacks more in Lecture 18.

The Lord's Resistance Army

And one of the more curious (and in my view, despicable) religious groups of the past few decades is called the **Lord's Resistance Army** (LRA). This group was founded in northern Uganda in 1992 by Joseph Kony, a self-proclaimed "prophet" and spiritual medium who preached an apocalyptic Christian worldview that blended some elements of mysticism and traditional African spirituality.[18] Eventually, he also called for overthrowing the Ugandan government and instituting a Christian holy land in which a new regime would rule by his interpretation of the Bible and the Ten Commandments. The group began to increase its ranks by raiding villages, kidnapping young boys and girls, and forcing them to become members of their terrorist group—boys as militants, girls as sex slaves.[19]

Under Kony's direction, the LRA also became increasingly violent, brutal, and indiscriminate in its violence. Between 2008 and 2010, according to a report by the U.N. High Commissioner for Refugees, the LRA murdered 2,000 people, abducted more than 2,600, and sent over 400,000 fleeing from their homes.[20] For several years, the LRA received some financial support from Sudan, but in July 2011, South Sudan seceded and effectively isolated the group from its former patrons in Khartoum. Reports then surfaced indicating differing factions of the LRA were roaming around the Central African Republic, the border region between northern Uganda and South Sudan, and the Democratic Republic of Congo's Garamba National Park. President Obama's announcement on October 14, 2011, that U.S. troops would be deployed to help the Ugandan government track down and apprehend Kony and his followers was widely welcomed, particularly by the thousands of beleaguered villagers throughout these regions who have suffered the most from nearly 20 years of LRA terror.[21] And the following year, a global Internet media campaign "Kony2012" was launched to bring additional pressure on governments to capture Joseph Kony and his remaining followers.

In recent years, the LRA has been estimated to have fewer than 200–300 fighters.[22] A series of defections and successful counterterrorism operations have greatly diminished their prospects for continuing the struggle much longer. In March 2014, the Pentagon announced the deployment of 150 Special Operations Forces, as well as aerial reconnaissance equipment, adding to the units deployed in 2011. Nobody knows for certain where Kony is, but according to at least two reports there is evidence to suggest he is hiding along with his closest associates in the Kafia Kingi enclave, one of the disputed areas on the border between Sudan and South Sudan.[23] The increasing constraints on the LRA's freedom of movement and resources lead many to suggest the end of its campaign of terror is drawing very near.

TERRORISM AND ISLAM

Okay, now let's turn to look at some examples of religious terrorism linked to the global religion of Islam. Within the category of religious terrorism, there are more groups associated with Islam than with any other monotheistic religion, and this has unfortunately given some observers a false sense of support for their misguided prejudices. Ever since the attacks of 9/11, I have been personally dismayed and disgusted by the way that some people in the United States have portrayed Muslims as inherently extremist. Please keep in mind that there is absolutely no evidence whatsoever to support assertions that Muslims are somehow culturally more accepting or promoting of terrorist activity. Now, with that said, let me climb off my soapbox and get back to business here. Since the next lecture in this book will focus on the global Salafi-jihadist movement—which includes al-Qaeda, the Islamic State, and many affiliated groups worldwide—I'm going to skip over them in this lecture and focus here on Islamist terror groups with a local or regional orientation. Let's start with the Middle East, where we find two of the most prominent and well-armed terrorist groups in the world: Hamas and Hizballah.

Hamas

Hamas is an Arabic acronym of *Harakat al-Muqawamah al-Islamiyya*, or "The Islamic Resistance Movement." It was founded in 1987 when the first *intifada*, a five-year uprising that began as a grassroots protest for the rights of Palestinians and escalated into full-blown riots with rock throwing and Molotov cocktails. The original leaders of this group were part of the local affiliate of the Muslim Brotherhood—a political Islamist movement founded in Egypt—before launching Hamas. According to the

Hamas charter, the land of "Palestine" [comprised today of Israel and the Palestinian Territories] is *waqf* (an endowment) of the Islamic world,[24] and thus Israel's very existence is a religious contradiction in terms. Hamas does not recognize Israel as a legitimate state, arguing that it is an illegal occupier of Palestinian land. Hamas portrays the conflict between Israel and the Palestinians as an Arab and Islamic nation occupied and oppressed by a Zionist movement with vastly superior military power and support from Western patrons like the United States and Europe. The group is completely against the Middle East peace process, and a negotiated settlement with Israel is viewed by most observers as something Hamas would never agree to.

Instead, Hamas seeks the destruction of Israel through violence.[25] The group's ideology articulates a belief that it is the duty of all Muslims to liberate Palestine through violent jihad.[26] Its attacks have included ambushing both Israeli soldiers and civilians alike, as well as suicide bombings, kidnappings, and rocket attacks. While bombings in Israel are relatively rare, knife attacks have increased in recent years. Hamas has workshops and factories scattered throughout Gaza that are used to manufacture explosives and weapons. The organization's funding comes from several sources, including *zakat* (alms giving) from Palestinian Muslims, profits from "legitimate" businesses, and fundraising throughout the Middle East, Europe, and North America. Several reports also indicate the group receives some financial support from Iran and Syria, and for years the group has received supplies smuggled into Gaza from Egypt using tunnels at the Raffah border crossing.

Hamas is rather different, however, from most of the other terrorist groups described in this lecture series. For starters, it runs a large social welfare network, providing support to basic services upon which millions of Palestinians rely.[27] As you can probably guess, life for most people in the Palestinian Territories is downright miserable. They are closed off from the rest of the world; they have a struggling economy and limited employment opportunities, with nearly three-fourths of the population living below the poverty line; occasionally the Israeli military comes in and bulldozes a few towns or neighborhoods (usually in retaliation for a terrorist attack); and for most of their existence the Palestinians have not had a government or leadership in whom they could trust to lead them toward a better future. A staggering level of corruption has been tied to the Palestinian Authority (PA), the PLO, and Fatah, and as noted in Lectures 3 and 4, corruption undermines a government's ability to establish legitimacy among the citizens it claims to govern.

In essence, both the Israeli government and Palestinian leadership have consistently failed to provide essential services to the Palestinian community, thus leaving a void that groups like Hamas are all too eager to fill. Recognizing the need to compete for hearts and minds against other Palestinian nationalist and political entities, Hamas began providing support to hospitals, schools, libraries, and recreation services. By 2006, the reputation and local popularity of Hamas allowed it to win a majority of seats in the parliamentary elections that year. Ordinary Palestinians felt the group offered a less corrupt alternative—and was also seen as a stronger opposition to Israel—than the existing government. However, in the years since Hamas was elected to power, it has not proven to be any more effective at governing. Further, after an armed conflict between Hamas and the Fatah-led Palestinian Authority, the Palestinian territories became split between the West Bank (under the control of PA) and Gaza Strip (under the control of Hamas). In 2012, Hamas signed a power-sharing deal with the PA, but everyday life has not significantly improved for the average Palestinian. Without some kind of major breakthrough, it seems that this conflict—and the terrorist groups involved, like Hamas—will not go away anytime soon.

Hizballah

Moving just a little north up the Mediterranean coast into Lebanon, we find another militant group that provides social services to local people while declaring its commitment to destroying the state of Israel. **Hizballah** is a Lebanese militia comprised of (and ostensibly fighting on behalf of) Shiite Muslims. There are several transliterations used for this group, like Hezbollah or Hizbollah, but to be precise, Hizballah is actually two words Hizb ("Party") and Allah ("God"), and joining them together you get Hizb'Allah, or "Party of God," which is why I use the version of the spelling you see here.

The Lebanese Civil War (1975–1990) created the chaotic backdrop for the emergence of this group, which was formally launched in 1982 when Israeli forces invaded Lebanon with the purpose of crushing the PLO, which had been launching attacks against Israel from its safe haven in southern Lebanon.[28] Leader Hassan Nasrallah described Hizballah as "a resistance movement and nothing else." Its founding statement—which was read by Sheikh Ibrahim al-Amin at the al-Ouzai Mosque in west Beirut and was then published on February 16, 1985 as an open letter "to all the Oppressed in Lebanon and the World" in *al-Safir* (Beirut)—states:

> We declare openly and loudly that we are an *umma* which fears God only and is by no means ready to tolerate injustice, aggression and humiliation. America, its Atlantic Pact allies, and the Zionist entity in the holy land of Palestine, attacked us and continue to do so without respite. . . . Our primary assumption in our fight against Israel states that the Zionist entity is aggressive from its inception, and built on lands wrested from their owners, at the expense of the rights of the Muslim people. Therefore our struggle will end only when this entity is obliterated. We recognize no treaty with it, no cease fire, and no peace agreements, whether separate or consolidated. We vigorously condemn all plans for negotiation with Israel, and regard all negotiators as enemies, for the reason that such negotiation is nothing but the recognition of the legitimacy of the Zionist occupation of Palestine.[29]

Spokesmen for the group have also declared its objectives as including the establishment of a Shiite theocracy in Lebanon and the elimination of Western influence in the Middle East.

During the 1980s, Hizballah launched several suicide car and truck bombings, including against the U.S. Marine barracks in Beirut in 1983, which killed 241 American peacekeepers. A separate truck bomb killed 58 French soldiers at their barracks nearby. Following these events, both the United States and France withdrew their peacekeeping forces from the country.[30] In addition to several attacks against Israeli forces, Hizballah was implicated in two attacks in the early 1990s against the Israeli Embassy and a Jewish cultural center in Argentina, and some reports indicate it may have been involved in the 1996 attack on a U.S. military housing complex in Saudi Arabia known as the Khobar Towers.

More recently, the group engaged in a full-scale military conflict with Israel in 2006. It started when Hizballah militants kidnapped two Israeli soldiers and threatened to kill them unless Israel agreed to release several Lebanese prisoners. Israel responded with airstrikes and artillery fire against a variety of targets, and then an invasion with ground forces. Hizballah employed guerilla warfare tactics, preventing any decisive victory for Israeli troops, and after 34 days a United Nations team negotiated a ceasefire. Hizballah claimed victory, primarily because it had stood up to a far superior military

Figure 11.2: Weapons and religious symbolism feature prominently in the logos of the Islamist extremist groups Hizballah in Lebanon and al-Shabaab in Somalia.

and was not defeated, which is more than we can say about the many Arab countries that went to war against Israel during the 1960s and '70s and were crushed.

Hizballah receives a significant amount of weapons and training from Iran and Syria. The United States believes the group has a significant stockpile of Katyusha rockets, anti-tank guided missiles, rocket-propelled grenade launchers, and anti-aircraft weapons. In the 2006 conflict, Hizballah also revealed an advanced information operations capability, to include jamming radars, hacking websites, and gathering signals intelligence.[31] And Hizballah also has an influential satellite TV station, al-Manar, through which it disseminates propaganda and promotes its ideology.[32]

Also, it is important to note that similar to Hamas in the Palestinian territories, Hizballah provides social services and health care to people in areas under its control. Following the 2006 conflict with Israel, Hizballah received a significant influx of cash from Iran and Syria that it used to rebuild bridges, schools, hospitals, and other places that had been damaged. As a result of these kinds of activities, the group has considerable popular support among the population of southern Lebanon. And, like Hamas, Hizballah has capitalized on this support through the political system, with members repeatedly winning seats in Lebanon's Parliament and even serving in the prime minister's cabinet. Finally, Hizballah has amassed a significant following in the broader Muslim world, not just among the Shia but among Sunnis as well, because it is seen by many as the only entity in the Arab world that has successfully stood up to Israel on multiple occasions.[33]

Al-Shabaab

Now we move a bit to the south, to the Horn of Africa, where we find a more recently created Islamist radical group known as **al-Shabaab** (Arabic for "the Youth"). This group emerged from the constant state of war and chaos that has characterized Somalia since 1990. Its founders were originally part of the military wing of the Islamic Courts Union, a Muslim extremist group that took power in southern Somalia and the capital Mogadishu in early 2006, but were driven out later that year when the Ethiopian army invaded the country. While al-Shabaab is mostly considered a religious insurgent group conducting guerilla attacks against the Somali Transitional Government, it has also been linked to attacks in other countries, including three bombings in the Ugandan capital Kampala, which killed nearly 80 people,[34] and several horrendous attacks in Kenya, including at a shopping mall and a university. The group also preaches an extremist brand of Sunni Islam and uses violence to try and coerce the behavior of the local population, like stoning people accused of adultery.[35] And it has intimidated, kidnapped and killed aid workers periodically, leading to a suspension of humanitarian operations and an exodus of relief agencies from Somalia, thus contributing to an already dire humanitarian situation. In 2011, a famine that killed an estimated 100,000 Somalis, with perhaps half that number being children, was largely attributed to al-Shabaab's refusal to allow Western aid workers to bring food and aid to the malnourished, starving people of the country.[36]

Since late 2011, al-Shabaab appears to have split into two factions, with the leader of one faction swearing allegiance to al-Qaeda (thereby indicating its support for a global jihadist ideology and welcoming foreign fighters to join them), and the other declaring itself committed to the original, exclusively Somali local conflict. Both factions, however, describe themselves as waging war against "enemies of Islam." More recently, the Islamic State has attempted to attract the allegiance of al-Shabaab members, but thus far it has been largely unsuccessful. The al-Qaeda affiliated faction of al-Shabaab has managed to recruit several foreigners, including young Americans growing up in Somali immigrant neighborhoods in places like Minneapolis and Newark, N.J. However, it is also apparent that this group's linkages with al-Qaeda are largely ideological, as opposed to operational. Instead of providing logistics or financial support, the most that Ayman al-Zawahiri and other senior figures in the global Salafi-jihadist movement have offered thus far is praise via online video and audio statements. We'll explore more about this in the next lecture.

In September 2013, al-Shabaab captured worldwide attention by staging a massive siege against a shopping center in Nairobi, Kenya. While militants rampaged through the complex, killing dozens and wounding nearly 200 more, other members of the group used social media (including the Twitter account described in Lecture 7) to announce their claim of responsibility and to taunt local authorities. In April 2015, they gained international headlines again following a massacre of 147 students at Garissa University in Kenya. Today, al-Shabaab fighters are believed to be sheltering primarily in a mountainous region in the north and in the heavy forests in the Lower Juba region. There is no telling how badly their capabilities have been degraded, or how many fighters have been lost to battle deaths and defections, but they are significant. However, the group's core force of approximately 3,500-5,000 fighters is mostly intact, making it well capable of carrying out more bloody attacks in the future.[37]

Boko Haram

A similar situation is found in northern Nigeria, where another local Islamist extremist group had for several years indicated an ideological affiliation with the global Salafi-jihadist movement, but little more than that. The group is known locally as **Boko Haram** (a Hausa term for "Western education is forbidden"), though it officially calls itself *Jama'atul Ahlul Sunnah Lidda'wati wal Jihad* which means "people committed to the propagation of the Prophet's teachings and jihad." As its name suggests, the group is adamantly opposed to what it sees as a Western-based incursion that threatens traditional values, beliefs, and customs among Muslim communities in northern Nigeria. In an audio tape posted on the Internet in January 2012, Abubakar Shekau, a spokesman for the group, even accused the United States of waging war on Islam.[38]

As is the case with many of the groups covered in this lecture series, Boko Haram is largely a product of widespread socioeconomic and religious insecurities, and its ideology resonates among certain communities because of both historical narratives and modern grievances like unemployment, corruption, and a lack of infrastructure.[39] Since 2009, the group has attacked police stations and patrols, politicians (including village chiefs and a member of parliament), religious leaders (both Christian and Muslim), and individuals whom the group deems to be engaged in un-Islamic activities, such as drinking beer. Boko Haram has also carried out several mass casualty attacks, and was the first militant group in Nigeria to embrace the use of suicide bombings, which it used in a June 2011 attack on the Nigeria Police Headquarters in Abuja.[40]

Later that year, Boko Haram expanded its terrorist attacks to include international targets, when on August 26, 2011, the group carried out its most notorious (and most international) attack to date using a suicide car bomber to blow up portions of the United Nations building in Abuja. At least 18 people were killed, and many more were injured when the blast destroyed the lower floors of the building. According to one report, the driver rammed the car into an exit gate and then drove into a parking garage before detonating his explosives.[41] In November 2011, the U.S. Department of State issued an alert for all U.S. and Western citizens in Abuja to avoid major hotels and landmarks, based on information about a potential Boko Haram attack. A 2011 report by the U.S. House of Representatives expressed concerns about Boko Haram attacks against the aviation and energy sectors as well.[42] However, the overwhelming majority of the group's attacks have been focused on local targets in Nigeria, which makes sense given the domestic orientation of their ideology and strategy. For example, a spate of attacks against churches from December 2011 through February 2012 were seen by many as attempts to provoke Christians into retaliatory attacks against Muslims, part of an overall effort to spark widespread sectarian conflict in order to destabilize the government.[43]

More recently, in April 2014, members of Boko Haram stormed a school in the village of Chibok, in Borno State, and kidnapped over 200 girls, mostly age 16–18. The Nigerian government's response was widely seen as inept, and a worldwide social media campaign "Bring Back our Girls" created some pressure on Western governments (including the U.S.) to send military advisors and aerial reconnaissance equipment to the region. While some of the kidnapped girls have been recovered in recent years, more young girls have been kidnapped, some as young as twelve years old. Abubakar Shekau, the leader of Boko Haram, has claimed responsibility for these acts, and in at least one video statement announced his intent to sell them into slavery.

In January, 2015, members of Boko Haram attacked the town of Baga, killing civilians and destroying thousands of homes in retaliation for their refusal to embrace its radical ideology. In addition to several other attacks in early 2015, many observers were alarmed when Boko Haram declared an oath of loyalty to the Islamic State later that year. More recently, in July 2017 members of the group killed 10 soldiers in an ambush on a Nigerian oil convoy, and, in August, several attacks by suicide bombers killed nearly 30 and injured dozens more around the city of Maiduguri. In sum, the bombings, kidnappings, and assassinations by Boko Haram have become all too common in northern Nigeria, and unless the government there makes drastic changes to its counterterrorism strategy, the situation could get even worse in the coming years.

Other Notable Islamist Extremist Groups

Finally, among the many other groups in this category, a handful of notables includes the **Abu Sayyaf Group** (ASG), an extremist Islamist group in the Philippines that developed out of the Moro independence movement led first by the Moro National Liberation Front, and then its splinter group, the Moro Islamic Liberation Front.[44] The ASG is responsible for several bombings, including an attack on a passenger ferry that killed 116, and an attack against the Philippine Congress, which killed a Congressman and three aides.[45] However, within the past decade, ASG has largely transformed from a religiously-motivated terrorist group into more of a kidnap-for-profit criminal network, targeting primarily Western tourists whom it takes hostage and threatens to kill unless huge ransoms are paid.[46]

Lashkar-e-Taiba (LeT) is a Pakistani-based extremist group that has targeted Indian forces and Hindus in Kashmir. Its most prominent attacks include the 2001 storming of the Indian Parliament with guns and grenades, killing 12 people and injuring dozens more; the 2006 bombing of several commuter trains in Mumbai, killing 180 people; and the 2008 attack on Mumbai, using heavily armed gunmen to kill and wound hundreds of Indians and Westerners. While I mentioned Lashkar-e-Taiba in the lecture on ethnonationalists, it is also characterized as a religious terrorist group because its leaders surround their political ideology with elements of radical Islam. The group's overall goal is to wrestle control of Kashmir from India and either place it under Pakistan's authority or gain independent statehood; in both cases, it would want the territory to be ruled by Shari'a law. Also, in the past few years, its ideological statements have suggested a more global vision of the future, to include "planting the flag of Islam" in New Delhi, Tel Aviv, and Washington. This indicates to some observers that LeT is perhaps transitioning toward becoming a part of the global Salafi-jihadist movement.[47]

Tehrik-i-Taliban Pakistan (TTP) is considered by some observers to be the largest and most lethal militant group in Pakistan today. Based in Southern Waziristan, TTP is comprised of several dozen Pakistani Taliban factions operating throughout the country as well as in the Afghanistan border regions. TTP attacks generally target Pakistani security forces and government facilities, and its overall goal is to overthrow the democratic government and establish an Islamic caliphate in Pakistan. The group has also targeted airports, hospitals, public markets, Christian churches, Sufi shrines, and schools (particularly those that educate girls), and attempted to assassinate Malala Yousafzai, a young advocate for female education. Since 2009, TTP has murdered thousands through car bombings in Peshawar, Karachi, and other cities throughout Pakistan.

Harkat-ul-Jihad-al-Islami (HuJI) is a militant group that originated in Pakistan but is now mostly active in Bangladesh. Founded in 1992, several leaders of the group have ties to the global Salafi-jihadist movement and aims to establish Islamic rule throughout the countries of this region, including Pakistan, India, and Bangladesh. Since 2000, the group has been responsible for numerous bombings and assassinations (or attempts) throughout Bangladesh. The country is also confronting a similar threat from another jihadist group known as **Jumatul Mujahideen Bangladesh** (JMB), founded in 1998 by Shaikh Abdur Rahman. JMB militants have carried out attacks against judges, foreigners, and others, and were responsible for a series of bombings across Bangladesh that killed over 30 people in 2005. And meanwhile, a third Islamist militant group known as the **Ansarullah Bangla Team** (ABT) has carried out dozens of attacks against bloggers, academics, and publishers in Bangladesh who have promoted democratic reform and have been openly critical of Islamist extremism and violence.

Jemaah Islamiyah (JI) is another Islamist group with a local agenda but with some ties to the global jihadist network. This group was formed in the early 1990s by two Indonesian clerics, Abdullah Sungkar and Abu Bakar Bashir, with the stated goal of establishing an Islamic state.[48] JI has been responsible for a number of lethal bombings targeting Western interests in Indonesia and the Philippines since 2000, including attacks in 2002 against two nightclubs in Bali, which killed 202 people (many of them Australian tourists[49]); an August 2003 car bombing of the JW Marriott hotel in Jakarta, killing 12; a 2004 truck bombing of the Australian Embassy in Jakarta; an October 2005 suicide bombing of three tourist establishments in Bali that killed 20 people; and the July 2009 bombings of the JW Marriott and Ritz-Carlton hotels in Jakarta, killing seven. Several reports have linked the group with the global Salafi-jihadist movement, mainly through personal relationships established by JI members who went to al-Qaeda training camps in Afghanistan during the 1990s.

And we also have instances of several religious groups operating within the same area, and where individuals may have their allegiances to more than one group. For example, there are three seemingly overlapping Islamist extremist groups in Morocco: **Salafia Jihadia**, the **Moroccan Islamic Combatant Group** (GICM), and a small ultraconservative group known as **Takfir wal-Hijra–Martyrs for Morocco** (also called "Takfiris" for short).[50] All three are dedicated to the creation of an Islamist state in Morocco. Several GICM members were trained in Afghanistan training camps, and there are alleged ties and personal relationships with members of al-Qaeda. Salafia Jihadia is considered responsible for a massive coordinated suicide bombing in Casablanca on May 16, 2003 that killed 45 people and injured dozens more. The attacks targeted a private Spanish club (Casa de España) near the Spanish consulate, as well as the Israeli Alliance Club, a Jewish cemetery, the Belgian consulate, and a hotel popular with businesspeople. And members of the third group, a local branch of the radical Islamist movement al-Takfir wal-Hijra, which originated in Egypt in the 1960s as a radical offshoot of the Muslim Brother-

> **TO THE POINT**
>
> Often, terrorists in this category are fueled by underlying religious insecurities.

hood, have been linked to the March 2004 commuter train bombings in Madrid and the November 2004 murder of Dutch filmmaker Theo van Gogh.

SUMMARY

So, these are just some of the many religiously-oriented terrorist groups seeking to bring about changes that are aligned with the values and doctrines of a particular religion—or, as in the case of Aum Shinrikyo, a religious cult. Because these changes are not seen as attainable through nonviolent means, these groups have adopted terrorism as a means to achieve their ideological goals. In several instances, a religious terrorist group emerged from a broader conflict, like the civil wars in Lebanon and Somalia, or the Palestinian struggle against Israel. But other religious groups have also emerged without any noticeable trigger.

We also have seen religious groups in many different kinds of countries, from industrialized liberal democracies in the West and Asia to authoritarian regimes in the Middle East and North Africa. A common theme among a majority of these religious groups is that they see themselves as defenders of the faithful, or defenders of those whom God wants them to defend. Often, this kind of terrorism is fueled by underlying religious insecurities.

This brings us back to a central point that was made in Lecture 1: terrorism as a means for pursuing power. In this light, religious terrorist groups are actually similar to the other categories we've looked at in previous lectures—they want the power to shape their socioeconomic and political future, and see the need to use violence in order to get that power. Concerns about their spiritual future, and that of their children, bring an added dimension that in some cases may bring a greater level of lethality that will be harder for governments to deal with.

Another important dimension that should be noted is that most of the groups we have covered thus far—ethnonationalist, left-wing, and right-wing—have almost all been oriented around a specific geographic entity, like a nation (or a territory within that nation, like Chechnya or a homeland for Basques, Tamils, or Kurds). Most religious terrorist groups also have local agendas and goals. However, religions can also be transnational. In other words, the reason for being an extremist may not be based on territory or political system as much as it is a set of religious principles that people in many other countries around the world also believe in. From this perspective, a Christian in Europe would probably have a similar view about their faith as a Christian in Asia, Africa, or North America. This dimension of crossing boundaries allows for an extremist ideology based upon interpretations of those religious principles to be a possible uniting and radicalizing force regardless of geographic location. As we turn now to focus on the global Salafi-jihadist movement in the next lecture, this transnational aspect of religious terrorism plays a central role. In essence, religious groups are often focused on local issues, but the jihadists' ability to attract support from others regardless of ethnicity or nationality sets that movement apart from other terrorist threats of the twenty-first century.

QUESTIONS FOR DISCUSSION

- Describe the ways in which terms such as martyrdom and leaderless resistance have similar connotations for groups like the Army of God, al-Qaeda, and others regardless of religious affiliation.
- Why do religious ideologies of violence seem to have more "staying power" than secular ideologies?
- What are some key challenges that liberal democracies face when trying to confront a religious-based terror threat?
- What can religious authorities do to undermine the resonance of a terrorist group's ideology?

RECOMMENDED READING

Aho, James. "Christian Fundamentalism and Militia Movements in the United States." In *The Making of a Terrorist*. Vol. 1. Edited by James J. F. Forest. Westport, CT: Praeger, 2005.

Abuza, Zachary. "Education and Radicalization: Jemaah Islamiyah Recruitment in Southeast Asia." In *The Making of a Terrorist*. Vol. 1. Edited by James J. F. Forest. Westport, CT: Praeger, 2005.

Azzam, Maha. "Political Islam: Violence and the Wahhabi Connection." In *The Making of a Terrorist*. Vol. 1. Edited by James J. F. Forest. Westport, CT: Praeger, 2005.

Brachman, Jarret. *Global Jihadism: Theory and Practice*. London: Routledge, 2008.

Brachman, Jarret. "Jihad Doctrine and Radical Islam." In *The Making of a Terrorist*. Vol. 1. Edited by James J. F. Forest. Westport, CT: Praeger, 2005.

Brownfeld, Allan C. "Zionism and the Pursuit of West Bank Settlements." In *The Making of a Terrorist*. Vol. 1. Edited by James J. F. Forest. Westport, CT: Praeger, 2005.

Byman, Daniel and Natan Sachs, "The Rise of Settler Terrorism: The West Bank's Other Violent Extremists." *Foreign Affairs* (September/October 2012).

Combs, Cindy C., Elizabeth A. Combs and Lydia Marsh. "Christian Militia Training: Arming the 'Troops' with Scripture, the Law and a Good Gun." In *The Making of a Terrorist*. Vol. 2. Edited by James J. F. Forest. Westport, CT: Praeger, 2005.

Davis, Danny W. *The Phinehas Priesthood: Violent Vanguard of the Christian Identity Movement*. Westport, CT: Praeger, 2010.

Dolnik, Adam. "Aum Shinrikyo's Path to Innovation." In *Terrorist Innovations in Weapons of Mass Effect: Preconditions, Causes and Predictive Behaviors*. Edited by Maria J. Rasmussen and Mohammed M. Hafez. Washington, D.C.: Defense Threat Reduction Agency, 2010.

Forest, James J. F. *Countering the Terror of Boko Haram in Nigeria*. Tampa, FL: JSOU Press, 2012.

Forest, James J. F. *U.S. Military Deployments to Africa: Lessons from the Hunt for Joseph Kony and the Lord's Resistance Army*. Tampa, FL: JSOU Press, 2014.

Gregg, Heather. "Defining and Distinguishing Traditional and Religious Terrorism." *Perspectives on Terrorism* 8, no. 2 (April 2014).

Habeck, Mary R. "The Jihadist Laws of War." *The Journal of International Security Affairs* 18 (2010).

Hoffman, Bruce. "Religion and Terrorism." In *Inside Terrorism*. New York: Columbia University Press, 2006: 81–129.

Jefferis, Jennifer. *Armed for Life: The Army of God and Anti-Abortion Terror in the United States*. Westport, CT: Praeger, 2010.

Juergensmeyer, Mark. *Terror in the Mind of God: the Global Rise of Religious Violence*. Berkeley: University of California Press, 2003.

Juergensmeyer, Mark. "Christian Violence in America," *Annals of the American Academy of Political and Social Science* 558 (1988).

Kohlmann, Evan. "The Mujahideen of Bosnia: Origins, Training and Implications." In *The Making of a Terrorist*. Vol. 2. Edited by James J. F. Forest. Westport, CT: Praeger, 2005.

Larsson, J. P. "The Role of Religious Ideology in Modern Terrorist Recruitment." In *The Making of a Terrorist*. Vol. 1. Edited by James J. F. Forest. Westport, CT: Praeger, 2005.

Levitt, Matthew A. "Hamas Social Welfare: In the Service of Terror." In *The Making of a Terrorist*. Vol. 1. Edited by James J. F. Forest. Westport, CT: Praeger, 2005.

Moghadam, Assaf. *Nexus of Global Jihad: Understanding Cooperation Among Terrorist Actors*. New York: Columbia University Press, 2017.

Parachini, John V. "The Making of Aum Shinrikyo's Chemical Weapons Program." In *The Making of a Terrorist*. Vol. 2. Edited by James J. F. Forest. Westport, CT: Praeger, 2005.

Pedahzur, Ami. *Jewish Terrorism in Israel*. New York: Columbia University Press, 2009.

Ramakrishna, Kumar. "Indoctrination Processes within Jemaah Islamiyah." In *The Making of a Terrorist*. Vol. 2. Edited by James J. F. Forest. Westport, CT: Praeger, 2005.

Ranstorp, Magnus. "Terrorism in the Name of Religion." In *Terrorism and Counterterrorism*. Edited by Russell Howard and Bruce Hoffman. New York: McGraw-Hill, 2011.

Rapoport, David C. "Fear and Trembling: Terrorism in Three Religious Traditions." *American Political Science Review* 78, no. 3 (1984).

Rashke, Diane. *The East Turkestan Islamic Movement: China's Islamic Militants and the Global Terrorist Threat*. Westport, CT: Praeger, 2010.

Reinares, Fernando. "The Madrid Bombings and Global Jihadism." *Survival* 52, no. 2 (2010).

Smith, James M. "Japan and Aum Shinrikyo." In *Countering Terrorism and Insurgency in the 21st Century*. Vol. 3. Edited by James J. F. Forest. Westport, CT: Praeger, 2007.

Stern, Jessica. *Terror in the Name of God: Why Religious Militants Kill*. New York: Harper Collins, 2003.

Turbiville, Graham, Josh Meservey and James Forest. *Countering the al-Shabaab Insurgency in Somalia: Lessons for U.S. Special Forces*. Tampa, FL: JSOU Press, 2013.

Wrona, Richard M. Jr. "Lebanon, Hizbollah, and the Patrons of Terrorism," In *Countering Terrorism and Insurgency in the 21st Century*. Vol. 3. Edited by James J. F. Forest. Westport, CT: Praeger, 2007.

Zuhur, Sherifa. "State Power and the Progress of Militant and Moderate Islamism in Egypt," In *Countering Terrorism and Insurgency in the 21st Century*. Vol. 3. Edited by James J. F. Forest. Westport, CT: Praeger, 2007.

WEBSITES

Mapping Militant Organizations
http://web.stanford.edu/group/mappingmilitants/cgi-bin/

START Terrorist Group Profiles ("Big, Allied and Dangerous") Database
http://www.start.umd.edu/baad/database

NOTES

1. John E. Mack, "Deeper Causes: Exploring the Role of Consciousness in Terrorism," *Ions Noetic Sciences Review* (June-August 2003): 14.

2. J. P. Larsson, "The Role of Religious Ideology in Modern Terrorist Recruitment," in *The Making of a Terrorist*, vol. 1, ed. James J. F. Forest (Westport, CT: Praeger, 2005).

3. For more on the concept of "othering," see Victor Asal and R. Karl Rethemeyer, "The Nature of the Beast: Organizational Structures and the Lethality of Terrorist Attacks," *Journal of Politics* 70, no. 2 (2008): 437–39.

4. Bruce Hoffman, *Inside Terrorism* (New York: Columbia University Press): 88.

5. Jessica Stern, *Terror in the Name of God* (New York: Ecco Trade Paperback Edition, 2004): 281.

6. Ibid., 282.

7. Ibid.

8. For more on this, see Jarret Brachman, "Jihad Doctrine and Radical Islam," in *The Making of a Terrorist*, vol. 1, 246–59.

9. Ibid.

10. "Rabbi Kahane Interview with Raphael Mergui and Philippe Simonnot," *Kahane Resources* (August 25, 2010).

11. For example, see Ami Pedahzur, *Jewish Terrorism in Israel* (New York: Columbia University Press, 2009): 84.

12. Jennifer Jefferis, *Armed for Life: The Army of God and Anti-Abortion Terror in the United States* (Westport, CT: Praeger, 2010): 55.

13. For more on this group, see ibid.

14. Frederick Clarkson, "Anti-Abortion Violence: Two Decades of Arson, Bomb and Murder," *SPLC Intelligence Report* 91 (1998): 2.

15. For more about this group, see Jefferis, *Armed for Life*.

16. John V. Parachini, "The Making of Aum Shinrikyo's Chemical Weapons Program," in *The Making of a Terrorist*, vol. 2.

17. Robert J. Lifton, *Destroying the World to Save it: Aum Shinrikyo, Apocalyptic Violence and the New Global Terrorism* (New York: Henry Holt and Company, 1999): 27.

18. For more information on the LRA, see James Forest, *U.S. Military Deployments to Africa: Lessons from the Hunt for Joseph Kony and the Lord's Resistance Army.* Tampa, FL: JSOU Press.

19. Lord's Resistant Army profile at the START database website: http://goo.gl/ZGols.

20. "UNHCR Seeing New Displacement Caused by Lord's Resistance Army" (October 15, 2010), http://www.unhcr.org/4cb832c29.html.

21. Jake Tapper and Luis Martinez, "Obama Sends 100 US Troops to Uganda to Help Combat Lord's Resistance Army," *ABC News* (October 14, 2011), http://goo.gl/XUuB1.

22. James J. F. Forest. *U.S. Military Deployments to Africa: Lessons from the Hunt for Joseph Kony and the Lord's Resistance Army*, JSOU Press, 2014. See also, Invisible Children, *LRA Crisis Tracking Report, 2013 Annual Security Brief.* Available at http://reports.lracrisistracker.com.

23. Ibid.

24. The Hamas Covenant is available at http://avalon.law.yale.edu/.

25. See the START Center profile on Hamas at: http://goo.gl/MqGmX.

26. Ibid.

27. See Matt Levitt, "Hamas Social Welfare: In the Service of Terror," in *The Making of a Terrorist*, vol. 1.

28. The Lebanese Civil War, which started in 1975 and continued until 1990, created the backdrop for the chaos in which these events took place.

29. "An Open Letter: The Hizballah Program [1988]," IDC Herzliya, International Institute for Counter-Terrorism, http://goo.gl/OEzXW.

30. See the START Center profile on Hizballah at: http://goo.gl/TM0y8.

31. Guermantes E. Lailari, "The Information Operations War Between Israel and Hizballah during the Summer of 2006," in *Influence Warfare,* ed. James J. F. Forest (Westport, CT: Praeger, 2009).

32. Maura Conway, "Terror TV? An Exploration Of Hizbollah's Al-Manar Television," in *Countering Terrorism and Insurgency in the 21st Century*, vol. 2, ed. James J. F. Forest (Westport, CT: Praeger, 2007).

33. For more on this group, see Hala Jaber, *Hezbollah: Born with a Vengeance* (New York: Columbia University Press, 1997), and Richard M. Wrona, Jr., "Lebanon, Hizballah, and the Patrons of Terrorism," in *Countering Terrorism and Insurgency in the 21st Century*, vol. 3.

34. Bariyo, Nicholas, "Militants Find Symbolic Targets in Uganda," *Wall Street Journal*, July 13, 2010, http://goo.gl/PBYzA.

35. Stephanie Hanson, "Al Shabaab," Council on Foreign Relations Backgrounder (August 10, 2011), http://goo.gl/1NjuX.

36. Jeffrey Gettleman, "Somalis Waste Away as Insurgents Block Escape from Famine," *New York Times*, August 2, 2011, http://goo.gl/kefBM.

37. While estimates of the group's size vary widely, one of the highest figures in recent years comes from Graham Turbiville, Josh Meservey and James Forest. *Countering the al-Shabaab Insurgency in Somalia: Lessons for U.S. Special Forces*. JSOU Press, 2013.

38. Mike Oboh, "Boko Haram leader tape threatens Nigeria forces," *Reuters*, January 27, 2012, http://goo.gl/tQTO1.

39. For a complete study of this group, see James J. F. Forest, *Countering the Terror of Boko Haram in Nigeria* (Tampa, FL: JSOU Press, 2012).

40. "Nigeria's Boko Haram Islamists 'bombed Abuja Police Headquarters," BBC (June 17, 2011), http://goo.gl/ksmmx; and John Campbell and Asch Harwood, "Nigeria's Challenge," *The Atlantic* (June 24, 2011).

41. Scott Stewart, "The Rising Threat from Nigeria's Boko Haram Militant Group," *STRATFOR Global Intelligence* (November 10, 2011), http://goo.gl/v12HQ.

42. U.S. House of Representatives Comm. on Homeland Security, Subcomm. on Counterterrorism and Intelligence, "Boko Haram: Emerging Threat to the U.S. Homeland" (November 30, 2011): 17–19.

43. For a detailed account, see Forest, *Countering the Terror Threat of Boko Haram.*

44. Robin L. Bowman, "Moro Insurgents and the Peace Process in the Philippines", *Countering Terrorism and Insurgency in the 21st Century*, vol. 3, 485–507.

45. See the START Center profile for the Abu Sayyaf Group at: http://goo.gl/Ci6bc.

46. See McKenzie O'Brien, "Kidnappings and Crime-Terror Oscillation: The Case of Abu Sayyaf," *Terrorism and Political Violence* 24, no. 2 (2012).

47. For more on this group, see Steve Coll, "Lashkar-e-Taiba," *New Yorker* (December 1, 2008), http://goo.gl/AkyXi.

48. See the NCTC profile at http://nctc.gov/site/groups/ji.html.

49. See the *BBC News* website, "Bali Terror Attack," for extensive details, http://goo.gl/ZEqBS.

51. The START group profile for Salafia Jihadia is online at http://goo.gl/A9rLV; the START group profile for GICM is online at http://goo.gl/eKJnN; and the START group profile for Takfir wal Hijra-Martyrs for Morocco is online at http://goo.gl/sP9kD.

12

Religious Terrorism, Part Two

In this lecture, we will look specifically at the history, evolution, and ideology of what many experts now call the global Salafi-jihadist movement, which has become the most prevalent form of religious terrorism worldwide. As we will discuss in this lecture, the modern threat from this movement involves groups like al-Qaeda and the Islamic State, as well as nonaffiliated individuals overseas and here within the United States who are inspired to carry out violent acts in the name of a religiously inspired political ideology.

The history of the Salafi-jihadist ideology dates all the way back to the thirteenth century, and is primarily focused on replacing a secular government with a system of governance based on a strict interpretation of Islam. I typically like to describe this ideology using the metaphor of a camera lens, where we start with the widest macro-lens possible by looking at the broader Muslim world, and then we zoom in closer to look at the broad landscape of Islamist ideologies, and then finally we focus on what we call the Salafi-jihadist ideology promoted by groups like al-Qaeda, al-Shabaab, Jemmah Islamiyyah, Boko Haram, the Islamic State, and many others described in previous lectures. So, let's begin with the wide-angle lens by touching on some brief background notes on Islam.

A BRIEF HISTORY OF ISLAM

In the late sixth century and early seventh century, the Arabian peninsula was mainly dominated by nomadic Arabic tribes who fought with each other and worshipped a whole range of idols. A city called Mecca near the Red Sea was a vibrant center for trade and gatherings, and it was here in 610 A.D. that a 40-year-old Arab named Muhammad announced that after meditating in a cave at Mount Hira (located on the outskirts of Mecca), he had received revelations from God. The message he began preaching, about believing in one God instead of worshipping idols, made some rich tribal leaders angry, and in 622 Muhammad was forced to flee Mecca along with his followers. They eventually settled in a place now called Medina, about 280 miles north of Mecca, where they established a theocracy—a system of rule in which a religious leader is given the power to resolve disputes and maintain public order. Their theocracy was guided by a collection of scholars, called **ulama**, and obedience was enforced by religious courts led by judges and jurists, called qadis and muftis, respectively.

The religious ideology that Muhammad taught became known as *Islam*, a word that means "submission to the will of God," and a follower of this religion was called *Muslim*, or "one who submits." Islam as a faith is meant to guide religious, political, and social life—in essence, governing all aspects of behavior. It was embraced by followers in part as a response to the barbaric chaos that existed in the region at that time. In 630 A.D., Muhammad had amassed such a large following that he was able to lead an army of 10,000 Muslims in conquering Mecca, after which he began to unify the various Arabic tribes throughout the peninsula under the same sort of theocracy that had been successful in Medina.

There are five basic pillars of Islam: **shahadah**, the profession of one's belief in one God, Allah, and that Muhammad was God's Prophet; daily prayer, called the **salah** or **salat**; **zakat** (a form of regular charitable giving); fasting during the month of Ramadan; and the **Hajj**—a pilgrimage to Mecca at least once in a person's lifetime. Note that the term *jihad* is not considered a central pillar of faith for most Muslims. Further, the true meaning of this term in the Islamic world is struggle or striving for a noble cause, though it is also used by radical extremists to denote a "holy war." As a struggle for continual improvement, jihad has generally been understood as an obligation of each individual Muslim as well as a general requirement of the Muslim community. Only in emergencies, when the Muslim community comes under attack, are all Muslims obligated to take up weapons and participate in a defensive jihad. Muslims have usually agreed that this kind of armed jihad applies to the defense of Islamic territory, faith, and lives; it is justified to repel invasion or its threat; and it is necessary to guarantee freedom for the spread of Islam. Although jihad has commonly been understood to have a religious aim, more important for the extremists is its political goal: to reestablish and then expand a single, unified Islamic realm which provides for a just political and social order. We will return to this topic in a few moments.

Other terms that are important to know include the ***umma***, or community; ***tawhid*** or "oneness"; ***Shari`a*** (sometimes called the Law of Islam); the ***Sunna***, the recorded behavior, practice, and sayings of the prophet in Medina; and the ***Hadith***, spoken decisions or judgments by Muslim leaders that have been written down and codified. Finally, it is important to keep in mind that several schools of thought emerged within Islam as it grew in popularity and membership. These different schools of thought, based on varying interpretations of the Quran and these other sacred texts, have led to a wide diversity in how the religion is taught and practiced throughout the Muslim world.

Today, there are roughly 1.8 billion Muslims worldwide, concentrated primarily in the Middle East, central and Southeast Asia, and Northern Africa. The countries with the largest Muslim populations are Indonesia, Pakistan, India, Bangladesh, Egypt, Nigeria, Iran, and Turkey. According to several estimates, less than one percent of the U.S. population is Muslim (roughly 3 million people), but the U.S. Census Bureau does not collect data on religious identification.

Within the Muslim world, an estimated 85 percent are Sunnis, and a majority of the rest are Shiites. The main differences between these two denominations involve recognizing the legitimacy of certain leadership transitions in the history of Islam, and in their interpretation of the Quran, the central text of this religion. For example, Sunnis have considered the caliphs (rulers selected by consensus of the community) as legitimate callers of jihad, so long as they had the support of the *ulama*; the Shia, however, see this power as having been meant for the Imams (rulers who descend directly from the bloodline of the Prophet Muhammad), but it has been wrongly denied by the majority Sunnis. All groups and individuals who embrace the ideology of Salafi-jihadism are Sunni Muslims, so we will focus primarily on them in this lecture.

As we move into our discussion of this ideology, please keep in mind some of the key points made in Lecture 11 about religions being vast, diverse, and sometimes contradictory. As noted earlier, much of the terrorist violence associated with religions (including Islam) is fueled not by the religious or sacred texts themselves, but by an individual's interpretations of those texts. Further, researchers have consistently shown that the kind of "othering" reflected in religious extremism of all kinds appeals particularly to people with binary and absolutist world views, and that the more knowledge of Islam an individual has, the less likely they are to become radicalized by the Salafi-jihadist interpretation of the religion. So with that as our launching point, let's begin.

EARLY FOUNDATIONS OF THE SALAFI-JIHADIST IDEOLOGY

During the late thirteenth and early fourteenth centuries, the Mongols invaded and conquered much of the Middle East. A popular religious scholar named **Taqi al-Din Ibn Taymiyya** wrote at this time that the reason the Muslim world had been conquered by outsiders was because leaders had not been true to the faith. He preached throughout the Arabian Peninsula, telling his followers that a leader who doesn't enforce Shari`a completely, and wage active jihad against infidels, is unfit to rule. He described jihad as fighting in the path of God in order to defend the *umma*, and then to spread the faith.[1]

In the early seventeenth century, another Arabian religious scholar named **Muhammad ibn Abd al-Wahhab** promoted a more conservative, strict interpretation of Islam, in which he argued that no compromise could be possible in how one practices the faith. To him, a pure fundamentalist version of Islam was meant to be the only guiding set of principles around which all human activity should be conducted. Wahhab was a religious reformer who sought to cleanse eighteenth century Islam of all unauthorized deviations from correct practice. He was influenced both by the Hanbali school of law (the smallest and strictest of the schools), and the ideas of Ibn Taymiyya, which he adapted and expanded upon.

A local tribal ruler named Muhammad bin Sa'ud became a big fan of Wahhab, and working together the religious leader and Saud's tribal leaders took control of the territory that is now known as the Kingdom of Saudi Arabia. Followers of Wahhab's strict interpretation of Islam are sometimes called Wahhabis, mainly within Saudi Arabia. However, in most countries (and often even in Saudi Arabia as well), devout followers of this conservative type of Islam prefer to use the term Salafis, which refers to those who follow the example of the companions (*salaf*) of the Prophet Muhammad. Salafis believe that because the companions learned about Islam directly from the Prophet, they commanded a pure understanding of the faith. Subsequent practices, in contrast, were sullied by religious innovations that infected the Muslim community over time. As a result, Muslims must purify the religion by strictly following the Quran, the Sunna (path or traditions of the Prophet Muhammad), and the consensus of the companions. Every behavior must be sanctioned by these religious sources.

Truly devout Salafis argue that they alone comprise the "saved sect" (*firqa al-najiyya*) and will avoid hell. Their approach to the religion ensures salvation. Though there is consensus among Salafis about this understanding of Islam, there are disagreements over the use of violence. The jihadi faction within the broader Salafist movement believes that violence can be used to establish Islamist governance and to confront the United States and its allies. The worldwide majority of nonviolent Salafis, on the other hand, emphatically reject the use of violence and instead emphasize propagation and advice to incumbent rulers in the Muslim world. In other words, the term "Salafi-jihadism" (the ideology promoted by groups like al-Qaeda and the Islamic State) represents a distinct minority opinion among those Muslims worldwide who embrace the conservative Salafist interpretation of Islam.

The next couple of centuries after the founding of the Salafist movement saw an increasing presence of Western powers throughout the Middle East. Colonies were established by Western European powers, which then imported their own financial and trade systems and sociopolitical ideas. Local rulers became increasingly seen by their subjects as inept and corrupt, and some followers of the faith became very angry at their seeming inability to restore the early purity of Islamic faith and practice, and to regain lost glory and prestige that was described in the sacred texts.

The peak of this dissatisfaction appears to have reached its highest point between the 1920s and 1970s when a number of radical groups were formed amid a larger population of Arabs throughout the Middle East who rejected the influences of Western civilization. The leaders of these radical groups described a crisis in the world where Islam was being threatened by Western influences. In response, they promoted a return to some sort of perfectionist, doctrinaire interpretation of Islam. Support for Salafist interpretations of Islam thus grew in response to local sociopolitical conditions, and from within this global expansion of Salafism emerged a small cadre of true believers who became convinced that violence was necessary in order to bring about the vision of a better future for all Muslims. These are the Salafi-jihadists who are responsible for the kinds of terrorist attacks we saw in the U.S. on September 11, 2001.

KEY IDEOLOGICAL INFLUENCES

From my perspective, there are at least seven key radical Islamist thinkers who reinterpreted traditionally accepted concepts of the faith, and who have authored the most significant works that still guide Salafi-jihadist groups today. I've already described Ibn

Taymiyya and Wahhab, two of the most popular sources of Islamist inspiration. The remaining five are Hassan al-Banna, an Egyptian teacher and founder of the Muslim Brotherhood; Sayyid Abul Ala Maududi, a Pakistani journalist and theological writer; Sayyid Qutb, an Egyptian and a civil servant at the famous Al-Azhar University; Abdullah Azzam, a Palestinian cleric who was instrumental in the Afghan jihad against the Soviets during the 1980s; and Ayman al-Zawahiri, a former leader of the Egyptian Islamic Jihad who joined Azzam and Osama bin Laden in Afghanistan during the late 1990s. Let's spend a few moments to look closely at what each one contributed to what we know today as the Salafi-jihadist ideology.

Hassan al-Banna was a former schoolteacher in Egypt who established the Muslim Brotherhood in 1928 as a response to what he saw as threats from both outside and within the Muslim world. Drawing on the earlier writings of Ibn Taymiyya, al-Banna redefined jihad as a God-ordained defensive requirement for all Muslims, as long as unbelievers still rule any Islamic lands. Al-Banna also argued that the greater jihad was not the internal spiritual struggle, but rather that it was the armed physical struggle against injustice and disbelief. His thoughts and writings on jihad are significant in that they helped to influence future

> **TO THE POINT**
>
> Al-Qaeda's ideology can be summed up in just four words: think globally, act locally.

Islamist radicals such as Qutb and Azzam. Because of his anti-regime views, al-Banna was eventually killed by the Egyptian government.

Sayyid Abul Ala Maududi was a journalist and prolific writer in Pakistan on issues of religion, politics, and law. He was also the founder and leader of Pakistan's Jemaat-e-Islami party, and following the end of the British colonial period, he became a significant voice in the negotiations to remake his nation into a true Islamic state after its partition from India in 1947. His ideas reached the Arabic speaking world in the 1950s and are known to have inspired Sayyid Qutb. Maududi advocated a kind of top-down reform in which truly devout Muslims gain power over key institutions through a political process and create a more just society ruled by Islamic law. Maududi also took a systematic approach to the topic of jihad as warfare, which should be conducted not only to expand Islamic political dominance, but also to establish just rule. For him, jihad was akin to a war of liberation that seeks to establish politically independent states. Through his popular writings, many in the Muslim world began to associate jihad with anti-colonialism and national liberation movements, and with the Palestinian resistance to Zionism and the creation of Israel.

Sayyid Qutb, a prominent Muslim Brotherhood member, has probably had a greater and more enduring effect on contemporary radical Islamist groups than any of the other men profiled in this lecture. He not only spent a large portion of his life in prison (where he wrote his popular book *Milestones*[2]), but the fact that he was executed for his views means that he is seen as a martyr in the eyes of Arab and Muslim revivalists.[3] *Milestones* is reportedly one of the most widely read books in the Muslim world besides the Quran and has become the ideological cornerstone of many Islamist reform movements. In the book, Qutb criticizes not only Western culture but also all Muslim societies where he described a loss of direction because the people are willfully ignorant of, and are not following, true Islam. He urged that Islamic societies be judged by how closely their leaders are adhering to the Shari`a, and those that are branded *kafir*, or apostate, must be forcefully replaced.

Qutb proposed a multistage process for reviving true Islam: First, a true Muslim movement would be formed, whose vanguard sounds the call to the community to return to sovereignty only under God and the Shari`a. Next, this group's message is ignored by the *jahili*, or ignorant, society and the government. Third, the movement then removes itself either spiritually or physically (or both) from the ignorant society in order to purify itself and to build up its strength. And the final stage is the movement's *jihad bil saif* (jihad by the sword) to overthrow the existing unbelieving regime and then restore justice and the practice of true Islam.

Qutb embraced Maududi's secular and nationalistic conception of jihad and its role in establishing a truly Islamic government, and he also incorporated Ibn Taymiyya's idea of jihad that includes the overthrow of regimes that fail to enforce the Shari`a. Because he advocated the use of violence to achieve political and societal change, Qutb was executed in 1966 by Nasser's

Figure 12.1: Sayyid Qutb in prison.

government in Egypt. However, he remains one of most enduring inspirations for most Sunni Islamist radical groups.

Then we have **Abdullah Azzam**, a Palestinian cleric who was inspired by both Maududi and Qutb, and wanted to organize a jihad of liberation against Israel. Some have called him the "Godfather of Jihad" because he tirelessly promoted Muslim global resistance to the Soviet Union's invasion and occupation of Afghanistan. Azzam was influenced by al-Banna's notion of jihad as required for all Muslims, and preached about an anti-Islam campaign being allegedly conducted by the Soviet Union, Israel, and the West. And also like al-Banna, he insisted that after devoting oneself to Islam, the second greatest obligation for Muslims was to wage jihad by force to defend the global *umma*.

Azzam is credited with establishing the training and support network for the foreign fighters in Afghanistan and Pakistan that eventually became al-Qaeda. He gave the Afghan conflict a religious justification and traveled widely to promote Muslim participation in the Afghan jihad. He also helped organize the Afghan resistance effort from a base in Pakistan, eventually forming a close working relationship with a wealthy Saudi dissident named Osama bin Laden. Azzam's books, *Defense of Muslim Lands* (1979) and *Join the Caravan* (1987), urged Muslims to come to Afghanistan and fight. He justified the jihad by claiming that all Muslim land that fell under infidel control had to be reclaimed. Notably, his books were publicly endorsed by Saudi Arabia's leading cleric, Sheikh Abdul Aziz bin Baz. Azzam is thought to have recruited a large number of Arab *mujahidin* (Islamic fighters) who, after receiving training and experience in Afghanistan, went on to engage in jihad in other parts of the world—places like Bosnia, Chechnya, Algeria, Morocco, and Indonesia. However, Azzam did not live long enough to mobilize these loose networks of jihadists to free Palestine from Israel's grip; in 1989, Azzam and his son were killed by a car bombing in Pakistan that has never been fully explained.

And next came **Ayman al-Zawahiri**, an Egyptian doctor and a leader of the Egyptian Islamic Jihad who was imprisoned and tortured by the government during the early 1980s after the assassination of Anwar Sadat.[4] After being released from prison, he made his way to Saudi Arabia, Sudan, Pakistan, and eventually Afghanistan, where he joined up with Osama bin Laden to form al-Qaeda. During these travels, al-Zawahiri wrote several articles and books in which he lamented the fall of the Ottoman Empire, arguing that the Ottomans had successfully defended the Muslim world for five centuries before the British-led Arab revolt against the Sultan during WWI. He also argued that the West was pursuing an agenda of intentionally marginalizing and weakening the Muslim world. In his book *Knights Under the Prophet's Banner*, al-Zawahiri wrote about the founding and development of a transnational Islamic extremist movement, something that dovetailed nicely with what Azzam and bin Laden had been developing in Afghanistan.[5] Al-Zawahiri suggested that the worldwide jihad should focus on small teams conducting suicide operations, and that a fundamentalist "base of operations" must be established in the Middle East to support and coordinate this campaign.

Al-Zawahiri agreed with the views of other Islamist thinkers that corrupt, apostate regimes in the Arab world needed to be overthrown, focusing the bulk of his terrorist efforts on overthrowing the Egyptian government. In time, however, he came to agree with bin Laden's argument that the "far enemy" (the West) must be hit first because the great oppressive powers would not allow the mujahidin to achieve power in their own societies. In 1998, al-Zawahiri was one of several senior Islamists who signed the so-called "Declaration of Jihad against the Jews and Crusaders" issued by al-Qaeda.[6]

Finally, in addition to these influential Islamist leaders, there are five other prominent figures in the recent history of Islamist ideologies who should at least be mentioned. Iran's **Ayatollah Ruholla Khomeini**, though he was a Shiite cleric, has been a significant inspiration to both Shiite and Sunni Muslim extremist groups, due to his successful creation of an Islamic theocracy as a result of the 1979 Islamic Revolution in Iran. Khomeini insisted that Muslims must resist the domination by and dependence on the decadent, infidel governments of the West and also, like Qutb, added to regional anti-Semitic sentiments by painting Jews and the West as enemies of the faith. **Muhammad Faraj** was the founder of the Egyptian Islamic Jihad, and was executed along with Anwar Sadat's killers following the Egyptian president's assassination in October 1981. Faraj authored "The Neglected Duty," a pamphlet that combined Qutb's ideas with Ibn Taymiyya's requirement to overthrow Muslim rulers who were un-Islamic.

Another significant author in the world of Salafi-jihadist terrorism is **Abu Bakr Naji**, whose *Management of Savagery* manuscript offers a variety of justifications for violence based on strict interpretations of the Quran and Hadith. He argued that violence acts are necessary to polarize the Muslim population, attract followers, and create an environment of chaos and savagery. This chaotic environment, in turn, offers the Salafi-jihadist vanguard an opportunity to gain local credibility by providing basic needs, maintaining order, and defending the *umma*. In essence, the successful "management of savagery" by a group like al-Qaeda or the Islamic State will then enable them to establish an Islamist caliphate.

Abu Musab al-Suri, born Mustafa Setmariam Nasar, is considered by many experts to be one of the most influential ideological and strategic thinkers related to the global Salafi-jihadist terrorism threat today. Al-Suri is a Syrian who speaks multiple languages and lived in several countries, including Spain and the U.K., before settling in Afghanistan in the late 1990s and joining al-Qaeda. A prolific writer, al-Suri built a reputation for his assistance with various jihadist media and propaganda efforts, but in 2000 he also gained prominence through a 20-hour video lecture series, released online, in which he argued that "individual terrorism" needed to replace the hierarchical, more traditional approach to terrorism that al-Qaeda had embraced thus far.[7] He envisioned a "mass participation jihadist movement" in which individuals would attack targets worldwide "where it hurts the enemy and costs him the most" and "where it awakens Muslims and revives the spirit of jihad and resistance."[8] Also, in December 2004, al-Suri published a 1,600-page book, *The Call for Global Islamic Resistance*, which became one of the most influential and widely circulated documents on jihadist web forums to date.

And finally, we must acknowledge the influence of an American cleric who was inspired by al-Suri and became a major creator and distributor of popular Salafi-jihadist propaganda: **Anwar al-Awlaki**. Born in New Mexico to Yemeni parents who were living in the United States (while his father was in graduate school), al-Awlaki lived roughly half his childhood in the U.S. and the other half in Yemen before studying education and religion at U.S. colleges and eventually becoming an imam of a mosque in San Diego during the late 1990s. He moved to Virginia in 2001, and then to the U.K. before eventually moving in 2004 to his ancestral homeland of Yemen, where he became a senior leader of the jihadist group al-Qaeda in the Arabian Peninsula. One of his most popular publications is the 21-page guide "44 Ways to Join the Jihad", in which he provides recommendations for individuals inspired to support the jihadist ideology—like how to raise funds for jihadist fighters, provide them with "moral support and encouragement," protect them, and contribute to their medical needs. But arguably his most important contribution to the spread of the Salafi-jihadist ideology has been the creation and dissemination of the popular online magazine *Inspire*, which I discussed in Lecture 7. Each issue of this English-language publication contains brief articles praising jihadist "heroes" along with ideological encouragement and useful operational instructions covering cybersecurity, personal fitness, and bomb-making. While he often cited the publications and lectures of al-Suri when encouraging followers to carry out individual "do-it-yourself" terrorist attacks, al-Awlaki added a unique, colloquial American flavor in his sermons, referencing pop culture and current events in a way that helped his messages resonate among a mainly Western audience. Despite his death in 2011, al-Awlaki's publications and his popular YouTube video sermons can still be found online, inspiring followers to carry out terrorist violence particularly against Western targets. According to several reports, al-Awlaki's sermons and other materials have been linked to over a hundred jihadist attacks and plots in the United States, and to many more around the world.

So, all together we have an emerging set of common themes and beliefs among a growing radical Islamist community, influenced significantly by the individuals I've just described. First, there is a sense of crisis about Muslim states' backwardness and apparent weaknesses, particularly when compared to the powerful West and its modernization; we see a historical pattern among these ideologues of victimization, blaming the problems faced in the Muslim world on others. We also see how the world is consistently described as a perpetual battlefield between faith and unbelief, a world in which there can be no coexistence or compromise. And finally, we have the notions of "vanguard" and self-motivated jihad—or what Marc Sageman has called a "leaderless jihad"[9]—in which members establish their own cells without linking up directly with the global Salafi-jihadist network, and carry out attacks in the name of the ideology.

THE GLOBAL SALAFI-JIHADIST IDEOLOGY TODAY

Each of the Islamist ideologues mentioned here describes their religion in terms of a revolutionary movement of "liberation," in which dramatic action is required to alter the unjust political, economic, and social status quo. They complain that because societies fear disorder and anarchy, they are willing to subject themselves to rule by authoritarian regimes and rulers who are corrupt and apostate: rulers who must therefore be overthrown. And overall, these Islamist ideologues argue that armed struggle is required until all lands are under Muslim control, and a global caliphate can be established in which the ideal society can be formed, governed only by Shari`a (Islamic law).[10]

Essentially, the groups and individuals who adhere to the global Salafi-jihadist ideology can be located within the broader Muslim world using the summary depicted in Table 12.1:

TABLE 12.1: Summary of Violent Jihadists' Connection to Islam

- **Islam**—A global religion of 1.8 billion people, with large concentrations in Southeast Asia, the Middle East, and North Africa. There are many divisions within, including Sunni, Shiite, Sufi, and Deobandi. There is considerable animosity between Sunni and Shia Muslims.
  - **Sunni** (roughly 85% of Muslims) follow the example of Muhammad and believe that the first four caliphs were legitimate rulers. Sunnis have no central religious organization or centers of authority.
  - **Shia** (roughly 15% of Muslims) believe that only the descendants and relatives of Muhammad are the legitimate rulers of all Muslims.
  - **Sufi** are mystics, found among both Sunni and Shiite Muslims, who seek to draw close to God through various rituals.
  - **Deobandi** is a popular revivalist movement among Sunni Muslims, particularly in Asia, that emphasizes scholastic traditions.
- **Islamism**: An ideological argument, supported by *some* Muslims, that politics and society must be organized according to Islamic doctrine.
  - **Salafism** is a Protestant-like fundamentalist version of Sunni Islamism that seeks to purify Islam from outside cultural influences. Salafists (also Wahhabists) want politics and society to be organized according to the ways in which the religions "forefathers" (*salaf*) lived, including the Prophet Muhammad and the first few generations of Muslims.
    - **Salafi-jihadism** is a subset of Salafism whose believers try to justify using violence to achieve the Salafist political agenda. Al-Qaeda, the Islamic State, and other terrorist groups support this Salafi-jihadist ideology.

This leads us to the specific ideology of promoting a global jihad.[11] Before the 9/11 attacks, Osama bin Laden had described al-Qaeda's goals, grievances, and tactics in detail in a series of statements and interviews. These statements provide insights into an ideology that may seem crazy to Americans, but it has been carefully crafted to appeal to the disgruntled and dispossessed of the Islamic world, and it is really more political than religious. At the heart of bin Laden's philosophy are two declarations of war against the United States. The first, in 1996, was directed at Americans occupying bin Laden's native Saudi Arabia; here he called upon Muslims all over the world to expel the infidels from his homeland. In his 1998 fatwa, which he issued along with the leaders of extremist groups in Egypt, Pakistan, and Bangladesh, bin Laden borrowed the ideas of Qutb, al-Banna, Faraj, and Azzam, and specified that the only appropriate response against the "crimes and sins" perpetrated by the United States against God and Muslims is a defensive struggle to repulse the aggressor; therefore, because it is defensive, such a war is a moral obligation incumbent upon all true Muslims. Although bin Laden's initial attacks against U.S. interests occurred in the Arabian Peninsula and East Africa, he had made it clear he would bring the war to the American homeland. Bin Laden told an ABC News reporter in May 1998 that the battle would inevitably move to American soil; however, al-Qaeda's targets would not be offending religious or cultural institutions, but rather symbolically important political, military, and economic targets.

The Salafi-jihadist ideology from which al-Qaeda, the Islamic State, and other groups have drawn support argues that Islam is the one and only way of ruling mankind that is acceptable to God. Pluralism, the idea that no one has a monopoly on truth, is a falsehood, and liberal democracy (rule by man's laws) is against God's will. In addition, Muslims should use force to establish a more just society—clearly a reference to Maududi's philosophy. Jihad is the only source of internal empowerment and reform in the Muslim world, and Muslims must resist the influences of Western institutions

Figure 12.2: Aftermath of September 11, 2001, attack on the Pentagon. U.S. Navy Photo by Photographer's Mate 2nd Class Lisa Borges.

and traditions that have poisoned mankind—arguments first made by Sayyid Qutb. And, they argue that there is a global conflict between Islam and the West. Islam is under siege and only we (the jihadis, the "pure" defenders of Islam) can lift it.

Today, the global Salafi-jihadist ideology can be summed up in just four words: **think globally, act locally**.[12] Their primary goal has always been to establish a base from which a global movement could be inspired and supported, a movement in which individuals anywhere in the world would carry out local acts of terrorism on behalf of the ideology. Plainly speaking, they argue that the world is messed up, and Islam is the only answer; therefore, "we the jihadists" (the self-appointed vanguard of the Muslim world) must do all that is necessary to tear down the existing order and replace it with one built on Islam. They seek to mobilize the entire Muslim community to join a global jihad, through which they can overthrow corrupt, incompetent "apostate" regimes in the Middle East and replace them with governments that rule by Shari`a (Islamic law). As bin Laden and al-Zawahiri have argued, doing this requires defeating the powerful Western patrons of these corrupt regimes, which is a core justification for attacking the United States and Western targets. Only after these corrupt regimes have been removed can they re-establish the Islamic caliphate to rule over the entire Muslim world. And from this perspective, they argue, the violence they inflict upon their own people, governments, and resources is (1) necessary, (2) religiously sanctioned, and (3) really the fault of the West, Israel, and apostate regimes.

> ## TO THE POINT
>
> Al-Qaeda's targets have typically been facilities of high economic, political and symbolic value.

So, to sum up, the ideology promoted by groups like al-Qaeda and the Islamic State is rooted in a much broader, conservative interpretation of Islam, but one that is not supported by many Muslims. The leaders of these Salafi-jihadist groups are engaged in a struggle for the hearts and minds of other Muslims; they see themselves as the vanguard of a global effort to establish Islam as the primary way of organizing political and social life worldwide. Their ideology, again, is all about thinking globally (in other words, envisioning changes on a global scale) and acting locally (using violent means to achieve these kinds of change). While members of the President Bush administration stated that the 9/11 attacks against the U.S. were carried out because "they hate us and our values," the deeper rationale behind the attacks is that we are seen as an obstacle in the way of achieving their long-term objectives of re-establishing an Islamist caliph-ate. Perhaps the most important takeaway from this discussion is that there is much more behind the violence than mere hatred; there are feelings of injustice, persecution, humiliation, and a thirst for revenge, even though in large measure the U.S. and the West really are not responsible for the current challenges faced by the Muslim world. Salafi-jihadist ideologues and strategists try very hard to justify their violent attacks by manipulating perceptions, as we have explored in previous lectures. But their ideology currently resonates among only a very small percentage of the Muslim world. In turn, this limited influence in the Muslim world is, in a way, a central reason why jihadists use terrorism in the first place.

EVOLUTION OF THE SALAFI-JIHADIST MOVEMENT

The first major group to promote this Islamist ideology was the Muslim Brotherhood, founded in 1928 by Hassan al-Banna. He and his colleagues felt that the Muslim world was increasingly threatened by Western culture, values, and policies. In response, they called for Muslims to rise up and defend the purity of their faith. Increasingly, Muslim Brotherhood leaders also argued that an armed physical struggle was necessary to over-throw governments responsible for the injustice and corruption that were contributing to the decay of the Muslim world. Because of the situation in Egypt during the 1930s and 1940s—including a significant British military presence—the Muslim Brother-hood gathered a large following, including some members of the Egyptian govern-ment. They established a network of schools and social gatherings, at which the central message was always "Islam is the answer" (thus the term "Islamist"). When World War II was fought on Egyptian soil, members of the Brotherhood protested the presence of alcohol, drugs, and prostitution that accompanied Western troops.

In 1948, Mahmud Fahmi al-Nuqrashi—a secular-minded Egyptian prime minister—banned the Muslim Brotherhood for its increasingly anti-government pro-tests, and shortly afterward he was assassinated. Egyptian authorities responded by killing Hassan al-Banna and several of his associates, sparking a brief Islamist armed uprising that was brutally suppressed. And yet, the Muslim Brotherhood continued to grow into a powerful political force, organizing protests and promoting its Islamist vision of governance. The Muslim Brotherhood also helped establish and nurture a vari-ety of groups throughout the Middle East and North Africa, from Morocco to Syria. In many cases, these groups initially built up popular support through educational programs, social services, and political activism. Mostly, these affiliate groups were concerned with local conditions, but through them, the Muslim Brotherhood was able to establish a transnational network that exists today.

For example, the Syrian branch of the Muslim Brotherhood rose in prominence during the 1960s and 1970s by portraying itself as representing the interests of the Sunni majority population (over two-thirds of the Syrian population is Sunni Muslim, but the country has been governed for nearly half a century by a Shia Alawite minority sect, led by President al-Assad). Some members of the Syrian Muslim Brotherhood decided that more direct action was needed to achieve the overall goals of establishing a system of Islamist governance, and led by Marwan Hadid, they founded a new militant group known as the Fighting Vanguard. After a few small-scale terrorist attacks, Hadid was arrested and later died in a military hospital. His replacement as leader of the Vanguard, Adnan Aqla, then launched a series of attacks against Syrian government targets as well as against Alawite community members throughout the country. In 1980, an Islamist uprising in the city of Hama led to a brutal government response in which thousands were killed, and shortly afterward the government passed a law banning the Muslim Brotherhood, and made membership in the organization punishable by death.

In Algeria, an Islamic political movement that began in the late 1970s led to the founding of the Islamic Salvation Front (FIS), a political party that attracted an increasingly large segment of the population throughout the 1980s. When polls seemed to indicate that FIS would win the 1992 national elections, the military government in Algeria annulled the election, sparking a bloody civil war. Several new Islamist militant groups emerged, including the Islamic Salvation Army and the Armed Islamic Group, leading to a flurry of attacks against members of the military and the government, as well as against foreigners. The overall goal of these groups was to undermine the perceived legitimacy of the Algerian government, creating an opportunity for the Islamist political organizations to seize power. The Islamists also wanted to make the situation intolerable for foreigners living in Algeria, believing that a massive flight of foreign capital would eventually lead to the collapse of economic stability, further eroding the Algerian government's ability to function.

Meanwhile, in the Palestinian Territories, decades of terrorist attacks by the mainly secular Palestinian Liberation Organization (and its various factions, including Fatah and the Popular Front for the Liberation of Palestine) had produced no beneficial outcomes in their struggle against the state of Israel. A growing dissatisfaction among the Palestinians led to the emergence of several Islamist groups, beginning in the 1970s.

The first of these was the Palestinian Islamic Jihad (PIJ), originally established in Egypt by Fathi Shaqaqi and Abd al-Aziz Awda. They argued that God would help truly faithful, devout Muslims defeat Israel. In July 1989, PIJ became the first Palestinian group to take responsibility for a suicide terrorist attack, when a member of the group seized the steering wheel of a crowded commuter bus and forced it over a steep cliff into a ravine, killing 16 passengers. However, while the PIJ eventually took responsibility for a series of suicide bombings, it was soon eclipsed by a different Islamist group that rose to prominence during this period: Hamas.

During the 1960s, Sheikh Ahmed Yassin founded a Palestinian branch of the Muslim Brotherhood, which focused mainly on preaching and performing charitable work in the West Bank and Gaza Strip. As a result, he and his close followers had developed deep roots and significant credibility among the Palestinian communities when they announced the establishment of Hamas, an acronym for *Harakat al-Muqawama al-Islamiyya* (Islamic Resistance Movement), in December 1987. The group's charter called for the destruction of Israel and the establishment of an Islamist government in the Palestinian Territories, and also called on Muslim clerics to help encourage the population to coordinate demonstrations, boycotts, and other political protest activities. Hamas also established a militant wing—the Izz al-Din al-Qassan Brigades—which carried out a series of terrorist attacks, including a campaign of suicide bombings that began in 1993.

By the late 1970s, dozens of locally-focused Islamist groups had emerged around the world, from the Moro Islamic Liberation Front in the Philippines to the Pakistani-based Lashkar-e-Taiba, to the Moroccan Islamic Combatant Group. For the most part, the central goal pursued by each of these groups has been to replace a secular government with a system of Islamist governance. Sometimes, members of different groups would collaborate on something specific (like an arms smuggling transaction), but for the most part there was no unifying network of Islamists during this period, nor any attempt to bring Islamists worldwide together as part of a global movement. This changed with the rise of al-Qaeda during the late 1980s.

A BRIEF HISTORY OF AL-QAEDA

You probably already know the basic timeline of how all this got started, but let's just review some of the most important points.[13] First, in 1979, the Soviet Union invaded Afghanistan (primarily to prop up a communist government in that country), and

Islamist extremists from the Middle East, North Africa, and Southeast Asia raised a call for jihad to expel this "infidel" invader from a Muslim country, a call to which thousands responded. Of course, Saudi Arabia and other governments were only too willing to see these radicals go abroad, instead of them causing trouble at home, and sometimes they even funded their trips, probably hoping that they would not make it back. Islamic charities were also a very important source of funding. And it's well known that the CIA and Pakistan's intelligence agency (the ISI) encouraged, armed, and trained some of these foreign jihadists, along with the Afghan mujahidin who were already fighting the Soviets there.

A young, wealthy Saudi named Osama bin Laden was among those who traveled to Afghanistan in pursuit of jihad. He had been inspired to do so by a charismatic Palestinian cleric named Abdullah Azzam, who traveled widely to promote Muslim participation in the Afghan jihad and had recently visited Saudi Arabia. Azzam also established a training and support network for foreign fighters, called the Mujahidin Services Bureau, and helped to organize the Afghan resistance effort locally, bringing together various armed militia leaders to discuss strategy and doctrines. Bin Laden used his personal wealth (and his connections to other wealthy donors) to support Azzam's work. He also had some limited battlefield experiences, but a myth soon developed that portrayed him as a charismatic and effective military leader.

In 1989, the Soviets pulled out, and shortly afterward the Soviet Union fell apart. The mujahidin declared victory, and the Arab foreign fighters took far more credit than they truthfully should have for the defeat of the Soviets. Azzam, bin Laden, and their colleagues became convinced of the superiority of Islamist guerilla fighters against a superpower, and this conviction led them to establish "al-Qaeda" (Arabic for "the Base"), to serve as a central hub of support for launching a jihad against apostate regimes and other perceived enemies of the Muslim world (eventually including their Western supporters like the United States). Azzam's long-term personal goal was to put together a global Muslim resistance movement to free Palestinians from Israel, though bin Laden had much loftier goals of launching a global jihad.

Later that year, however, Azzam and his son were killed in a mysterious car bomb in Pakistan, and bin Laden assumed full control over al-Qaeda. A couple years later bin Laden moved to Sudan, establishing a collection of training camps and legitimate businesses, while also providing some financial support to the country's leader Hasan al-Turabi. The following year, in 1992, al-Qaeda operatives were caught at an airport in Aden, Yemen, preparing to launch rockets at U.S. military planes. This is the first known attempt by al-Qaeda operatives to attack U.S. targets.[14]

On February 26, 1993, a truck bomb exploded in the parking garage of the World Trade Center towers in New York City, killing six and injuring over a thousand.[15] The leader of the Islamist cell responsible for this attack was Ramzi Yousef, a Pakistani who grew up in Kuwait and England, and was a follower of a New York-based radical cleric named Sheikh Omar Abdel al-Rahman (also known as the "Blind Sheikh"), who had been expelled from Egypt for preaching an extreme Islamist ideology. Yousef was also the nephew of Khalid Sheikh Muhammad, another Egyptian who later became the architect of the 9/11 attacks. According to court testimony, the plan for this attack in 1993 was to cripple the support beams of the corner of the north tower so it would topple over and knock the south tower down at the same time.[16]

Later in 1993, a special unit of the U.S. military on a peacekeeping mission came under heavy fire in Mogadishu, Somalia, killing 18 servicemen. This event, which was later made into a book and a movie called *Black Hawk Down*, prompted President Clinton to withdraw all U.S. forces from the country. A few years later, Osama bin Laden took credit for helping to train Somali militants (though whether or not this is true is widely debated). He also celebrated the withdrawal of U.S. forces from Somalia as a victory for al-Qaeda and for the Islamic world. As we've discussed earlier in these lectures, perceptions matter tremendously in the world of terrorism, and an ideology (or in this case, a claim for which no evidence has ever been found) does not necessarily have to be true to be believed. This also highlights the important role that bin Laden's audio and video tapes have had in the evolution of al-Qaeda over the past three decades.

In 1994, the Saudi government stripped bin Laden of his citizenship because of "his irresponsible behavior that contradicts the interests of Saudi Arabia and harms sisterly countries."[17] Meanwhile, Ramzi Yousef had relocated to the Philippines and was hatching various plots, including one to assassinate the pope, and another to assassinate President Clinton during a visit to Manila.[18] In late 1994, Yousef collaborated with his uncle Khalid Sheikh Muhammad to develop what became known as *Oplan Bojinka*, an effort to blow up 10 airliners en route to the United States from Southeast Asia using explosives smuggled in children's toys.[19] In preparation for this attack, he planted a small bomb aboard a plane bound for Tokyo that killed a Japanese businessman but did not destroy the plane. In January the following year, a fire broke out in Yousef's apartment in Manila, and he was forced to abandon his plan and fled to

Pakistan, where he was eventually captured and brought back to the United States to face trial.

In May 1996, Sudan—under pressure by the governments of Saudi Arabia, Egypt, the United States, and others—ordered bin Laden to leave the country. He returned to Afghanistan, along with a number of followers and family members, and began establishing new training camps there under the protection of the Taliban regime. In August of that year, Osama bin Laden issued a "Declaration of War Against the Americans Occupying the Land of the Two Holy Places."[20] He was quite angry at the continued presence of U.S. forces in Saudi Arabia, placed there by request of the Saudi government as a security measure against Saddam Hussein's regime in Iraq following the 1991 Gulf War. Bin Laden warned that these "crusader forces" in Saudi Arabia would become a beachhead to impose a new imperialism on the region and steal oil from the Muslim world. He portrayed the United States as an invading enemy, and declared it a duty of all Muslims to resist and expel it from the Middle East. In 1997, bin Laden gave a rare interview to CNN in which he said that the United States must pay for its support of Israel. He applauded the 1996 attack against U.S. military personnel at the Khobar Towers residence facility in Saudi Arabia, noting, "Only Americans were killed in the explosions. No Saudi suffered any injury."[21]

Meanwhile, the Egyptian Islamic Jihad, led by Ayman al-Zawahiri, had been coming under increasing pressure from the government following a series of assassination attempts against Hosni Mubarak, and several leaders fled the country. Al-Zawahiri traveled to various parts of Europe before eventually making his way to Afghanistan, and in 1998 he merged the remnants of his jihadist group with al-Qaeda (along with a few others) to establish what formally became known as the International Front for Fighting Jews and Crusaders (though everyone refers to them as al-Qaeda).[22] This new organization then issued a second fatwa, in which bin Laden declared it was a duty of all Muslims to kill Americans anytime, anywhere. In a subsequent statement, bin Laden also reiterated his intention that al-Qaeda was not meant to be a global organization, but rather a base of support and guidance for motivated believers. Al-Zawahiri also took the post as second in command of al-Qaeda. Shortly afterward, in August 1998, the U.S. embassies in Tanzania and Kenya were attacked, nearly simultaneously, killing over 200 people from several countries and injuring over 5,000.[23]

The end of 1999 saw the disruption of a few al-Qaeda–related millennium plots. In mid-December, Jordanian authorities arrested more than 20 alleged al-Qaeda operatives who were planning to bomb three locations where American tourists gather: Mt.

Nebo, where Moses first saw the Promised Land; the Ramada Hotel in Amman, a stopover for tour groups; and the spot on the Jordan River where tradition holds John the Baptist baptized Christ.

Meanwhile, on the other side of the world, U.S. border control authorities at Port Angeles (northwest of Seattle) disrupted a plot to bomb Los Angeles International Airport.[24] In December 1999, an Algerian named Ahmed Ressam was trying to cross by ferry from Canada to the United States. An alert border guard noticed him acting strangely and nervously, so she confronted him and asked to see identification and to search the trunk of his car, which she then discovered was full of bomb-making equipment, cash, and weapons. Ressam was immediately arrested, and he eventually admitted to authorities that he had been planning to blow up the airport in the name of al-Qaeda. Ressam had belonged to Algeria's Armed Islamic Group before being recruited to al-Qaeda. He had traveled to Afghanistan, where he received some basic terrorist training, and then was given nonspecific, virtually open-ended targeting instructions before flying to Montreal. He was given $12,000 in "seed money" and instructed to raise the rest of his operational funds from petty crime. He was also instructed to recruit members for his terrorist cell from among the expatriate Muslim communities in Canada and the United States. (As an aside, this case serves as a great example of the nexus between criminal and terrorist activity, the role of diaspora communities, and the importance of training provided by al-Qaeda in its Afghanistan safe haven.[25])

Back to our history lesson. Attacks against U.S. targets continued into the new millennium, beginning in January 2000 with an attempt against a U.S. naval destroyer called the *USS The Sullivans* (named after five brothers from the same family who were all killed on the same ship during WWII). In this instance, the al-Qaeda operatives loaded up a small Zodiac powerboat with explosives and headed across the Port of Aden in Yemen toward the ship on what was meant to be a suicide bombing mission. However, they put too much weight in the front, and the boat sank almost immediately. So, they swam back to shore, got some friends, pulled the boat out of the water, and loaded up everything into a truck. Nobody reported anything to the authorities. The same boat, most of the same explosives, and the same suicide bombers were used again in October 2000 in an attack against the *USS Cole*, which was refueling in the Port of Aden. This time, the operatives pulled the boat almost right next to the ship, detonated their explosives, and killed 17 U.S. sailors.[26]

One of the interesting points to note here is that the tactic of suicide boat bombs was actually pioneered years earlier by the Tamil Tigers in Sri Lanka, who attacked

various military and commercial ships throughout the late 1990s. Al-Qaeda operatives also used this tactic for a 2002 attack against the French tanker *MV Limburg* in
the Persian Gulf. This demonstrates the organizational learning aspect of sophisticated
terrorist organizations, which we'll examine in Lecture 13. Those we fear most are able
and willing to learn from others regardless of ideology or geography. Further, they
learn from their failures—in this case, figuring out what they did wrong in their first
attempt, fixing it, and then succeeding the next time around.[27]

And then, in September 2001, we all know what happened. If you have not read
the official 9/11 Commission Report, I strongly encourage it.[28] Also, National Geographic produced an excellent four-hour documentary on what happened that day,
and the events that led up to the worst terrorist attack in U.S. history.[29] We may never
know if bin Laden knew what forces he was going to unleash against him by carrying
out this attack, or if he underestimated America's response. In several of his statements
about the attacks of 9/11, bin Laden refers to the United States as a paper tiger, noting that when America was attacked in Beirut, the United States sent its troops home.
When we were attacked in Somalia, we pulled our troops out. His argument was that if
al-Qaeda inflicted enough pain and suffering, Americans will abandon their support of
regimes in Israel, Egypt, Saudi Arabia, and so forth, which (as described earlier) would
then create an opportunity to begin establishing a global caliphate.

Later in 2001, passengers and crew of an American Airlines flight from Paris to
Miami subdued Richard Reid after he attempted to light a bomb hidden inside his
shoe. Of course, this led to the Transportation Security Administration (TSA) requirements that we all have to remove our shoes and put them through a scanner at airports in the United States. In January 2002, al-Qaeda militants released a video which
showed the beheading of *Wall Street Journal* reporter Daniel Pearl, who had traveled
to Pakistan to conduct a prearranged interview. In June 2002, a suicide bomb attack
at the U.S. Consulate in Karachi killed 11 locals, and in October of that year, a U.S.
Agency for International Development (USAID) worker named Laurence Foley was
killed by al-Qaeda operatives outside his residence in Amman, Jordan.

In 2003, the United States led a coalition of forces in an invasion of Iraq to oust the
regime of Saddam Hussein. While several Sunni and Shiite militant groups eventually
formed to conduct insurgent attacks against these forces (and against each other), one
of the most lethal was known as al-Tawhid wal-Jihad, led by Abu Musab al-Zarqawi,
a Jordanian who had trained in an al-Qaeda camp in Afghanistan. In late 2004, he
pledged his loyalty to Osama bin Laden, renamed his group al-Qaeda in Iraq, and
orchestrated a campaign of suicide bombings throughout the country.

During the next couple of years, there were also dozens of al-Qaeda linked attacks all around the world: from hotels in Indonesia, to banks in Turkey, to train stations in Spain. Some of the targets (but not a majority) were U.S.-related, such as the Marriott hotel in Jakarta. Beheadings were videotaped and published on the Internet by Zarqawi's terrorist cell in Iraq, and these actions were mimicked by terrorists in other countries, including Saudi Arabia. In October 2004, four days before the presidential election in the United States, the Arabic satellite TV network Al Jazeera aired a video in which Osama bin Laden threatened fresh attacks on the U.S., noting that the reasons behind the events of 9/11 still existed. In a statement later that year, al-Qaeda claimed responsibility for an attack on the U.S. Consulate in Jiddah, Saudi Arabia, that left five employees dead.

In 2005, al-Qaeda operatives bombed three American-owned hotels in Amman, Jordan, one of which killed several local attendees at a wedding party, producing some bad publicity for al-Qaeda throughout the Muslim world. Curiously, in January 2006 Osama bin Laden offered the United States a "long term truce" through an audio tape aired by Al Jazeera—an offer that, naturally, the United States rejected. But bin Laden also warned that new attacks on the United States were being planned. In June 2006, Abu Musab al-Zarqawi was killed by U.S. forces in an air strike. But the most dramatic event of that year was the disruption by Pakistani, British, and U.S. authorities of a plot that could have caused more deaths than the attacks of 9/11. Here, al-Qaeda operatives intended to smuggle liquid explosives (disguised as energy drinks) onto flights bound for Canada and the United States. Once over the Atlantic Ocean, the operatives were going to mix the explosives and then ignite them using an electrical charge from the flash bulb of a disposable camera.

Their plan was to simultaneously bomb at least 10 U.S. and Canadian airliners while en route from London to the U.S. and Canada. Some reports indicate they hoped to have enough operatives and explosives to attack 17 planes. This plot was clearly based on Ramzi Yousef's design of *Oplan Bojinka*. The plot was only uncovered after Pakistani authorities arrested some individuals on weapons and drug smuggling charges, and under interrogation two of these individuals provided details about the airplane plot. The Pakistanis contacted the Brits, who then contacted the Americans, and together they identified and rounded up dozens of suspects—most of whom were British Muslims. One of the most interesting aspects of this plot was that it was not directed against more vulnerable targets like metros or commuter trains, hotels and tourist destinations, but against arguably the most internationally hardened target set since 9/11: commercial aviation. This raises questions about whether we truly appreciate al-Qaeda's ability to adapt to counterterrorism and security measures.

During their investigation, British authorities found martyrdom tapes made by at least six of the perpetrators. In these tapes, the operatives reiterate the usual sort of al-Qaeda propaganda about defending the Muslim world from the evil West and the United States, and talk about their desire for revenge and retaliation for all the suffering the United States has caused in the Muslim world. Echoing the 1998 fatwa issued by bin Laden, which calls upon Muslims to kill Americans anywhere, anytime, these operatives declare that there are no innocents in this struggle against evil.

Since this plot was thwarted in 2006, there have been no uncovered plots of this magnitude (at least, nothing that has been acknowledged in public), involving multiple simultaneous targets—a favored modus operandi of al-Qaeda. However, there have been an increasing number of attempted smaller scale attacks against the U.S. and its allies over the past decade, including plots involving aviation targets, which I'll discuss in a moment. But first, an important point to make here is that for the first 10 to 15 years of its existence, the primary threat posed by al-Qaeda originated from a core group of senior members hiding out in caves along the Afghanistan-Pakistan border region. Today, however, the threat is much more likely to come from al-Qaeda affiliate groups in Yemen or North Africa, or from individual citizens—including in Western countries—who are inspired by the Salafi-jihadist ideology.[30]

THE MODERN EVOLUTION OF AL-QAEDA

Al-Qaeda is thus understood as both a centralized group (with affiliate relationships) as well as a movement of loosely connected individuals. The evolution in structure and scope of al-Qaeda over the past three decades has produced a global dispersion of knowledge and capabilities. For example, when foreigners who were fighting in Iraq against coalition forces began leaving to join the fight in Afghanistan, they brought with them tactics and strategies learned in Iraq, which explains to some degree the rise of suicide bombings and new kinds of roadside improvised explosive devices (IEDs) in Afghanistan over the last several years. Further, a growing number of fighters left Iraq and Afghanistan and traveled to Yemen, where a full-blown insurgency is still underway. Here, they are likely to join up with perhaps the most active al-Qaeda affiliate group today, which calls itself al-Qaeda in the Arabian Peninsula. Of course, they could also travel to several other countries where we find affiliate groups, like Algeria and Mali, where al-Qaeda in the Islamic Maghreb is carrying out terrorist attacks; or

Indonesia, where the group Jemmah Islamiyyah has claimed its support for al-Qaeda; or Somalia, where the Islamist militant group al-Shabaab has declared itself an affiliate of al-Qaeda; or most prominently these days, Syria, where several groups are linked to al-Qaeda.

Affiliate groups like these have been responsible for many more terrorist attacks than the original core group of al-Qaeda leaders. This is in part because of the concerted effort by U.S. government and its allies to disrupt and defeat that core group of al-Qaeda that was responsible for the 1998 embassy bombings, the *USS Cole* attack, and of course the 9/11 attacks. In the most notable event of this effort, on May 1, 2011, after nearly fifteen years of trying to locate and capture him, Osama bin Laden was killed in a raid by a U.S. Navy Seal team. As President Obama said in his speech to the nation, "[W]e went to war against al-Qaeda, to protect our citizens, our friends, and our allies. . . . For over two decades, bin Laden has been al-Qaeda's leader and symbol and has continued to plot attacks against our country and our friends and allies. The death of bin Laden marks the most significant achievement to date in our nation's effort to defeat al-Qaeda."[31]

However, as President Obama noted, "his death does not mark the end of our effort. There's no doubt that al-Qaeda will continue to pursue attacks against us."[32] This reflects a stark reality about al-Qaeda today—it has evolved from a centralized entity into a global network of affiliates and individuals who are basically just people who believe in the need for violent action, but are not really members of any formally recognized group. These disparate entities reflect the complex, multifaceted terrain of the global Salafi-jihadist movement that exists today.

Al-Qaeda's core leaders are interested in supporting and maintaining relationships with affiliate groups for several reasons. First, their hope is that over time these geographically scattered, disparate entities will one day coalesce into a single, unstoppable force. Second, the terrorist activities carried out by these groups is often attributed in the media and by government leaders as having something to do with al-Qaeda, and this in turn gives al-Qaeda a much-needed perception of having a global presence and influence, which they can use to attract new recruits. And at the same time, there are basic operational reasons for maintaining affiliate relationships. For example, members of these affiliate groups could carry out attacks at al-Qaeda's behest, or provide essential local, logistical and other support to other affiliates within the movement when necessary. For their part, these affiliate groups benefit in several ways from becoming affiliated with al-Qaeda. First, they can gain some amount of legitimacy within the global Salafi-jihad movement. This can open the doors to new kinds of logistical support and other opportunities, and can also help attract new recruits from throughout their areas of operation. They may be provided support for their operations from within the al-Qaeda network. Further, members of these affiliate groups might raise their personal stature and prestige by being seen as close associates of al-Qaeda's leaders, as these individuals are revered among many in the world of Salafi-jihadist extremism.

While al-Qaeda affiliates in Yemen and Mali have been significantly active in recent years, arguably the most worrisome events have recently taken place in Syria, where various jihadist groups have joined the ongoing civil war against the Bashar al-Assad regime. The most active group aligned with al-Qaeda is called Hayat Tahrir al-Sham (formerly known as "Jabhat Fateh al-Sham" "Jabhat al-Nusra" or "al-Nusra Front"), and some of its leaders received training in Afghanistan during the previous decade. In addition to fighting Syrian government forces, this group has also been engaged in a struggle for power and influence against another jihadist group calling itself the Islamic State, which we'll discuss below.

But the most pressing threat we face today is arguably the "inspired Salafi-jihadists," primarily homegrown Islamic radicals whose families are sometimes (but not always) originally from North Africa, the Middle East, and South and Southeast Asia. They also include local converts to Islam mostly living in Europe, Africa, and perhaps Latin America and North America. The one thing they all have in common that places them in this category is that they have had no direct connection with al-Qaeda (or any other identifiable terrorist group), and yet are prepared to carry out attacks in solidarity with or without support of al-Qaeda's radical jihadi agenda. This is perhaps where the ideology described early in this lecture has its greatest impact, in motivating these kinds of individuals who develop a sense of enmity and grievance toward the United States and the West.

Individuals in this category are described as having a relationship with al-Qaeda that is *more inspirational than actual*, fueled by profound rage over foreign events, such as U.S. troops in a Muslim country and the perceived oppression of Muslims in Palestine, Kashmir, Chechnya, and elsewhere. These are often small collections of like-minded locals who gravitate toward one leader to plan and mount terrorist attacks completely independent of any direction provided by al-Qaeda. Examples include the group of jihadists responsible for the 2004 attack against commuter trains in Madrid,[33] and the four young men who carried out the 2005 suicide bombing attack in London.[34] Other examples of the al-Qaeda-inspired cells or individuals include the so-called Hofstad Group in the Netherlands, whose member Mohammed Bouyeri murdered the Dutch filmmaker Theo van Gogh in Amsterdam in November 2004, and the so-called "trolley bombers"—the two Lebanese nationals who in July 2006 placed bombs (that failed to explode) on two German commuter trains near Dortmund and Koblenz. And of course, the 2013 bombing of the Boston Marathon by two brothers highlighted the impact of al-Qaeda's online propaganda (particular its magazine *Inspire,* discussed in Lecture 7). However, individuals in this category are neither directly members of a known, organized terrorist group, nor necessarily even a very cohesive entity unto themselves.

There have been only a small handful of cases where an individual terrorist did have some kind of connection to an al-Qaeda affiliate group. For example, a young Nigerian named Umar Farouk Abdulmutallab was radicalized mainly by what he found on the Internet, but he may have received his training and the explosives for his December 2009 attempted attack in Yemen by members of the group al-Qaeda in the Arabian Peninsula. As another example, several Somali-Americans, including a group of young men from Minneapolis, have been radicalized and recruited by the group al-Shabaab, which declared itself an affiliate of al-Qaeda. In mid-September 2009, a naturalized U.S. citizen of Afghan heritage named Najibullah Zazi was arrested during the last stages of a plot to bomb the New York subway system. And in April 2010, Faisal Shahzad—a U.S. citizen born in Pakistan but who lived for many years in Connecticut—tried to detonate his SUV in New York City's Times Square. Officials believe he may have been trained for this attack by members of an al-Qaeda affiliate group calling itself the Pakistani Taliban.

Overall, there has been an increase since 2001 in the cases of domestic radicalization and recruitment to jihadist terrorism occurring in the United States. Most of these so-called aspirational terrorists had limited skills or experience with weapons, criminal activity, or violence, which is probably a big reason why their attacks failed. But of course, what keeps intelligence and law enforcement leaders up late at night is the worry that someone else, a U.S. citizen radicalized by the Salafi-jihad ideology, will get lucky one day. This is what al-Qaeda wants most—individuals who embrace a "do it yourself" model of terrorism inspired by the "think global, act local" ideology of the global jihadist movement. We will cover this topic much more in Lecture 15.

THE ISLAMIC STATE

Finally, the most recent major development in the global Salafi-jihadist movement has been the rise and fall of the so-called Islamic State, currently led by Abu Bakr al-Baghdadi. The origins of this group can be traced to 2002, when it was called Jama`at al-Tawhid wa`al Jihad, and was led by a Jordanian militant named Abu Musab al-Zarqawi.[35] After murdering USAID officer Laurence Foley, the group moved into Iraq following the 2003 U.S. invasion and began attacking coalition forces and transitional Iraqi government targets. In October 2004, following a series of high profile kidnappings and suicide bombings, Zarqawi pledged his group's allegiance to Osama bin Laden and renamed his group al-Qaeda in Iraq (AQI). His group became increasingly notorious for its violent brutality and attacks against civilians at Shiite mosques and other religious sites, as well as a bombing at a hotel in Amman, Jordan. Retaliatory strikes against Sunni mosques in Baghdad and elsewhere escalated into a nationwide cycle of sectarian violence that continued even after Zarqawi was killed in a 2006 American airstrike.

His successor as AQI leader, Abu Ayub al-Masri, was an Egyptian bomb maker who had trained in Afghanistan and shared Zarqawi's commitment to provoking sectarian violence between Shiite and Sunni communities throughout Iraq.[36] However, an organized resistance began to emerge, eventually forming into what became known as the Anbar Awakening—a collection of powerful Sunni tribes that cooperated with U.S. and coalition forces in tracking down and eliminating AQI cells. Al-Masri tried to rebrand his group as more distinctly pro-Iraq by announcing the establishment of the Islamic State of Iraq (ISI), and naming an Iraqi, Abu Umar al-Baghdadi, as its leader. However, both al-Masri and al-Baghdadi were killed in April 2010, and a new leader—Abu Bakr al-Baghdadi—took control of the group's remnants. Then in 2011, coalition forces withdrew from Iraq, providing an opportunity for ISI to re-establish its logistics and recruitment efforts.

During this time, the Shiite-dominated central government of Iraq initiated several policies that alienated the country's Sunni minority. As a result, some disenchanted and angry young Iraqis joined ISI, and Sunni attacks against Shiite targets increased rapidly through 2012 and 2013. Meanwhile, the civil war in neighboring Syria offered al-Baghdadi a useful training ground for new recruits, and in 2013 he renamed his group Islamist State in Iraq and Syria (ISIS) as a reflection of their presence in both countries (note that some have translated the group's official Arabic name as Islamic State in Iraq and the Levant, or ISIL). A dispute with al-Qaeda's affiliate group in Syria (known then as Jabhat al-Nusra) led to a public rebuke of ISIS by Ayman al-Zawahiri, and in February 2014 al-Qaeda officially renounced any connection with ISIS.

Early in 2014, ISIS began capturing significant amounts of territory, including the Iraqi cities of Fallujah, Mosul, and Tikrit. The oil production facilities within these territories helped generate billions of dollars in revenue for ISIS, which it used to provide services to the people living in the regions under their control. On June 29, 2014 the group changed its name again, this time to "Islamic State," and declared the establishment of an Islamist caliphate, with al-Baghdadi as the new caliph (leader of all Muslims worldwide).[37] They called for all Muslims to declare allegiance to al-Baghdadi and encouraged them to come defend the Islamic State's territories in Iraq and Syria. By some estimates, tens of thousands of young Muslims from all over the world responded to this appeal, often making their way into Syria through the Turkish border. Obviously, al-Zawahiri did not take kindly to al-Baghdadi's attempt to displace him and al-Qaeda as the leading vanguard of the global Salafi-jihadist movement. The publicly expressed acrimony between al-Qaeda and the Islamic State over the past few years reflects the fact that the two groups are seen primarily as peer competitors; thus it is unlikely we will see any kind of unity or collaboration between them in the near future.

The good news is that since early 2016, military forces in Iraq and Syria (backed by numerous other countries, including Russia, Turkey, and the U.S.) have turned the tide against the Islamic State. As of late 2017, the group has lost almost all of the territory and resources it once controlled, and thousands of fighters have died, been captured and imprisoned, or fled to neighboring countries. However, the bad news is that in some cases these former fighters of Islamic State have managed to return to their home countries, bringing with them a range of skills and network connections useful for planning and executing terrorist attacks. Recent incidents in France, Belgium, Sweden, and the U.K. are considered by some experts as an indication of the kinds of terrorism we should expect in the future as a result of this process.

Further, over the last several years, the Islamic State has established a network of affiliates (called *wilayat*) in various corners of the world, from the Philippines to Nigeria. In some cases, a group that had originally declared its allegiance to al-Qaeda has switched and proclaimed its loyalty (*bayat*) to the Islamic State. These affiliates offer a range of opportunities for Islamic State veterans to continue their efforts to plan and carry out terrorist attacks in pursuit of the broader political goal of establishing an Islamic caliphate. Unfortunately, while the centrally-organized entity known as the Islamic State may be defeated soon, the inspired, loosely-connected network of affiliates and individuals that the group has nurtured will endure for at least a while longer.

SUMMARY

So, to sum up this brief history of the global Salafi-jihadist movement, there have been a variety of Islamist groups throughout the past century, though most of them have focused exclusively on a local political agenda. Al-Qaeda and the Islamic State have been exceptions in terms of pursuing a more global vision of establishing a transnational caliphate. We have seen al-Qaeda evolve from a small, centralized entity headquartered in Afghanistan into a global movement in which affiliates and individuals play an increasingly prominent role. We have also seen an increase in affiliates and alliances in which al-Qaeda co-opts a group's ideology, rebranding their local grievances as part of a global struggle. Both al-Qaeda and these local affiliate groups benefit from such relationships, although there are some risks involved—not the least of which is that the more affiliates al-Qaeda has, the broader the potential for infiltration by a country's intelligence services that could undermine the operational security of the whole movement. But through groups like al-Qaeda in the Islamic Maghreb, al-Qaeda in the Arabian Peninsula, al-Qaeda in Iraq, and al-Shabaab, we have seen an evolution of al-Qaeda toward multipolarity. Fifteen years ago, al-Qaeda's presence was primarily limited to the tribal region of eastern Afghanistan and western Pakistan. Today, there is an al-Qaeda presence in many countries, and on every continent except Antarctica.

Meanwhile, the Islamic State stormed onto the scene in 2011, and within a couple of years had managed to do something al-Qaeda has never done: capture and control large swaths of territory. At one point, the Islamic State controlled more territory than a medium-sized European country and had an estimated income in the billions of dollars (including from the sale of oil production facilities under its control). However, its extreme brutality toward the people under its control, combined with increasingly effective military efforts to defeat the group, has resulted in rapid deterioration of the Islamic State's power and presence in this region.

Both al-Qaeda and the Islamic State face huge challenges and obstacles before they could ever hope to achieve their long-term vision of establishing an Islamist caliphate. But both groups—along with several others—are committed to inspiring a global movement of individuals to use violence against civilians in pursuit of this objective. It is likely that we may see a new Salafi-jihadist group take center stage of this movement in the future. It could be a current affiliate of al-Qaeda or the Islamic State, or even some entirely new group that has not yet formed, perhaps in Southeast Asia or in North Africa. At the same time, recent efforts to inspire and mobilize new jihadists in

Western countries, largely through videos and websites, pose one of the largest security challenges facing the United States today. As we will examine much further in Lecture 15, the nature of the threat to the U.S. homeland is thus an ideologically-fueled movement, through which global relationships can lead to "do it yourself" attacks by U.S. citizens or residents as well as by foreigners.

QUESTIONS FOR DISCUSSION

- Is al-Qaeda a different kind of terrorist organization than others we have discussed in this course? If yes, should countries respond to al-Qaeda in a different way than they have responded to terrorist threats in the past?
- How is the Salafi-jihadist ideology similar to that of other religious terrorist movements described in previous lectures? How does it differ?
- Under what local or regional circumstances could the Salafi-jihadist ideology resonate with larger segments of the Muslim world?
- Will the Islamic State and al-Qaeda ever reconcile their differences and join forces in pursuit of the global Salafi-jihadist movement's goals?
- What have been the Salafi-jihadist movement's major strategic (as opposed to tactical or operational) achievements as of today?
- Under what circumstances could Salafi-jihadist groups be more successful in achieving the goals and objectives articulated in their ideology?
- How well, in your opinion, do national, state, and local law enforcement officials understand the evolving nature of the global Salafi-jihadist movement today?
- Based on this lecture, how and where might counterterrorism actors best coordinate their actions and policies to prevent the further spread of Salafi-jihadist terrorism?
- What might local, state, and national law enforcement officials best learn from the evolution of Salafi-jihadism and their own past successes and failures when combating this threat?

RECOMMENDED READING

9/11 Commission. *The Final Report of the National Commission on Terrorist Attacks Upon the United States*. Washington, DC: Government Printing Office, 2004. https://www.9-11commission .gov.

Al-Zawahiri, Ayman. *Knights Under the Prophet's Banner*. London: Al-Sharq al-Awsat, 2011.

Ackerman, Gary A. and Sundara Vadlamudi. "The Case of Ramzi Youssef." In *Countering Terrorism and Insurgency in the 21st Century*. Vol. 3. Edited by James J. F. Forest. Westport, CT: Praeger, 2007.

Alonso, Rogelio. "The Madrid Attacks on March 11: An Analysis of the Jihadist Threat in Spain and Main Counterterrorist Measures." In *Countering Terrorism and Insurgency in the 21st Century*. Vol. 3. Edited by James J. F. Forest. Westport, CT: Praeger, 2007.

"Al-Qaeda's Five Aspects of Power." *CTC Sentinel* 2, no. 1 (2009).

Azzam, Maha. "Political Islam: Violence and the Wahhabi Connection." In *The Making of a Terrorist*. Vol. 1. Edited by James J. F. Forest. Westport, CT: Praeger, 2005.

Baracskay, Daniel. "The February 1993 Attack on the World Trade Center." In *Countering Terrorism and Insurgency in the 21st Century*. Vol. 3. Edited by James J. F. Forest. Westport, CT: Praeger, 2007.

Barber, Victoria. "The Evolution of al Qaeda's Global Network and al Qaeda Core's Position Within It: A Network Analysis." *Perspectives on Terrorism* 9, No. 6 (2015).

Beitler, Ruth Margolies. "Yemen and the Attack on the USS Cole." In *Countering Terrorism and Insurgency in the 21st Century*. Vol. 3. Edited by James J. F. Forest. Westport, CT: Praeger, 2007.

Bergen, Peter. *Holy War, Inc.: Inside the Secret World of Bin Laden*. New York: Free Press, 2002.

Bergen, Peter. *The Longest War: The Enduring Conflict between America and al-Qaeda*. New York: Free Press, 2011.

Berger, J. M. and Jessica Stern. *ISIS: The State of Terror*. New York: Harper Collins, 2015.

Bhatt, Chetan. "The Virtues of Violence: The Salafi-Jihadi Political Universe." *Theory Culture Society* 31, no. 1 (2014): 25–48.

Bjelopera, Jerome P. *American Jihadist Terrorism: Combating a Complex Threat*. Washington, DC: Congressional Research Service, January 23, 2013.

Brachman, Jarret. *Global Jihadism: Theory and Practice*. London: Routledge, 2008.

Brachman, Jarret. "Jihad Doctrine and Radical Islam." In *The Making of a Terrorist*. Vol. 1. Edited by James J. F. Forest. Westport, CT: Praeger, 2005.

Braniff, Bill and Assaf Moghadam. "Al Qaeda's Post-9/11 Evolution: An Assessment." In *Terrorism and Counterterrorism*. Edited by James J. F. Forest, Bruce Hoffman, and Russell Howard. New York: McGraw-Hill, 2014.

Burke, Jason. *Al-Qaeda: The True Story of Radical Islam*. London: IB Taurus, 2004.

Cook, David. *Understanding Jihad*. University of California Press, 2005.

Cruickshank, Paul and Mohannad Hage Ali. "Abu Musab al Suri: Architect of the New Al Qaeda." *Studies in Conflict & Terrorism* 30 (2007).

Dar, Rashid and Shadi Hami. "Islamism, Salafism and Jihadism: A Primer." Brookings Institution (July 15, 2016). http://brook.gs/2mkTk0F.

Forest, James J. F. and Sammy Salama. "Jihadist Tactics and Targeting." In *Jihadists and Weapons of Mass Destruction: A Growing Threat*. Edited by Gary Ackerman and Jeremy Tamsett. Washington, DC: CRC Press, 2008.

Gerges, Fawaz A. *The Far Enemy: Why Jihad Went Global*. Cambridge University Press, 2005.

Gunaratna, Rohan. *Inside Al-Qaeda*. New York: Columbia University Press, 2002.

Gunaratna, Rohan. "Al Qaeda's Trajectory During and After Bin Laden." In *Terrorism and Counterterrorism*. Edited by Bruce Hoffman and Russell Howard. New York: McGraw-Hill, 2011.

Habeck, Mary. "Jihadist Laws of War." *Journal of International Security Affairs* 18 (2010).

Heffelfinger, Chris. *Radical Islam in America: Salafism's Journey from Arabia to the West*. Washington, DC: Potomac Books, Inc., 2011.

Hegghammer, Thomas and Petter Nesser. "Assessing the Islamic State's Commitment to Attacking the West." *Perspectives on Terrorism* 9, no. 4 (2015).

Hegghammer, Thomas. "The Rise of Muslim Foreign Fighters." *International Security* 35, no. 3 (Winter 2010/11).

Hegghammer, Thomas. *Jihadi Culture: The Art and Social Practices of Militant Islamists*. London: Cambridge University Press, 2017.

Hoffman, Bruce. "American Jihad." *National Interest* (April 20, 2010).

Hoffman, Bruce. "The Leaderless Jihad's Leader: Why Osama Bin Laden Mattered." *Foreign Affairs* (May 13, 2011).

Hoffman, Bruce. "Bin Ladin's Killing and Its Effect on Al-Qa'ida: What Comes Next?" In *Terrorism and Counterterrorism*. Edited by Russell Howard and Bruce Hoffman. New York: McGraw-Hill, 2011.

Hoffman, Bruce. "Al Qaeda's Uncertain Future." *Studies in Conflict and Terrorism* 36, no. 8 (2013): 635–53.

Hussain, Ghaffar and Erin Marie Saltman, *Jihad Trending: A Comprehensive Analysis of Online Extremism and How to Counter It*. London: Quilliam Foundation, May 2014.

Jenkins, Brian Michael. *Would-Be Warriors: Incidents of Jihadist Terrorist Radicalization in the United States since September 11, 2001*. Santa Monica, CA: RAND Corporation, 2010.

Jones, Seth G. "Syria's Growing Jihad." *Survival: Global Politics and Strategy* 55, no. 4 (2013): 53–72.

Lemieux, Anthony, Jarret Brachman, Jason Levitt, and Jay Wood. "Inspire Magazine: A Critical Analysis of its Significance and Potential Impact through the Lens of the Information, Motivation and Behavioral Skills Model." *Terrorism and Political Violence* 1, no. 1 (2014): 1–18.

Lia, Brynjar. *Architect of Global Jihad: The Life of Al Qaeda Strategist Abu Musab Al-Suri*. Columbia University Press, 2009.

Lia, Brynjar. "Doctrines for Jihadi Terrorist Training." *Terrorism and Political Violence* 20 (2008).

Lindo, Samuel, Michael Schoder, and Tyler Jones. *Al-Qaeda in the Arabian Peninsula*. CSIS Case Study (2011).

Maher, Shiraz. *Salafi-Jihadism: The History of an Idea*. London: Hurst & Company, 2016.

Maley, Tom. "The London Terrorist Attacks of July 7, 2005." In *Countering Terrorism and Insurgency in the 21st Century*. Vol. 3. Edited by James J. F. Forest. Westport, CT: Praeger, 2007.

McCants, William. *The ISIS Apocalypse: The History, Strategy and Doomsday Vision of the Islamic State*. New York: St. Martin's Press, 2015.

Moghadam, Assaf. *Nexus of Global Jihad: Understanding Cooperation Among Terrorist Actors*. New York: Columbia University Press, 2017.

Moghadam, Assaf. "Terrorist Innovation: The Case of 9/11." In *Terrorist Innovations in Weapons of Mass Effect: Preconditions, Causes and Predictive Behaviors*. Edited by Maria J. Rasmussen and Mohammed M. Hafez. Washington, DC: Defense Threat Reduction Agency, 2010.

Nesser, Petter, Anne Stenersen, and Emile Oftedal, "Jihadi Terrorism in Europe: The IS-Effect." *Perspectives on Terrorism* 10, no. 6 (2016).

Obama, Barack. "Remarks by the President on Osama bin Laden." White House Address (May 2011). In *Terrorism and Counterterrorism*. Edited by Russell Howard and Bruce Hoffman. New York: McGraw-Hill, 2011.

Reidel, Bruce. *The Search for Al-Qaeda*. Washington, DC: Brookings Institution Press, 2008.

Rollins, John. "Al-Qaeda and Affiliates: Historical Perspective, Global Presence, and Implications for U.S. Policy." CRS Report for Congress (February 5, 2010).

Sageman, Marc. *Leaderless Jihad: Terror Networks in the Twenty-First Century*. University of Pennsylvania Press, 2008.

Shane, Scott. "The Enduring Influence of Anwar al-Awlaki in the Age of the Islamic State." *CTC Sentinel* 9, no. 7 (July 2016).

Tawil, Camille. "How Bin Ladin's Death Will Affect Al-Qa'ida's Regional Franchises." In *Terrorism and Counterterrorism*. Edited by Russell Howard and Bruce Hoffman. New York: McGraw-Hill, 2011.

Thornberry, William and Jaclyn Levy. "Al-Qaeda in the Islamic Maghreb." CSIS Case Study (September 2011).

Tierney, Dominic. "The Twenty Years' War." *The Atlantic* (August 23, 2016). https://www.theatlantic.com/international/archive/2016/08/twenty-years-war/496736/.

Vadlamudi, Sundara. "The U.S. Embassy Bombings in Kenya and Tanzania." In *Countering Terrorism and Insurgency in the 21st Century*. Vol. 3. Edited by James J. F. Forest. Westport, CT: Praeger, 2007.

Watts, Clint. "Deciphering Competition Between al-Qaida and the Islamic State." *CTC Sentinel* (July 2016).

Wesley, Robert. "Capturing Khalid Sheik Mohammad." In *Countering Terrorism and Insurgency in the 21st Century*. Vol. 3. Edited by James J. F. Forest. Westport, CT: Praeger, 2007.

Whiteside, Craig. "New Masters of Revolutionary Warfare: The Islamic State Movement (2002-2016). *Perspectives on Terrorism* 10, no. 4 (2016).

Wiktorowicz, Quintan. "The Anatomy of the Salafi Movement." *Studies in Conflict and Terrorism* 29 (2006).

Wiktorowicz, Quintan. "A Genealogy of Radical Islam." *Studies in Conflict and Terrorism* 28 (2005): 75–97.

Wilson, Lydia. "What I discovered from interviewing captured ISIS Fighters." *The Nation* (October 21, 2015). http://bit.ly/1PGeXTe.

Winter, Charlie. "Why is Islamic State Group so Violent?" BBC Video (December 8, 2015). http://www.bbc.com/news/world-middle-east-34966674.

Wood, Graeme. *The Way of the Strangers: Encounters with the Islamic State.* New York: Random House, 2017.

Wood, Graeme. "What ISIS Really Wants." *The Atlantic* (March 2015). http://www.theatlantic.com/features/archive/2015/02/what-isis-really-wants/384980/.

Wright, Lawrence. *The Looming Tower: Al-Qaeda and the Road to 9/11.* New York: Knopf, 2006.

WEBSITES

Al-Qaeda's Fatwa "Declaration of War Against the Americans Occupying the Land of the Two Holy Places" (August 23, 1996)
http://bit.ly/2xR50zu

Al-Qaeda's Fatwa: "World Islamic Front Declaration of Jihad Against Jews and Crusaders" (1998)
https://fas.org/irp/world/para/docs/980223-fatwa.htm

Jihadology
http://jihadology.net

Selected al-Qaeda Documents (captured in Afghanistan, Pakistan, and elsewhere)
https://ctc.usma.edu/programs-resources/harmony-program

NOTES

1. This was a much different conception of jihad than what the Sufi sects throughout North Africa and some parts of Asia promoted, where they embraced a concept of "greater jihad" as being an internal struggle necessary for spiritual insight.

2. Sayyid Qutb, *Milestones* [English translation] (New Delhi: Islamic Book Service, 2001).

3. For more on Sayyid Qutb, see Emmanuel Sivan, *Radical Islam: Medieval Theology and Modern Politics* (Yale University Press, 1985); Gilles Kepel, *Muslim Extremism in Egypt: The Prophet and the Pharaoh*, trans. Jon Rothschild (Berkeley: University of California Press, 1993): 26–43; Yvonne Haddad, "Sayyid Qutb: Ideologue of Islamic Revival," in *Voices of Resurgent Islam*, ed. John Esposito (New York: Oxford University Press, 1983).

4. For more detail on Ayman al-Zawahiri, see the excellent biography by Montasser al Zayyat, *The Road to Al Qaeda: The Story of Bin Laden's Right Hand Man* (London: Pluto Press, 2004).

5. Ayman al-Zawahiri, *Knights Under the Prophet's Banner* (London: Al-Sharq al-Awsat, December 2011).

6. Fawaz A. Gerges, *The Far Enemy: Why Jihad Went Global* (Cambridge University Press, 2005): 11–13. Also, the original Arabic and a translated English version of this declaration can be found http://www.fas.org/irp/world/para/docs/980223-fatwa.htm.

7. Paul Cruickshank and Mohannad Hage Ali, "Abu Musab al Suri: Architect of the New Al Qaeda," *Studies in Conflict & Terrorism* 30 (2007): 8.

8. Abu Musab al Suri, jihadist training videos, dated August 2000. Cited in Cruickshank, p. 9.

9. Marc Sageman, *Leaderless Jihad: Terror Networks in the Twenty-First Century* (Philadelphia: University of Pennsylvania Press, 2008).

10. This description of al-Qaeda's ideology summarizes much more extensive and thorough explanations contained in the following: Jarret Brachman, *Global Jihadism* (London: Routledge, 2008); David Cook, *Understanding Jihad* (Berkeley, CA: University of California Press, 2005); Bruce Reidel, *The Search for al Qaeda* (Brookings Institution, 2008); Jarret Brachman, "Jihad Doctrine and Radical Islam," in *The Making of a Terrorist*, vol. 1, ed. James J. F. Forest (Westport, CT: Praeger, 2005); Quintan Wiktorowicz, "A Genealogy of Radical Islam," in *Terrorism and Counterterrorism*, ed. Russell Howard and Bruce Hoffman (New York: McGraw-Hill, 2011); and Maha Azzam, "Political Islam: Violence and the Wahhabi Connection," in *The Making of a Terrorist*, vol. 1, ed. Forest.

11. See Brachman, *Global Jihadism*.

12. As noted in Lecture 1, an ideology is generally defined as an articulation of grievances and what to do about them.

13. Many of the sources for this historical summary are a matter of public record, but also see Lawrence Wright, *The Looming Tower: Al-Qaeda and the Road to 9/11* (New York: Alfred A. Knopf, 2006); The 9/11 Commission Report (particularly Chapter 2: "The Foundations of the New Terrorism"), http://www.9-11commission.gov/report/index.htm; and Bruce Reidel, *The Search for Al-Qaeda* (Washington, DC: Brookings Institution Press, 2008).

14. The 9/11 Commission Report, Chapter 2: "The Foundations of the New Terrorism," http://www.9-11commission.gov/report/index.htm.

15. Daniel Baracskay, "The February 1993 Attack on the World Trade Center," in *Countering Terrorism and Insurgency in the 21st Century*, vol. 3, ed. James J. F. Forest (Westport, CT: Praeger, 2007).

16. Gary A. Ackerman and Sundara Vadlamudi, "The Case of Ramzi Youssef," in *Countering Terrorism and Insurgency in the 21st Century*, vol. 3.

17. Youussef M. Ibrahim, "Saudis Strip Citizenship from Backers of Militants," *New York Times* April 10, 1994, http://goo.gl/pBtRB.

18. Gary A. Ackerman and Sundara Vadlamudi, "The Case of Ramzi Youssef," in *Countering Terrorism and Insurgency in the 21st Century*, vol. 3.

19. Rohan Gunaratna, "Al Qaeda's Lose and Learn Doctrine: The Trajectory from Oplan Bokinka to 9/11," in *Teaching Terror*, ed. James J. F. Forest (Lanham, MD: Rowman & Littlefield, 2007).

20. PBS *Newshour*, "Bin Laden's Fatwa" ("Declaration of War Against the Americans Occupying the Land of the Two Holy Places") (August 23, 1996),http://goo.gl/vYqbw.

21. "Al-Qaida timeline: Plots and attacks," MSNBC (n.d.), http://goo.gl/LkAHz.

22. PBS *Newshour*, "Al Qaeda's Fatwa" ("World Islamic Front Declaration of Jihad Against Jews and Crusaders") (February 23, 1998), http://goo.gl/6nNz2.

23. Sundara Vadlamudi, "The U.S. Embassy Bombings in Kenya and Tanzania," in *Countering Terrorism and Insurgency in the 21st Century*, vol. 3.

24. The 9/11 Commission Report, Chapter 2: "The Foundations of the New Terrorism," http://www.9-11commission.gov/report/index.htm.

25. Ibid.

26. Ruth Margolies Beitler, "Yemen and the Attack on the USS Cole," in *Countering Terrorism and Insurgency in the 21st Century*, vol. 3.

27. For more on this dimension of organizational learning among terrorist groups, see *Teaching Terror, ed.* Forest.

28. Available online at http://www.9-11commission.gov/report/index.htm. For additional analysis, see Assaf Moghadam, "Terrorist Innovation: The Case of 9/11," in *Terrorist Innovations in Weapons of Mass Effect: Preconditions, Causes and Predictive Behaviors*, ed. Maria J. Rasmussen and Mohammed M. Hafez (Washington, DC: Defense Threat Reduction Agency, 2010).

29. In addition to the DVD videos, *National Geographic* also offers an archive of interviews, documents, and other materials online at http://goo.gl/nkejp.

30. See Brian Michael Jenkins, "Would-Be Warriors: Incidents of Jihadist Terrorist Radicalization in the United States since September 11, 2001" (Santa Monica, CA: RAND Corporation, 2010); and Bruce Hoffman, "American Jihad," *National Interest* (April 20, 2010).

31. President Obama speech on the death of Osama bin Laden, http://www.whitehouse.gov/blog/2011/05/02/osama-bin-laden-dead.

32. Ibid.

33. See Rogelio Alonso, "The Madrid Attacks on March 11: An Analysis of the Jihadist Threat in Spain and Main Counterterrorist Measures," in *Countering Terrorism and Insurgency in the 21st Century*, vol. 3.

34. Tom Maley, "The London Terrorist Attacks of July 7, 2005," in *Countering Terrorism and Insurgency in the 21st Century*, vol. 3.

35. This section's description of the Islamic State draws significantly from the profile published online by the Mapping Militant Organizations project at Stanford University, led by Professor Martha Crenshaw, http://web.stanford.edu/group/mappingmilitants/cgi-bin/groups/view/1.

36. Ibid., notes 42–44.

37. Ibid., note 78.

13

Terrorist Group Decision-Making

In this lecture, we examine the attributes of terrorist organizations that have managed to survive for long periods of time. Obviously, each terrorist organization has a different history and trajectory; some have survived for many years, while most terrorist organizations fail relatively quickly. According to a study by David Rapoport published in the early 1990s, roughly 90 percent of all terrorist organizations in history have had a life span of less than one year.[1] Further, of the remaining 10 percent that survived for more than a year, half of them disappeared within a decade. In fact, only a small handful of terrorist groups have survived over multiple decades, and fewer still have lasted over multiple generations. Because of this, we can learn a lot about the nature of terrorism by looking closely at what makes these long-lasting organizations different from the majority that have had short lives.

> **TO THE POINT**
>
> Terrorists require a significant breadth of knowledge to be successful.

To begin with, the capabilities of a group's leaders and members play a central role in their prospects for long-term survival and effectiveness. These capabilities may include access to financial support and weapons, but arguably none are more important than the capability to make good strategic, tactical, and operational decisions. Every day, terrorist groups make a variety of decisions about strategy, tactics, personnel, finances, and much more. These decisions impact the likelihood of their success or failure. Thus, a number of researchers have studied terrorist group decision-making, the factors that may influence or shape those decisions, and the outcomes of those decisions.

For example, research by Gordon McCormick explores several overlapping types of theories about terrorist decision-making. Strategic theories focus on the use of violence as a means to an end and highlight the need for a group's tactical decisions to be based on accurate information, while other theories explain decision-making as a product of internal organizational dynamics and individual psychological issues that may have little or nothing to do with reality.[2] Indeed, as discussed in several other lectures of this series, terrorism is a distinctly human behavior (albeit an awfully inhumane one); thus at some level it should be intuitive that there is a complex array of factors (internal and external) that influence a human's decision to engage in terrorism.

Jacob Shapiro is one of several scholars to explore how terrorist groups must calibrate their violence in order to avoid alienating the very people whose support is crucial to their survival.[3] This need to avoid counterproductive violence is different for each terrorist group depending on a variety of political, social, economic, and other dimensions of their local operating environment. As he explains, "terrorism is a contextual phenomenon and it thus makes sense that successful analysis of terrorist group decision-making needs to take into account a variety of contextual factors."[4] His book *The Terrorist's Dilemma* also explains how the challenges that a terrorist organization must overcome are similar to many other kinds of organizations. They must have competent bookkeeping and human resources personnel, expected behavioral protocols and disciplinary procedures, training programs, and so forth. Basically, terrorist groups require many of the same kind of managerial and bureaucratic roles that we find in public and private sector organizations worldwide.[5]

Max Abrahms, another well-known scholar, has published several in-depth research articles on how terrorist leaders try to accurately interpret information available to them but then make bad decisions—particularly about terrorist attacks against civilian targets—that lower the chances of a government's leaders making concessions to their demands.[6] In fact, his very popular 2006 article "Why Terrorism Does Not Work" reveals that the vast majority of terrorist groups have perpetrated terrorism "without any real signs of political progress."[7] Further, some of the influential writers on guerilla warfare mentioned in Lecture 2—whose ideas about organized political violence still influence terrorist groups today—actually recommended against the use of terrorism as a strategy to bring about change. Che Guevara, for example, stressed that terrorism "is of negative value" and is "generally ineffective and indiscriminate in its results, since it often makes victims of innocent people and destroys a large number of lives that would be valuable to the revolution."[8] Likewise, Carlos Marighella tells his readers not to "attack indiscriminately without distinguishing between the exploiters and the exploited"[9] And recently, Abrahms and his colleagues found statistical support for the argument that terrorist leaders tend to favor significantly less indiscriminate violence than their lower-level operatives actually commit. They also note that terrorist leaders are significantly more likely to assume organizational responsibility for attacks that avoid civilian targets.[10]

Of course, this is not to suggest that all terrorist groups are similar in their decision--making or other aspects—as noted earlier, there is a lot of diversity in this area. For example, the terrorism studies literature also provides ample research on how the different kinds of goals and objectives of a terrorist group directly impact the decisions they make. A study by Andrew Kydd and Barbara Walter identified five categories of the most common goals pursued by terrorist groups throughout history: regime change, territorial change, policy change, social control, and status quo maintenance. Regime change (sought by many left-wing groups like Baader-Meinhof, Italian Red Brigades, and Sendero Luminoso) is defined as the overthrow of a government and its replacement with one more to their liking. Territorial change, common among ethnonationalist groups like the Liberation Tigers of Tamil Eelam (LTTE) or Euzkadi ta Askatasuna (ETA), typically involves taking land away from a nation-state in order to establish a new one. Policy change is a broader category of goals that are pursued by (for example) environmental and animal rights extremists, or reflected by al-Qaeda's demands for the U.S. to stop supporting Israel and regimes such as in Saudi Arabia and Egypt that it considers to be apostate. Social control involves the use of terrorism to compel the behavior of a population—for example, abortion clinic bombers or the KKK. And the final category of status quo maintenance is something we see most often among right-wing extremists.[11] Each of these kinds of terrorism is described in more detail in previous lectures in this book.

In all five of these strategies of terrorism, the central purpose is to coerce the behavior of the target government or population in ways that the terrorist group believes will help it achieve its goals. Once a group has decided to use terrorist violence as a means to achieve its goals and objectives, it must then decide on the kind of strategy this violence is meant to achieve. For example, terrorist campaigns typically pursue one or more of the "five principal strategic logics" identified by Kydd and Walter: (1) attrition, (2) intimidation, (3) provocation, (4) spoiling, and (5) outbidding.[12] An attrition strategy involves convincing the target government (or the population writ large) that the terrorist group is strong enough to cause significant damage and costs unless their demands are met. Similarly, an intimidation strategy is meant to convince the population that resistance is futile—the terrorists are too strong, and the government is too weak to stop them. A provocation strategy involves doing things that the government responds to with increasing repression, and perhaps even indiscriminate violence. This will, in theory, radicalize the population by revealing the "truly evil nature" of the government, and lead to change.[13]

The spoiler strategy is used by terrorists when more moderate factions are negotiating for peace. For example, shortly after the 1998 Good Friday Agreement in Northern Ireland was signed, a dissident group called the Real IRA bombed the town of Omagh, killing 29 people in what became the worst terrorist attack of the entire multi-decade conflict known as "The Struggles." This was an attempt at derailing the peace process, an attempt that fortunately failed. In contrast, the 1995 assassination of Prime Minister Yitzak Rabin (by Jewish extremist Yigal Amir) was followed by several other acts of terrorism by Hamas and the Palestinian Islamic Jihad that prevented the implementation of the Oslo Peace Accords in the Middle East. Examples include bus bombings in Jerusalem in August 1995 and February 1996, and three simultaneous suicide bombings in September 1997 at the Ben Yehuda shopping mall in Jerusalem.[14]

And the final strategic logic identified by Kydd and Walter only applies when there are conflicts involving multiple terrorist groups (like the Middle East), where peer competition can be a factor that influences a group's decision-making. According to Mia Bloom's "outbidding thesis," some groups in this context have chosen to use suicide bombings in their terrorist campaigns as a way of demonstrating greater strength and commitment to the cause than other groups competing for local support.[15]

Many terrorist groups have also pursued multiple goals and strategic objectives at the same time. Anti-abortion clinic bombers want to reverse the *Roe v. Wade* decision of the Supreme Court as well as coerce the behavior of individuals throughout the United States with regard to abortions. Ethnonationalists may want both territorial change and regime change. But the important takeaway from this discussion is that all these strategic dimensions inform the decisions a group makes about tactical operations, including weapons to use and targets of terrorist attacks. For example, the KKK would have no reason to attack a church attended exclusively by white people; ethnonationalists would have no reason to attack an abortion clinic; the tactic of suicide bombings has not been adopted by terrorist groups in the left-wing, right-wing, or environmental extremist categories. In recent years, jihadists have attacked targets largely related to public transportation (subways, commuter trains, airports, ferries, and airlines), commerce (hotels, office buildings, cafes, nightclubs, etc.), and civil authority (government offices, police stations, etc.). Most of what we know about the objectives of these attacks—as well as the tactical and operational means by which they seek to achieve these objectives—is drawn from documents disseminated by key ideologues and thinkers within the Salafi-jihadist movement. Thus, an assessment of al-Qaeda's operational manuals and literature provides a valuable case study for how jihadists choose their targets.

To begin with, the primary strategic objective of the network has direct relevance for the question of targeting: *to "bleed" (exhaust) the United States economically and militarily both by directly causing inordinate economic losses and forcing the U.S. to spend excessive amounts of money to protect its vast infrastructure.*[16] A variety of jihadist literature and manuals describe how the United States derives its considerable military power and political influence from its superior economy. It is believed, therefore, that disrupting the American economy will in turn defeat the U.S. as an opponent and end its military hegemony and presence overseas. Impeding Western economies is therefore, as one al-Qaeda member aptly stated, "the most dangerous and effective arena of Jihad, because we live in a materialistic world."[17] Consequently, jihadist cells are encouraged to attack targets with high economic value that will result in serious economic losses in the United States.

The following excerpt from *Sawt al-Jihad* (The Voice of Jihad), an al-Qaeda publication distributed in Saudi Arabia during the last decade, underscores the network's primary strategic objective of weakening the United States economically by forcing it to expend enormous sums of money on protecting its vast infrastructure, as well as by attacking its economic assets directly: "If the enemy used his economy to rule the world and hire collaborators, then we need to strike this economy with harsh attacks to bring it down on the heads of its owners. If the enemy has built its economy on the basis of open markets and free trade by getting the monies of investors, then we have to prove to these investors that the enemy's land is not safe for them, that his economy is not capable of guarding their monies, so they would abandon him to suffer alone the fall of his economy."[18]

In October 2005, Abu Mus`ab al-Najadi, another Saudi al-Qaeda affiliate, published a short manuscript titled "*Al-Qaeda's Battle is Economic not Military*," in which he also outlines in significant detail the rationale behind attacking soft targets of high economic value:

> Anything that negatively affects their [America's] economy is considered for us a step in the right direction in the path to victory. Military defeats do not greatly affect how we measure total victory, but these defeats indirectly impinge on the economy, which can be demonstrated with breaching the confidence of capitalists and investors in this nation's ability to safeguard its various trade and dealings . . . For example, if a hotel that caters to Western tourists in Indonesia is targeted, the enemy will be required to protect all hotels that cater to Western tourists in all countries, which may become a target of similar attacks.[19]

An assessment of jihadists' targeting rationale reveals that these terrorists' most likely targets will be facilities of high economic value in the United States and Europe. Although the network's literature does not specify which precise sectors it intends to target, such facilities would most likely include financial districts and buildings, airports and planes, train and bus stations, ports and ships, subways, shopping malls, hotels, resorts, tourist attractions, sports arenas, entertainment centers, and embassies. An attack on a critical component of a country's transportation infrastructure would impact such things as power distribution, food and water supply chains, waste management, the domestic retail sector, and so forth.

In addition to "bleeding" the United States economically, attacking American targets in Muslim countries is also aimed at discouraging alliances between the United States and regional "apostate" governments; deterring Western corporations and Western individuals from conducting business in Muslim countries (described in one manual as "removal of foreign capitalists from domestic markets");[20] and "breaching the security and climate of stability that is necessary for economic growth, such as the bombing of oil pipelines in Iraq."[21] Attacks by various terrorist groups on the global energy infrastructure are something that the world governments now expect and have to guard against. In a December 2005 video distributed online, Ayman al-Zawahiri encourages "mujahideen to concentrate their attacks on Muslims' stolen oil, most of the revenues of which go to the enemies of Islam while most of what they leave is seized by the thieves who rule our countries."[22] And in one of the most popular al-Qaeda strategic documents in recent years, *The Management of Savagery* (described in Lecture 12), Abu Bakr Naji justifies attacks on petroleum facilities and lays out a media-savvy game plan to disrupt the flow of oil.[23]

Meanwhile, we have seen an increasing number of jihadist attacks against public gatherings, like plowing a truck into a promenade filled with people in Nice, France. Other recent attacks have targeted a school in Peshawar, nightclubs in Istanbul and Orlando, concert venues in Paris and Manchester, an airport in Brussels, and underground trains in Russia, Belgium, and the U.K., just to name a handful. Even unsophisticated knife attacks against local citizens in Sweden, France, Spain, and the U.K. are meant to generate a climate of fear that jihadists believe will have political, economic and psychological effects that will help them achieve their overall goals and objectives.

Overall, the tactical decisions made by a terrorist movement like the Salafi-jihadists are influenced by many factors, including their goals and objectives as well as their access to weapons and meaningful targets, their opportunities to attract financial support and new recruits, and the personal attributes of key leaders within the movement. And, as described in Lecture 18 of this book, most terrorist groups have consciously avoided using weapons of mass destruction in their attacks—even when such weapons are relatively easy and accessible. Basically, weapons of mass destruction really don't offer many strategically useful benefits to most terrorist groups, and certainly not commensurate with the level of costs and resource investments it would take to acquire and use those weapons effectively. Further, a significant majority of terrorist groups have recognized the need to impose constraints on their violence, in order to maintain the popular support necessary for financing their operations and recruiting new members to their ranks. In fact, many terrorists throughout history have pursued a vision of the future in which they will someday be in charge of a particular governable space, and this vision may require them to overthrow an existing government but ensure that the space and people they seek to govern are left relatively undamaged. In this sense, using a weapon of mass destruction that makes an entire population sick (or worse), or that renders a particular location uninhabitable (e.g., contaminated by radiological, biological, or chemical agents) seems counterproductive.

All these attributes of a group and its operating environment can influence the kinds of decisions they make, and even the kinds of things they can make decisions about. But perhaps no attribute is more important than knowledge. Clearly, nobody is born with the knowledge and skills needed to be a competent and effective terrorist. Thus, a very important topic within the research on effective decision-making among terrorists is the role of learning and knowledge transfer.

TERRORIST GROUP LEARNING AND INNOVATION

Obviously, terrorist groups that make good, informed decisions tend to fare better than their counterparts, underscoring the importance of knowledge and the capacity for terrorists to learn and innovate. As analysts Horacio Trujillo and Brian Jackson of the think tank RAND have noted, combating terrorism effectively requires us to recognize these attributes, as well as *how* these groups learn and change: "Understanding this learning process can both improve our knowledge of terrorist groups' current capabilities and help us to predict how those capabilities may evolve or shift in the future."[24]

Of course, knowledge is widely recognized as a vital resource for any organization, and can make the difference between success and failure, perhaps even life and death. This holds true for terrorist organizations as well. Successful terrorist attacks are rarely accomplished by idiots; rather, in order to carry out their lethal agenda, terrorists require a broad range of knowledge that incorporates skills, competency, creative thinking, some understanding of engineering, coded communications, and so forth. Without such knowledge, terrorists are more easily thwarted, apprehended, or otherwise likely to fail. Of course, this is not to say that all terrorists are smart. Within any terrorist organization, you will find members with different levels of capabilities and knowledge, and they have different roles to play. But the important point to make here is that the history of terrorism is fueled by a body of strategic and tactical knowledge that has expanded over time. How organizations draw from and contribute to this body of knowledge is an important aspect to the study of terrorism.

Generally speaking, terrorist organizations move through several phases from inception to dissolution. They start with a core of individuals who share an idea, and they try to convince others to join their group. If they are successful in expanding the group's size and capabilities, they may grow stronger and more capable of withstanding the inevitable counterterrorism response by the government. They may accumulate various kinds of resources that help sustain their operations and long-term survival. But over time, if they are unable to achieve any of their significant objectives (and very, very few ever do), the terrorist group's membership declines. Members are captured or killed, or may just abandon the cause as hopeless. Some groups may fall apart because of infighting among leaders; others may negotiate a political settlement to their grievances; and others may transform from a politically-oriented terrorist group into a profit-oriented criminal organization.[25]

Understanding the breadth and depth of a terrorist group's knowledge base allows us to better anticipate its capabilities, including the likelihood that it may be able to successfully adapt to our counterterrorism efforts. Terrorist groups that survive for more than a few years tend to learn and draw inspiration from others, and commit resources toward developing their strategic and tactical capabilities over the long term. They scan the environment for the successes (and failures) of other terrorist groups, and invest time and energy in sharing knowledge among members of the group, often by writing their own training manuals and running training camps. In short, they demonstrate the attributes of a learning organization.

The term "learning organization" describes an organization that, through purposefully applying its resources toward the acquisition of knowledge about itself and its environment, is continually expanding its capacity to meet present and future challenges with increasing sophistication and success.[3] Attributes of a learning organization include the ability to identify knowledge useful to its long-term success, and incorporate that knowledge into the operations and future plans of the organization. In doing so, it creates for itself a competitive advantage: learning allows it to adapt to an increasingly fluid environment faster and more effectively than other organizations.[26]

These concepts were advanced during the 1990s through a book by Peter Senge, in which he described learning organizations as "organizations where people continually expand their capacity to create the results they truly desire, where new and expansive patterns of thinking are nurtured, where collective aspiration is set free, and where people are continually learning to see the whole together."[27] In some cases, organizations have even taken the extra step of identifying individuals or units who are responsible for facilitating organizational learning, sometimes reflected in an organizational learning plan with measurable objectives. An overarching question which all learning organizations ask themselves is, "What do we need to learn in the process of achieving our goals?" Questions such as this reflect a relatively high level of pragmatic flexibility and encourage an organization to think about the strategic environment and their future within it. This, in turn, helps the organization anticipate and respond to change more effectively.

An example of this organizational learning and adaptation was seen among the militant groups in Iraq during the mid-2000s, when they continually adapted their use of improvised explosive devices (IEDs) to achieve greater effectiveness in their attacks on U.S. and Iraqi security forces. According to one report, the first IEDs were triggered by wires and batteries; insurgents waited on the roadside and detonated the primitive devices when Americans drove past. After a while, U.S. troops improved their ability to spot and eliminate the triggermen before the bombs went off. That led the insurgents to replace their wires with radio signals. The Pentagon then equipped its forces with jammers to block those signals. In response, the insurgents adapted by sending a continuous radio signal to the IED; when the signal stopped or was jammed, the bomb exploded. The military solution was to try and track the signal, and then mimic it to make sure it continues. However, the main challenge here was that the signals were encrypted, which led to the additional task of cracking the encryption of the signal and then replicating it—all within a very short time span, in order to ensure the safety of the convoy.[28] In some instances, insurgents also began detonating their explosives by using infrared lasers, an innovation aimed at bypassing electronic jammers used to block radio-wave detonators. In essence, these terrorists learned and adapted in order to increase their effectiveness.

Of course, terrorist organizations require a significant breadth of operational knowledge before they can be truly effective. Examples of the types of knowledge needed include document falsification, sabotage, target vulnerability assessment, and artillery training. Capturing knowledge and expertise in these areas, and then committing it to organizational memory, is essential. This is why several groups have invested time and effort in writing their own training manuals, like al-Qaeda's *Encyclopedia of Afghan Jihad*, the *Mujahideen Poisons Handbook*, the *Handbook for Volunteers of the Irish Republican Army: Notes on Guerilla Warfare*, Che Guevara's *Guerilla Warfare* (1961), Carlos Marighella's *Mini-Manual of the Urban Guerrilla* (1969), and the Red Army Faction's *The Urban Guerilla Concept* (1971). The primary purpose is to identify and provide core elements of knowledge needed to sustain an organization from one generation to the next.

Historically, the most common and important places where operational learning has taken place are the various terrorists training camps scattered throughout the globe. Research in the field of terrorism studies over the past several decades has given us a pretty good understanding of what goes on in these training camps. For example, according to a study conducted in the 1990s by a member of the U.S. Marine Corps, a typical day at a PLO training camp began with early morning physical fitness exercises, and included education in explosives and detonators, the art of setting mines in munitions dumps and on bridges and vehicles, the rudiments of chemical and biological warfare, field command and escape tactics, marksmanship and camouflage, and the use and employment of Soviet RPG rockets and shoulder borne Strela missiles.[29]

In a remarkable 2003 *Foreign Policy* article, researchers Martha Brill Olcott and Bakhtiyar Babadjanov describe their analysis of 10 notebooks that once belonged to young men who were recruited for jihad and attended terrorist training camps in Central Asia (most likely Uzbekistan) during the 1990s.[30] They describe how students learned cartography (map-making), the use of small firearms (mainly Soviet-era rifles and the occasional Egyptian rocket-propelled grenade launcher), tactics for targeting the enemy (both on the ground and in the air), explosive device construction (including antipersonnel mines), and how to make poison using corn, flour, beef, yak dung, alcohol, and water. While the motivational knowledge represented in these students' notebooks reflects a clear radical Islamist influence, it is equally interesting to note that, according to Olcott and Babadjanov, "the teachers who used Russian terminology clearly had experience with the Red Army and Soviet system of military instruction, and those who used Arabic likely passed through terrorist camps in Afghanistan and maybe even those of the Middle East."[31]

In 2002, *New York Times* reporters C. J. Chivers and David Rohde examined hundreds of documents collected from "terrorist training schools" during the U.S. military assault on the Taliban in Afghanistan, and found "signs that in developing martial curriculums, the [terrorist] groups were cannily resourceful in amassing knowledge."[32] The documents included student notebooks, instructor lessons plans, course curricula, training manuals, reference books and memoranda—collectively, the same sorts of materials one would expect to find at a conventional military academy. Analysis of the documents revealed that students began their training by learning all about Kalashnikov rifles, the ubiquitous Soviet-era weapon used by many insurgent organizations around the world. Once the history, design, and operation of these weapons were mastered—mainly through rote memorization—students turned their attention to "PK machine guns, 82-millimeter mortars and the RPG-7, a shoulder-fired rocket effective against armored vehicles and trucks."[33]

In this program of study, the next course was a sort of "infantry weapons 201," with some students learning sniper rifle skills and how to fine-tune a rifle sight at short range to ensure accuracy at longer distances, while others studied how to direct weapon fire at targets on the ground and in the air. Training in four-man unit deployments and formations—including wedges, columns, echelons, and lines—reflected similar techniques used by U.S. Marines and Army Rangers. Demolition instruction was also provided, covering mines and grenades, pressure and tripwire booby traps, and the basic knowledge of electrical engineering that would allow students to figure out "the wiring, power sources and fuses required to spark an explosive charge."[34]

Al-Qaeda also trained recruits in a variety of urban guerilla tactics. An archive of videotapes obtained by CNN in 2002 shows how the group "replicated a small Western-style city on a hillside in eastern Afghanistan, using canvas and stone," and how trainees used explosives to destroy simulated houses, office buildings, and bridges.[35] Also included on the tapes were "step-by-step instructions on how to use a surface-to-air missile" and "lessons on complex hostage-taking techniques and assassination operations."[36] And according to court records and other sources, many training camps have offered instruction in basic hand-to-hand combat skills, including the use of knives and martial arts.[37] Similar kinds of instruction were seen among militant groups in Iraq after the 2003 invasion by the U.S.-led coalition, and more recently a variety of training campus were established in Iraq and Syria over the last decade to provide instruction to thousands of foreign fighters who came to join the Islamic State. These jihadists also learned about using videos of beheadings (distributed via social media) to draw attention to their cause, as well as making and deploying IEDs, using drones for surveillance, and other newer technologies.

Another example of knowledge transfer was seen among one of the most sophisticated terrorist groups in recent history, the Revolutionary Armed Forces of Colombia (FARC). Studies by Román Ortiz have described how FARC's survival and expansion was possible thanks to its notable capacity for learning.[38] In addition to recruiting university students, and sending a number of the group's members to universities throughout the country to study science and engineering, FARC also established training centers to provide programs, sometimes three months long, attended by dozens of guerrillas removed from their usual duties in order to receive training in new weapons like anti-aircraft defenses, or specific guerilla warfare tactics like mine warfare, sniping, intelligence gathering, and the use of explosives. They also developed the ability to manufacture their own weapons, including mortars and land mines, and they resolved their constant shortage of ammunition for certain types of machine guns and assault rifles by developing the capacity to recharge and reuse the cartridges fired by these weapons.

FARC also learned to become financially self-sufficient through its increasing involvement in drug trafficking. Initially, toward the beginning of the 1980s, it merely provided military protection to drug traffickers in exchange for a percentage of the value of the drugs produced or transported. However, this type of association provided relatively limited economic benefits; moreover, FARC had to depend on the management of this illegal trade by drug cartels. Consequently, during the early 1990s, FARC decided to independently produce its own narcotics and develop its own networks to market them. This decision forced the organization to learn how to be effective in activities such as cocaine production, trafficking, and laundering of substantial assets. In other words, the demand for financial autonomy served as a powerful driving force to stimulate technological innovation.[39] More recently, FARC leaders entered into a five-year nego-tiation process with the Colombian government, and in 2016 signed a peace treaty that ended this long conflict. In June 2017, the group completed its demobilization and dis-armament obligations, and also launched a political party. In essence, its future survival as a political movement will now depend on different kinds of organizational learning.

Nearby in Peru, Sendero Luminoso also established schools in which it taught new recruits about guerilla warfare strategy, as well as the use of firearms and explosives.[40] During the late 1990s, the Islamist terrorist group Jemmah Islamiyyah (JI) established several training facilities in the southern Philippines, providing courses in weapons and explosives.[41] Hizballah, Hamas, and many other terrorist groups in the Middle East have had training camps in the Bekaa Valley of eastern Lebanon, which was controlled by Syria until 2005.

Beyond written manuals and training camps, the most sophisticated terrorist groups have invested in structural mechanisms and pathways for knowledge to be shared throughout an organization. Instead of compartmentalizing knowledge accord-ing to a person's function within the organization—a "need to know" approach that we often see in the intelligence community—groups like the Provisional IRA ensured that cross-training among cells within a group would provide a mechanism for knowl-edge diffusion throughout an organization.[42] Also, when members of the PIRA were captured and sent to British or Irish prisons, they were immediately debriefed by other inmates, who then smuggled the information (and lessons learned) to PIRA members outside the prison walls. Particularly useful information passed on by the imprisoned terrorists could include how they were caught, what information the captors were look-ing for, what (if anything) might have gone awry with a planned attack being carried out, and who (if anyone) might have played a role in their capture.[43] This process of debriefing and knowledge transfer reflects the fact that learning organizations require the ability and willingness to examine both success and failure.

These examples of operational learning demonstrate how the most effective *ter-rorist organizations study the counterterrorism strategies of governments and adapt accord-ingly*. They learn by studying publicly available doctrines, statements, public court records, investigative news stories of counterterrorism successes, and various infor-mation resources available on the Internet. As terrorism expert Bruce Hoffman once observed, "success for the terrorist is dependent on their ability to keep one step ahead not only of the authorities but also of counterterrorist technology."[44] The IRA offers a prime example of this adaptation, particularly in how their bomb makers adapted new triggering devices to circumvent the scanners and other technological advances developed by Scotland Yard. Another famous example is the story of Osama bin Laden's satellite phone: in 2001, when it was reported in the news media that the U.S. was tracking bin Laden in Afghanistan by targeting his satellite phone, he gave the phone to someone moving in an opposite direction, thus thwarting America's efforts to catch him.

Al-Qaeda learned to adapt and evolve through the diffusion of knowledge and capabilities, and by responding to publicly available knowledge about U.S. counterterrorism efforts. What started out as a traditionally hierarchical organization, established by the Palestinian cleric Abdullah Azzam and Osama bin Laden, became more of a global "leaderless resistance" movement in which individuals inspired by al-Qaeda's ideology of anti-Western jihad carry out terrorist attacks with little or no direct involvement or coordination with the original core members of the group. This kind of transformation was articulated most forcefully by prolific al-Qaeda ideologue Abu Musab al-Suri, who argued that "individual terrorism" needed to replace the hierarchical, more traditional

Figure 13.1: Abu Musab al-Suri (a.k.a. Mustafa Setmariam Nasar), a prolific author of jihadist strategies and other documents popular among al-Qaeda members.

approach to terrorism that al-Qaeda had embraced thus far.[45] He envisioned a "mass participation jihadist movement" in which individuals would attack targets worldwide "where it hurts the enemy and costs them the most" and "where it awakens Muslims and revives the spirit of jihad and resistance."[46] More on the history and evolution of al-Qaeda and the global Salafi-jihadist movement is provided in Lecture 12, while the individualized form of "do it yourself" terrorism that al-Suri envisioned is addressed in Lecture 15.

While these and other examples reflect the ways in which knowledge is transferred among members within an organization, we have also seen how knowledge is transferred from one organization to another, even across significant distance in time, space, and ideological orientation. For example, innovations by the Tamil Tigers in the development and use of suicide bombers and improvised explosive devices have been emulated by other terrorist groups worldwide, from al-Qaeda to Hizballah.[47] They also pioneered the use of boats on suicide bombing missions. For example, they used this tactic in an attack on May 4, 1991 against the *Abheetha*, a Sri Lankan Navy supply ship, and conducted similar attacks throughout the 1990s. And in October 2001, they carried out a coordinated suicide attack on the *MV Silk Pride*, an oil tanker carrying more than 650 tons of diesel and kerosene to the port of Jaffna, in northern Sri Lanka. In this instance, the attackers used five boats in the attack. One rammed the tanker, triggering an explosion on board, and three sailors died in the attack.[48]

October is the same month in which al-Qaeda had attacked the *USS Cole*, a U.S. Navy destroyer, while it was visiting the port of Aden, Yemen, back in 2000. Here, a small boat laden with explosives pulled up next to the ship and detonated, killing 17 sailors and injuring 39 others. In October 2002, an explosive-laden boat driven by members of al-Qaeda slammed into the French oil tanker *MV Limburg* in the port of Ash Shihr, off the coast of Yemen, splitting the vessel's hull. At the time of the blast, which killed one crew member and sent more than 90,000 barrels of Iranian crude oil pouring into the Gulf of Aden, the *MV Limburg* was picking up a pilot to guide it into the terminal.[49] The naval wing of the Tamil Tigers—the so-called "Black Sea Tiger Suicide Squad"—also developed underwater bombs, based on the explosive RDX and a timer detonator, which were used in suicide attacks by members who received scuba training. Knowing this, the FBI began investigating reports of possible al-Qaeda suspects approaching scuba diving clubs in America and inquiring about training, and a diving school in the Netherlands was investigated after a diving instructor and three students were suspected of al-Qaeda links.[50]

AT A GLANCE

The level of threat posed by a terrorist group is determined in large part by its ability to build its organizational capabilities and make effective decisions. Characteristics that affect terrorist group learning and decision-making include:

- Resources devoted to learning (including personnel, documentation and finances)
- Connections to external knowledge sources
- Group operational environment (including political and socioeconomic conditions)
- Stability and longevity of group membership and leaders
- Personal experiences and other attributes of members
- Absorption capacity for new knowledge
- Ability to communicate effectively throughout the organization
- Structure and command relationships

Sources: Adapted from two RAND Corporation reports, *Aptitude for Destruction* (2005), and *Breaching the Fortress Wall* (2007)

Finally, we have seen terrorist innovations most recently among members of the so-called Islamic State, where drones have been used to drop explosives on Iraqi forces.[51] IS members have used rudimentary chemical weapons dozens of times over the past several years, according to at least one report.[52] As noted earlier, the group became notorious for its innovative online propaganda, including popular music videos and documentaries portraying life in their so-called caliphate as blissful and exciting. Some members of IS even stole airport screening machines and used them to test whether various kinds of weapons could be smuggled onto airplanes.[53] In these and other ways, the Islamic State has continued to demonstrate the attributes of organizational learning and innovation described in this lecture, one of several reasons the U.S. and other countries are focusing a great deal of effort to confront them and diminish their capabilities.

SUMMARY

To conclude, our analysis of terrorist group decision-making requires an appreciation for the different kinds of ways that terrorists commit resources (finances, personnel, and time) to learning and innovation. Scholars like Paul Gill refer to a certain "malevolent creativity" when describing the attributes of terrorist groups that seem to have a knack for innovating in ways that help improve their effectiveness and chances of survival.[54] We know that some (but certainly not all) terrorist groups innovate for a variety of reasons, sometimes in an attempt to solve a specific tactical or operational problem, and other times because new resources or personnel suddenly became available. Rivalries and competition, as described earlier in this lecture, can also motivate certain kinds of innovation. In turn, these kinds of innovations are also learning opportunities, and allow the terrorist group's leaders to make new kinds of decisions based on the nature of those innovations.[55]

Terrorist organizations that have survived over multiple generations appear to have made a clear commitment to improving their ability to motivate new members, equip them with new skills, and become smarter and more lethal terrorists. Let's conclude this lecture with a handful of observations about organizational learning in the world of terrorism. First, *knowledge is a critical asset for any terrorist organization.* In a sense, knowledge can be seen as information that becomes useful upon human interpretation. Whether this knowledge is developed from within the organization or acquired by studying other organizations that have developed useful expertise, a terrorist organization must continually obtain, analyze, assimilate, and operationalize certain kinds of knowledge in order to effectively achieve its goals. Further, beyond tactical and operational learning, a terrorist group also needs to invest in strategic learning—that is, it needs to constantly monitor and adapt to its environment in ways that will ensure sustained support and long-term survival. In essence, learning impacts a group's decision-making and the potential for positive outcomes from those decisions. As we will discuss in Lectures 16 through 18, decision-making about weapons—particularly suicide bombings and weapons of mass destruction—is uniquely dependent upon a terrorist group's knowledge base.

Second, a review of the history of terrorism reveals that *successful terrorist organizations are committed to the long-term training and education of their members.* Clearly, the attributes of a learning organization (e.g., fostering the ability to adapt to a changing strategic environment) can be seen among the more sophisticated terrorist organizations like al-Qaeda, Hamas, Jemmah Islamiyyah, and the FARC. Through the development of doctrines, training manuals, military exercises, and educational programs (often, but not necessarily, provided at remote training camps), the most lethal terrorist organizations work hard to continually improve their capabilities. From a counterterrorism and law enforcement perspective, it is important to recognize that some terrorist groups will respond to whatever efforts might be undertaken to degrade their capabilities by adapting new tactics, changing their group and command structures, selecting new targets, or even developing new organizational objectives or missions.[29]

> **TO THE POINT**
>
> Relatively few terrorist groups have survived over multiple generations.

Third, *successful terrorist organizations learn from the strategies and tactics of other organizations.* They learn by studying each other's training manuals, videos, and other forms of information (particularly via the Internet). They also learn from media accounts of terrorist events (both successes and failures) conducted by other organizations. Over time, a global network of information knowledge sharing has come to play a key role in developing the operational capabilities of learning organizations in the world of terrorism. Further, while the formal means and locations of knowledge sharing are important (for example, Jemmah Islamiyyah members trained in al-Qaeda's Afghanistan camps; members of the Lebanese Hizballah helped to train the Palestinian group Hamas), it is the informal knowledge networks among terrorists and their organizations that contribute the most to learning in the terrorist world.

And finally, we should recognize that *a variety of social institutions support knowledge transfer in the terrorist world.* While much has been written in recent years about the role of training camps in developing a terrorist group's capabilities, we must also recognize that terrorists can exchange or acquire knowledge in many other ways, from attending a particular madrasa or university to surfing the Internet or simply following the news on CNN or Al Jazeera. From this perspective, the modern information age has now made possible a whole variety of new strategic and tactical capabilities, knowledge sharing, and potential collaboration for terrorist organizations. This is one of the most fundamental ways in which today's terrorism differs from that of a hundred years ago. This information-rich environment may also be a major reason why the modern religious "wave" of terrorism may be here for many years to come.

QUESTIONS FOR DISCUSSION

- What factors influence a terrorist group's decision-making?
- What do terrorist organizations need to know in order to survive?
- How does "knowledge" differ from "intelligence"?
- How can a terrorist group find out what a government will try to do to defeat it?
- If you have already begun studying a particular terrorist group, what indications of strategic, tactical, and organizational learning have you found?

RECOMMENDED READING

Abrahms, Max and Karolina Lula. "Why Terrorists Overestimate the Odds of Victory." *Perspectives on Terrorism* 6, no. 4 (August 2012): 46–62.

Arquilla, John, David Ronfeldt, and Michele Zanini. "Networks, Netwar and Information Age Terrorism." In *Networks and Netwars*. Edited by John Arquilla and David Ronfeldt. Santa Monica, CA: Rand Corporation, 2001.

Bell, J. Bowyer. "The Armed Struggle and Underground Intelligence: An Overview." *Studies in Conflict and Terrorism* 17 (1994).

Gill, Paul et al. "Malevolent Creativity in Terrorist Organizations." *Journal of Creative Behavior* 47, no. 2 (2013): 121–51.

Gunaratna, Rohan and Arabinda Acharya. "The Terrorist Training Camps of al Qaeda." In *The Making of a Terrorist*. Vol. 2. Edited by James J. F. Forest. Westport, CT: Praeger, 2005.

Heyman, Edward and Edward Mickolus. "Imitation by Terrorists: Quantitative Approaches to the Study of Diffusion Patterns in Transnational Terrorism." In *Behavioral and Quantitative Perspectives on Terrorism*. Edited by Yonah Alexander and John M. Gleason. New York: Pergamon Press, 1981.

Hoffman, Bruce. "Terrorism Trends and Prospect." In *Countering the New Terrorism*. Edited by Ian O. Lesser et al. Santa Monica: RAND, 1999.

Jackson, Brian A. *Aptitude for Destruction, Volume 1: Organizational Learning in Terrorist Groups and its Implications for Combating Terrorism*. Santa Monica, CA: Rand Corporation, 2005.

Jackson, Brian A. "Training for Urban Resistance: The Case of the Provisional Irish Republican Army." In *The Making of a Terrorist*. Vol. 2. Edited by James J. F. Forest. Wesport, CT: Praeger, 2005.

Jackson, Brian A., Peter Chalk, Kim Cragin, et al. B*reaching the Fortress Wall: Understanding Terrorist Efforts to Overcome Defensive Technologies*. Santa Monica, CA: RAND Corporation, 2007.

Kenney, Michael. "How Terrorists Learn." In *Teaching Terror*. Edited by James J. F. Forest. Lanham, MD: Rowman & Littlefield, 2006.

Levitt, Barbara and James G. March. "Organizational Learning." *Annual Review of Sociology* 14, no. 324 (1988).

Lia, Brynjar. *Architect of Global Jihad: The Life of al-Qaeda Strategist Abu Musab al-Suri*. Oxford University Press, 2008.

Moghadam, Assaf. "How Al-Qaeda Innovates." *Security Studies* 22, no. 3 (2013): 466–97.

Olcott, Martha Brill. "Teaching New Terrorist Recruits: A Review of Training Manuals from the Uzbekistan Mujahideen." In *The Making of a Terrorist*. Vol. 2. Edited by James J. F. Forest. Westport, CT: Praeger, 2005.

Ortiz, Román D. "Renew to Last: Innovation and Strategy of the Revolutionary Armed Forces of Colombia (FARC)." In *Teaching Terror*. Edited by James J. F. Forest. Lanham, MD: Rowman & Littlefield, 2006.

Parachini, John V. "The Making of Aum Shinrikyo's Chemical Weapons Program." In *The Making of a Terrorist*. Vol. 2. Edited by James J. F. Forest. Westport, CT: Praeger, 2005.

Rasmussen, Maria J. and Mohammed M. Hafez, eds. *Terrorist Innovations in Weapons of Mass Effect: Preconditions, Causes and Predictive Behaviors*. (August 2010 Workshop Report). Washington, DC: Defense Threat Reduction Agency.

Shapiro, Jacob N. *The Terrorist's Dilemma: Managing Violent Covert Organizations*. Princeton University Press, 2013.

Shapiro, Jacob. "Terrorist Decision-Making: Insights from Economics and Political Science." *Perspectives on Terrorism* 6, no. 4 (August 2012): 5–20.

Trujillo, Horacio R. and Brian A. Jackson. "Organizational Learning and Terrorist Groups." In *Teaching Terror*. Edited by James J. F. Forest. Lanham, MD: Rowman & Littlefield, 2006.

WEBSITES

Center for Terrorism and Security Studies, UMass Lowell
http://www.uml.edu/ctss

Combating Terrorism Center at West Point
http://www.ctc.usma.edu

RAND Corporation
http://www.rand.org

NOTES

1. David C. Rapoport, "Terrorism," in *Routledge Encyclopedia of Government and Politics*, vol. 2, ed. Mary Hawkesworth and Maurice Kogan (London: Routledge, 1992): 1067.

2. Gordon H. McCormick, "Terrorist Decision Making," *Annual Review of Political Science* 6 (2003): 500.

3. Jacob Shapiro, *The Terrorist's Dilemma: Managing Violent Covert Organizations* (Princeton University Press, 2013): 4.

4. Jacob N. Shapiro, "Terrorist Decision-Making: Insights from Economics and Political Science," *Perspectives on Terrorism* 6, no. 4–5 (2012): 5.

5. Jacob Shapiro, *The Terrorist's Dilemma: Managing Violent Covert Organizations* (Princeton University Press, 2013): 1–4.

6. Max Abrahms and Karolina Lula, "Why Terrorists Overestimate the Odds of Victory," *Perspectives on Terrorism* 6, no. 4–5 (2012): 46–47.

7. Max Abrahms, "Why Terrorism Does Not Work," *International Security* 31 (2006): 42–78.

8. Che Guevara, *Guerrilla Warfare* (Harmondsworth: Penguin Books, 1969): 26. See also Wilkinson, Terrorism and the Liberal State, 59. Cited in Max Abrahms, "Why Terrorism Does Not Work," *International Security* 31, no. 2 (2006).

9. Carlos Marighella. Minimanual of the Urban Guerrilla (1969), http://www.marxists.org /archive/marighella-carlos/1969/06/minimanual-urban-guerrilla/index.htm. Cited in Abrahms, 2006.

10. Max Abrahms, Nicholas Beauchamp, and Joseph Mroszczyk. "What Terrorist Leaders Want: A Content Analysis of Terrorist Propaganda Videos," *Studies in Conflict & Terrorism* 40, no. 11 (2017): 899–916.

11. Kydd, Andrew H. and Barbara F. Walter, "The Strategies of Terrorism," *International Security* 31, no. 1 (Summer 2006): 52–53.

12. Ibid., 51.

13. Ibid.

14. Ibid., 51–52.

15. For more on this, see Mia Bloom, *Dying to Kill: The Allure of Suicide Terrorism* (New York: Columbia University Press, 2005).

16. See Bruce Hoffman, *Inside Terrorism* (New York: Columbia University, 2006): 280–90.

17. Nur al-Din al-Kurdi, "The Arenas of Jihad," *Dharwat al-Sunam* 3 (2006): 27-28.

18. Akhu Man Ta`a Allah, "What Else is There to Say About September 11," *Sawt al-Jihad* 26 (2004): 35–42.

19. Abu Mus`ab al-Najadi, "al Qaeda's Battle is Economic not Military" (October 3, 2005).

20. Abi Hajer Abd al-Aziz al-Muqrin, "Military Sciences—Targets in the Cities," *Mu`askar al-Battar* 7: 23–27.

21. Ibid.

22. *Softpedia*, "Fuel Depot Explosion in London Covers the Sky with Huge Smoke Cloud" (December 12, 2005).

23. Abu Bakr Naji, *The Management of Savagery: The Most Critical Stage through which the Umma Will Pass*, translated by William McCants (2006), available on the Combating Terrorism Center at West Point website, http://www.ctc.usma.edu/naji.asp.

24. Horacio R. Trujillo and Brian A. Jackson, "Organizational Learning and Terrorist Groups," in *Teaching Terror*, ed. James J. F. Forest (Lanham, MD: Rowman & Littlefield, 2006): 53.

25. For more on this, see Audrey Kurth Cronin, "How Al Qaeda Ends," *International Security* 31, no.1 (2006).

26. Case Willoughby, "Learning Organizations," in *Higher Education in the United States: An Encyclopedia*, ed. James J. F. Forest and Kevin Kinser (Santa Barbara, CA: ABC-CLIO, 2002): 391–93.

27. Peter Senge, *The Fifth Discipline: The Art and Practice of the Learning Organization* (New York: Doubleday, 1990): 3.

28. Scott Johnson and Melinda Liu, "The Enemy Spies," *Newsweek*, June 27, 2005.

29. See David E. Smith, "The Training of Terrorist Organizations," CSC Report (1995): 7.

30. See Martha Brill Olcott and Bakhtiyar Babadjanov, "The Terrorist Notebooks," *Foreign Policy* (March–April 2003): 30-40.

31. Ibid., 33.

32. See C. J. Chivers and David Rohde, "Turning out Guerillas and Terrorists to Wage a Holy War," *New York Times*, March 18, 2002, A1.

33. Ibid.

34. Ibid.

35. See Nic Robertson, "Tapes Show al Qaeda Trained for Urban Jihad on West," CNN (August 20, 2002), http://goo.gl/T2EWA.

36. Ibid.

37. See John J. Lumpkin, "Bin Laden's Terrorist Training Combined Math, Missiles," *Associated Press* (October 9, 2001).

38. Román D. Ortiz, "Renew to Last: Innovation and Strategy of the Revolutionary Armed Forces of Colombia (FARC)," in *Teaching Terror*, ed. Forest.

39. Ibid.

40. See David E. Smith, "The Training of Terrorist Organizations," 25, and Thomas Bedford and Frank Jones, "Sendero Luminoso: Origins, Outlooks and Implications" (Monterey, CA: Naval Postgraduate School, June 1986): 53.

41. For more on these, see Zachary Abuza, "Education and Radicalization: Jemaah Islamiyah Recruitment in Southeast Asia," and Kumar Ramakrishna, "Indoctrination Processes Within Jemaah Islamiyah," in *The Making of a Terrorist*, ed. James J. F. Forest (Westport, CT: Praeger, 2005).

42. See J. Bowyer Bell, *The IRA, 1968-2000: Analysis of a Secret Army* (London: Frank Cass, 2000); and "The Training of Terrorist Organizations."

43. Ibid.

44. Bruce Hoffman, *Inside Terrorism* (Columbia University Press, 1998): 180.

45. Paul Cruickshank and Mohannad Hage Ali, "Abu Musab al Suri: Architect of the New Al Qaeda," *Studies in Conflict & Terrorism* 30 (2007): 8.

46. Abu Musab al-Suri, jihadist training videos, dated August 2000. Cited in Cruickshank, 9.

47. Mia Bloom, "What the Tigers Taught Al-Qaeda," *Washington Post*, May 24, 2009.

48. Tamil Tigers Claim Tanker Attack," *BBC News* (October 31, 2001), http://goo.gl/WJpYp.

49. "Yemen Says Tanker Blast was Terrorism," *BBC News* (October 16, 2002), http://goo.gl /I0SQF; and "Craft 'Rammed' Yemen Oil Tanker," *BBC News* (October 6, 2002), http://goo.gl /XAnLv.

50. Michael Smith, "Al-Qaeda Threat to Trafalgar Fleet," *Sunday Times* (April 24, 2005), http://goo.gl/MdbOr; and "Divers at Eindhoven Dive School Suspected of Al-Qaeda Connection," *Divernet News* (August 22, 2003).

51. Joby Warrick, "Use of weaponized drones by ISIS spurs terrorism fears," *Washington Post* (February 21, 2017), http://wapo.st/2DQONvg.

52. Eric Schmitt, "ISIS Used Chemical Arms at Least 52 Times in Syria and Iraq, Report Says," *New York Times* (November 21, 2016), http://nyti.ms/2oQkRut.

53. Pierre Thomas et al., "Intel suggests terrorists got airport screening equipment to test concealing bombs," ABC News (March 31, 2017), http://abcn.ws/2nsHuRB.

54. Paul Gill, et al., "Malevolent Creativity in Terrorist Organizations," *Journal of Creative Behavior* 47, no. 2 (2013): 121–51.

55. For more on terrorist group innovation and creativity, see Assaf Moghadam, "How Al-Qaeda Innovates," *Security Studies* 22, no. 3 (2013): 466–97; and *Terrorist Innovations in Weapons of Mass Effect: Preconditions, Causes and Predictive Behaviors*, ed. Maria J. Rasmussen and Mohammed M. Hafez (August 2010 Workshop Report) (Washington, DC: Defense Threat Reduction Agency).

56. Trujillo, Horacio R. and Brian A. Jackson, "Organizational Learning and Terrorist Groups," in *Teaching Terror*, ed. Forest, p. 53.

IV

Contemporary Challenges

14

Engagement, Recruitment, and Radicalization

This lecture examines how an individual's perceptions and beliefs about the world, along with their interpersonal relationships, are at the core of most terrorist activity. As Lorenzo Vidino has described, engagement in terrorism often takes place at the "intersection of an enabling environment and a personal trajectory."[1] Thus, to understand what leads a person to become a terrorist, we have to gather information on both the local context and that person's situation.

As discussed in Lecture 3, grievances (political, social, economic, and many others) may lead to various kinds of radical or extremist ideas. Thus, ideological motivations for terrorism have been a central aspect of research literature and mainstream news reporting. For example, research by a team of psychologists identified five "belief domains" that have motivated individuals and groups toward violent behavior.[2] The first of these is superiority, which revolves around the conviction that one type of people is better than others and thus entitled to a better future, a special destiny. For centuries, the manifestations of this have included widespread violence such as ethnic cleansing and religious wars. A second belief domain is injustice, which fuels grievances based on perceived mistreatment by specific others or by the world at large. Next is vulnerability, a feeling (common among minority ethnic and religious groups within a society) that others seek to harm them, which leads to group behavior that may include hostility toward the source of the perceived threat, heightened in-group solidarity, ethnocentrism, and a tightening of group boundaries. The fourth belief domain of distrust is directly related to the other beliefs described here, with its presumption of hostility and malign intent of others. And the fifth core belief they identify is helplessness, a conviction that the current sociopolitical environment lacks opportunities for creating a better future. Each of these beliefs alone can be linked to many historical and contemporary examples of individual and group conflict; when several of these beliefs are prevalent within the same context, they can produce a very powerful combination of rationalizations and motivations for engaging in terrorism.

However, it is also important to recognize that individuals may engage in (or support) terrorist activity for reasons that have nothing to do with radicalization or extremist ideologies. In some cases, a person's involvement in terrorist activity may have more to do with a sense of loyalty, kinship, or duty. In fact, some scholars have even suggested that the term "radicalization" has become overused and meaningless in our search to determine why individuals become involved in terrorist activity. For example, John Horgan encourages us to focus on "engagement" in (and disengagement from) terrorism, in order to avoid the false assumption that without radicalization there can be no terrorist recruitment.[3]

Of course, we know that some individuals get involved in a terrorist movement because they want to, often driven by dissatisfaction with their lives, and searching for something that gives them a sense of purpose. But as Marc Sageman and other researchers have found, some terrorists have been drawn into a movement by their family members or close friends.[4] According to a recent study by William Rosenau and others, personal connections have been "a factor of recruitment into a wide variety of clandestine, underground and violent extremist groups."[5] In his personal account of how he joined (and eventually left) al-Qaeda, Omar Nasiri describes in detail the various personal relationships that led him into the terrorist network, and helped him survive the difficult ordeals in the training camps and living a life on the run from government authorities.[6]

Meanwhile, many other individuals have become involved in terrorist activity entirely by accident, agreeing to help someone they trust only to discover afterward that their actions were related to terrorism. An even uglier and more worrisome trend involves terrorist groups using children to do their bidding. They are easy prey for a terrorist group—young, impressionable, and often dependent on adults for their survival. A recent study of children recruited by the FARC (a left-wing terrorist group in Colombia) found that several had joined because of "the tediousness of their former lives, family ties to armed groups, and the desire for a better quality of life."[7] One 13-year-old joined after having worked in a mine, and a 17-year-old joined after what he called "an ill-paying job on a rice plantation." Throughout Afghanistan, Iraq, Nigeria, and Pakistan, children as young as 10 years old have been recruited, forced, or tricked into various kinds of terrorist operations, in some cases even becoming a suicide bomber. In other cases, their parents simply handed them over to a terrorist group in response to threats, extortion, to pay off a debt, or even due to a misplaced belief that their child would be better off in the hands of militants.[8]

Essentially there are many different reasons why a person can become a terrorist. So, if we accept the premise that a person's decision to engage in terrorist activity may not necessarily be related to any radicalization process, this naturally impacts our understanding of so-called "recruitment" of terrorists. For example, while there is considerable concern (and rightly so) about the role of the Internet in mobilizing individuals toward terrorist activity, it appears that for some terrorists the actual radicalization process may take place *after* they have already joined a terrorist movement. Certainly when it comes to young children being used by Taliban and other militants in Afghanistan, or by Boko Haram in Nigeria, if any radicalization takes place at all, it does so long after they have become involved in terrorist activity.

The implications of this discussion for counterterrorism strategies and policies are important to keep in mind. For those terrorists who get involved in terrorist activity because they want to, we might be able to identify some broad risk factors, like grievances or a level of dissatisfaction with life that lead a person to feel that he or she has to do something dramatic. But these risk factors don't apply to those who become involved in terrorism by accident (or by force).

Further, the nature of engagement in terrorism is not always clearly defined or easily discernable. At what point can we say, based on a person's behavior and communication, that they have become a terrorist? Some (including a court of law) may require evidence that the person has committed an act of ideologically motivated violence against persons or property before they can be officially labeled a terrorist. Others, like Max Taylor and John Horgan, argue for a more nuanced understanding of a person's "incremental and changing involvement" in terrorism, taking into account how social learning and context influence behavior.[9] This implies a kind of change or process through which life events and decisions may lead a person into—and perhaps even out of—terrorism. Naturally, the critical elements of this process differ from person to person, making it virtually impossible to describe a single common framework for understanding the transformation from "Joe the citizen" into "Joe the terrorist."

As a result, the many pathways into (and out of) terrorism are more fluid and complex than we have time to adequately explore in this brief overview. But it is important to recognize that while the bulk of the rest of this lecture focuses on issues surrounding the problem of radicalization, there is much more to terrorist involvement than radical ideologies. Further, to reiterate, we have to recognize that ideological radicalization could take place before or after an individual becomes part of a terrorist movement. With this in mind, we now turn to examine some research-based ideas on the nature of radicalization.

RADICALIZATION

In general, the term "radicalization" is meant to describe the ways in which a terrorist group mobilizes people and convinces them to support their strategy and tactics. A person can become radicalized through a variety of complex and dynamic interactions with the terrorist group's ideology and other characteristics (including leadership, reputation, history, etc.), often (but not always) combined with personal motivations (including revenge, psychological attributes, belief systems, personal grievances, and so forth), and influenced by their family, friends, religious or community leaders, and many others. The bottom line here is that while previous lectures highlighted a bunch of grievances and facilitators that are connected to outbreaks of terrorist activity, the real "root" of terrorism lies in the mind of the individual. Thus, it is important to understand the emotional and intellectual aspects of this problem.

As mentioned several times earlier in this book, the ideologies of terrorist groups typically articulate and explain a set of grievances, including socioeconomic disadvantages, and a lack of justice or political freedoms.[10] Usually, but not always, the strategies that terrorist groups put forward require joining or at least supporting their organization—thus, an ideology also provides a group identity and highlights the common characteristics of individuals who adhere to it. According to Assaf Moghadam, "ideologies are links between thoughts, beliefs and myths on the one hand, and action on the other hand . . . [providing] a 'cognitive map' that filters the way social realities are perceived, rendering that reality easier to grasp, more coherent, and thus more meaningful."[11]

Research by Andrew Kydd and Barbara Walter indicates that terrorist organizations are usually driven by political objectives, and in particular, "five have had enduring importance: regime change, territorial change, policy change, social control and status quo maintenance."[12] These objectives have led to terrorist group formation in Northern Ireland, Italy, Egypt, Germany, Sri Lanka, Japan, Indonesia, the Philippines, the United States, and many other countries around the world. The members of these groups have viewed terrorism as an effective and necessary vehicle for political change, often pointing to historical examples of terrorist attacks producing results, like driving the United States (and later Israel) out of Lebanon, and convincing the French to pull out of Algeria. Ethnic separatist groups want the power to form their own recognized, sovereign entity, carved out of an existing nation-state, and believe terrorist attacks can help them achieve this objective. Several religious extremist groups engaged in the Middle East want the power to establish an Islamic Palestinian state, while others want the power to establish an Islamic state in their own region. In these and other instances, people seek power to change the status quo, to forge a future that they do not believe will come about peacefully, and are determined to use terrorism to achieve their objectives. In other cases, particularly among right-wing terrorist groups, violence is used to defend a status quo that is perceived to be threatened by various sociopolitical changes or "outside" forces.

We have already spent considerable time in this lecture series examining different kinds of ideologies that have compelled individuals to carry out terrorist acts. Several of the most prominent terrorist ideologies draw on revolutionary theorists of the past half-century, like Mao, who called for uniting the classes in a mass revolution; Che Guevara, who argued that a small dedicated cadre of fighters could create the conditions for popular revolution; Frantz Fanon, who argued that political violence is a *necessary* instrument of liberation; and Carlos Marighella, who argued that terrorism should move from the countryside to the cities, because urban violence will have a greater impact on the most influential decision-makers of a country. Even al-Qaeda and the Islamic State have embraced elements of these revolutionary narratives, as reflected in their "vanguard" ideology and commitment to urban terrorist attacks.

Across the spectrum, from political revolutionaries to religious militants, ideologies of violence and terrorism must strike a chord; that is, an ideology has no power unless it resonates with the social, political, and historical context of those whose support the organization requires. As we explored in Lecture 3, the resonance of an organization's ideology is largely based on a combination of persuasive communicators, the compelling nature of the grievances articulated, and the pervasiveness of local conditions that seem to justify an organization's rationale for the use of violence. In other words, local context is a critical element of radicalization. When an organization's ideology resonates among its target audience, it can influence an individual's perceptions and help determine the form of their "decision tree," a menu of potential options for future action that may include terrorism (see Figure 14.1).

Thus, in addition to studying the attributes of terrorist organizations and the environments in which they operate, we also have to examine the characteristics of individuals who join or support terrorist groups. There has of course been ample research in this area. An abundance of scholarly books and journal articles describe various kinds of psychological influences, including kinship, belief systems, and personal grievances, which contribute to a person's motivations for engaging in terrorist activity. Scholars have also cited the importance of a person's hatred of others, desire for power, risk tolerance, unbreakable loyalty to friends or family who are already involved in a violent movement, prior participation in a radical political movement, thirst for excitement and adventure, and many other types of motivations.

Terrorism is a distinctly human endeavor—that is, of all species on Earth, only humans have been known to engage in terrorist activity, either individually or as members of an organization, and victims and targets of terrorism are always human.[13]

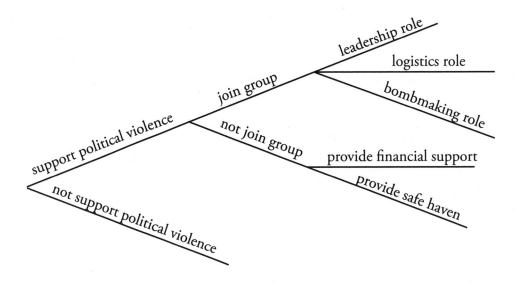

Figure 14.1: A decision tree such as this illustrates the kinds of decisions a potential terrorist would have to make.

Thus, academic disciplines that study human behavior, and particularly the field of psychology, can contribute much to our understanding of what motivates individuals to choose terrorism. According to renowned psychologist Max Taylor, much of the research in this field has attempted to describe personal characteristics of terrorists, on the assumption that terrorists can be identified by these attributes.[14] Surely, many have argued, terrorists are sociopaths, psychopaths, paranoid, or pathological narcissists—individuals with anti-social or other personality disorders that drive them toward terrorist activity. Therefore, through rigorous research, they suggest it is possible to derive some form of a "terrorist mindset."

Psychologist Jerrold Post has suggested that a person's need to belong and to exercise control in their own lives is intensified in communities where segments of the population are ostracized or persecuted based on ethnic, religious, or social background. By belonging to a radical group, otherwise powerless individuals become powerful. Group identity provides a foundation of relative stability upon which disenfranchised or isolated members of a society build a base of commonality and join together.[15] His research also led him to coin the term "psycho-logic" to describe how the terrorist constructs a personal rationalization for acts they are psychologically compelled to commit.[16] In essence, a polarizing and absolutist "us versus them" rhetoric reflects terrorists' underlying views of "the establishment" as the source of all evil, and provides a psychologically satisfying explanation for what has gone wrong in their lives; a "psychopolitics of hatred."[17]

Other researchers, such as Bard O'Neill and Donald Alberts, have described how organizations provide a blend of ideological and material incentives that meet an individual's need for belonging, identity, and for rectifying a perceived injustice. Once individuals have joined or otherwise actively supported terrorist groups for ideological reasons, it is difficult to win them back because of the psychological and emotional investments they have made.[18] Other reasons individuals join these groups include a perception of rewards for participating in terrorism; friendships and camaraderie that lead to and are solidified within the terror cell or organization; and the perceived opportunity to attain a higher social status derived from group membership.[19]

Proponents of similar psychological explanations for terrorism describe individuals consumed by hatred toward others and willing to kill without remorse.[20] Walter Lacqueur has argued that "madness, especially paranoia, plays a role in contemporary terrorism. Not all paranoiacs are terrorists, but all terrorists believe in conspiracies by powerful, hostile forces and suffer from some form of delusion and persecution mania."[21] Others have suggested that an education system that places a heavy emphasis on rote memorization and an unwillingness to challenge authority may contribute to an individual's susceptibility to indoctrination by terrorist groups.[22]

Overall, these and various other studies in psychology have sought to illuminate a unique set of attributes that contribute to terrorism. There is clearly a demand for this among policymakers and the general public who seek clarity about what is in fact a very complex problem.[23] However, the most common result of research in this area actually reveals a pattern of "normalcy"—that is, the absence of any unique attribute or identifier that would distinguish one individual from another. Andrew Silke observed how research on the mental state of terrorists has found that they are rarely mad, and very few suffer from personality disorders.[24] According to John Horgan, "Many of the personal traits or characteristics [identified in this research] as belonging to the terrorist are neither specific to the terrorist nor serve to distinguish one type of terrorist from another. . . . There are no a-priori qualities of the terrorist that enable us to predict the likelihood of risk of involvement and engagement (which is, after all, the true scientific test of such profiles) in any particular person or social group that is valid or reliable over a meaningful period of time."[25]

> **TO THE POINT**
>
> Psychological research indicates that terrorists are rarely mad, and very few suffer from personality disorders.

Clark McCauley has observed that "30 years of research has found little evidence that terrorists are suffering from psychopathology,"[26] and Marc Sageman agrees, noting how "experts on terrorism have tried in vain for three decades to identify a common predisposition for terrorism."[27] Sociologist Martha Crenshaw also agrees with these scholars in declining to ascribe abnormal pathology to terrorists, arguing instead that terrorists' actions are the product of a strategic, rational choice.[28] Overall, there is no single psychology of terrorism, no unified theory.[29] The broad diversity of personal motivations for becoming a terrorist undermines the possibility of a single, common "terrorist mindset." Thus, profiling individuals based on some type of perceived propensity to conduct terrorist attacks becomes extremely difficult, if not altogether impossible.[30]

This reinforces the importance of individual choice; that is, individuals from virtually *any* background can choose to engage in terrorist activity. Thus, an especially promising area of research on the individual risk of terrorist activity uses phrases and metaphors like "pathways to radicalization" and "staircase to terrorism" to describe a dynamic process of psychological development that leads an individual to participate in terrorist activity.[31] In one noteworthy example, Max Taylor and John Horgan offer a framework for analyzing developmental processes—that is, "a sequence of events involving steps or operations that are usefully ordered and/or interdependent"— through which an individual becomes involved with, and sometimes abandons, terrorist activity.[32] Their research highlights the importance of understanding the dynamic context in which individuals operate, and how the relationships between contexts, organizations and individuals affect behavior.[33]

Each day, countless individuals grapple with situations and environmental conditions that may generate feelings of outrage and powerlessness, among many other potential motivators for becoming violent. But an individual's view of these situations and conditions—and how to respond appropriately to them—is clearly influenced by their family members, peers and personal role models, educators, religious leaders and others who help interpret and contextualize local and global conditions. Because these interpretive influences play such a key role in how an individual responds to the challenges of everyday life events and trends that generate political grievances among members of a particular community, we sometimes see a contagion effect, whereby an individual's likelihood of becoming involved in terrorism is increased because they know or respect others who have already done so. Further, as Taylor and Horgan note, "There is never one route to terrorism, but rather there are individual routes, and furthermore those routes and activities as experienced by the individual change over time."[34]

The dynamics of an individual's connections to others—including, for example, family, friends, small groups, clubs, gangs, and diasporas—also help an individual interpret the potential legitimacy of an organization that has adopted terrorism as a strategy. According to Michael Leiter, a former director of the National Counterterrorism Center, individuals are often introduced to the fringes of violent extremist groups by friends, family members, and authority figures in their community, among others.[35] Similarly, Sageman has found that social bonds have played a central role in the emergence of the global Salafi-jihadist movement, whose members comprise organizations such as al-Qaeda, the Islamic State, and their affiliates in North Africa and Southeast Asia.[36]

In essence, a central component of any terrorism analysis is the need to understand the dynamic nature of an individual's interactions with and perceptions toward their environment, along with the many developmental processes that lead into, through, and out of terrorist activity. We have to take into account the tools and mechanisms of radicalization, like myths, symbols, history, educational and religious leaders, family members, social networks, and so forth, as well as the temporal nature of the interactions that lead to terrorist radicalization. We also have to study how environmental conditions and individual belief systems interact with each other, and how we know what we know, and why we believe what we believe.

SIX PROPOSITIONS ABOUT RADICALIZATION

Overall, I have come to view *radicalization as an interactive process that begins with communication.* By extension, terrorism can be seen as the product of individual and organizational choices influenced by complex relationships that are dynamic, fluid, and changing over time. Thinking about these kinds of interactions eventually led me to formulate six propositions about the risks of terrorism that highlight the centrality of ideas, perceptions, and beliefs, and how these can be influenced as part of a comprehensive counterterrorism strategy.[37] I will review each of them here, and then conclude this lecture with some final thoughts about the complex challenges of studying terrorist radicalization.

The first proposition is that *the primary cause of terrorism is a human being's decision to commit some form of terrorist activity.* In other words, whatever an individual does that is terrorist-related, the chances are fairly good that he or she chose to do it. While we have seen a few instances here or there of individuals reluctantly coerced into carrying out some sort of terrorist act (for example, the case of the Iraqi father who detonated a car bomb at a checkpoint because his family was being held hostage by al-Qaeda militants, or the children abducted by the Lord's Resistance Army and forced to become militants), these are a minority in the world of terrorism. For the most part, people who get involved in terrorist activity do so by intention, making a conscious choice whether to pull that trigger, detonate that bomb, transfer those funds, or carry out some other act that leads to death and destruction. Some individuals choose direct involvement in actions that kill, while others choose to engage in support activities like providing funding, safe haven, or ideological support. From this perspective, it is critical for us to understand what influences and motivates an individual to make such choices.

This brings us to the second proposition, that *an individual's choice to engage in (or disengage from) terrorist activity occurs at the intersection of ideas, perceptions, and opportunities, and these can change over time.* A person's decisions to do anything in this realm are influenced by personal characteristics (like personality traits, gender, age, kinship, socioeconomic status, religiosity, etc.) as well as by their perceptions toward and interactions with specific organizations. Further, the nature of these characteristics, perceptions, and interactions change over time.

The third proposition explores this conceptual intersection further by suggesting that *an individual's perceptions toward and interactions with terrorist organizations and environmental conditions are influenced by their family, peers, and personal role models, as well as educators, religious leaders, and others who help interpret and contextualize local and global conditions.* This reflects the importance of ignorance as an enabling condition for interpretive influences that direct an individual toward terrorist activity. When individuals are prevented from encountering alternative viewpoints or open debate, when their parents, teachers, friends, and religious leaders all reinforce a common theme of hatred toward others, "radicalization" can become the norm.

> ## TO THE POINT
>
> If a person *chooses* to engage in terrorism, who or what influenced that choice, and how?

The fourth proposition is that members of terrorist organizations influence an individual's decisions about terrorist activity *by providing ideological justification for violence, along with training and expertise, material support, connections with others, and so forth.* This emphasizes the importance of understanding terrorist ideology, as well as where and why a particular organization's ideology resonates. For example, there are some contexts in which an ethnonationalist ideology will have more resonance than in others. Often, a terrorist group's ideology resonates among a population because of underlying socioeconomic and political grievances. Essentially, this proposition reinforces a central theme found in many of the lectures in this series: terrorism is a highly *contextual* phenomenon.

The fifth proposition is that *individual decisions (within and outside the organization) shape the choices and trajectory of an organization and the kinds of terrorist activity its members may pursue.* Simplistically speaking, organizations are made of people, without whom there is no organization. Thus, a terrorist organization's actions are determined by individual perceptions—including perceptions of success or failure of a particular strategy or tactic. Further, perceptions of an organization's leadership, especially its competence and personal agendas, are vital to its efforts at attracting followers of its ideology.

Members of terrorist groups, like all people, make mistakes. As a result, we have seen a number of instances where the decisions made by leaders of a terrorist group actually led to a diminished ability to gain acceptance of their ideology among their target

Figure 14.2: Palestinian child emulating a suicide bomber.

population. Examples include high profile kidnappings by the Red Army Faction in Germany, involvement in the drug trade by the FARC in Colombia, or the killing of children by militants (both Republican and Unionist) in Northern Ireland. By many accounts, the extreme level of brutality carried out by al-Qaeda in Iraq during the mid-2000s led directly to a number of powerful Sunni tribal militias turning against the group, resulting in the death of its leader Abu Musab al-Zarqawi. Essentially, a group can undermine its own ability to radicalize others, and eventually the loss of support becomes their undoing. This is an important vulnerability to keep in mind when formulating counterterrorism strategies.

The last proposition is that *the motivations and opportunities for individuals to engage in terrorism are framed by their perceptions about socioeconomic conditions and policies* (domestic and foreign), some of which are used to legitimate the grievances articulated in an organization's ideology. The reason I emphasize the word "perceptions" here is that an ideology does not have to be true to be believed. Certainly, as noted earlier, there are many kinds of contexts and conditions (and perceptions thereof) that can lend themselves to ideological resonance, radicalization and terrorist actions. But often a terrorist group will try to make a person believe that things are far worse than they really are, in order to drum up support for their radical ideology. If the terrorist group fails to do so, its ability to radicalize others to do their bidding is weakened.

INFLUENCING

Now, let's take a few moments to look at how this research on radicalization informs our understanding of the modern threat of so-called "homegrown terrorism." First, it should be clear that beliefs and ideologies are core aspects of terrorism, and thus influencing perceptions through words and images becomes a key mission of any terrorist group or movement. Note that in recent years, some media and political pundits have suggested that certain populations are easier to influence than others. This is very false and creates dangerous misperceptions. For example, despite the anti-Muslim hysteria fomented by certain individuals in the United States and Western Europe, a huge majority of Muslims reject the jihadist worldview of groups like al-Qaeda and the Islamic State. As world-renowned expert Peter Neumann accurately explains, "the 'average Muslim' is as unreachable for the jihadists as the 'average German' is for violent neo-Nazis."[38]

As a result of this challenge that all terrorist groups face, there are individuals in the world of terrorism who play the critical role of "**influencer**." These are ideological entrepreneurs, individuals whose contribution to a terrorist group's cause may be more intellectual and emotional than operational, but their ability to influence others becomes a critical asset for the group's ability to recruit and radicalize new members and supporters. Examples of these critical influencers include Abu Bakr al-Baghdadi (Islamic State), Michael Bray (Army of God), Richard Butler (Aryan Nations), Ayman al-Zawahiri and Abu Musab al-Suri (al-Qaeda), Anwar al-Awlaki (al-Qaeda in the Arabian Peninsula), Manuel Maralundo (FARC), Gerry Adams (Republican militants in Northern Ireland), and Ian Paisley (Protestant militants in Northern Ireland). For the most part, these are individuals who have not carried out major terrorist attacks on their own, but who have inspired and influenced others to do so on behalf of an ideology.

Influencers are communicators who articulate an ideology in ways that people can connect with. And there has never been a more powerful means of connecting with others worldwide than the Internet. Thus, over the past 20 years, we have seen an increasing number of these influencers using the Internet to facilitate their radicalizing efforts. Through audio and video statements, web forum discussions, and other virtual means (rather than any face-to-face communication), terrorist groups today have the capability to radicalize scores of potential followers anywhere in the world. The challenge for them in doing so, however, is to communicate in ways that will connect and resonate with people in very diverse kinds of contexts. This is an underlying reason why over a decade ago al-Qaeda began publishing videos and audios in several different languages, and with different kinds of messages tailored for different audiences. For example, in a video from Ayman al-Zawahiri that was clearly meant for an American audience, references were made to Malcolm X, the economic recession, and high profile corruption scandals—all with English subtitles. These kinds of Internet-facilitated radicalization efforts have not yet produced the kind of global "leaderless resistance" movement that Osama bin Laden and the other founders of al-Qaeda had envisioned. But as we'll discuss further in the next lecture, a significant number of recent terrorist plots within the United States have involved individuals whose radicalization process—and their only real link to al-Qaeda—has been through the Internet.

As explained earlier, an even more powerful "influencer" in a person's life is found among their family and friends. Research on terrorism by Marc Sageman and others highlight the "importance of kinship" and how "tight bonds of family and friendship" contribute to a person's membership in the al-Qaeda terror network.[39] Research by Rogelio Alonso on the IRA and the Provisional IRA found similar patterns.[40] In some cases, an individual may join a terrorist group before he or she has been radicalized; they do so out of loyalty to someone already in the group, and then become indoctrinated and radicalized by the other group members over time. Family relationships were also prominent in the case of the 2013 Boston Marathon attacks, where 19-year-old Dzhokhar Tsarnaev was significantly influenced by his older brother Tamerlan, who had been radicalized and spent time in Dagestan learning how to construct the weapons they detonated on that fateful day. Sadly, the history of terrorism is replete with stories of individuals who have been led astray by someone they trusted and believed in.

SUMMARY

To sum up, what we know today about terrorist engagement, recruitment, and radicalization is informed by analysis on the interactions between individuals and ideas. An individual's behavior is influenced by perceptions of trust, legitimacy, power, competence, and mutual benefit, among many others. Further, as emphasized throughout this lecture series, terrorist activity is a contextual phenomenon. When an individual's local community reinforces the ideological views promoted by a terrorist group, acts of terrorism become more likely. The specific pathway or process of radicalization may differ from one person to the next, but the underlying mechanisms and interactive relationships of radicalization appear rather similar. That is, the radicalization of an individual by the PKK in Turkey, Jemmah Islamiyyah in Indonesia, or the Army of God in the U.S. may follow a similar pattern, even though the terrorist ideologies and enabling contexts are very much different.

Terrorist groups also influence an individual's decisions about engaging in terrorist activity by providing training and expertise, material support, connections with others, and socialization. And, as noted earlier, an increasing body of research has shown that some individuals engage in terrorist activity without being radicalized at all. Instead, their support for—or direct involvement in—a terrorist movement may be driven by close bonds of loyalty to family members or friends. Thus, it is a mistake to oversimplify the pathways into terrorism as merely "recruitment" or "radicalization." As we'll discuss toward the end of this lecture series, this has implications for how we should think about combating terrorism. For example, if radicalization is not the primary force behind terrorist activity, programs that focus on "deradicalization" may not be a meaningful investment of resources. In fact, if an individual effectively chooses their pathway into a terrorist movement, and then chooses the roles they play within that movement, then we must learn how and why they choose to leave that group, and how we can influence those choices.

QUESTIONS FOR DISCUSSION

- Think about how you have formed your view of the world, and your place within it. Who in your life has most influenced your perceptions of the world? What events or other factors have also influenced you the most?
- What if your "influencers" were considered "extremists" by others? Would you know? How would you react if your personal "influencers" were considered "extremists" by others?
- How should a society respond when individuals are making decisions based on popular sources of information that are biased and untrustworthy?

RECOMMENDED READING

Abuza, Zachary. "Education and Radicalization: Jemaah Islamiyah Recruitment in Southeast Asia." In *The Making of a Terrorist*. Vol. 1. Edited by James J. F. Forest. Westport, CT: Praeger, 2005.

Abrahms, Max. "What Terrorists Really Want.." *International Security* 32, no. 4 (Spring 2008): 78–105.

Cragin, R. Kim. "Resisting Violent Extremism: A Conceptual Model for Non-Radicalization." *Terrorism and Political Violence* 26, no. 2 (2014): 337–53.

Crenshaw, Martha. *Explaining Terrorism: Causes, Processes and Consequences.* London: Routledge, 2010.

Eidelson, Roy and Judy Eidelson. "Dangerous Ideas: Five beliefs that propel groups toward conflict." *American Psychologist* 58 (2003).

Forest, James J. F. "Terrorism as a Product of Choices and Perceptions." In *Terrorism and Counterterrorism.* Edited by Russell Howard and Bruce Hoffman. New York: McGraw-Hill, 2011.

Forest, James J. F. "Influence Warfare and Modern Terrorism." *Georgetown Journal of International Affairs* 10, no. 1 (2009).

Horgan, John. "The Search for the Terrorist Personality." In *Terrorists, Victims and Society: Psychological Perspectives on Terrorism and its Consequences.* Edited by Andrew Silke. Chichester, UK: John Wiley and Sons, 2003.

Horgan, John. "The Social and Psychological Characteristics of Terrorism and Terrorists." In *Root Causes of Terrorism: Myths, Realities and Ways Forward.* Edited by Tore Bjorgo. London: Routledge, 2005.

Horgan, John and Max Taylor. "A Conceptual Framework for Addressing Psychological Process in the Development of the Terrorist." *Terrorism and Political Violence* 18, no. 4 (2006): 585–601.

Kydd, Andrew and Barbara Walter. "The Strategies of Terrorism." *International Security* 31, no. 1 (Summer 2006): 52.

Lia, Brynjar. "Doctrines for Jihadi Terrorist Training." *Terrorism and Political Violence* 20, no. 4 (2008).

Magouirk, Justin, Scott Atran and Marc Sageman. "Connecting Terrorist Networks." *Studies in Conflict & Terrorism* 31, no. 2 (2008): 1–16.

McCauley, Clark. "Psychological Issues in Understanding Terrorism and Response to Terrorism." In *Psychology of Terrorism: Coping with the Continuing Threat.* (Condensed Edition). Edited by Chris Stout. Westport, CT: Praeger, 2004.

McCauley, Clark and Sophia Moskalenko. "Mechanisms of Political Radicalization: Pathways Toward Terrorism." *Terrorism and Political Violence* 20, no. 3 (2008).

Nasiri, Omar. *Inside the Jihad: My Life with Al Qaeda.* New York: Basic Books, 2006.

Neumann, Peter R. *Radicalized: New Jihadists and the Threat to the West.* London: I.B. Tauris, 2017.

Robbins, James S. "Battlefronts in the War of Ideas." In *Countering Terrorism and Insurgency in the 21st Century.* Vol. 1. Edited by James J. F. Forest. Westport, CT: Praeger, 2007.

Rosenau, William, et al. "Why They Join, Why They Fight, and Why They Leave: Learning from Colombia's Database of Demobilized Militants." *Terrorism and Political Violence* 26, no. 1 (2012): 277–85.

Richardson, Louise. *What Terrorists Want.* New York: Random House, 2007.

Sageman, Marc. *Understanding Terror Networks.* Philadelphia: University of Pennsylvania Press, 2004.

Sageman, Marc. *Turning to Political Violence: The Emergence of Terrorism.* University of Pennsylvania Press, 2017.

Taylor, Max and John Horgan. "A Conceptual Framework for Addressing Psychological Process in the Development of the Terrorist." *Terrorism and Political Violence* 18, no. 4 (2006).

Lorenzo Vidino, Francesco Marone, and Eva Entenmann. *Fear Thy Neighbor: Radicalization and Jihadist Attacks in the West.* ISPI/ICCT/GWPOE Joint Report, July 2017.

WEBSITES

German Institute on Radicalization and De-Radicalization Studies
http://girds.org/

International Center for the Study of Radicalization, King's College, London
http://icsr.info/

International Center for the Study of Violent Extremism
http://www.icsve.org/

Program on Extremism, George Washington University
https://extremism.gwu.edu/

START Profiles of Individual Radicalization in the U.S.
http://www.start.umd.edu/profiles-individual-radicalization-united-states-pirus-keshif

NOTES

1. Lorenzo Vidino, "The Buccinaso Pentiti: A Unique Case Study of Radicalization," *Terrorism and Political Violence* 23, no. 3 (2011): 407.

2. Roy J. Eidelson and Judy I. Eidelson, "Dangerous Ideas: Five Beliefs That Propel Groups Toward Conflict," *American Psychologist* 58, no. 3 (March 2003): 182–92.

3. John Horgan, *Walking Away from Terrorism: Accounts of Disengagement from Radical and Extremist Movements*. (London: Routledge, 2009).

4. Marc Sageman, *Understanding Terror Networks*. (Philadelphia: University of Pennsylvania Press, 2004).

5. William Rosenau, Ralph Espach, Roman D.Ortiz, and Natalia Herrera, "Why They Join, Why They Fight, and Why They Leave: Learning from Colombia's Database of Demobilized Militants," *Terrorism and Political Violence* 26 (Spring 2014): 277–85 at 283.

6. Omar Nasiri, *Inside the Jihad: My Life with Al Qaeda*. (New York: Basic Books, 2006).

7. William Rosenau, Ralph Espach, Roman D. Ortiz, and Natalia Herrera, "Why They Join, Why They Fight, and Why They Leave: Learning from Colombia's Database of Demobilized Militants," *Terrorism and Political Violence* 26 (Spring 2014): 277–85 at 282.

8. John Horgan, "Child Suicide Bombers Find Safe Haven," CNN (March 27, 2013), http://www.cnn.com/2013/03/27/world/asia/pakistan-anti-taliban/.

9. John Horgan and Max Taylor, "A Conceptual Framework for Addressing Psychological Process in the Development of the Terrorist," *Terrorism and Political Violence* 18, no. 4 (2006): 585–601.

10. See James J. F. Forest, "The Final Act: Ideologies of Catastrophic Terror," published by the Fund for Peace Expert Series, http://www.fundforpeace.org/web/images/pdf/forest.pdf; and James J. F. Forest, "Influence Warfare and Modern Terrorism," *Georgetown Journal of International Affairs* 10, no. 1 (2009).

11. Assaf Moghadam, "The Salafi-Jihad as a Religious Ideology," *CTC Sentinel* 1, no. 3 (2008): 14–16.

12. According to Andrew Kydd and Barbara Walter, "of the forty-two groups currently designated as foreign terrorist organizations by the U.S. State Department, thirty-one seek regime change, nineteen seek territorial change, four seek policy change, and one seeks to maintain the status quo." Andrew Kydd and Barbara Walter, "The Strategies of Terrorism," *International Security* 31, no. 1, (2006): 52.

13. Even though environmental extremists or animal rights activists may attack logging operations, fur warehouses, and research laboratories, and typically try to avoid human casualties, the victims of these attacks suffer financially and economically (from property damage), as well as psychologically. As with all other kinds of terrorism, the overall goal of these extremists is to influence human behavior through violence.

14. Maxwell Taylor, *The Terrorist* (London: Brassey's, 1988).

15. Jerrold M. Post, "When Hatred is Bred in the Bone: The Socio-Cultural Underpinnings of Terrorist Psychology," in *The Making of a Terrorist*, vol. 2, ed. James J. F. Forest (Westport, CT: Praeger, 2005).

16. Jerrold M. Post, "Terrorist Psycho-logic: Terrorist Behavior as a Product of Psychological Forces," in *Origins of Terrorism: Psychologies, Ideologies, Theologies, States of Mind*, ed. Walter Reich (Baltimore: Woodrow Wilson Center Press, 1998): 25–40.

17. Robert Robins and Jerrold M. Post, *Political Paranoia: The Psychopolitics of Hatred* (New Haven, CT: Yale University Press, 1997).

18. Bard O'Neill and Donald J. Alberts, "Responding to Psychological, Social, Economic and Political Roots of Terrorism," in *Countering Terrorism and Insurgency in the 21st Century*, vol. 2, ed. James J. F. Forest (Westport, CT: Praeger, 2007).

19. For an analysis of how personal relationships contribute to terrorist group formation and recruitment, see Sageman, *Understanding Terror Networks*.

20. See for example, Raymond H. Hamden, "Unresolved Trauma and the Thirst for Revenge: The Retributional Terrorist," in *The Making of a Terrorist*, vol. 1, ed. James J. F. Forest; Albert Bandura, "Mechanisms of Moral Disengagement," in *The Making of a Terrorist*, vol. 2; and Chris Stout, "Introduction," in *Psychology of Terrorism: Coping with the Continuing Threat* (Condensed Edition), ed. Chris Stout (Westport, CT: Praeger, 2004).

21. Walter Lacqueur, "Left, Right and Beyond: The Changing Face of Terror," in *How Did This Happen? Terrorism and the New War*, ed. James Hoge and Gideon Rose (Oxford: Public Affairs, 2001): 71–82.

22. *Testimony (Statement for the Record) before the Senate Comm. on Homeland Security and Governmental Affairs* (July 10, 2008) (testimony of Michael E. Leiter).

23. John Horgan, "The Social and Psychological Characteristics of Terrorism and Terrorists," in *Root Causes of Terrorism: Myths, Realities and Ways Forward*, ed. Tore Bjorgo (London: Routledge, 2005): 45.

24. Andrew Silke, "An Introduction to Terrorism Research," in *Research on Terrorism: Trends, Achievements and Failures*, ed. Andrew Silke (London: Frank Cass, 2004): 20.

25. John Horgan, "The Social and Psychological Characteristics of Terrorism and Terrorists," in *Root Causes of Terrorism*, ed. Bjorgo, p. 49.

26. Clark McCauley, "Psychological Issues in Understanding Terrorism and Response to Terrorism," in *Psychology of Terrorism*, ed. Stout, p. 35.

27. Sageman, *Understanding Terror Networks*, p. 91.

28. Martha Crenshaw, "The Logic of Terrorism: Terrorist Behavior as a Product of Strategic Choice," in *Origins of Terrorism*, ed. Reich, pp. 7–24.

29. Chris Stout, "Introduction," in *Psychology of Terrorism*, ed. Stout, p. xiv. See also Rex A. Hudson, *Who Becomes a Terrorist and Why: The 1999 Government Report on Profiling Terrorists* (Guilford, CT: Lyons Press, 2001); and Robert A. Pape, "The Strategic Logic of Suicide Terrorism," *American Political Science Review* 97, no. 3 (2003).

30. For more on this, see John Horgan, "The Search for the Terrorist Personality," in *Terrorists, Victims and Society: Psychological Perspectives on Terrorism and its Consequences*, ed. Andrew Silke (Chichester, UK: John Wiley and Sons, 2003); and Andrew Silke, "Cheshire-Cat Logic: The Recurring Theme of Terrorist Abnormality in Psychological Research," *Psychology, Crime and Law* 4 (1998): 51–69.

31. For example, see Leiter, Testimony; Fathali M. Moghaddam, "The Staircase to Terrorism: A Psychological Exploration," *American Psychologist* 60 (2005): 161-69; and Clark McCauley, "Pathways Towards Radicalization," *START Research Brief* (National Consortium for the Study of Terrorism and Responses to Terrorism, October 2008).

32. Max Taylor and John Horgan, "A Conceptual Framework for Addressing Psychological Process in the Development of the Terrorist," *Terrorism and Political Violence* 18, no. 4 (2006): 2.

33. Ibid.

34. Ibid., 13.

35. Leiter, Testimony.

36. Sageman, p. 178.

37. These six propositions were originally published in James J. F. Forest, "Terrorism as a Product of Choices and Perceptions," in *Terrorizing Ourselves*, ed. Benjamin H. Friedman, Jim Harper and Christopher A. Preble (Washington, DC: Cato Institute, 2010).

38. Peter R. Neumann, *Radicalized: New Jihadists and the Threat to the West* (London: I.B. Taurus, 2016): 5.

39. Sageman, *Understanding Terror Networks*; and Justin Magouirk, Scott Atran, and Marc Sageman. "Connecting Terrorist Networks," *Studies in Conflict & Terrorism* 31, no. 2 (2008): 1–16.

40. Rogelio Alonso, *The IRA and Armed Struggle* (London: Routledge, 2007); and Rogelio Alonso, "Individual Motivations for Joining Terrorist Organizations: A Comparative Qualitative Study on Members of ETA and IRA," in *Tangled Roots: Social and Psychological Factors in the Genesis of Terrorism*, ed. Jeffrey Ivan Victoroff (The Netherlands: IOS Press, 2006).

15

"Do-It-Yourself" Terrorism: No Group Required

It is a tragic reality that virtually anyone could plan and carry out a terrorist attack. Most humans have a natural understanding of how fragile and vulnerable life is, and how technically easy it is to kill. Thankfully, an overwhelming majority of us do not have the motivation or will to kill others. But when the knowledge of how to kill is combined with a resonating ideology and an effective radicalization process, the result has too often been a personal commitment to carry out some kind of terrorist act. These are the thoughts that came to mind on April 15, 2013, as I watched the tragedy of the Boston Marathon bombing unfold not far from where I live. The facts surrounding that event, which I'll describe later in this lecture, reflect the increasingly complicated security challenge of "do-it-yourself" terrorism.

Several of the previous lectures in this book have already described individuals who have been inspired by resonating ideologies to conceive and carry out various kinds of terrorist attacks, but had no clear ties to an established organization responsible for funding, directing or supervising their operation. This phenomenon has roots in the anarchist movement of the nineteenth century as well as late twentieth-century white supremacists and anti-abortionists. As described in Lecture 2 of this book, anarchists generally believe that formal governments of any kind are harmful and unnecessary, and that all human interactions should be organized by voluntary associations. Individuals inspired by anarchist ideologies were responsible for the assassination of Spanish Prime Minister Antonio Cánovas del Castillo in 1897, the assassination of U.S. President William McKinley in 1901, and a September 1920 bombing in downtown New York City (which killed nearly 40 people and wounded more than 150), among several other high profile terrorist attacks. Often (though not always) the perpetrators of these attacks acted alone, with little or no operational assistance from others within the anarchist movement.

More recently (as discussed in Lecture 10), right-wing extremists have embraced a form of "leaderless resistance"—a concept promoted by white supremacist Louis Beam in 1983 as a method to attack the federal government.[1] Beam argued that highly centralized organizations were vulnerable to infiltration and arrest by federal agents, particularly in highly technical societies where the authorities had a wide variety of means by which they could conduct surveillance.[2] Therefore, he argued, the movement needed to abandon hierarchical arrangements, and instead establish "phantom cells" tied together only by common philosophy and ideology. Right-wing extremists have in several instances acted alone in their attacks, from Eric Rudolph to Dylan Roof and James Fields, Jr. (all of whom are described later in this lecture).

As described in Lectures 12 and 13, the Salafi-jihadist movement (based on ideas promoted by senior al-Qaeda ideologue Abu Musab al-Suri) has adopted a similar "leaderless jihad" style of motivating do-it-yourself terrorist attacks. Recent examples of these kinds of attacks have been seen in Paris, Brussels, Nice, Berlin, London, Stockholm, New York, and many other cities in Western Europe and the U.S. In many cases, these attackers have been inspired by al-Qaeda or Islamic State to use guns, knives, a truck, or some other uncomplicated weapon for killing or injuring as many innocent bystanders as they could before (in almost every instance) getting killed by local law enforcement.

And of course, there have also been adopters of the "do-it-yourself" mode of terrorism beyond the ideological categories of right-wing extremism and Islamic jihad. In fact, we see a leaderless resistance approach embraced by individuals motivated by environmental and animal rights extremism, anti-abortion, and other ideological categories. Environmental extremists, for example, have attacked timber and logging companies, SUV dealerships, pharmaceutical companies, and private homes. Animal rights extremists have attacked fur and leather companies, university research labs, and a variety of other targets.

Regardless of ideology, this kind of "do-it-yourself" terrorism involves individuals committing terrorist attacks autonomously, independent of any operational direction or support from a formal organization. They can choose their own target, day, time, and mode of attack. In their popular book *The Next Attack*, Daniel Benjamin and Steven Simon used the term "self-starter" to describe these individuals.[3] Their analysis revealed that modestly intelligent, highly motivated, and resourceful individuals can obtain (or fabricate) weapons and deploy them to deadly effect, without any help from anyone else. They don't really need to attend a training camp, receive funding or operational direction, or meet with key members or leaders of an established terrorist group prior to carrying out their attack. Of course, as Beam noted in his treatise, these individuals must "acquire the necessary skills and information as to what is to be done,"[4] as well as the resources (money, weapons, transportation, etc.) necessary to put their plan into operation. But as discussed in Lectures 7 and 13, these individuals can now use the Internet to find most of what they need. There are a wide variety of training manuals and instructions for building improvised explosive devices, often translated into multiple languages. Weapons and other technologies can be ordered online and delivered in unmarked packages, particularly using deep web resources and Bitcoin payments.[5] The Internet can also be used to gather information on potential targets and conduct surveillance. Meanwhile, Internet discussion forums and social media also serve a particularly important role as ideological incubators, connecting people around the world and legitimating their shared ideas, beliefs, and values. The online radicalization process can then meld with local socioeconomic or political conditions that lead to the kinds of contextual grievances described in previous lectures in this book—and perhaps even social alienation or other personal issues—to produce lethal results.

From this perspective, the 2013 Boston Marathon attacks and other recent incidents have been reminders of how so-called true believers—encouraged by ideological entrepreneurs to "think globally, and act locally"—have been able to kill and injure scores of innocent people. In some cases, individuals have worked together as a kind of team, while in other cases they have acted entirely alone. These individuals typically share goals and philosophies with others and believe they are part of a larger "political resistance" movement in which violence is a necessary means to achieve the movement's goals.[6] The attacks they have been responsible for, several of which are described in this lecture, typically come in the form of the self-starter team or the lone attacker. These do-it-yourself attackers are a significant dimension of the contemporary terrorist threat we face today, and unfortunately we are unlikely to see it fade away anytime soon.

SELF-STARTER TERRORIST TEAMS

A self-starter team is sometimes mistaken as an autonomous cell of a terrorist movement, but there are key differences. For example, on November 13, 2015, a series of explosions at the Stade de France (a sports stadium in a suburb north of Paris) signaled the beginning of a multilocation terrorist attack involving guns and suicide bombings throughout the city, including bars and restaurants. The attackers killed 130 people and injured over 400 more. In the worst of these attacks, 89 were gunned down at the Bataclan concert hall. Shortly afterward, the Islamic State (IS) took credit for the attacks, and later investigations pointed to an extensive network of operatives that IS had developed throughout Western Europe. Several months later, on March 22, 2016, another group of jihadists (who were allegedly part of this European IS network) bombed the airport and a metro station in Brussels, killing 32 and injuring over 300 others. In both these instances, the attacks were orchestrated by cells trained and dispatched to Europe by IS, and thus are not examples of do-it-yourself terrorism.

In contrast, the self-starter team involves two or more individuals who are inspired to work together to carry out a terrorist attack, but have no known direct links with an established terrorist organization. One of the most bloody examples of this type of "do-it-yourself" terrorism that comes to mind is the attack against the Alfred P. Murrah Federal Building in Oklahoma City,[7] which killed 168 people and wounded over 800 others.[8] The building housed a variety of federal agencies—including Housing and Urban Development, General Services Administration, and military recruitment offices—as well as a daycare center on the second floor for children of the more than 500 federal employees who worked there. On April 19, 1995, a truck parked in front of the northern section of the building and containing nearly 5,000 pounds of explosive chemicals, detonated at 9:02 a.m. The blast was felt 55 miles away and registered a 6.0 on the Richter scale, blowing out windows and doors in a 50-block area.[9] Originally constructed of reinforced concrete, the front and middle portions of the nine-floor building crumbled without the support of a steel frame.[10]

Within 90 minutes of the explosion, U.S. Army veteran Timothy McVeigh was arrested after drawing the attention of an Oklahoma state trooper by driving a motor vehicle without a license plate. The subsequent investigation found that he and his accomplice Terry Nichols were responsible for this attack, inspired by the ideology of a right-wing militia movement in the U.S. that renounced the policies of the federal government as hostile and antagonistic.[11] Portions of William Pierce's *The Turner Diaries*, a violent portrayal of a racially-based revolutionary movement that declares genocide against all non-Caucasian people, were found in McVeigh's vehicle.[12] As Lou Michel and Dan Herbeck note, "Timothy McVeigh was preparing to teach the government a lesson . . . [motivated by] a list of grievances he'd been amassing for years: crooked politicians, overzealous government agents, high taxes, political correctness, and gun laws."[13] McVeigh was convicted of the attack and his death sentence was carried out on June 1, 2001. Nichols was eventually sentenced to 160 consecutive life sentences in prison without the possibility of parole. The judge in the final court proceedings noted that no additional evidence existed to implicate involvement by any persons other than McVeigh and Nichols.[14]

Two other well-known examples of the self-starter team "do-it-yourself" terrorism model occurred in Europe, and in these cases the perpetrators were motivated by a much different kind of ideology. Following the attacks of September 11, 2001, the world's attention was focused on efforts by U.S. and NATO forces to drive the Taliban out of Afghanistan and capture senior leaders of the global al-Qaeda network. Until, that is, U.S. President George W. Bush and his administration orchestrated an invasion of Iraq, under the premises that overthrowing an allegedly WMD-armed Saddam Hussein was a necessary part of the so-called Global War on Terrorism. A few countries eventually provided some troops and assistance, particularly Spain and the United Kingdom. As described in previous lectures, these events helped bolster the resonance of the global Salafi-jihadist ideology and led some young Muslims in Europe to believe

Figures 15.1 and 15.2: Terry Nichols (left) and Timothy McVeigh.

Osama bin Laden's claim that the West was at war with Islam. This, in turn, contributed to some of the most significant terrorist attacks of the last two decades.

On March 11, 2004, bombs placed aboard four different trains filled with thousands of commuters on their way to Madrid, Spain were detonated between 7:37 and 7:40 am, killing 191 people.[15] Authorities later determined through video statements and a communiqué sent to a newspaper that a small group of Muslim extremists had been responsible for the attack. In one video, a man armed with a 9mm pistol looked into the camera and stated: "This is a response to the crimes you have committed in the world, and particularly in Iraq and Afghanistan, and there will be more if God so desires . . . If you don't stop your injustices there will be more and more blood."[16] Another video recording stated: "We are continuing the path of our blessed jihad until the defeat of all of those who may consider following Bush's example of combating Muslims in the name of the war against terrorism . . . You must know that you will never be safe . . . We will kill you at any time and place. We will not distinguish between the military and civilians."[17]

The bombings of March 11 were meant by the terrorists to be the beginning of a campaign that was going to continue weeks afterward. However, the investigation by Spanish authorities eventually thwarted their plans. An unexploded device left by the terrorists on one of the trains proved especially valuable in identifying key individuals behind the attack, and led police to Jamal Zougam, a Moroccan who had lived in Spain for 20 years. As described briefly in Lecture 6, the perpetrators of the Madrid bombing were young men like Zougam who were mostly known by local authorities as petty criminals, involved in various kinds of theft, fraud, drugs, and other low-level street crimes. Most of them had immigrated from Morocco, Tunisia, or Algeria, but had lived in Spain for long periods of time. What authorities did not realize until later was that all of them had been radicalized (often while serving time in prison) and had formed deep bonds of loyalty to each other. The ties they had with the criminal world also allowed them to acquire the high-grade explosives (stolen from a mine in northern Spain) used in their attacks.

On April 2, 2004 an explosive device was found on a railway line in the province of Toledo, near Madrid, which had similar attributes to the devices used on March 11. Forensic evidence gathered from these devices indicated the involvement of several of Zougam's close associates, like Jamal Ahmidan, Said Berraj, Allekema Lamari, Abdennabi Kounjaa, Anwar Asrih Rifaat, and Rachid Oulad Akcha. Spanish authorities then discovered that seven of the suspects were hiding out together at an apartment in Leganés. On April 3, after police surrounded the apartment building, the terrorists initiated a shoot-out and the GEO (*Grupo Especial de Operaciones*), a special unit of the Spanish police trained for siege situations, was deployed. Government negotiators attempted to reason with the terrorists, but they continued shooting from inside the apartment, and eventually—realizing they were besieged with no prospect of escaping—they detonated their explosives, killing themselves and one of the police squad members. The subsequent court proceedings identified 29 individuals who had some level of involvement in these terrorist incidents. While there was no clear evidence of any formal *operational* links to al-Qaeda, this self-starter team clearly had an affinity for, and affiliation with, the Salafi-jihadist ideology that al-Qaeda had been promoting for several years (see Lecture 12).

The same ideological inspiration was seen in the July 7, 2005 terrorist attacks in London.[18] At 8:50am that morning, a bomb exploded on an eastbound Circle Line train traveling from Liverpool Street station to Aldgate station in the heart of the financial district. Within a minute, a second bomb detonated on another Circle Line train traveling westbound, just moments after it had left Edgware Road station for Paddington station, and then a third, approximately two minutes later, on a southbound Piccadilly Line train traveling from King's Cross station to Russell Square station. At that point, authorities immediately shut down the entire London Underground system and evacuated the passengers. Then almost an hour later, at 9:47 a.m., a double-decker bus crowded with passengers was entering Tavistock Square when a bomb exploded on the upper deck toward the back, almost completely blowing the roof off the bus. In total, these four bombings killed 52 people and injured 784.[19]

This self-starter team in London was much smaller than the Madrid group of attackers, with just four men ranging in age from 18 to 30. The oldest (and presumably the leader) of this team, Mohammad Sidique Khan, was considered a respected member of his community. Locals describe "Sid" as a thoughtful, soft-spoken man with a graduate degree, a wife and daughter, who did not openly display any outward hostility or anger toward the government or people of Great Britain.[20] A friend (and fellow bomber), Shehzad Tanweer, was the son of a prosperous owner of several fish and chips stores, and drove a Mercedes Benz sports car that was the envy of many neighborhood friends. Hasib Hussein, the youngest member of the team, was described as an impressionable high school dropout who had dabbled in drugs before a pilgrimage to Mecca led him

Figure 15.3: Mohammad Sidique Khan
30 years old

Figure 15.4: Germaine Lindsay
19 years old

to embrace a more devout Muslim lifestyle, wearing traditional Islamic clothing and praying five times daily.[21] These three were British nationals of Pakistani origin, who were born and raised in the U.K. and were living in the Leeds and Dewsbury areas north of London. The fourth team member, Germaine Lindsay, was born in Jamaica but also became a British national and lived in the same region north of London.[22]

On the morning of their attack, closed circuit television (CCTV) recordings showed all four young men in the parking lot of the Luton railway station, putting on large backpacks and heading into the station. Watching their behavior on the video, you might have thought these were four young friends heading off on a hiking trip somewhere. It has been estimated that the bombs in each backpack contained between 2–5 kilograms (roughly 5–11 pounds) of hexamethylene triperoxide diamine (HMTD) explosive, a homemade organic peroxide-based substance, relatively straightforward to make, although very dangerous because of its instability.[23] After the group arrived at the King's Cross station in London, cameras recorded them hugging each other before splitting up to

carry out their deadly suicide missions. The motivations for their attack were articulated most poignantly by Khan in a video statement recorded earlier in 2005, and published online in September of that year on various web forums:

I and thousands like me are forsaking everything for what we believe . . . Your democratically elected governments continuously perpetuate atrocities against my people all over the world. And your support of them makes you directly responsible, just as I am directly responsible for protecting and avenging my Muslim brothers and sisters. Until we feel security, you will be our targets. And until you stop the bombing, gassing, imprisonment and torture of my people we will not stop this fight. We are at war and I am a soldier.[24]

These, and similar statements made by Tanweer in his own video recording, indicate a strong affinity with the Salafi-jihadist ideology described in Lecture 12. In various statements following the attacks, Ayman al-Zawahiri claimed that al-Qaeda operatives helped train Sid and Tanweer during an extended visit to Pakistan, which is where they also recorded their martyrdom videos claiming the attacks were on behalf of grievances shared by al-Qaeda's leaders and the global *umma*. As Brian Jenkins noted, attacks like this are meant to provide inspiration for other adherents of the Salafi-jihadist ideology and strategy.[25]

Another example of the jihadist self-starter team approach was seen in a 2006 plot in Toronto in which 18 young men (including some in their teens) came together and crafted an ambitious plan to attack Parliament buildings, the CBC Broadcasting Centre, and the Canadian Security and Intelligence Service offices.[26] They were arrested after trying to acquire three tons of ammonium nitrate (the same kind of explosives used by Timothy McVeigh in the Oklahoma City bombing). The team members came from diverse backgrounds, and included Arabs, Pakistanis, Somalis, and a man from the Caribbean. All were Canadian born or legal residents. None of them are known to have had any direct ties to al-Qaeda leaders or affiliate groups. Reports on this plot have described these individuals as inspired by the Salafi-jihadist ideology and guided by 43-year-old Salafist cleric Qayyum Abdul Jamal, whose sermons at a local mosque, the Al-Rahman Islamic Centre for Islamic Education, were "filled with hate" against Canada.[27]

Most of this team's members were very active online, and the Internet served an important role in providing indoctrination and information on targets and weapons. One of the group members, Saad Khalid—in a series of interviews from his prison cell in 2014—described how he was influenced by a series of online lectures by the fiery American-born cleric Anwar al-Awlaki (see Lectures 7 and 14): "He had a knack for telling a good story, so when I came across his lectures on jihad I was hooked . . .Here was someone I respected and he was connecting global grievances that Muslims share with what your responsibility is in terms of these issues."[28] Another of the group's members, Fahim Ahmed, distributed DVDs after Friday prayers containing jihadi videos glorifying the 9/11 hijackers, videos he had downloaded from various websites and discussion forums. Thankfully, this self-starter team was infiltrated by a police informant, without whose assistance it would have been very difficult to learn the details of this plot and disrupt it.[29]

The case of the would-be jihadists who wanted to attack a military base in New Jersey is illustrative of the security challenges we face here in the United States. In May 2007, the U.S. Department of Justice announced the arrest of six men who had been conspiring to attack Fort Dix and kill soldiers there with assault rifles and grenades. The court proceedings described a 16-month operation to infiltrate and monitor the group, and portrayed this as "a leaderless, homegrown cell of immigrants from Jordan, Turkey and the former Yugoslavia who came together because of a shared infatuation with Internet images of jihad, or holy war."[30] As we have seen in several other cases like this, the conspirators had very limited skills or abilities. Their extremist zeal led them to pursue weapons training at shooting ranges and an attempt to purchase assault rifles, but the 26-page indictment noted that the group "did not appear close to being able to pull off an attack."[31]

In September 2008, Najibullah Zazi (a naturalized U.S. citizen of Afghan heritage) and two of his former high school classmates traveled to Pakistan in an attempt to gain training from al-Qaeda operatives. They were motivated by the jihadist ideology and had expressed increasing anger about the U.S. and coalition military attacks in Afghanistan. Court records indicate that they spent time at a training camp in the mountains of Pakistan's Waziristan region, and then by late January 2009 each had returned to the U.S. After moving from New York to Colorado, where he found work as an airport shuttle driver, Zazi began acquiring materials and constructing explosives based on hydrogen peroxide, acetone, and acid. In early September 2009, he and his friends were arrested in the final stages of a plot to bomb the New York subway system on the eighth anniversary of the 9/11 attacks.[32]

Then there's the May 2009 case of four guys who planned to bomb a couple of synagogues in New York and shoot down military airplanes at the Stewart Air National Guard Base, near Newburgh, N.Y. (which is quite close to West Point).[33] All of the suspects lived in Newburgh, but were allegedly radicalized in prison or at a mosque in the Bronx. Authorities arrested them on May 9 after they attempted to detonate what they believed to be bombs in cars outside the Riverdale Temple and the nearby Riverdale Jewish Center (the bombs, obtained with the help of an FBI informant, were fake).[34] While there is much that could be discussed from these cases about the debate over FBI sting operations and possible entrapment, the point that needs to be made in this lecture is that these were highly motivated and determined individuals who simply lacked the ability to carry out their intended attack without some help. And, lucky for us, the people they turned to for assistance happened to be police or FBI informants.

But there are also cases in which the terrorists have unfortunately succeeded. For example, on April 3, 2017, an explosion near a metro station in St. Petersburg, Russia, killed 15 people and injured several dozen others. An explosive device was also found at another metro station and defused. Initially, the authorities thought it was the work of a lone suicide bomber, a Russian citizen named Akbarzhon Jalilov who was an ethnic Uzbek born in Kyrgyzstan. But they later charged an accomplice in the attack, Abror Azimov (also Kyrgyz-born), who said he was "just following orders and did not realize what he was doing."[35]

Closer to home, on April 15, 2013—as mentioned at the beginning of this lecture—a team of two young men with no discernible connection to an established terrorist group or organization built, deployed and detonated two bombs near the finish line of the Boston Marathon. A young boy and two young women were killed, and over 260 other participants were injured.[36] Some of the victims who survived will never walk again. The perpetrators of this attack were two brothers who had immigrated to the U.S. from Chechnya with their parents and had lived for several years in the Boston area. The younger brother exhibited various signs of normal integration into society—attending a local public university, partying with friends, and networking via social media. In contrast, the older brother appears to have become increasingly radicalized by anti-Western jihadist ideology, to a point where he was expelled from a local mosque after one of his extremist outbursts. He traveled to Dagestan (a neighboring province of Chechnya), where authorities believe he may have received some training from a local militant group. But according to the investigation into the attack, the Internet played a key role in the radicalization process that led to the brothers' eventual decision to carry out a terrorist attack on U.S. soil, as well as the weapons-making instructions that culminated in the bombing.[37] The al-Qaeda magazine *Inspire*, described in Lecture 7, has been cited by authorities as playing a particularly influential role in this attack, not only in inspiring and motivating their actions but also in providing detailed instructions on making the pressure-cooker explosive devices they used.

Figures 15.5 and 15.6 : Tamerlan Tsarnaev (age 26) and Dzhokhar Tsarnaev (age 19)

Online jihadist materials were also allegedly a source of inspiration for Syed Rizwan Farooq and his wife Tashfeen Malik, who killed 14 people and injured over 20 others at a social services center in San Bernardino, Calif. in early December, 2015. While investigators have uncovered no indication of direct operational, financial or logistical links with any known terrorist organization, the January 2016 issue of the Islamic State's online magazine *Dabiq* praised the shooting and the perpetrators. As of this writing, the San Bernardino attack is still considered an example of a self-starter team, similar to the Tsarnaev brothers, in the do-it-yourself model of terrorist attacks. It is not unusual to see friends, siblings, and even spouses become members of such teams, given what we know from research on radicalization and engagement (as described in the previous lecture). When we make decisions in our lives—particular decisions about doing something dramatic—those with whom we are closest tend to have the most influence on those decisions.

According to a May 2013 report for the Department of Homeland Security, most of the environmental extremist and animal rights extremist self-starter teams "came together informally through friends and personal contacts" and were "not linked to groups with any substantial organizational capacity."[38] Their terrorist attacks were fueled by a recognizable ideology of political violence, articulated on the Internet by self-appointed spokespeople of "leaderless" movements like Earth First, the Earth Liberation Front, the Animal Liberation Front, and Stop Huntingdon Animal Cruelty. But again, all operational details of these attacks (targets, timing, weapons, etc.) were completely at the discretion of those who were motivated to act on behalf of the ideology. Some self-starter teams have carried out multiple attacks over an extended period of time, and even adopted formal names (for example, "The Family," a small but particularly active cell of radical environmentalists),[39] but most have been one-hit wonders, perhaps owing to the aforementioned lack of sophisticated training or skills among their members. These teams have been formed within a variety of contexts, particularly in Europe and North America. In many of those instances, it seems that the grievances motivating the self-starter terrorists have been linked to a perceived identity affiliation with others in different parts of the world who are viewed as suffering from some kind of socioeconomic or political conditions.

Within each of these cases of self-starter teams we find some common elements of in-group cohesion, where belief in an ideology unites the members of the team toward a shared goal. This can become a transformative experience, in which individual identity becomes subsumed by group identity. The group and the individual may form a symbiotic relationship, serving each other's needs. Terrorist attacks are justified as serving the needs of the group, taking primacy over the individual's desires, but at the same time belonging to the group fulfills a primal need of the individual.[40]

Finally, a core trait found among the self-starter teams is that two or more individuals worked together to conduct a terrorist attack. We can presume that they shared ideas, deliberated, and collectively decided on an attack plan, including targets, weapons, and timing. As the number of individuals with this operational knowledge increases, there is a concurrent increase in the possibility that an intelligence or law enforcement agency could get lucky and learn about the attack from one of the team's members. In contrast, it is considerably more difficult to prevent an attack that is crafted within the mind of only one individual: the "lone actor" terrorist.

LONE ACTOR TERRORISTS

In recent years, scholars and policymakers have offered various phrases—including lone wolves or stray dogs[41]—to try and characterize the kind of terrorism in which an individual carries out a terrorist attack entirely of their own volition. If we view terrorism as a theater of violence, this individual steps out onto the stage alone to deliver his or her own script and choreography; there is no director, stage manager, orchestra conductor, or supporting cast. The term "lone actor" should not be confused with "lone attacker," where the perpetrator is a single individual who is trained, financed, and sent on an attack mission by an established terrorist organization. Examples of the lone attacker include hundreds of individual suicide bombers responsible for attacks in Sri Lanka, Israel, Lebanon, Iraq, Afghanistan, Nigeria, Somalia, Syria, Europe, and elsewhere. In these instances, established organizations like LTTE, Hamas, Hizballah, al-Qaeda in Iraq, the Islamic State, al-Shabaab, Boko Haram, and the Taliban have all deployed suicide bombers as a strategically and tactically effective weapon.

Examples of the lone attacker include a young woman in Sri Lanka named Thenmozhi Rajaratnam (but known locally as Dhanu), who was trained by the LTTE and sent to murder Rajiv Gandhi, a former prime minister of India. Late at night on May 21, 1991, Gandhi was attending a campaign rally, and he greeted a young woman in glasses who bent down in a traditional act of respect and then detonated the vest bomb that she was wearing beneath her green and orange dress. In addition to the two of them, 17 other bystanders in the crowd were also killed in the explosion.[42]

A decade later, on January 27, 2002, a young Palestinian woman by the name of Wafa Idris—a paramedic who lived in Ramallah—entered a shopping district in Jerusalem and detonated a 22-pound bomb filled with nails and metal objects, killing an 81-year-old man and injuring more than 100 bystanders. Idris, a member of the al-Aqsa Martyr's Brigade, was the first known *istish-hadiyat* (female martyr) in the Middle East—but others soon followed, including Dareen Abu Aisheh, who wounded two Israeli policemen when she detonated her bomb at a roadblock near Maccabim on February 27, 2002; Aayat al-Akhras, who strolled into a supermarket in the neighborhood of Kiryat Yovel in Jerusalem and killed two Israeli civilians and wounded 22 more on March 29, 2002; and Hanadi Jaradat, a 29-year-old lawyer who calmly entered a highly popular restaurant on October 4, 2003 and killed 21 Israeli and Arab men, women, and children.[43]

Each of these tragedies was the result of a lone attacker who was trained, equipped, and in most cases accompanied to the target by members of a known terrorist organization. More recent examples of this mode of terrorist attack include the May 24, 2014 attack at the Jewish Museum of Belgium, in which Mehdi Nemmouche shot and killed four people. A French national of Algerian origin, Nemmouche had previously spent a year fighting alongside ISIS in Syria and Iraq, and carried out this attack on behalf of the jihadist group. On December 31, 2016, an Uzbek national named Abdulkadir Masharipov (alias Muhammed Horasani) was sent by ISIS to carry out an attack at the Reina nightclub in Istanbul, where he used an AK-47 to kill 39 people.

The "lone attacker" category also accounts for several well-known recent cases of failed bombers, including:

- Richard Reid, who was deployed by al-Qaeda on a suicide mission against a transatlantic flight in December 2001. Passengers jumped on him after he tried to ignite explosives hidden in his shoes.
- Ahmed Ressam, a lone attacker dispatched from an al-Qaeda cell in Montreal who was foiled by law enforcement in the state of Washington while trying to transport his explosives to the Los Angeles International Airport.
- Farouk Abdulmutallab, a young Nigerian radicalized mainly by information found on the Internet, but who received training and explosives in Yemen from members of the group al-Qaeda in the Arabian Peninsula. His attempt to blow up a transatlantic flight in December 2009 was foiled when the explosives in his underwear fizzled and sparked but did not detonate.
- Faisal Shahzad, a U.S. citizen born in Pakistan but who lived for many years in Connecticut. In April 2010, he tried to detonate a bomb inside his SUV while parked in Times Square in New York City, but here again the explosives smoked and sparked but did not detonate. Officials believe he was trained for this attack by members of an al-Qaeda affiliate group calling itself Tehrik-i-Taliban Pakistan (aka the Pakistani Taliban).

Again, in each of these cases, the individuals had operational links to established organizations, with clearly identifiable leaders and mentors telling the lone attacker what to do, and how and when to do it. A lone attacker may have carried out the attack on their own (or at least attempted to do so), but a terrorist organization provided them with training, weapons, financial resources, transportation, or some other kind of direct assistance, which means they are *not* an example of the "do-it-yourself" model of terrorism described in this lecture.[44]

In contrast, true "lone actors" (who embody the working definition of "do-it-yourself" terrorism) include Eric Rudolph, a young man who (like Timothy McVeigh) was motivated by a mix of right-wing anti-government ideologies and personal grievances to carry out terrorist attacks. On July 27, 1996, Rudolph placed a bag at the Centennial Olympic Park containing dynamite and nails. This park was a venue for concerts and events celebrating the Atlanta Olympics that month, and was often crowded during the evenings. The detonation of this bomb killed one person and injured over 100 others. Rudolph (see Lecture 10) also used similar bombs to attack an abortion clinic in Atlanta (January 1997), a gay bar in Atlanta (February 1997), and an abortion clinic in Alabama (January 1998).[45] He spent more than five years on the run from the authorities, mostly living off the land in the Appalachian mountains, until the early morning of May 31, 2003, when an alert rookie police officer in the small town of Murphy, N.C. went to investigate a strange man digging through a dumpster behind a convenience store and discovered he had found one of the FBI's most wanted fugitives.

Rudolph later provided numerous statements describing the motivations behind his attacks as driven by his opposition to abortion and homosexuality.[46] From that perspective, he joined a long line of other lone actors who attacked abortion clinics and their staff throughout the 1980s and 1990s. Examples include Paul Hill, who killed doctor John Britton and his bodyguard outside an abortion clinic in Pensacola, Fla. on July 29, 1994. In December of that year, John Salvi walked into a Planned Parenthood clinic in Brookline, Mass. and killed receptionist Shannon Lowney and wounded a clinical assistant. He then drove down the street to another abortion clinic, where he killed receptionist Leeann Nichols and wounded a security guard before fleeing. He was eventually apprehended in Norfolk, Va. after firing multiple times into an abortion clinic there.

On October 23, 1998, James Kopp used a sniper rifle to kill doctor Barnett Slepian in Amherst, N.Y. In late 2001, Clayton Lee Waagner sent several hundred letters to abortion clinics that claimed to contain anthrax, a type of terror-by-mail that was emulated by Paul Ross Evans in December 2006 when he mailed explosive devices to abortion providers, pornographers, and others. Then in April 2007, Evans was arrested after leaving a large explosive device outside a clinic in Austin, Texas that was detected by an employee and then destroyed in a controlled detonation by the local bomb squad.[47] On May 31, 2009, doctor George Tiller was shot at point-blank range in Wichita, Kansas, by Scott Roeder.[48] And on November 27, 2009, Robert Lewis Dear, Jr. attacked a Planned Parenthood clinic in Colorado Springs, Colo., calling himself "a warrior for the babies." During his attack and five-hour standoff, he killed a police officer and two civilians, and injured nine others, before police SWAT teams crashed armored vehicles into the lobby and forced his surrender.

In each of these cases, the attacker acted alone, and rationalized their use of violence as necessary "to protect the unborn child"—a catchphrase common among members of the anti-abortion movement in America. Proponents of this ideology argue that "an individual who kills to save a life has not committed murder, but has in fact prevented it."[49] The attacks are considered a form of terrorism because the intent was not just to kill, but also to use fear and violence to coerce the behavior of other doctors, staff and patrons of abortion clinics throughout the country.

Because the anti-abortion attacks had a common and exclusive target set, the U.S. government response was largely effective in preventing these kinds of attacks by providing more security for abortion clinics and practitioners, and enforcing new laws under the Freedom of Access to Clinic Entrances Act (passed in May 1994). But their limited target focus has been the exception among lone actor terrorists worldwide, who have actually attacked a very wide variety of targets over the past several decades. For example, Jewish extremist Yigal Amir killed Israeli Prime Minister Yitzhak Rabin at a campaign rally on November 4, 1995, having become convinced that doing so was a necessary form of God's retribution for signing the Oslo Peace Accord with Palestinian leader Yassir Arafat. On July 4, 2002, an Egyptian immigrant named Hesham Mohamed Hadayet opened fired at the El Al Israeli Airlines ticket counter at Los Angeles International Airport, killing two people and wounding four others before he was killed by security personnel. Carlos Bledsoe (aka Abdulhakim Mujahid Muhammad) killed a U.S. military recruiter and wounded another in Arkansas on June 1, 2009, acknowledging after the attack that he was inspired by the Salafi-jihadist ideology. Similarly, Ayanle Hassan Ali attacked soldiers at a Canadian Forces recruiting center in Toronto in March, 2016.

Places of worship have also been attacked by lone actor terrorists. On February 25, 1994, Jewish extremist Baruch Goldstein entered a mosque in Israel and began shooting indiscriminately, killing 29 worshippers and wounding more than 125. Wade Page, a white supremacist, killed six people and wounded four more at a Sikh temple in Wisconsin on August 5, 2012. In Charleston, S.C., white supremacist Dylan Roof killed nine people at the Emanuel African Methodist Episcopal Church on June 17, 2015. And on January 29, 2017, Alexandre Bissonnette entered a mosque in Quebec City and began shooting, eventually killing six people and injuring 19 others before he ran out of bullets. According to press reports and court records, each of these attacks were not only hate crimes, they were acts of terrorism linked to right-wing extremist ideologies described in Lecture 10 of this book.

Even a well-fortified U.S. military base can be the target of a lone actor terrorist attack. On November 5, 2009, U.S. Army Major Nidal Malik Hasan calmly entered Fort Hood, a large Army base near Killeen, Texas, and began shooting anyone he saw. While the U.S. Department of Defense eventually classified the shootings as an act of workplace violence, this attack—which killed 13 people and injured more than 30 others—has been deemed a terrorist incident by most scholars, policymakers, media experts, and others, based on the tomes of evidence compiled by the FBI that Hasan was motivated and inspired by the Salafi-jihadist ideology, and even communicated directly with the radical cleric Anwar al-Awlaki.

Lone actor terrorists have sometimes targeted public gatherings, like clubs and concert arenas. For example, on June 12, 2016, Omar Mateen carried out a mass shooting at the Pulse nightclub in Orlando, Fla., killing 49 people and wounding 58 others. During a break in the shooting, Mateen made a phone call in which he declared his loyalty to the leader of the Islamic State—even though IS had never heard of him before. Less than a year later, a suicide bomber attacked the Manchester Arena in the U.K. on May 22, 2017. The explosion ripped through the arena foyer as thousands of fans, mostly young girls and their parents, were leaving the venue after a performance by the pop star Ariana Grande. A 22-year-old college student named Salman Ramadan Abedi carried out this suicide bomb attack, and an investigation later found no direct links with any known terrorist organization.[50]

Historical analysis shows that bombings, shootings, and knife attacks are the most common type of lone actor terrorist attacks. Indeed, these are also the most common types of weapons used by terrorists in general, regardless of whether they are members of an established organization. But in recent years, we have also seen an increase in attacks using motor vehicles to plow into a crowd of people, a mode of attack that has been encouraged and praised by various online materials produced by al-Qaeda and the Islamic State, including their English-language magazines *Inspire* and *Rumiyah*.

For example, on July 14, 2016, Mohamed Lahouaiej Bouhlel drove a 19-tonne truck through a crowd of over 30,000 people watching a Bastille Day fireworks show along a promenade in Nice, France. He killed 84 people in this attack, and injured over 300 others before he was killed in a firefight with police. Later that year, on December 19, a Tunisian immigrant named Anis Amri drove a stolen truck into a Christmas market next to a church in Berlin, killing 12 and injuring 56 others. As in other instances, a spokesman for IS later took credit for the attack, but there is thus far no evidence that the group provided anything more than ideological encouragement to the attacker, indicating this was another example of "do-it-yourself" terrorism.

The year 2017 saw several more terrorist attacks using motor vehicles. On March 22, 2017, Khalid Masood drove a car into a crowd of pedestrians on the pavement of a popular street near Westminster Bridge in London, killing four and injuring more than 50 people. After crashing the rented vehicle into the gates of Parliament, Masood ran into New Palace Yard and stabbed an unarmed policeman to death before being shot and killed by plainclothes officers. On April 7, an Uzbek national named Rakhmat

Akilov used a truck to mow down pedestrians in Stockholm, killing four and injuring 15. On August 12, James Alex Fields, Jr. killed a young woman when he rammed his car into a crowd of anti-racist protestors at a rally in Charlottesville, Va. On October 31, Sayfullo Saipov—a 29-year-old immigrant from Uzbekistan—drove a rented truck into a crowd of people walking on the sidewalk in New York City, killing eight people and injuring a dozen others. In short, this mode of attack appears to be increasingly popular (and not just among jihadists, as demonstrated in the Charlottesville incident), and authorities are faced with a very complex challenge in trying to prevent them, particularly in an open society like ours.

And in one of the most lethal "do-it-yourself" attacks in recent years, white supremacist Anders Breivik carried out a bombing of a government building in Oslo, Norway on July 22, 2011, and then hours later murdered 69 people, mostly teenagers, at a camp on the island of Utoya. Hours before his attacks, Breivik uploaded to several websites a very lengthy manifesto (over 1,600 pages, which he titled "2083: A European Declaration of Independence") describing his far-right ideology and his perceived justification for committing these acts of mass killing. An extreme white nationalist, Breivik was highly anti-Muslim and felt that political leaders in his country had betrayed his race. As Raffaello Pantucci noted, "the vast majority of the document quotes others, with much of the rest made up of a detailed manifesto for what his perfect society and army should look like. Breivik goes into particular detail providing future followers with an outline of how they should go about building bombs, weaponry and military equipment."[51] At his trial, Breivik acknowledged that a primary reason for his terrorist attack was to draw attention to this manifesto. One could argue that in this regard he was partly successful, although the mass movement of white nationalists that he hoped to inspire has thankfully not materialized. In fact, this has been the most common outcome of lone actor terrorist attacks: the perpetrator often has some warped sense of their own importance in the trajectory of history, but while their use of violence to kill or maim others has drawn attention to their grievances, they have not inspired others to follow in their footsteps.

As we review the list of attacks conducted by lone actors, our natural instinct is to try and discern some kind of patterns or common traits among the targets or the attackers that might give us clues for preventing these kinds of tragedies in the future. Ideological orientation is certainly an important factor in a terrorist's target selection, but there is such a diverse array of targets and perpetrators, the "do-it-yourself" model of terrorism does not fit neatly into any particular categorization.

At the very least, we have learned that the nature of this threat is less related to jihadist ideology than certain media outlets or politicians would have us believe. For example, according to a report by the New America Foundation, from 2001 to 2015, right-wing terrorists in the U.S. have killed almost twice as many Americans in home-grown attacks than jihadists have.[52] In a June 2015 report, based on a survey of 382 state, county, and municipal law enforcement agencies, Kurzman and Schanzer found that "law enforcement agencies in the U.S. consider anti-government violent extremists, not radicalized Muslims, to be the most severe threat" they face.[53] A similar report by the Center for Investigative Reporting found that far-right plots and attacks outnumber jihadist incidents by almost 2 to 1 during the 9-year period 2008 thru 2016.[54]

A different study released in 2012 by researchers at Penn State University found a handful of patterns related to the ideological orientation of the attackers. For example, "al-Qaeda-related lone-actor terrorists were younger and more likely to be students, seek legitimization from others, learn through virtual sources, and display command and control links. They were less likely to have previous criminal convictions and less likely to execute their attacks successfully." In contrast, "right-wing lone-actor terrorists were more likely to be unemployed. They were less likely [than terrorists in other ideological categories] to have any university experience, make verbal statements to friends and family about their intent or beliefs, engage in dry-runs, or obtain help in procuring weaponry."[55] However, this study also found that "there were no uniform characteristics across all or even a majority of lone-actor terrorists." Similarly, a 2015 study released by the Center for the Study of Terrorism and Responses to Terrorism (at the University of Maryland) found a significant amount of demographic diversity among the perpetrators of lone actor terrorist attacks in the U.S. from 1980 to 2014.[56]

Some scholars have looked at mental illness as a potential attribute among lone actor terrorists. For example, a 2016 study by experts in the Netherlands examined 72 cases of lone actor terrorist attacks in Europe (and an additional 98 failed plots) between 2000 and 2014, and found that only a third of the perpetrators "suffered from some kind of mental health disorder" (like schizophrenia, depression, or bipolar disorder).[57] Researchers have found that in a few cases, a perpetrator of ideologically-motivated violence was mentally ill yet highly functional (e.g. Ted Kaczynski or Bruce Ivins), but these are also shown to be relatively rare cases within the broader spectrum of "do-it-yourself" terrorists.

In sum, the unfortunate truth is that scholarly research has thus far proven unable to identify any clear indicators of emotional or psychological instability, or any other personal or background profile attributes that might help us identify these kinds of attackers before they strike. This brings us back to a fundamental theme addressed throughout this book: terrorism is a contextual phenomenon, therefore identifying and preventing terrorist attacks—particular those orchestrated by lone actors—requires a great deal of human intelligence and contextually relevant knowledge.

CONCLUSION: THE ENDURING CHALLENGE OF "DO-IT-YOURSELF" TERRORISM

As this brief summary demonstrates, there has been a wide variety of team-based and individual forms of "do-it-yourself" terrorism. Often, the perpetrators of these attacks have been characterized as "homegrown" terrorists, meaning they were citizens or legal residents of the country in which they carried out their attack. In the U.S. and many other countries, law enforcement agencies have built a fairly extensive track record curtailing the activities of domestic terrorist groups by arresting and imprisoning leaders, disrupting their financial and weapons transactions, and deterring others from joining or supporting the group. But homegrown self-starter teams and lone actor terrorists present a tremendous challenge, as in many cases the perpetrators had clean police records, and no detectable affiliation with an extremist movement or group. There were no indications that they might be planning a lethal terrorist attack. The perpetrators chose their own timing and target of the attack, and in several cases they did not even try to acquire explosives or any other kind of traditional weapon—they simply got behind the wheel of a car or truck and plowed it into an innocent group of bystanders on a busy street.

Frequently, as described in Lectures 7 and 14, the Internet has played a significant role in facilitating the kinds of information and communication that motivated and inspired these individuals to carry out their attacks. Many attackers found various kinds of detailed instructions on weapons and targets, as well as ideological support and encouragement for their attack among those whom they interacted with online. However, research also shows that lone actors interact just as frequently with others in person as they do online. That is, they are equally likely to find ideological support and encouragement, and perhaps even some ideas for targets and weapons, through communication with someone in person as they are online. For example, research by Paul Gill found that "there is a lot of evidence to suggest that many of these lone-actors interact with co-ideologues during their radicalization and/or attack-planning process.

Just less than half (47.9%) interacted face-to-face with members of a wider network of political activists, and 35.3% did so virtually."[58]

Regardless of the specific kind of ideology motivating their attack, their state of mental health, or the weapons and targeting choices they make, these attackers have led to an alarming number of deaths and injuries among innocent civilians. However, the good news is that when we look at the broader picture of those who have attempted these kinds of "do-it-yourself" terrorist attacks, we find that a significant number of them have failed. Many aspiring lone actor terrorists have been amateurs, "wannabes" who were easily lured into law enforcement sting operations. In some cases they injured or killed themselves in the process of assembling or testing a weapon. In other cases, their lack of sophisticated preparation or training prevented their attack from succeeding. Faisal Shahzad's car bomb attempt in New York's Times Square only fizzled and smoked; Joseph Brice was building a bomb that prematurely detonated; the Fort Dix plotters, the wanna-be jihadists in Newburgh, Rezwan Ferdaus, Michael Finton, Hosam Smadi, and many others were caught in sting operations because they naively sought help from others who turned out to be FBI or police informants.

The bottom line here is that from a terrorist movement's strategic viewpoint, the "do-it-yourself" approach may offer advantages in terms of influencing a perception that the threat is widespread, there is a terrorist around every corner or under every bed, an existential threat to the very survival of our society or way of life. This perception creates the kind of fear that, the terrorists hope, will lead to policy changes or social behavior that will help them achieve their overall objectives. The "do-it-yourself" model of terrorism also affords the terrorist organization some level of protection from infiltration by law enforcement and intelligence agencies.

However, the reality is that this form of terrorism is inefficient and largely ineffective in achieving the core political and strategic objectives of a terrorist movement. As noted in previous lectures, the "leaderless resistance" or "leaderless jihad" model of terrorism is meant to inspire individuals toward action on behalf of a violent ideology. One assumption behind this strategy is that successful (or almost successful) "do-it-yourself" attacks could inspire others by their examples ("if they can do that, so can I"). Essentially, it lowers the threshold for what it takes to become part of a terrorist movement. However, a movement's leaders seeking to encourage these kinds of attacks have no power to select targets, weapons, or the timing of attacks. Their role is mainly limited to certain kinds of activities like motivating, inspiring, and teaching. In comparison, organized terrorist groups like Hizballah or Hamas—with significant resources and a centralized hierarchy of decision-making authority—have far greater capabilities to sustain a campaign of carnage over long periods of time, and to direct that carnage toward the achievement of strategic objectives. Clearly, as exemplified by a number of prominent attacks over the past three decades, the security challenge we face today from the "do-it-yourself" terrorist is very real. But this form of terrorism is highly unlikely to result in the kind of catastrophic, game-changing attack that will bring about any kind of real political or social change.

QUESTIONS FOR DISCUSSION

- What do we know about the kinds of motivations behind "lone actor" or "self-starter team" terrorist attacks?
- What knowledge, skills, and abilities would a do-it-yourself lone actor or self-starter team need to successfully carry out a significant terrorist attack in your local area?
- Are the targets chosen by lone actors or self-starter teams different from what an established terrorist organization might choose to attack? Why or why not?
- What can be done, if anything, to improve the quality of U.S. intelligence in ways that could help prevent the next "do-it-yourself" attack?
- Is this a kind of terrorism that cannot be prevented or deterred? Why or why not?
- How are U.S. government agencies responding to (or working to mitigate) the threat of "do-it-yourself" terrorist attacks? What could be done to improve this response?

RECOMMENDED READING

Alonso, Rogelio. "The Madrid Attacks on March 11: An Analysis of the Jihadist Threat in Spain and Main Counterterrorist Measures." In *Countering Terrorism and Insurgency in the 21st Century*. Vol. 3. Edited by James J. F. Forest. Westport, CT: Praeger, 2007.

Baracskay, Daniel. "The April 1995 Bombing of the Murrah Federal Building in Oklahoma City." In *Countering Terrorism and Insurgency in the 21st Century*. Vol. 3. Edited by James J. F. Forest. Westport, CT: Praeger, 2007.

Benjamin, Daniel and Steven Simon. *The Next Attack*. New York: Times Books, 2005.

Bergen, Peter L. *United States of Jihad: Investigating America's Homegrown Terrorists*. New York: Crown Publishers, 2016.

Bjelopera, Jerome P. *American Jihadist Terrorism: Combating a Complex Threat*. Washington, DC: Congressional Research Service, January 23, 2013.

Davis, Danny W. *The Phinehas Priesthood: Violent Vanguard of the Christian Identity Movement*. Westport, CT: Praeger, 2010.

Deloughery, Kathleen, Ryan D. King, and Victor Asal. "Understanding Lone-actor Terrorism: A Comparative Analysis with Violent Hate Crimes and Group-based Terrorism." Final Report to the Resilient Systems Division, Science and Technology Directorate, U.S. Department of Homeland Security. College Park, MD: START, 2013.

Ellis, Clare. "With a Little Help From My Friends: An Exploration of the Tactical Use of Single-Actor Terrorism by the Islamic State." *Perspectives on Terrorism* 10, no. 6 (December 2016), http://bit.ly/2ngHUeJ.

Galanter, Marc and James J. F. Forest. "Cults, Charismatic Groups and Social Systems: Understanding the Transformation of Terrorist Recruits." In *The Making of a Terrorist*. Vol. 2. Edited by James J. F. Forest. Westport, CT: Praeger, 2005. Pp. 51–70.

Gill, Paul "Tracing the Motivations and Antecedent Behaviors of Lone-Actor Terrorism." International Center for the Study of Terrorism, Pennsylvania State University, 2012.

Gill, Paul. *Lone Actor Terrorists: A Behavioral Analysis*. London, Routledge (2015).

Gill, Paul and Emily Corner. "Lone-Actor Terrorist Target Choice." *Behavioral Sciences & the Law* 34, no. 5 (2016): 693–705.

Hughes, Seamus. "Low Cost, High Impact: Combatting the Financing of Lone-Wolf and Small-Scale Terrorist Attacks." *Written Testimony for U.S. House of Representatives Financial Services Committee*. September 6, 2017. http://bit.ly/2neNpLa.

Jenkins, Brian M. "Stray Dogs and Virtual Armies: Radicalization and Recruitment to Jihadist Terrorism in the United States Since 9/11." RAND Corporation, 2011.

Jenkins, Brian M. *The Origins of America's Jihadists*. Santa Monica, CA: RAND Corporation, 2017.

Joosse, Paul. "Leaderless Resistance and the Loneliness of Lone Wolves: Exploring the Rhetorical Dynamics of Lone Actor Violence." *Terrorism & Political Violence* 29, no. 1 (2017): 52–78.

Kirby, Aidan. "The London Bombers as 'Self-Starters': A Case Study in Indigenous Radicalization and the Emergence of Autonomous Cliques." *Studies in Conflict & Terrorism* 30 (2007): 415–28.

Kurzman, Charles and David Schanzer. Law Enforcement Assessment of the Violent Extremist Threat. Durham, NC: Triangle Center on Terrorism and Homeland Security, June 25, 2015. http://bit.ly/1oUeKBJ.

Lemieux, Anthony, Jarret Brachman, Jason Levitt, and Jay Wood. "Inspire Magazine: A Critical Analysis of its Significance and Potential Impact thorough the Lens of the Information, Motivation and Behavioral Skills Model." *Terrorism and Political Violence* 1, no. 1 (2014): 1–18.

Maley, Tom. "The London Terrorist Attacks of July 7, 2005." In *Countering Terrorism and Insurgency in the 21st Century*. Vol. 3. Edited by James J. F. Forest. Westport, CT: Praeger, 2007.

Michel, Lou and Dan Herbeck. *American Terrorist: Timothy McVeigh and the Oklahoma City Bombing*. New York: Regan Books, 2001.

Mullins, Sam. "Lone-Actor vs. Remote-Controlled Jihadi Terrorism: Rethinking the threat to the West." *War on the Rocks*, April 20, 2017. http://bit.ly/2pH4T5T.

Mullins, Sam. *Home-Grown Jihad: Understanding Islamist Terrorism in the US and UK*. London; New Jersey: Imperial College Press, 2016.

Pantucci, Raffaello. "What Have We Learned about Lone Wolves from Anders Behring Breivik?" *Perspectives on Terrorism* 5, no. 5–6 (2011).

Sageman, Marc. *Leaderless Jihad: Terror Networks in the Twenty-First Century*. University of Pennsylvania Press, 2008.

Schuster, Henry and Charles Stone. *Hunting Eric Rudolph*. Berkley Books, 2005.

Shibuya, Eric Y. "The Struggle with Violent Right-Wing Extremist Groups in the United States" In *Countering Terrorism and Insurgency in the 21st Century*. Vol. 2. Edited by James J. F. Forest. Westport, CT: Praeger, 2007.Pp. 574–75.

Simon, Jeffrey. *Lone Wolf Terrorism: Understanding the Growing Threat*. New York: Prometheus Books, 2013.

Sinai, Joshua. "Najibullah Zazi's Plot to Bomb the New York City Subway System: A Case Study of How U.S. Domestic Counterterrorism Operates." In *Homeland Security and Terrorism*. Edited by James J. F. Forest et al. New York: McGraw-Hill, 2012.

Smith, Brent L., and Paxton Roberts, Jeff Gruenewald, and Brent Klein. "Patterns of Lone Actor Terrorism in the United States: Research Brief." College Park, MD: START, June 2015.

van Zuijdewijn, Jeanine de Roy, and Edwin Bakker. "Analyzing Personal Characteristics of Lone-Actor Terrorists: Research Findings and Recommendations." *Perspectives on Terrorism* 10, no. 2 (2016).

Vidino, Lorenzo et al. "Fear They Neighbor: Radicalization and Jihadist Attacks in the West." George Washington University, Program on Extremism, June 2017. http://bit.ly/2rHRSWL.

WEBSITES

Global Terrorism Database
https://www.start.umd.edu/gtd/

George Washington University, Program on Extremism
https://extremism.gwu.edu/

NOTES

1. Eric Y. Shibuya, "The Struggle with Violent Right-Wing Extremist Groups in the United States," in *Countering Terrorism and Insurgency in the 21st Century*, ed. James J. F. Forest (Westport, CT: Praeger, 2007): 574–75.

2. Louis Beam, "Leaderless Resistance," *Seditionist* 12 (February 1992).

3. Daniel Benjamin and Steven Simon, *The Next Attack* (New York: Times Books, 2005).

4. Beam, "Leaderless Resistance."

5. For a brief description of the deep web and Bitcoin, see Jay Newton-Small, "Why the Deep Web Has Washington Worried," *Time* (October 31, 2013).

6. Aidan Kirby, "The London Bombers as 'Self-Starters': A case study in indigenous radicalization and the emergence of autonomous cliques," *Studies in Conflict & Terrorism* 30 (2007): 415–28; and Daniel Levitas, *The Terrorist Next Door: The Militia and the Radical Right* (London: St. Martin's Griffin, 2004).

7. The building, which housed several federal agencies and bureaus, was constructed in 1997 and named after federal judge Alfred P. Murrah, who was appointed to the U.S. District Court for Oklahoma in 1937, and the 10th U.S. Circuit Court of Appeals in 1940, and retired in 1970.

8. This description of the attack is drawn from Daniel Baracskay, "The April 1995 Bombing of the Murrah Federal Building in Oklahoma City," in *Countering Terrorism and Insurgency in the 21st Century*, ed. James J. F. Forest (Westport, CT: Praeger, 2007).

9. U.S. Department of Justice, *Responding to Terrorism Victims: Oklahoma City and Beyond* (Washington, DC: Office of Justice Programs, October 2000).

10. S. A. Pressley, "Bomb Kills Dozens in Oklahoma Federal Building," *Washington Post*, April 20, 1995, A1.

11. For more on this topic, please see Lecture 10.

12. Brian L. Keeley, "Of Conspiracy Theories," *Journal of Philosophy* 96, no. 3. (March 1999): 109–126.

13. Lou Michel and Dan Herbeck, *American Terrorist: Timothy McVeigh & the Oklahoma City Bombing* (New York: Regan Books, 2001): 2.

14. Ibid.

15. This description of the Madrid attack is drawn from Rogelio Alonso, "The Madrid Attacks on March 11: An Analysis of the Jihadist Threat in Spain and Main Counterterrorist Measures," in *Countering Terrorism and Insurgency in the 21st Century*, ed. James J. F. Forest (Westport, CT: Praeger, 2007).

16. Juzgado Central de Instrucción Número 6, Audiencia Nacional (April 10, 2006): 339–40.

17. Ibid., 336. As cited in Rogelio Alonso, "The Madrid Attacks on March 11."

18. This description of the attack is drawn from Tom Maley, "The London Terrorist Attacks of July 7, 2005," in *Countering Terrorism and Insurgency in the 21st Century*, ed. James J. F. Forest (Westport, CT: Praeger, 2007); and from Kirby, "The London Bombers as 'Self-Starters,'" 415–28.

19. Tom Maley, "The London Terrorist Attacks of July 7, 2005."

20. Intelligence and Security Committee, UK Parliament. *Report into the London Terrorist Attacks on 7 July 2005.* Cm 6785. (London, UK: The Stationery Office, 2006): 2.

21. Kirby, "The London Bombers as 'Self-Starters,'" 417.

22. Maley, "The London Terrorist Attacks of July 7, 2005."

23. Greg McNeal, "London casts long shadow in New York," *New York Times,* August 3, 2005. See also Intelligence and Security Committee, UK Parliament, *Report into the London Terrorist Attacks,* 11.

24. Ibid.

25. Brian M. Jenkins, "Stray Dogs and Virtual Armies: Radicalization and Recruitment to Jihadist Terrorism in the United States Since 9/11," RAND Corporation, 2011.

26. For an overview of this attack, see "Toronto 18: Key events in the Case," CBC News (June 4, 2008), http://www.cbc.ca/news/canada/toronto-18-key-events-in-the-case-1.715266.

27. "Canada Prime Minister Reportedly Target of Plot," NBC News (June 7, 2006), http://www.nbcnews.com/id/13150516/.

28. Janet Davison and Janet Thomson, "Homegrown Terrorist: Toronto 18 Bomb Plotter Saad Khalid Recalls his Radicalization," CBC News [Canada] (April 16, 2014), http://news360.com/article/234215435.

29. For a full account of Mubin Shaikh's role in this incident, please see Stefano Bonino, "In Conversation with Mubin Shaikh: From Salafi Jihadist to Undercover Agent inside the 'Toronto 18' Terrorist Group," *Perspectives on Terrorism* 10, no. 2 (2016); and his November 2016 TED talk, https://youtu.be/RK8zb8dA4G4.

30. Dale Russakoff and Dan Eggen, "Six Charged in Plot to Attack Fort Dix," *Washington Post,* May 9, 2007, http://www.washingtonpost.com/wp-dyn/content/article/2007/05/08/AR2007050 800465.html.

31. Ibid.

32. Joshua Sinai, "Najibullah Zazi's Plot to Bomb the New York City Subway System: A Case Study of How U.S. Domestic Counterterrorism Operates," in *Homeland Security and Terrorism,* ed. James J. F. Forest et al. (McGraw-Hill, 2012).

33. Jerome P. Bjelopera, *American Jihadist Terrorism: Combating a Complex Threat* (Washington, DC: Congressional Research Service, January 23, 2013), http://www.fas.org/sgp/crs/terror/R41416.pdf.

34. Al Baker and Javier C. Hernandez, "4 Accused of Bombing Plot at Bronx Synagogues," *New York Times,* May 20, 2009, http://www.nytimes.com/2009/05/21/nyregion/21arrests.html?_r=0.

35. "St. Petersburg Attack: What we know," BBC News (April 19, 2017), http://www.bbc.com/news/world-europe-39481067; and "St. Petersburg Attack: Suspect says he only 'followed orders," BBC News (April 18, 2017), http://www.bbc.com/news/world-europe-39629875.

36. For details of this incident and its immediate aftermath, see the CNN Fast Facts website, http://www.cnn.com/2013/06/03/us/boston-marathon-terror-attack-fast-facts/.

37. For more information, see the formal indictment Boston Marathon Attack: Grand Jury Indictment, United States v. Dzhokhar A. Tsarnaev, June 2013.

38. Steven M. Chermak, Joshua Freilich, Celinet Duran, and William S. Parkin, "An Overview of Bombing and Arson Attacks by Environmental and Animal Rights Extremists in the United States, 1995–2010," Final Report to the Resilient Systems Division, Science and Technology Directorate, U.S. Department of Homeland Security (College Park, MD: START, May 2013): 14.

39. "Countering Eco-Terrorism in the United States: The Case of Operation Backfire," START Report for the Science & Technology Directorate, U.S. Department of Homeland Security (September 2012), http://www.start.umd.edu/start/publications/Countermeasures_OperationBackfire.pdf.

40. For more on this, see Marc Galanter and James J. F. Forest, "Cults, Charismatic Groups and Social Systems: Understanding the Transformation of Terrorist Recruits," in *The Making of a Terrorist*, vol. 2, ed. James J. F. Forest (Westport, CT: Praeger, 2005): 51–70.

41. Brian M. Jenkins, "Stray Dogs and Virtual Armies: Radicalization and Recruitment to Jihadist Terrorism in the United States Since 9/11," RAND Corporation, 2011.

42. For more on this attack, see Mia Bloom, *Bombshell: Women and Terrorism* (New York: Penguin, 2011); and Michael Roberts, "Killing Rajiv Gandhi: Dhanu's sacrificial metaporphosis in death," *South Asian History and Culture* 1, no. 1 (January 2010): 25–41.

43. For more on these attacks, see Mia Bloom, *Bombshell: Women and Terrorism* (New York: Penguin, 2011); and Yoram Schweitzer, "Palestinian Female Suicide Bombers," in *Female Terrorism and Militancy: Agency, Utility, and Organization,* ed. Cindy Ness (London: Routledge, February 2008).

44. For more on these kinds of attacks, see Clare Ellis, "With a Little Help From My Friends: An Exploration of the Tactical Use of Single-Actor Terrorism by the Islamic State," *Perspectives on Terrorism* 10, no. 6 (December 2016).

45. Henry Schuster and Charles Stone, *Hunting Eric Rudolph*(Berkley Books, 2005).

46. "Rudolph reveals motives," CNN (April 10, 2005), http://www.cnn.com/2005/LAW/04/13/eric.rudolph/. Also, a number of Rudolph's personal writings are made available by the Army of God on its website at http://www.armyofgod.com/EricRudolphHomepage.html.

47. For more on these and other individuals linked to the Phineas Priesthood, see Danny W. Davis, *The Phinehas Priesthood: Violent Vanguard of the Christian Identity Movement* (Westport, CT: Praeger, 2010).

48. For more on these and other individuals responsible for anti-abortion violence, see Jennifer Jefferis, *Armed for Life: The Army of God and Anti-Abortion Terror in the United States* (Westport, CT: Praeger, 2010).

49. Ibid., 55.

50. Nazia Parveen, "Manchester Bombing," *Guardian*, July 7, 2017; and "Manchester Attack: Who was Salman Abedi?," BBC News (June 12, 2017), http://www.bbc.com/news/uk-40019135.

51. Raffaello Pantucci, "What Have We Learned about Lone Wolves from Anders Behring Breivik?," *Perspectives on Terrorism* 5, no. 5–6 (2011).

52. New America Foundation, "Terrorism in America After 9/11" (updated November, 2017), http://bit.ly/2Ee42i6.

53. Charles Kurzman and David Schanzer. *Law Enforcement Assessment of the Violent Extremist Threat* (Durham, NC: Triangle Center on Terrorism and Homeland Security, June 25, 2015), http://bit.ly/1oUeKBJ.

54. David Neiwert, et al., "Homegrown Terror," Center for Investigative Reporting (June 22, 2017), https://apps.revealnews.org/homegrown-terror/.

55. Paul Gill, "Tracing the Motivations and Antecedent Behaviors of Lone-Actor Terrorism," International Center for the Study of Terrorism, Pennsylvania State University (2012).

56. Brent L. Smith, Paxton Roberts, Jeff Gruenewald, and Brent Klein, "Patterns of Lone Actor Terrorism in the United States: Research Brief" (College Park, MD: START, June, 2015).

57. Jeanine de Roy van Zuijdewijn and Edwin Bakker, "Analyzing Personal Characteristics of Lone-Actor Terrorists: Research Findings and Recommendations," *Perspectives on Terrorism* 10, no. 2 (2016).

58. Paul Gill, *Lone Actor Terrorists: A Behavioral Analysis* (London: Routledge, 2015). Also, see Paul Gill and Emily Corner, "Lone-Actor Terrorist Target Choice," *Behavioral Sciences & the Law* 34, no. 5 (2016): 693–705.

16

Suicide Terrorist Attacks

In this lecture, we are going to examine the nature of suicide terrorism from two different angles. First, we will look at some global trends and the intentions of groups that use this tactic. And then we will examine what the research literature can tell us about individual suicide attackers. In most cases, suicide terrorist attacks involve bombs, with individuals using their bodies as a delivery mechanism for the explosives to reach the target. But sometimes knives, guns, trucks, and so forth have been used by attackers who anticipate that their own death will result from their actions. However, while similar motivations can be seen among suicide attackers regardless of specific weapons used in their attacks, we will focus mainly on suicide bombings throughout most of this lecture.

But before we get started we need to have a definition of "suicide terrorism" to work from. The most common definition of the term, as it is used in the literature, is the intentional killing of oneself for the purpose of killing others in the service of a political or ideological goal. This is not to be confused with other types of attacks in which an individual is killed in the process of the attack, including high-risk missions, fooled couriers, or suicide—without homicide—for a political cause (e.g., several instances of Tibetan monks setting themselves on fire to protest the oppressive regime in China, or similar cases in Tunisia and elsewhere at the start of the Arab Spring). Essentially, a suicide bomber is for the most part simply viewed as a weapon in the arsenal of some (but not all) terrorist groups.

Now, let's look at how terrorist groups have employed this type of weapon. The Islamist group al-Dawa is credited with the first modern suicide car bomb attack, which destroyed the Iraqi Embassy in Beirut on December 15, 1981, killing 16 people and injuring 110 more. The Lebanese group Hizballah embraced this tactic shortly after it was founded a couple years later, with six attacks using a combination of cars, trucks, grenades, and explosive belts that killed almost 400 people. These included a suicide car bomb attack against the U.S. Embassy in Beirut in April 1983, and simultaneous suicide truck bomb attacks in October 1983 against the U.S. Marine barracks and the French Paratroops barracks, again in Beirut. During the 1990s, this tactic became widely associated with the conflict between the Palestinians and Israel. In July

Figure 16.1: Aftermath of the 1983 Hizballah bombing of the U.S. Marine barracks in Beirut, Lebanon. Credit: U.S. Marine Corps. Photo by SSgt Randy Gaddo, USMC.

1989, the Palestinian Islamic Jihad (a group affiliated with the Muslim Brotherhood in Egypt) became the first group to take responsibility for a suicide terrorist attack in this region. A PIJ member of the group named Abd al-Hadi Ghanim seized the steering wheel of a crowded commuter bus and forced it over a steep cliff into a ravine, killing 16 passengers. Several years later, the group took responsibility for a series of suicide bombings, but soon a different Islamist group known as Hamas took its place as the premier suicide bombing terrorists in this region. However, as we'll discuss in a moment, the real leaders in the use of suicide bombings throughout the 1990s were the Tamil Tigers, an ethnonationalist terrorist group in Sri Lanka.

Worldwide, the use of suicide terrorism as a tactic has grown exponentially over the last three decades.[1] It has become more global, meaning that suicide terrorist attacks have occurred in an increasing number of countries, including Nigeria, Somalia, Iraq, Syria, Turkey, and France. The tactic has been used with greater frequency, and by a larger number of different terrorist groups (though predominately by Salafi-jihadist groups, described in Lecture 12). And by several accounts, suicide attacks have become more lethal over time. For example, Robert Pape's research on suicide attacks indicates that between 1980 and 2003, this tactic actually accounted for only three percent of terrorist events worldwide, but almost half of all casualties related to terrorism were caused by suicide attacks.[2] As we'll discuss later in this lecture, the tactic of suicide terrorism appears to be gaining in strategic importance among terrorists and insurgents because it brings an array of disruptive effects that cascade upon the political, economic, and social routines of national life and international relations. In addition, suicide attacks garner more media coverage than most other kinds of terrorist attacks.

One of the key challenges to combating suicide terrorism is that there are so many delivery mechanisms. We have seen cars and trucks loaded with explosives driven to their targets and detonated by the drivers. We have seen small boats doing the same off the coast of Sri Lanka and in the Persian Gulf, including attacks on U.S. warships in Yemen; we have seen terrorists use (or try to use) airplanes full of fuel as a form of suicide bomb. September 11 wasn't the first instance of this, by the way. In 1994, a group of Algerian Islamists hijacked an Air France flight on its way to Greece and forced it to land in Marseille, near the French Mediterranean coast. The hijackers demanded that the airplane be filled with fuel, but then indicated their intention to fly to Paris, which would have used very little of the fuel they were demanding. At this point, French Special Forces stormed the plane and took down the hijackers, although a few hostages were also killed. It turns out the hijackers had planned to fly the plane to Paris, but crash it into the Eiffel Tower, creating a massive fireball and killing untold hundreds of people.

And of course, the most common form of suicide bomber has been the individual with explosives wrapped around them like a belt, or tucked inside a jacket, or carried in a backpack or other sort of personal bag. In December 2001, Richard Reid hid explosives in his shoes as part of a failed suicide bombing attempt aboard a U.S.-bound transatlantic flight, which is why we all have to remove our shoes at TSA checkpoints today. In a suicide attack in 2008 against the Marriott Hotel in Islamabad, Pakistan, the bomber took his explosives into the lobby inside a large, ordinary-looking wheeled suitcase. Nigerian jihadist Umar Farouk Abdulmutallab hid plastic explosives in his underwear in his failed suicide bombing attempt against a transatlantic flight to Detroit in December 2009. Most suicide terrorist attacks involve so-called "soft targets," mainly civilian gathering places like shopping malls, buses, airports, train terminals, restaurants, hotels, and so forth. As a result, the overwhelming majority of suicide bombings have killed civilians as opposed to members of a government's security forces. This holds true even when we take into account the U.S. military deployments in Iraq and Afghanistan since 2001. In those countries, the pattern has remained the same. While military bases are obviously high on most terrorists' target lists, they are usually difficult to penetrate. Several suicide bombers have attacked checkpoints and military convoys, but by and large the terrorists have more commonly targeted publicly accessible, less protected targets.

It is important to note that of the hundreds of terrorist groups that have come and gone over the past few decades, including those that are still active today, only a small portion of them have adopted the tactics of suicide terrorism. Those that have include members of the global Salafi-jihadist movement, including groups like al-Qaeda and the Islamic State, and their affiliates in Afghanistan, Pakistan, Syria, Iraq, Nigeria, Algeria, and Somalia; Palestinian groups like Hamas, the Palestinian Islamic Jihad, the Popular Front for the Liberation of Palestine, the al-Aqsa Martyr Brigades, and a few others; Hizballah in Lebanon; Chechen separatists, some of whom have ties to Salafi-jihadist groups and fought alongside the Taliban during the initial American invasion in 2001; the PKK, a separatist group that seeks to create an independent Kurdish state in southeastern Turkey and parts of neighboring countries inhabited by Kurds; the Taliban and the Haqqani militant networks in Afghanistan; and the Tamil Tigers in Sri Lanka.

There are of course several others as well. However, note from this list of groups that there is a distinct pattern among the groups who have adopted the use of suicide bombings. We do not see any environmentalist or animal rights groups on this list, for example. We also see no right-wing racist or reactionary groups, no anti-abortion or other Christian extremists, and none of the communist left-wing revolutionary groups that terrorized Europe and Latin America during the last half-century.

Further, there are only a few ethnonationalist groups among the ranks of suicide bombing terrorists, and several highly prominent groups in that category, like the ETA and the IRA, have not used suicide bombers in their attacks. The Tamil Tigers, on the other hand, pioneered several kinds of suicide bombings, and led the world in the use of this tactic throughout the 1990s. They deployed suicide bombers using cars, boats, even bicycles, and both men and women were used in these attacks. Over time, they became increasingly efficient and deadly in their use of this weapon. But as I mentioned, and as my friend Assaf Moghadam details in his excellent book *The Globalization of Martyrdom*, Salafi-jihadist groups account for the majority of suicide attacks worldwide.[3] This raises a fundamental question: *Why have these groups, and not others, chosen to embrace the tactic of suicide bombings?*

The question itself reveals an important point about all this: personal attributes tend to be less critical to understanding suicide bombers than group attributes. Most suicide attacks have been carried out by groups, as opposed to individuals acting on their own whims. A primary goal of the organization using this tactic may be to inflict as many casualties as possible, but other objectives include causing widespread fear and panic; exploiting the targeted government's "weakness"; and demonstrating the kind of commitment that can't be deterred.

> **TO THE POINT**
>
> A wide variety of terrorist groups have found suicide bombings to be tactically and strategically beneficial.

This is an important point to make because there is a perception, often perpetrated by the media, that suicide terrorism is a seemingly irrational act, but from the perspective of a terrorist organization it's a strategy that is well planned, logical, and designed to achieve specific political objectives. From this perspective, it may be intuitive that suicide attacks have increased over the past three decades because—as discussed in Lecture 13—many terrorist groups learn and adapt new ideas from others that seem to be effective. So, let's explore some of the strategic advantages and reasons behind this trend. To begin with, traditional concepts of security are based on deterring terrorist attacks, and these approaches to deterrence typically assume that the terrorist fears death or capture. However, suicide attacks *depend* on the death of the terrorist. In other words, the suicide bomber doesn't care about his or her death, imprisonment, or torture at the time of the attack. They have no need for an escape plan, which is traditionally the most difficult part of a terrorist operation. Both the terrorist group and the suicide bomber have a strong desire for the mission to succeed.

Some refer to suicide terrorists as the "ultimate smart bomb." What is meant by the use of this term? A suicide bomber is the only weapon that can respond to unforeseen changes in the targeting environment and make split-second decisions that can help them achieve their mission. For example, imagine a suicide attack is planned at a shopping mall in Tel Aviv. But on the day of the attack, as the bomber approaches the entrance to the mall, he sees that there are some Israeli Defense Forces (IDF) soldiers guarding the door and stopping people at random for security screening. So, to avoid risking the failure of his mission, the bomber looks around, sees a crowded bus stop, and goes over there to detonate his backpack filled with explosives. Or consider the case of 18-year old Hasib Hussein, one of the suicide bombers in the July 7, 2005 attacks on the Underground in London. While his three friends successfully detonated their backpack bombs on separate underground trains at almost exactly the same time, Hussein's malfunctioned. So, based on evidence from closed-circuit television cameras that day, we know that he calmly walked into a nearby drug store, bought a new 9-volt battery, boarded a double-decker bus at Tavistock Square and then repaired and successfully detonated his bomb. No other weapon can do such things.

Groups also benefit from public perception when using a suicide bomber, because employing this tactic demonstrates the commitment of the group and of those they recruit. Research by Mia Bloom has shown that among those communities that accept its legitimacy, the use of this tactic *underpins trust in the organization*, thus *increasing* the organization's *political "market share"* in the community.[4] In other words, some groups may adopt this tactic as a way of demonstrating greater commitment than other groups competing for support within the same community. This is why we have frequently seen competing claims for particular suicide attacks, especially in the Israel-Palestinian conflict. On the other hand, a group that refuses this tactic can find itself losing public support. For example, the Popular Front for the Liberation of Palestine— a nationalist Marxist group—refused to embrace suicide terrorism, and was seeing rapidly diminishing public support (compared to other groups) in Palestinian polls until they changed policy and adopted suicide attacks in 2001. This issue of demonstrating greater commitment illustrates how important public support is in terms of influencing a terrorist group's decision over whether or not to adopt this tactic. It also influences the number of volunteers the group can attract for terrorist activity in general and for suicide attacks in particular.

Another important aspect of a group's decision to adopt suicide terrorism is based on whether or not this tactic is viewed as effective. According to a study by Robert Pape, terrorists achieved some political gains in over half of the major suicide terror campaigns between 1980 and 2003. In these instances, the states involved in the attacks either fully or partially withdrew from territory they were occupying; began negotiations with the terrorist group; or released a terrorist leader.[5] Pape also notes that suicide campaigns have been particularly successful against a variety of democratic governments—even hawkish ones like the United States under Ronald Reagan, and Israel under Benjamin Netanyahu. For example, the United States pulled its troops out of Lebanon shortly after the 1983 suicide attacks against the embassy and the Marine barracks. In his memoirs, President Reagan reflected that, "We couldn't stay there and run the risk of another suicide attack on the Marines"[6]—in essence, a public confirmation that suicide attacks were effective in forcing concessions by a powerful government.

If suicide terrorism is indeed effective, at least to some degree, the next question to ask is why. When looking at this from the perspective of asymmetric warfare strategies, suicide terrorism does seem to offer a useful counter to traditional military force. That is, with suicide terrorism the *weaker acts as coercer* and the stronger actor becomes the target.[7] Through the use of suicide terrorism, groups of Palestinians, Kurds, Tamils, and others have felt a rising sense of empowerment. In the Palestinian case, they feel they finally have a weapon that creates a balance of power with Israel and, in their fantasies at least, can defeat Israel. Also, protecting against human bombs is nearly impossible; the very nature of this kind of weapon can reduce the effectiveness of even the most draconian security measures. This reflects a historical fact that terrorist groups have long proven an ability to find their way around whatever challenges are placed in their way—they are, after all, human, and humans have always had a knack for figuring out things like this. The importance of appreciating this history is that underestimating a terrorist group's capability for innovation or malevolent creativity is a road to disastrous consequences.

However, it is also important to note that from a long-term perspective, terrorist groups have realized only limited gains from using suicide attacks. To date, no studies have indicated that suicide terrorism *per se* has enabled any group to achieve its central core objectives. Even when the United States withdrew from Lebanon, America really only had humanitarian interests at stake since it was there on a peacekeeping mission. No real political or economic damage was inflicted upon the United States in that instance (though the death of 241 U.S. Marines was certainly tragic). Similarly, when Israel withdrew from Lebanon in 1985, its troops remained in a security buffer along the border for another 15 years. And when Israel withdrew its troops from the West Bank and Gaza Strip in 1995, it increased the scope and breadth of Jewish settlements in the Palestinian Territories, and the IDF has had no problem going back in whenever they have felt necessary. Thus, any claims that suicide terrorism is a strategically effective tactic should be met with some skepticism.[8]

> **TO THE POINT**
>
> There is no common profile of a suicide bomber—there are many differences in age, gender, socioeconomic background, religious identification, ethnicity, and much more.

To sum up, suicide terrorism is considered by most scholars and policymakers to be a unique phenomenon in the world of political violence. It is driven by group strategies and decisions, more than by individuals, and relies heavily on public support (or acquiescence). Traditional concepts of deterrence and security are ineffective in preventing the use of this tactic. Rather, suicide terror campaigns can only be stopped by the right mix of intelligence infiltration, counterideology efforts, and diminished public support for the tactic. This leads us to the second part of this lecture: the role of the individual who decides to become a suicide bomber.

INDIVIDUAL DIMENSIONS

There are several basic dimensions of a suicide attack. A group first needs to recruit individuals to serve as suicide bombers (we have yet to find a suicide bomber without at least some connection to an established terrorist group or network). Research in the Palestinian Territories, Iraq, and Afghanistan indicates that often the suicide bombers volunteered to become martyrs, while in Sri Lanka the Tamil Tigers considered it an honor to be selected for a suicide bombing mission. A terrorist group's ideology and proficiency in radicalization and indoctrination plays an important role here, as described in Lectures 7 and 14. Then, after recruitment, there are various kinds of preparations that must be made before the bomber can be sent on his or her way to the target for what they hope will be a successful mission.

First, let's take a look at what the research literature tells us about recruitment for suicide terrorism. Among the many attempts to try and describe the types of individuals who would agree to become a suicide bomber, the most common themes include some kind of religious fanaticism; poverty and economic desperation; ignorance, owing to a lack of decent education in the region; revenge for personal suffering, or for the suffering of a loved one; or some form of psychopathology—that is, mental or emotional imbalance that makes them susceptible to the lure of suicide terrorism. However, *none of these explanations are supported by significant data*. As noted in Lectures 3 and 14, these are largely the same problems we encounter when studying the individual motivations behind terrorist activity in general. Thus, to truly understand the individual dimension of suicide terrorism, we need to find sources of empirical data—not an easy task, considering that the prime subjects of this research kill themselves before we can ask them any questions.

Still, there are some sources of empirical data that can be used to paint a more complete and clear portrait of suicide bombers. These sources include: media accounts, particularly in which the journalists interview friends and families of the suicide bomber; interviews with captured would-be suicide bombers, which have been done mostly in Israel and the Palestinian territories, Jordan, Lebanon, Syria, and Russia; interviews with trainers and launchers of suicide bombers who have been incarcerated in Israel, Saudi Arabia, Jordan, Egypt, and elsewhere; and so-called "psychological autopsies" of suicide bombers (predominately, these are based on interviews with families and close friends of the bombers by established scholars like Jerrold Post, Scott Atran, John Horgan, Ehud Sprinzak, Mia Bloom, Yoram Schweitzer, and a host of others).

From these sources of data, we are able to determine a number of demographic details most common to suicide terrorists. For example, we have learned that the mean average age of suicide bombers is in the mid-twenties, but there has been a wide range of ages observed, from as young as 11 years old to over 60. We have also learned that most suicide bombers have been male, but there have been a significant number of female suicide bombers in Chechnya, Sri Lanka, Lebanon, and the Palestinian territories (we'll discuss some examples of these in a moment). Some suicide bombers were married, but more often they were single. Regarding the role of poverty and economic desperation, the research indicates that bombers have come from a cross-section of the population—no single socioeconomic category is common to a significant proportion of them. And in terms of education, there's a lot of variety here as well: a majority of Palestinian, Lebanese, and European suicide bombers had at least a high school education, while this was far less common among the suicide bombers in Sri Lanka, Afghanistan, Iraq, Turkey, and Chechnya. Several of the 9/11 suicide attackers from al-Qaeda had college degrees, even at the graduate level, while at the opposite end of the spectrum there are thousands of terrorists in Nigeria, Somalia, and Mali who are basically uneducated and illiterate.

In terms of gender, a book by Mia Bloom, called *Bombshell*, notes that more than 230 suicide attacks between 1985 and 2008 were carried out by women.[9] So, let's look at some examples of women who have chosen to become suicide bombers. On May 21, 1991, Rajiv Gandhi, a former prime minister of India, was killed by a young woman named Dhanu who was sent on a suicide bombing mission by the Tamil Tigers. She concealed the bomb under her dress and smuggled it through security. Then, when she knelt down to touch Gandhi's feet, in a traditional show of respect, she detonated the bomb, killing them both as well as 17 others in the crowd.

On January 27, 2002, a young Palestinian woman by the name of Wafa Idris—a paramedic who lived in Ramallah—entered a shopping district in Jerusalem and detonated a 22-pound bomb filled with nails and metal objects, killing an 81-year-old man and injuring more than 100 bystanders. Idris, a member of the al-Aqsa Martyr's Brigade, was the first known *istish-hadiyat* (female martyr) in the Middle East—but others soon followed, including Dareen Abu Aisheh, who wounded two Israeli policeman when she detonated her bomb at a roadblock near Maccabim on February 27, 2002; Aayat al-Akhras, who strolled into a supermarket in the neighborhood of Kiryat Yovel in Jerusalem and killed two Israeli civilians and wounded 22 more on March 29, 2002; and Hanadi Jaradat, a 29-year-old lawyer who calmly entered a highly popular restaurant on October 4, 2003 and killed 21 Israeli and Arab men, women, and children.[10]

Russia has also suffered multiple attacks by female suicide terrorists, particularly by some we refer to as Black Widows—young Chechen women whose husbands, brothers, or close relatives have been killed by Russian forces in one of the two Chechen wars or as a result of that country's fight against terrorism. For example, on August 24, 2004, two aircraft left from the same Moscow airport, and dropped off the radar screens within 60 seconds of each other. The investigation by Russian authorities revealed that both had been blown up by young women, resulting in the deaths of 90 people. Then on August 31 of that year, another female suicide bomber attacked the Rizhskaya station of Moscow's metro subway system, killing ten. And on March

29, 2010, two young Chechen women blew themselves up on separate metro trains in Moscow, killing 40 and injuring an additional 160. One was Maryam Sharipova, a 28-year-old married woman with an honors degree in mathematics and psychology from a local university, and the other was Djennet Abdurakhmenova, a petite 17-year-old young woman. Both had been married to jihadists in their home province of Dagestan; Sharipova's husband was still alive and apparently had encouraged her mission to martyrdom, while Abdurakhmenova's had recently been killed by Russian authorities.[11] In all these cases, women have been suicide bombers within the context of a group and a local conflict, with other participants in that conflict playing a role in helping equip or otherwise facilitate the attacks.

Of particular note is the fact that groups like Boko Haram in Nigeria, al-Shabaab in Somalia, and Islamic State in Iraq and Syria have all increasingly used women and children as suicide bombers. In fact, researchers at the Combating Terrorism Center at West Point and Yale University analyzed 434 suicide bombings carried out by Boko Haram since 2011, and found that at least 244 (73%) of the 338 attacks in which the bomber's gender could be identified were carried out by women.[12] The tactical rationale for doing so is fairly straightforward: women and children tend to attract less attention by security guards at checkpoints and so forth. In Somalia and Afghanistan, men have actually disguised themselves as women in an effort to evade security forces and detonate their explosives at their intended target.

The bottom line is that the data indicate there is no real demographic profile of a suicide terrorist. Most are male and single, but obviously they can also be female. They can be any race, color, gender, age, and marital status. We also know that even if there were a common demographic profile, terrorist groups would employ bombers and disguises most likely to defeat security measures, altering their appearance to help them blend into a crowd and thereby have a better chance to reach their target.

Research has also suggested that the factors motivating an individual's choice to become a suicide bomber are often politically oriented. Personal humiliation and a thirst for revenge are also mentioned in the literature as important, as are perceptions of injustice, particularly when family or close friends are seen as victimized by a government's actions. Military occupation has been cited as a motivator behind many Lebanese and Palestinian suicide bombers, and this became a much more predominant theme among the suicide terrorism research after the invasion of Iraq in 2003.

Despite the common portrayals in the media, religious motivation, seeking paradise, or doing "God's will" has seemed a less important motivator overall when compared to these politically oriented and personal reasons. There is also no credence to the oft-cited myth that suicide bombers are driven to carry out their attacks because they want to meet their promised "72 virgins" in heaven. Not only is this not true, I especially doubt this alleged motivation has any relevance for the many female suicide bombers we have seen over the past two decades.

In truth, much of the terrorism studies scholarship these days has noted that religious fanaticism is neither a necessary nor a sufficient factor behind suicide terrorism. For example, most of the suicide attacks in Lebanon were carried out by secular groups. Both the Tamil Tigers in Sri Lanka and the PLO's militant wing, Fatah, are neither, nor are religious groups. The PKK in Turkey and the Popular Front for the Liberation of Palestine are pseudo-Marxist groups. And most members of both Hamas and the Palestinian Islamic Jihad do not mention religion as the main cause behind the use of suicide terrorist attacks. Granted, religion has played a role in the use of suicide bombings by sectarian militants in Iraq and Pakistan over the last decade. And as I noted earlier, the majority of groups that use suicide bombings today are categorized as Islamic extremist. But at the individual level, we see a variety of other nonreligious motivations among men and women who decide to strap on a bomb and go blow themselves up somewhere.

Another common misperception about suicide terrorism is that the bombers are psychologically or emotionally abnormal in some way. As described in Lecture 14, researchers from the field of psychology have attempted to describe personal characteristics of terrorists based on the hope that terrorists can be identified by these attributes. Some people assume that there must be a "terrorist mindset." Surely, they argue, terrorists are sociopaths, psychopaths, paranoid, pathological narcissist, etc.— individuals with some kind of personality disorders that drive them toward terrorist activity. Some have suggested that suicide bombers tend to have weak personalities and are easily manipulated; or they are socially marginal and have low self-esteem. They view "the establishment" as the source of all evil—as Walter Lacqueur argued, "all terrorists believe in conspiracies by the powerful, hostile forces and suffer from some form of delusion and persecution mania."[13]

However, the most recent scholarship in this area indicates that suicide bombers are not mentally ill and do not display major suicidal risk factors. In fact, the most common result of research on the relationship between terrorism and psychology actually reveals a pattern of "normalcy"—that is, the absence of any unique attribute or identifier that would distinguish one individual from another. Andrew Silke observed how research on the mental state of terrorists has found that they are rarely mad, and very few suffer from personality disorders.[14] Renowned psychologist John Horgan has noted that "many of the personal traits or characteristics [identified in this research] as belonging to the terrorist are neither specific to the terrorist nor serve to distinguish one type of terrorist from another. . . . There are no qualities of the terrorist that enable us to predict the likelihood of risk of involvement and engagement in any particular person or social group that is valid or reliable over a meaningful period of time."[15] Clark McCauley has observed that "30 years of research has found little evidence that terrorists are suffering from psychopathology."[16] I would also note that terrorist groups in general are reluctant to accept psychologically unstable individuals into their group—they typically prove to be an operational security risk. So, essentially, one could argue that when studying the unique phenomenon of suicide terrorism, it is really the group factors, more than the individual factors, that matter most.

OPERATIONS

Before we conclude this lecture, let's take a quick look at a few operational aspects of suicide terrorism. There are at least three elements of the recruitment and so-called "production process" behind a typical suicide terrorist event. First, there has to be a general public atmosphere in which suicide terrorism will be seen as acceptable. Without this, the group risks losing legitimacy and the kind of community support that is critical for its own survival. This is one of several reasons why suicide terrorism was never adopted by the IRA, PIRA, UDA, UVF, or other participants in the Northern Ireland conflict. Further, there have to be appropriate targets to select within this environment. For example, suicide bomb attacks by Jemmah Islamiyyah in Bali, Jakarta, and elsewhere in Indonesia have targeted Western hotels, restaurants, and nightclubs popular among Western tourists. The "othering" described in previous lectures can play a significant role here.

The second element is a group commitment to the individual chosen for this type of attack. The group members agree, in a sort of contractual arrangement, to train and equip the bomber and help ensure that he or she has a successful mission. Often, they also agree to help provide for the suicide bomber's family and loved ones after the attack. And third, the individual demonstrates a personal commitment, a will to kill and to use his or her body as a primary delivery mechanism for the explosives. When all three of these elements are present, the preparations for the attack can begin.

Typical preparations for a suicide bombing may take as little as a week, or perhaps even a couple months, but in rare cases we may see the preparation phase last quite a long time—like in the case of the 9/11 hijackers, who knew about and prepared for their mission, in some cases over the course of several years. During this very important phase, the group will make all the logistical arrangements—creating or acquiring the explosive charges, conducting surveillance of the target, arranging for transportation and escorts, and so forth. Sometimes the individual may arrange to settle some debts and provide farewell gifts to loved ones after the attack has taken place. They may also acquire some new clothes and a haircut, in the assumption that their neat appearance will help them pass through security checkpoints without suspicion.

Sometimes the group orchestrating the attack will isolate the future martyr from others, sheltering them from outside influences while ensuring the proper level of indoctrination and technical capability to carry out the mission successfully. But here, too, there is a considerable variety. For example, as described in Lecture 15, the four young men who carried out the suicide bombing in London on July 7, 2005, regularly interacted with their families (and in two cases, with their wives). They rented an apartment in a different neighborhood, where they assembled their bombs, but they also went on a whitewater rafting trip with some friends, and by all outward appearances did not attract suspicion that they might be planning to carry out any kind of terrorist attack, much less a suicide bombing.[17] Further, there was no group orchestrating the operation; it was just them, on their own, inspired by al-Qaeda's ideology to carry out a terrorist attack using their own means (although two of them likely received bomb-making instruction during a March 2005 trip to Pakistan).[18]

The preparation phase is also where we see a good deal of moral disengagement, a process that Stanford psychology professor Albert Bandura describes (and which I discussed in Lecture 1).[19] Moral disengagement is essential for enabling a person to strap on a bomb and then walk into a crowded café or board a bus where, after looking into the faces of people of all ages, even children, they are still able to push that button and detonate their explosives. Also, videos of the suicide bomber are often prepared at this stage. Even the perpetrators of the London attack made their own videos. The leader among them, Mohammad Sidique Khan, stated in his video that "I and thousands like me are forsaking everything for what we believe. Our words are dead until we give them life with our blood. Our religion is Islam. Your democratically elected governments continuously perpetuate atrocities against my people all over the world. We are at war and I am a soldier."[20] When you look at these videos, many of which you can find easily on YouTube and other Internet services, you find some common themes of strategic justification, anger, grievances, and so forth, but what you don't really see are any signs that the individual is somehow abnormal, crazy, or desperate.

For terrorist groups orchestrating a suicide bombing, the videos serve not only to reinforce the indoctrination process, but also makes it very difficult, embarrassing, and humiliating for the individual to chicken out at the last moment and not complete his or her mission. The group can also use the video in its propaganda effort to inspire and motivate others to follow "in the footsteps of this heroic martyr." And the video also serves another important objective: as mentioned earlier in this lecture, we have frequently seen competing claims for particular suicide attacks, especially in the Israel-Palestinian conflict, as groups compete against each other for support and influence among potential backers. Once an attack has taken place, a group is able to use the video as proof that they were the ones responsible for the attack, discrediting any claims made by other groups.

Success of the suicide bombing attack depends on several elements. For example, secrecy is essential to the planning and execution of the mission. Thorough reconnaissance and surveillance is required to choose a meaningful target and identify its weakness. Most terrorist groups that use suicide bombers don't just send them off to attack whatever kind of target at random that they choose. However, as mentioned earlier, the suicide bomber is sometimes referred to as the "ultimate smart bomb" because they can always choose an alternate target if the situation requires. Sometimes extensive rehearsals and "dry runs" are necessary to ensure stealth and speed during the attack. Some terrorist groups will use escorts to help the bomber reach their target, and sometimes that escort may have a remote secondary trigger device in case the bomber fails to detonate the explosives for whatever reason. Cell phones may be used for both communications and for secondary trigger devices in these attacks. And, as noted earlier, no escape plan is needed; this is a strategic advantage of suicide terrorism, because escape plans are often the most difficult part of many terrorist plots. Understanding these logistical and operational aspects of a suicide terrorist attack can be useful because there are some points at which the preparation activities—like surveillance, communication, acquiring explosives or chemical precursors, making trigger switches, and so forth—can provide opportunities for intelligence and law enforcement professionals to detect a potential threat and take action before it is too late.

SUMMARY

Let's wrap up this overview of suicide terrorism with a few final thoughts. First, we need to keep in mind that media accounts of suicide terrorists should be read or viewed with caution; too often they rely more on assumptions and prejudices than on empirical data and scholarly research. With few exceptions, suicide attacks are not the desperate actions of wild-eyed, crazy idiots with nothing to live for, nor are suicide bombers typically motivated by any number of supposed virgins in the afterlife. In truth, the majority of suicide terrorists are no more "abnormal" than you or I. As a result, strategies for combating suicide terrorism require a strong commitment to public diplomacy and communications, especially involving counterideology narratives that discredit and delegitimize this tactic. Until families in places like Iraq, Pakistan, or the Palestinian Territories are embarrassed to have a son or daughter martyr themselves, instead of being honored, this problem will not go away anytime soon. And clearly, the most critically important resource for combating suicide terrorist attacks is the quality and quantity of intelligence on groups and the communities they recruit from.

Finally, our experience (and the research literature) indicates that suicide terrorism is mainly a group phenomenon—that is, organizational strategies and ideologies have been more important than individual attributes. Again, lone wolf attackers are not typically suicide bombers. However, within the past decade we are seeing some changes here. The 2005 attacks in London and other examples of the so-called "homegrown terrorist threat" reflect the emergence of a kind of "do it yourself" approach to suicide terrorism, encouraged by the Salafi-jihadists' "think globally, act locally" ideology that described in Lecture 12.[21] Here we have a group (al-Qaeda or Islamic State) that is merely inspiring individuals, but not directing or orchestrating the suicide terrorism attacks. In these instances, the ideology has become the central factor, creating new challenges for intelligence and law enforcement in combating this unique and very lethal form of terrorism.

QUESTIONS FOR DISCUSSION

- Throughout history, why have only a handful of terrorist groups and their members adopted the tactic of suicide bombing?
- Why have more groups worldwide adopted this tactic only within the past decade?
- In contrast to what the media and policymakers typically portray about suicide terrorism being associated with Islamist extremism, the Tamil Tigers—a Hindu ethno-separatist group in Sri Lanka—were by far the world leaders in suicide bombings between 1988 and 2001. Why? How did the nature of that conflict sustain local Tamil support for this tactic?
- What lessons can the United States and other countries learn from the experiences of Israel?
- What does the recent increase in suicide terrorism tell us about the commitment of religious terrorists? What impact does it have on recruitment?

RECOMMENDED READING

Alakoc, Burcu Pinar. "Competing to Kill: Terrorist Organizations Versus Lone Wolf Terrorists." *Terrorism and Political Violence* 29, no. 3 (2017): 509–32.

Atran, Scott. "The Moral Logic and Growth of Suicide Terrorism." *Washington Quarterly* 29, no. 2 (2006).

Bandura, Albert. "Training for Terrorism through Selective Moral Disengagement." In *The Making of a Terrorist*. Vol. 2. Edited by James J. F. Forest. Westport, CT: Praeger, 2005.

Bloom, Mia. *Bombshell: Women and Terrorism*. New York: Penguin, 2011.

Bloom, Mia. "Female Suicide Bombers: A Global Trend." *Daedalus* (2007).

Bloom, Mia. *Dying to Kill: The Allure of Suicide Terrorism*. New York: Columbia University Press, 2005.

Hassan, Nasra. "An Arsenal of Believers: Talking to the 'Human Bombs.'" *New Yorker*, June 11, 2011.

Hoffman, Bruce. *Inside Terrorism*. New York: Columbia University Press, 2006.

Hoffman, Bruce. "The Logic of Suicide Terrorism." In *Terrorism and Counterterrorism*. Edited by Russell Howard and Bruce Hoffman. New York: McGraw-Hill, 2011.

Horgan, John. "The Social and Psychological Characteristics of Terrorism and Terrorists." In *Root Causes of Terrorism: Myths, Realities and Ways Forward*. Edited by Tore Bjorgo. London: Routledge, 2005.

Merari, Ariel et al. "Personality Characteristics of 'Self-Martyrs/Suicide Bombers' and Organizers of Suicide Attacks." *Terrorism and Political Violence* 22, no. 1 (2010).

Moghadam, Assaf. *The Globalization of Martydom: Al Qaeda, Salafi Jihad and the Diffusion of Suicide Attacks.* Johns Hopkins University Press, 2008.

Moghadam, Assaf. "Motives for Martyrdom: Al Qaeda, Salafi Jihad, and the Proliferation of Suicide Attacks." *International Security* 33, no. 3 (2008–2009).

Nasra, Hassan. "An Arsenal of Believers." *New Yorker*, November 19, 2001. http://bit.ly/2D48SAi.

Pedahzur, Ami and Arie Perliger. "The Making of Suicide Bombers: A Comparative Perspective." In *The Making of a Terrorist*. Vol. 1. Edited by James J. F. Forest. Westport, CT: Praeger, 2005.

Pape, Robert. "The Strategic Logic of Suicide Terrorism." *American Political Science Review* 97, no. 3 (2003).

Piazza, James. "A Supply Side View of Suicide Terrorism." *Journal of Politics* 70, no. 1 (2008).

Roberts, Michael. "Killing Rajiv Gandhi: Dhanu's sacrificial metaporphosis in death." *South Asian History and Culture* 1, no. 1 (January 2010): 25–41.

Speckhard, Anne and Khapta Akhmedova. "The Making of a Martyr: Chechen Suicide Terrorism." *Studies in Conflict and Terrorism* 29 (2006).

WEBSITES

Global Terrorism Database
https://www.start.umd.edu/gtd/

University of Chicago, Project on Security and Threats
https://cpost.uchicago.edu/focus/terrorism/

NOTES

1. Assaf Moghadam, *The Globalization of Martydom: Al Qaeda, Salafi Jihad and the Diffusion of Suicide Attacks* (Baltimore, MD: Johns Hopkins University Press, 2008).

2. Robert Pape, *Dying to Win: The Strategic Logic of Suicide Terrorism* (New York: Random House, 2005): 6.

3. Moghadam, *The Globalization of Martydom*.

4. Mia Bloom, *Dying to Kill: The Allure of Suicide Terrorism* (New York: Columbia University Press, 2005).

5. Robert Pape, "The Strategic Logic of Suicide Terrorism," *American Political Science Review* 97, no. 3 (2003): 344.

6. Ronald Reagan, *An American Life* (New York: Simon and Schuster, 1990): 456.

7. Pape, "The Strategic Logic of Suicide Terrorism," 343–45.

8. For example, see the analysis of Robert Pape's research deficiencies in Max Abrahms and Karolina Lula, "Why Terrorists Overestimate the Odds of Victory," *Perspectives on Terrorism* 6, no. 4 (2012), http://www.terrorismanalysts.com/pt/index.php/pot/article/view/216/html.

9. Mia Bloom, *Bombshell: Women and Terrorism* (New York: Penguin, 2011).

10. For more on these attacks, see Mia Bloom, *Bombshell: Women and Terrorism* (New York: Penguin, 2011); and Yoram Schweitzer, "Palestinian Female Suicide Bombers," in *Female Terrorism and Militancy: Agency, Utility, and Organization*, ed. Cindy Ness (London: Routledge, February 2008).

11. See Bloom, *Bombshell*, 1–7.

12. Jason Warner and Hilary Matfess, "Exploding Stereotypes: The Unexpected Operational And Demographic Characteristics of Boko Haram's Suicide Bombers," Combating Terrorism Center at West Point (August 9, 2017), http://bit.ly/2vjanmj.

13. Walter Lacqueur, "Left, Right and Beyond: The Changing Face of Terror," in *How Did This Happen? Terrorism and the New War*, ed. James F. Hoge, Jr. and Gideon Rose (New York: Council on Foreign Relations, 2001): 80.

14. Andrew Silke, "An Introduction to Terrorism Research," in *Research on Terrorism: Trends, Achievements and Failures*, ed. Andrew Silke (London: Frank Cass, 2004): 20.

15. John Horgan, "The Social and Psychological Characteristics of Terrorism and Terrorists," in *Root Causes of Terrorism: Myths, Realities and Ways Forward*, ed. Tore Bjorgo (London: Routledge, 2005): 49.

16. Clark McCauley, "Psychological Issues in Understanding Terrorism and Response to Terrorism," in *Psychology of Terrorism: Coping with the Continuing Threat* (Condensed Edition), ed. Chris Stout (Westport, CT: Praeger, 2004): 35.

17. For a detailed analysis of the days and weeks leading up to the attack in London, see *Report of the Official Account of the Bombings in London on 7th July 2005*, Home Office, HC 1087 (May 11, 2006), http://goo.gl/Uqxzv.

18. Ibid.

19. See Albert Bandura, "Training for Terrorism through Selective Moral Disengagement," in *The Making of a Terrorist*, vol. 2, ed. James J. F. Forest (Westport, CT: Praeger, 2005): 34–50.

20. The full text of Khan's martyrdom tape is available online via the BBC at http://goo.gl/L7ifz.

21. For example, see Joshua Sinai, "Najibullah Zazi's Plot to Bomb the New York City Subway System: A Case Study of How Domestic Counterterrorism Works," in *Homeland Security and Terrorism*, ed. James J. F. Forest, Russell Howard, and Joanne Moore (New York: McGraw-Hill, 2012); and Tom Maley "The London Terrorist Attacks of July 7, 2005," in *Countering Terrorism and Insurgency in the 21st Century*, vol. 3, ed. James J. F. Forest (Westport, CT: Praeger, 2007).

17

Terrorism and Weapons of Mass Destruction

Having examined the nature of suicide bombings, we are now going to tackle the more complicated and frightening issue of terrorists acquiring and using weapons of mass destruction (WMD). In this lecture we examine the basic scientific and technological aspects of the main kinds of WMD, and then in the next lecture we will look at terrorist group opportunities and capabilities to acquire or develop these weapons, and their intentions to use these weapons.

First, let's define what we mean by the term "weapons of mass destruction." The general definition of the term is weapons that have a relatively large-scale impact on people, property, and/or infrastructure. The FBI uses a more specific definition that encompasses an explosive device or "weapon that is designed or intended to cause death or serious bodily injury through the release, dissemination, or impact of toxic or poisonous chemicals; any weapon involving a biological agent or toxin; or any weapon that is designed to release radiation or radioactivity at a level dangerous to human life."[1] Essentially, any kind of weapon that involves biological, chemical, or radiological materials can be considered a WMD. In fact, many scholars and intelligence agencies prefer to use the term "CBRN weapons" instead of WMD, because it further specifies that these are primarily chemical, biological, radiological, or nuclear weapons. Increasingly, we are seeing the acronym CRBNE used in official reports and academic research, which includes a fifth category of high explosives. And of course, it's understood that mass casualty attacks don't require a WMD—for example, mass casualties have been caused by attackers using assault rifles, and significant destruction can be caused by incendiary devices.[2] In truth, there are many ways that someone can cause massive amounts of destruction and casualties—like flying a fully-fueled 747 airplane into a skyscraper, as we saw on September 11, 2001. But what we'll cover in this lecture are just the four traditional WMD categories of chemical, biological, radiological, or nuclear weapons.

CHEMICALS

The first category of WMD includes weapons that use the toxic properties of chemical substances, rather than their explosive properties, to cause physical or psychological harm. These chemical substances can be gases, liquids, or solids, and are used because of their direct toxic effects on humans, animals, and plants. Some poisonous gases enter the victim's lungs when inhaled and cause respiratory damage. Other chemical agents cause damage upon skin contact or can get through a person's skin and enter the bloodstream and nervous system.

There are several kinds of chemical substances that can cause this kind of damage.[3] Most frequently found among chemical weapons are choking agents, which are chemicals that cause severe irritation or swelling of the respiratory tract. Some cause fluids to build up in the lungs, which can cause death through asphyxiation or oxygen deficiency if the lungs are badly damaged. Others, like chlorine gas, produce a damaging acid when it comes into contact with moist tissues such as the eyes, throat, and lungs. When weaponized, these choking agents are delivered as gas clouds to the target area, where individuals become casualties through inhalation of the vapor. The effect of the chemical agent, once an individual is exposed to the vapor, may be immediate or can take up to several hours.

Examples of choking agents include phosgene, which is an industrial chemical used to make plastics and pesticides. Today, more than a billion pounds of phosgene are produced and consumed in the United States each year for the production of plastics.[4] Chlorine is another chemical used by many industries around the world as a bleach in making paper or cloth, or in making pesticides, rubber, and solvents. Chlorine is also used in drinking water and swimming pool water to kill harmful bacteria, and it is used as part of the sanitation process for municipal sewage and industrial waste. It is also found in some household products.*

Blistering agents are chemicals that severely burn and blister the eyes, respiratory tract, and skin upon contact. Depending on an individual's level of exposure, these physical symptoms might be immediate or might appear after several hours. Although lethal in high concentrations, blister agents seldom kill. Mustard gas is the most common blistering agent used in chemical weapons because it is easy to produce, cheap, predictable, and can penetrate leather and fabrics. It can also cause the targeted population or military to spend a lot of resources and effort dealing with large numbers of suffering casualties, rather than fatalities. Mustard gas was the most frequently used chemical weapon in World War I, and there are many stockpiles of these weapons today, including here in the United States.

Blood agents are poisons that affect the body by being absorbed into the blood and then preventing the transfer of oxygen to the cells, causing the body to asphyxiate. One example is hydrogen cyanide, which is used worldwide in the manufacture of acrylic polymers and pesticides, among other industrial uses. A pesticide based on hydrogen cyanide known as Zyklon B was used extensively by Nazi Germany in its gas chambers during WWII. Other cyanide-based chemicals are utilized in a wide variety of industrial applications such as mineral extraction, printing, photography, agriculture, and the production of paper, textiles, and plastics. Industries in the United States alone produce and use several hundred thousand metric tons of cyanides each year.[5]

The most lethal chemical weapons today contain nerve agents, which block an enzyme that is necessary for the proper functioning of the central nervous system, causing a loss of muscle control, respiratory failure, and eventually death. A single drop on the skin or inhaled into the lungs can cause a person's nervous system to shut down muscles, the lungs, and the heart. Some nerve agents cause intense sweating, loss of vision, uncontrollable vomiting, convulsions, and finally paralysis and respiratory failure. Death can result within a few minutes of inhalation or within hours if the person had skin contact with a liquid nerve agent.

---

*Note that household chlorine bleach can release chlorine gas if it is mixed with other cleaning agents. Also, by itself, chlorine is not flammable, but it can react explosively or form explosive compounds with other chemicals such as turpentine and ammonia. If you have children at home, please take extra caution with how and where you store any bottles of bleach and your cleaning supplies.

Nerve agents produced for chemical warfare purposes are all stored as liquids at room temperature. Similar in action to many pesticides, they are lethal in much lower quantities than classic choking, blood, or blistering agents. Nerve gases were discovered by the Germans in the 1930s and were developed during World War II. In 1936, during studies of possible pesticides, the German chemist Gerhard Schrader discovered a chemical compound which he called "tabun" and two years later he discovered the even more toxic "sarin." These chemicals were found to be significantly more lethal than those used in World War I, and the Germans produced a large number of tabun-filled munitions. However, fortunately for the Allies, these weapons were never used. After the war, the United States and the Soviet Union seized these weapons, and eventually began producing their own nerve agents as weapons.

VX is the deadliest nerve agent in existence today. It was developed by chemists at a British government facility in 1952. Britain renounced all chemical and biological weapons in 1956 but traded information on the production of VX with the United States in exchange for technical information on the production of thermonuclear bombs. In 1961 the United States began large-scale production of VX. The only other countries believed to have built up VX arsenals are Russia and Syria, though some reports have suggested France and Iraq also may have at one time had a VX weapons program. Also, Aum Shinrikyo, a religious cult in Japan (described in Lecture 11) used VX injections in assassination attempts of perceived enemies in 1994 and 1995, though only one person died.[6] This group is far better known for its attacks using sarin nerve agent, which we'll discuss in the next lecture.

Other chemical substances include biotoxins, which are poisons that come from plants or animals; caustics, which are general acids that burn or corrode people's skin, eyes, nose, lungs, and so forth on contact; and incapacitating agents, which are chemical substances that make people unable to think clearly or that cause an altered state of consciousness or even unconsciousness. Overall, there are many kinds of chemical weapons, some newer and more lethal than others. Their attributes vary—many are gases that kill or incapacitate anyone who inhales them; others are absorbed through the skin and can cause blisters or severe damage to the nervous system. These weapons deliver the chemicals to the target through bombs, rockets, artillery shells, spray tanks, and missile warheads, using a building's heating, ventilation, and air conditioning (HVAC) system, introducing it to a water supply, and several other means.

Compared with the other categories of WMD, chemical weapons are the least expensive and easiest to manufacture. They have been part of the operational arsenals of sizable militaries, and have been used more often than any other kind of WMD.[7] Precursor materials for many weapons (like chemicals that can be combined with others to form harmful ones) can be found in virtually any country that has industrial manufacturing facilities, leading to what many describe as a "dual-use" problem we face when trying to keep chemical weapons out of the hands of terrorists.

TABLE 17.1: "CBRN" Weapons of Mass Destruction

Type	Attributes
Chemical	Harmful chemicals including choking, blood, blister, and nerve agents. Examples include chlorine, phosgene, lewisite, mustard, cyanide, tabun, sarin, and VX.
Biological	Harmful pathogens, viruses, toxins, and bacteria. Examples include anthrax, smallpox, tularemia, plague, Ebola, Marburg, botulinum, and ricin.
Radiological	Materials that emit harmful kinds of radioactivity. Examples include cesium-137, iridium-192, cobalt-60, strontium-90, and radium-226.
Nuclear	Fissile material—highly-enriched uranium-235 or plutonium 239—that releases a massive energy burst in an explosion that causes widespread destruction.

BIOLOGICAL

Next we have the biological weapons, which intentionally disseminate agents of infectious diseases to harm or kill others. Some can be similar to chemical weapons in terms of how the harmful agents can hurt or kill large numbers of people. However, biological weapons are also much different than any other kind of weapon, in that human beings can be a means for dissemination or delivery of the harmful agent to the target populations. Further, in some cases an infectious disease can be modified in a laboratory to increase its effectiveness as a weapon.

Today there are over 80 biological agents, pathogens, and toxins that the government believes may pose a severe threat to human or animal health. But while there are many kinds of infectious diseases that we worry about, those that are considered the most useful as a potential weapon have similar features, including: infectivity, which is the ability of a pathogen to establish an infection; virulence, which is the ability of that infection to produce a disease; toxicity, the damage to humans or agriculture that can be caused by that disease; the incubation period between infection and the symptoms of the disease; the lethality or killing power of that disease; and the stability of the pathogen—that is, how well the virus or bacteria can survive in various environments.[8]

The agents most commonly associated with biological weapons can be divided into bacteria (such as anthrax, tularemia, and plague), viruses (like smallpox, Marburg or yellow fever), rickettsia (which are microorganisms that are similar to bacteria and viruses and cause typhus fever, spotted fever, and other diseases), chlamydia, fungi (like the molds that cause stem rust of wheat and rye), and toxins (such as ricin, botulinum, and saxitoxin). Note that toxins are sometimes called a "midspectrum weapon," and can be considered both biological and chemical, because they basically involve using poisonous substances produced by living organisms like plants, animals, or algae. Bacteria and viruses are relatively cost-effective weapons, because the dosage needed to induce illness can be very low, an amount much smaller by weight than the amount required of chemicals. Also, while chemical agents require a manufacturing process, biological agents can be grown and multiplied from a tiny initial sample, and in some cases (like anthrax) can be found naturally in some parts of the world.

This also means production and storage facilities for these weapons can be very small: you can hide a bio weapons lab, or thousands of deployable weapons, in the basement of a normal-sized home. There are several ways you can deploy a biological weapon effectively, like using a building's HVAC system, contaminating your enemy's food or water supply, sending the biological agents through the mail in envelopes or packages, distributing infected items like blankets to an unsuspecting population, or by using pressurized sprayers mounted on a truck, or in a small plane—even an unmanned aerial vehicle, or drone, would work. You could also disperse your biological agents using explosive pressurized munitions, similar to what is used for chemical weapons. Explosive munitions distribute the agent more rapidly, but tend to destroy much of the agent (sometimes as much as 50%).

From the perspective of national security and public health, the most worrisome biological agents include anthrax, botulism, plague, smallpox, tularemia, and viral hemorrhagic fevers, like the dreaded Ebola or Marburg viruses that we have seen in parts of Africa over the last several years.[9] Several of these can be easily spread or transmitted from person to person, result in high death rates, are highly likely to cause public panic and social disruption, and require special action for public health preparedness.

In October 2001, anthrax was deliberately spread through the U.S. postal system by sending letters with powder containing the potentially deadly bacteria. This caused

22 cases of anthrax infection (six of them fatal), and generated a lot of media and public policy attention toward anthrax, so let's take a close look at what this really is. First of all, anthrax is a serious disease caused by a bacterium, which is a very small organism made up of one cell. Many kinds of bacteria can cause disease. The anthrax bacteria forms spores, which are cells that remain dormant but can come to life with the right conditions.

There are three ways a human can become infected with anthrax: skin, lungs, and digestion. In most cases, early treatment with antibiotics can cure skin—also called "cutaneous"—anthrax. Even when untreated, 80% of people who became infected with cutaneous anthrax did not die, while the other 20% of cases have been fatal. Gastrointestinal anthrax is more serious, and the fatality rate is higher, between 25% and 50%. The most lethal type of anthrax is inhalation, where about half of all cases have been fatal. This is the form of anthrax that was used during the October 2001 attacks.

The symptoms of an anthrax infection are different depending on the type of the disease. For cutaneous anthrax, the first symptom is a small sore that develops into a blister, which then develops into a skin ulcer with a black area in the center. For gastrointestinal anthrax, the first symptoms are nausea, loss of appetite, bloody diarrhea, and fever, followed by bad stomach pain. The first symptoms of inhalation anthrax are like cold or flu symptoms and can include a sore throat, mild fever, and muscle aches. Later symptoms include cough, chest discomfort, shortness of breath, tiredness, and muscle aches. For all three types of anthrax, these symptoms can appear within seven days of coming in contact with the bacterium. Antibiotics are used to treat all three types of anthrax. There is also a vaccine to prevent anthrax, but it has only been provided to laboratory workers and certain members of the military, and has not been made available to the public yet.

Some have suggested that anthrax is a preferred kind of biological weapon because it is both dangerous and easy to acquire. It has become less dependent on having access to advanced technology, and information about anthrax cultures, transportation, and dispersion is widely available in libraries and on the Internet. With the exception of the powderized form used for inhalation anthrax, the disease is relatively easy to produce in large quantities and to weaponize. It is extremely stable, it can be stored indefinitely as a dry powder, and the bacteria can multiply even in its dormant stage. And, unlike many other biological weapons, anthrax is not contagious. Although anthrax bacterium exists in nature, it is not known to spread from one person to another. However, humans can become infected with anthrax by handling products from infected animals or by breathing in anthrax spores from infected animal products (like wool, for example). People also can become infected with gastrointestinal anthrax by eating undercooked meat from infected animals. And as we saw in the October 2001 attacks, a powderized form of anthrax can be delivered through the mail. However, because it is not contagious, the effects of weaponized anthrax can be contained.

In contrast to anthrax, however, smallpox is very contagious and infections of this disease can be more fatal. Smallpox is caused by the variola virus. It emerged in human populations thousands of years ago, but naturally occurring smallpox was eradicated in 1980 by a major effort led by the World Health Organization. Today the virus is only known to exist in certain laboratories in Russia and the United States. For the most part, it takes direct face-to-face contact to spread smallpox from one person to another. Smallpox also can be spread through direct contact with infected bodily fluids or contaminated objects such as bedding or clothing. In some rare cases, smallpox has been spread by a virus carried in the air in enclosed settings such as buildings, buses, and trains.

Symptoms of the disease vary according to how long the individual has had it. For example, during the first 1–2 weeks there is an incubation period in which people do not have any symptoms and may feel fine. They are not contagious during this period. But after this period the first symptoms begin to show—things like high fever, head and body aches, and sometimes vomiting. This will last for 2–4 days, and then the tell-tale smallpox rash emerges, beginning with small red spots on the tongue and in the mouth. For the next four days, the person is the most contagious they will be. The rash will spread to all parts of the body, starting on the face and spreading to the arms, legs, hands and feet. By the third day of the rash, you will see several raised bumps. For the next three weeks, the rash will develop into bumps, which then scab over and often leave permanent marks on the skin. Assuming the person survives the infection, they will still be contagious until all of these scabs fall off.

There are four major types of smallpox, tied to the four categories of variola virus. First, there is the ordinary type, which is the most frequent, accounting for over 90% of cases. The overall fatality rate for ordinary smallpox is about 30%. Then there is a modified type, a sort of mutated form of the virus that can infect a person who has been previously vaccinated for smallpox. The last two types are called flat and hemorrhagic; both of these are rare, and are usually fatal.

Humans are the only natural hosts of the variola virus. Smallpox is not known to be transmitted by insects or animals. However, it should also be noted that smallpox is not as contagious as the measles, the flu, or whooping cough. There is no specific treatment for smallpox disease, and the only prevention is vaccination. Right now, the U.S. government has enough smallpox vaccine to vaccinate every person in the United States in the case of a smallpox emergency.

Ricin has also received considerable media attention in recent years, so let's take a closer look at it for just a moment. To begin with, ricin is a poison found naturally in castor beans. Like other toxins, it is considered both a biological agent and a chemical agent, because it is a nonliving toxic product produced by a living organism, in this case a plant. And, like other toxins, ricin poisoning is not contagious—it cannot be spread from person to person through casual contact. Once ricin gets inside you it prevents your cells from making the proteins they need. Without those proteins, your cells die, and then the body dies.

Castor beans are processed to make castor oil, which is a product people use all over the world. The process of making castor oil also leaves a waste product that contains ricin, so this is a toxin which is fairly easy to acquire for anyone wanting to turn it into a weapon. Weaponized ricin can be in the form of a powder, a mist, or a pellet, or it can be dissolved in water or weak acid. The effects of ricin poisoning depend on whether ricin was inhaled, ingested, or injected.

For inhalation exposure to ricin, initial symptoms may appear within eight hours, and include difficulty breathing, fever, cough, nausea, and tightness in the chest. Heavy sweating may follow as well as fluid building up in the lungs, and the skin might turn blue. Finally, low blood pressure and respiratory failure may occur, leading to death within 2–3 days.

If someone were to swallow at least 500 micrograms of weaponized ricin (like a ricin pellet, roughly the size of the head of a pin), he or she would develop vomiting and diarrhea, severe dehydration, and low blood pressure, all within less than six hours. Other symptoms may include hallucinations, seizures, and bleeding from the stomach and intestines. In a couple days the person's liver, spleen, and kidneys would probably stop working, causing them to die. At one point, the Soviet Union was suspected of developing these kinds of ricin pellets for use in targeted killings. For example, in 1978, an anti-Soviet journalist named Georgi Markov, a Bulgarian who was living in London at the time, was killed after being injected with a ricin pellet.

It is important to note that there is no antidote for ricin poisoning. If your skin or eyes are exposed to ricin, the first thing you need to do is remove all clothing as quickly as you can.[10] Then get in the shower or bath, wash thoroughly, and go get medical attention. If you breathe in ricin, get outside quickly for fresh air and then go get medical attention. If you swallow or have been injected with ricin, get to a hospital as fast as you can where they might be able to flush your stomach and potentially save your life.

To sum up, there are several different kinds of biological weapons, including bacteria, viruses, and toxins. Biological weapons are also considered by many to be the most insidious and indefensible type of weapons. Diseases don't discriminate by race, ethnicity, or political or ideological orientation, and most contagious diseases aren't constrained by physical or geographic borders. Worse, several pathogens can reproduce and multiply within infected individuals—thus humans become both victims and a potential weapon delivery system to harm or kill others.

RADIOLOGICAL

The third major category of WMD involves the use of radioactive materials. At the outset, it must be emphasized that a radiological weapon is not a nuclear weapon or atomic bomb. Nuclear weapons, like the bombs dropped on Hiroshima and Nagasaki at the end of World War II, involve the splitting of atoms and a huge release of energy that produces the iconic mushroom cloud. In contrast, radiological weapons cannot create an atomic blast and do not produce the same kind of massive destruction. Rather, the primary effect of these weapons is to infect large numbers of people with radioactive poisoning, and in that way they are similar to many of the chemical weapons discussed earlier in this lecture.

There are actually two kinds of radiological weapons. The first is a radiological dispersal device, or RDD. This is the kind that gets the most attention, and is often called a "**dirty bomb**." In general, this kind of weapon uses conventional explosives (like C4, RDX, or TNT) to scatter radioactive powder, pellets, dust, smoke, or other material in order to cause radioactive contamination. Examples of a dirty bomb could include a backpack, truck, boat, etc.—really, any kind of improvised explosive device could be modified into a dirty bomb by incorporating the kinds of radiological materials I'll describe in a moment.

The second, called a radiation-emitting device, or RED, does not involve any kind of explosion, so we really can't call it a "dirty bomb" or really any kind of bomb. Here, the attackers will simply place highly radioactive objects or materials in a location where people can be affected by the radiation—for example, a highly trafficked place like a subway station or airport, or a place where many people gather, such as an indoor stadium, a church, a government center, or an office building. The objective here would be to expose a large number of people to an intense radioactive source over a short period of time—a similar kind of attack as placing an open container of a highly toxic chemical in a public area, where the fumes could harm many people. But unlike chemical weapons, you would not be able to see or smell the radioactive materials that are making people sick.[11]

Both kinds of radiological weapons can be built in a variety of sizes, and the radiation they spread can cause sickness, even death. These weapons can also produce widespread panic, and cause physical and environmental contamination, which at the very least complicates emergency response efforts following an attack. In some cases, radiological attacks could even cause economic damage.[12]

The main element of these weapons, obviously, is the radioactive material. But what does this term "radioactive" mean? Every day, we are surrounded by sources of radioactivity, almost all of it harmless particles or electromagnetic waves, like alpha and beta radiation generated by earth or outer space. Gamma radiation and neutrons are more dangerous, and more rare, and harder to shield against—usually requiring some kind of lead, steel, concrete, or large pools of water. Many kinds of radioactive materials produced by the nuclear fuel cycle emit gamma radiation, which I will discuss in a moment. But first, without getting too much into the physics and science of this, let's review just a few of the most important terms and definitions we need to know when talking about radiological weapons.

The first term is isotopes. In general, isotopes are atoms of the same chemical element having different numbers of neutrons in their nucleus. An isotope is specified by its atomic weight and a symbol denoting the chemical element, such as uranium-235, which stands for uranium with 235 neutrons and protons. Isotopes can be either stable or unstable. Radioactivity is the property or condition of some elements that results in the spontaneous transformation, or decay, of the nucleus of an unstable atom. When these atoms decay, they release excess energy in the form of radiation. Substances that undergo this transformation process are called radioisotopes, or more generally, radioactive materials. Once these substances are processed into a usable form, such as pellets or powder, they are called radioactive sources.[13]

In general, the faster the atoms decay, the higher the level of radiation they produce. The time it takes for the elements to decay is called a "half-life." Highly radioactive materials, which have a short half-life, are the most lethal. Things that decay much slower, meaning they have a longer half-life, are much less radioactive, and thus are not useful in a radiological weapon. For example, cobalt-60 has a half-life of just over five years, and is highly radioactive; in contrast, uranium-235, with a half-life of over 700 million years, is not very radioactive at all, and thus makes a poor choice of material for a radiological weapon.[14]

Elements with an intermediate half-life are the most useful for a radiological weapon. Unfortunately, these are also the same kinds of radioactive materials that are used every day for peaceful purposes in the fields of medicine, industry, agriculture, and research. For example, tiny amounts of the radioactive material americium-241 can be found in the smoke detectors used in many homes worldwide. This small quantity of radioactive material would not be harmful if used in a dirty bomb. However, factories where these smoke detectors are manufactured may contain enough americium-241 to pose a security concern.[15]

The things that make a radioisotope most hazardous include the amount of energy and type of radiation it produces; its half-life, as mentioned a moment ago; the amount of the radioactive material that is available and how prevalent it is; the shape, size, and portability of the material; and how easy it is to disperse the material over a wide area. Together, this collection of attributes helps us identify which are the most high-risk radioisotopes. Thus, while hundreds of radioactive isotopes exist, there are really only a small number that are of major concern for the threat of radiological weapons.[16] Further, most of these are byproducts of the fission process or other processes in nuclear reactors, which means we should have a good handle on where the majority of these radioisotopes may be found. But because radiological source materials are widely used for industrial and medical purposes, governments face a similar kind of "dual-use" security challenge as I described earlier regarding chemical weapons.

There are three kinds of radioisotopes that are classified as high risk because they are widely available and are strong emitters of gamma and beta radiation.[17] Cobalt-60 is mostly known for its use in irradiating or killing bacteria in spices and other food products. Direct exposure to cobalt-60 can be very harmful, with a high risk of cancer or radiation sickness if inhaled or ingested in large enough amounts. Cesium-137 has a half-life of about 30 years, and can emit a strong level of beta radiation. It is most commonly used in radiation devices to treat cancer, but has also been used in X-ray machines and equipment to monitor wells for oil.

Iridium-192 emits powerful gamma and beta radiation that has a half-life of 74 days. It is often used in treating prostate cancer, and in detecting faults below the surface of certain materials. Because of its strong gamma radiation, iridium-192 can be harmful in cases of direct external exposure, in addition to being dangerous if inhaled or ingested in large enough amounts. Another strong beta emitter is strontium-90, which has a half-life of just over 29 years. Strontium-90 has been used in medical and agricultural research, and has several industrial applications. Also, the heat produced by this radioisotope can provide a source of electricity, and has often been used as a power source for remote lighthouses, weather stations, and space vehicles. Direct exposure is harmful; if ingested or inhaled, strontium-90 deposits itself in bone and bone marrow, which can increase the risk of leukemia and other cancers.

Another category of high-risk isotopes includes three strong emitters of alpha radiation. These are also byproducts of the nuclear fuel cycle and processes at nuclear reactors. Americium-241 is commonly known for its use in household and industrial smoke detectors, and is also used in a number of other commercial applications, including oil wells and small diagnostic devices for medicine and research. It has a half-life of almost 433 years and emits mostly alpha as well as some gamma radiation, both of which can cause harm to body tissue, especially if inhaled or ingested. Californium-252 has several medical and industrial applications, including its use in cancer therapy. It is also used to detect explosive devices in airline luggage. It has a relatively short half-life of less than three years and emits both alpha radiation and neutrons (the most harmful kind of radiation).

Then we have plutonium-238 and plutonium-239, both of which emit alpha radiation as well as small amounts of gamma radiation. Plutonium-238 has a half-life of about 88 years, and gives off heat that can be used as an energy source. For example, plutonium-238 has been used as a power source for orbiting satellites. Plutonium-238 cannot be used in nuclear weapons, but its elemental sibling plutonium-239 *is* used in nuclear weapons, such as the atomic bomb that was dropped on Nagasaki, Japan in 1945. Plutonium-239 has a half-life of 24,100 years, meaning it is much less radioactive than plutonium-238 and can actually be handled fairly safely. However, inhalation or ingestion of any kind of plutonium poses a great danger to bodily organs, since plutonium can stay in the body for decades and can greatly increase the risk of cancer and kidney damage.

And finally, there is radium-226, which is a *naturally occurring* radioisotope that is formed by the decay of uranium-238. Radium-226 emits alpha and gamma radiation and has an intermediate half-life of about 1,600 years. Before the dangers of radium were understood, the glow-in-the-dark property of radium-226 was commonly used for clock faces, paint for aircraft dials and gauges, and other industrial products.

Radium-226 was also used for cancer treatment and to scan for flaws below the surface in metal parts. Like the other high-risk isotopes, radium-226 can cause harm if large enough amounts are inhaled, ingested, or if the body is directly exposed to the material. Once in the body, radium-226 can settle in the bones and increase the risk of cancer and blood diseases.

To sum up, there are several important radioactive materials in use today throughout the world, in millions of places where medical and scientific research is conducted as well as at industrial manufacturing plants. These materials are used in gauges, static eliminators, X-ray machines, sterilizers, processors, particle accelerators, power sources, mineral extraction and processing, and much more. Unfortunately, some of these facilities may lack significant physical security, increasing the chances that terrorists could acquire radioactive materials. Some radioactive materials pose a greater threat depending on a number of factors including the source's energy and type of radiation, the half-life of the isotope, and the amount of material. For example, if a radioisotope produces strong gamma radiation, but has a very short half-life of 12 hours, it is probably not very appealing to a terrorist because the radioactive contamination would not last long enough to cause real harm. The portability of the radioactive material (especially its weight and size) and the ease with which it can be scattered or dispersed also impacts its potential desirability to a terrorist. For example, radioisotopes that are easily made into a dispersible powder would be more attractive to terrorists.[18]

People will be affected differently by an RED than by an RDD, or dirty bomb. In an attack using an RED, the exposure to radiation is the primary objective. Some victims may suffer from acute exposure within a short amount of time, or others may be exposed to lower doses over an extended period of time, called chronic exposure. Low levels of radiation exposure generally do not cause any immediate symptoms, but higher levels of radiation exposure may produce symptoms such as nausea, vomiting, diarrhea, and swelling and redness of the skin. Other symptoms may include fatigue, increased temperature, blood changes, hair loss, bleeding gums, and convulsions. In general, radiation interacts with DNA, potentially causing cell malfunction or death.

In contrast, the main danger from a dirty bomb is actually from the explosion, which can cause serious injuries, death, and property damage. The radioactive materials used in a dirty bomb would probably not create enough radiation exposure to cause immediate serious illness, except to those people who are very close to the blast site. However, the radioactive dust and smoke spread farther away could be dangerous to health if it is inhaled, absorbed through cuts in the skin, or ingested.[19] Please keep in mind: people cannot see, smell, feel, or taste radiation, so if there is a dirty bomb attack in your area you may not know whether you have been exposed. Police or firefighters will quickly check for radiation by using special equipment to determine how much radiation is present and whether it poses any danger in your area. Of course, if you develop any of these symptoms, you should contact your doctor or hospital right away.

NUCLEAR

Finally, we have the category most often associated with WMD: nuclear weapons. These weapons are unique in their explosive energy, most or all of which is derived from fission or a combination of fission and fusion processes, which I'll describe in a moment. Nuclear weapons are by far the most powerfully destructive weapons ever created. Explosions from such devices can cause catastrophic damage due both to the high temperatures and ground shocks produced by the initial blast and the lasting residual radiation.

Before we look at the details of these weapons, let's review some basic terms of physics.[20] You and I are a type of matter called organisms, an individual life form like a plant or an animal. The smallest structural unit of organisms that is capable of independent functioning is called a cell. Within a cell are molecules, which are groups of atoms that are linked or bound together. An atom, the building block of molecules, is of course even smaller, and consists of a nucleus, or central core, in which there are protons and neutrons surrounded by orbiting electrons that are bound to the nucleus by electrical attraction. An atom is classified by the number of protons and neutrons in its nucleus.

An element is a substance composed of atoms in which there are an identical number of protons in each nucleus. About 100 elements make up all substances on Earth.[21] Elements, such as hydrogen, iron, uranium, and plutonium, are all different in composition and weight. Further, a given element generally occurs in several forms, called isotopes (described earlier). Different isotopes of an element are distinguished by the number of neutrons in their nuclei. Each type of isotope is distinguished by an atomic number that reflects the number of protons in its nucleus. This is how we get the numbers associated with the kinds of isotopes mentioned above in describing radiological sources: Cesium-137, strontium-90, iridium-192, and so forth. Uranium has an atomic number of 92, meaning these isotopes have 92 protons in their nucleus; they also have between 140 and 146 neutrons, which gives us the element range of uranium-232 to uranium-238. In contrast, plutonium has an atomic number of 94, meaning these isotopes have 94 protons in their nucleus; they also have between 144 and 148 neutrons, which gives us the element range of plutonium-238 to plutonium-242. Higher element range numbers indicate greater density, meaning uranium and plutonium are physically heavier than (for example) cobalt or strontium.

The isotopes of most concern to any discussion about nuclear weapons are uranium-235 and plutonium-239, which are commonly referred to as fissile materials. These have an odd number of neutrons in their nuclei, and when the nuclei are struck by neutrons, they can split into lighter elements, or fragments. This splitting of atoms that occurs within these nuclei, called **nuclear fission**, produces a significant amount of energy. Fission produces new atoms as well as free-floating neutrons, which then go on to split apart other atoms, and the fission of those atoms generates even more neutrons that then go on to split apart even more atoms, and so forth, in a **chain reaction**. The energy released from this chain reaction can be harnessed and used in nuclear reactors for generating heat and electricity, or it can be used in a weapon.

Fissile material is required to make a nuclear bomb. Many heavy isotopes are fissionable (meaning they can split apart to form other atoms), but relatively few of them are also **fissile** (meaning they can cause a chain reaction), and almost all of these are isotopes of uranium or plutonium. All fissile materials and some fissionable materials are usable in weapons. Odd-numbered isotopes of uranium and plutonium are fissile (uranium-233 and uranium-235 and plutonium-239 and plutonium-241), but uranium-235 and plutonium-239 are the most common materials used in nuclear weapons. Uranium is far more prevalent than plutonium—in fact, the first fissile material to be discovered was the isotope uranium-235. However, plutonium-239 emits more neutrons in its fission process, so it takes less plutonium-239 than uranium-235 to sustain a fission chain reaction. One thing to keep in mind here is that the radioactive processes in which isotopes decay and give off energy in the form of radiation are also taking place here at the same time in these isotopes that are being put into weapons. This is particularly important with regard to certain types of plutonium. For example, plutonium-241 has a short half-life of 14 years, and plutonium-238 has a relatively short half-life of 88 years, while plutonium-239 has a much longer half-life of 24,100 years (and is the type of plutonium most often used in nuclear weapons).

There are two structural types of nuclear weapons. The first is called gun-type. Here, nuclear fission is produced when one of two subcritical pieces of highly enriched uranium is slammed against the other, usually from the force of a small but powerful conventional explosive. In a typical gun-type design, a shell of fissile material is fired down a gun barrel into a hollow fissile target fastened to the other end of the barrel, thus creating a supercritical mass. Once the two pieces of uranium are brought together, the initiator introduces a burst of neutrons and then the fission reaction and the chain reaction begins, continuing until the energy released becomes so great that the bomb simply blows itself apart.

The other type is called an "implosion" weapon, and requires a core of fissile material that becomes critical when compressed by the force of an explosion around it. In a typical implosion design, explosive charges are used to compress a sphere of plutonium very rapidly to a density sufficient to make it go critical and produce a nuclear explosion. Surrounding the core with a layer of beryllium (as a reflector, or tamper) amplifies and magnifies the power of the explosion because it keeps most of the fissile material and neutrons from escaping when the core becomes critical. This type of nuclear weapon is more powerful than the gun-type device, but is also more complicated. For example, the explosive charges surrounding the core must all go off at exactly the same instant in order to create a uniform shockwave that compresses the core and leads to the fission reaction. Further, the reflector, or tamper, surrounding the core must be of a heavy material. An implosion weapon would thus likely be heavier and significantly less portable than a gun-type weapon. Both kinds of weapons were used by the United States in attacking Japan at the end of World War II. Compared to the implosion-type nuclear weapon, the gun-type design requires a larger amount of fissile material, and much of it is used inefficiently. However, gun-type weapons using highly enriched uranium are less technically difficult than implosion devices, making them more attractive to a terrorist group.

In addition to nuclear fission, there is another method to create a nuclear explosion called "fusion." As mentioned above, atoms have different weights as well as different compositions of protons and neutrons. **Nuclear fusion** is a nuclear reaction in which the nuclei of two light atoms (such as hydrogen) combine to form a heavier atom (such as helium). This process releases excess binding energy from the reaction, based upon the binding energies of the atoms involved in the process. At extremely high temperatures—in the range of tens of millions of degrees—the nuclei of isotopes of hydrogen (and some other light elements) can readily combine to form heavier elements and in the process release considerable energy. The sun's power (about 386 billion megawatts) is produced by nuclear fusion reactions. Each second about 700 million tons of hydrogen are converted to about 695 million tons of helium and 5 million tons of energy are released in

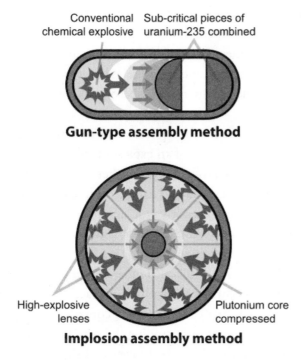

Conventional chemical explosive   Sub-critical pieces of uranium-235 combined

Gun-type assembly method

High-explosive lenses   Plutonium core compressed

Implosion assembly method

Figure 17.1: Gun-type and implosion fission bomb designs.

the form of gamma rays. In general, fusion produces five to six times more energy than fission.

Making fusion happen is not easy, however. The electrostatic nature of atoms—the makeup of protons and neutrons—means that they typically bounce off each other or repel each other like the same sides of two magnets. Thus, for fusion to occur, you have to smash the two nuclei together with enough force to overcome the electrostatic force of repulsion. Again, this can only be achieved in conditions of extremely high temperatures. And to date, the only way that scientists have been able to produce that kind of heat is through a **nuclear fission** reaction. Thus, scientists combined the basic designs of nuclear fission with a source of fusion to create the most powerful weapons ever known to mankind: the thermonuclear bomb. The enormous technical difficulties involved in creating and deploying such a weapon, however, make it highly unlikely that terrorists or other violent nonstate actors would ever have them.

The bottom line here is that since their introduction in 1945, nuclear bombs have become the most feared weapon of mass destruction. These are the most powerful, most destructive weapons ever known. There are currently more than enough nuclear warheads in the world to completely destroy every major population center in the world. In addition to physical destruction, these weapons also leave behind a large area of radioactive contamination. Those people who survive the blast would likely die from radiation sickness or other related illnesses, and a large area would be uninhabitable for quite a while.

If there is any silver lining in these terrible weapons, it is that they are very complicated and difficult to make (especially fusion-type nuclear weapons), which is why only a handful of countries have them. Currently the countries that have nuclear weapons are China, France, India, North Korea, Pakistan, Russia, the United Kingdom, and the United States. Israel is widely known to have nuclear weapons, but has never officially acknowledged this. South Africa developed nuclear weapons, but then abandoned the program and disassembled its weapons. And when the Soviet Union collapsed, three countries that became independent—Belarus, Kazakhstan, and Ukraine—turned over their nuclear weapons to Russian control. Some states (like Iraq, Libya, and Syria) have tried to develop but eventually abandoned their own nuclear weapons programs, while others (allegedly Iran) appear to be trying to secretly build a nuclear weapons capability. And because a nuclear terrorist attack would be absolutely devastating, virtually all the countries of the world are working together to prevent that worst-case scenario from ever happening.

SUMMARY

This was a fairly broad overview of the four main categories of WMD. Chemical weapons are the most common and easiest to make. Biological weapons are unique in the way humans can be victims as well as delivery systems of an infectious disease. Radiological weapons have some similarities to chemical weapons, but use radioactive materials and are more difficult to develop and handle. And nuclear weapons are by far the most destructive, but also the most difficult to build or acquire. In the next lecture, we will briefly explore the history of states developing and using these weapons, where we find CBRN weapons and materials today, and what all of this means for the threat of WMD terrorism.

QUESTIONS FOR DISCUSSION

- Why did countries like Germany develop and use chemical weapons in WWI?
- In what ways do biological weapons differ from chemical weapons?
- In what ways are radiological weapons similar to chemical weapons?
- In what ways do radiological weapons differ from biological weapons?
- Do these differences matter in terms of how states (or terrorists) view their potential usefulness?

RECOMMENDED READING

Carter, Ashton B., Michael W. May, and William J. Perry. "The Day After: Action Following a Nuclear Blast in a U.S. City." *Washington Quarterly* 30, no. 4 (2007).

Caves, Jr., John P. and W. Seth Carus. *The Future of Weapons of Mass Destruction: Their Nature and Role in 2030.* Washington, DC: NDU Press, 2014.

Cote, Jr., Owen R. "A Primer on Fissile Materials and Nuclear Weapon Design." In *Avoiding Nuclear Anarchy: Containing the Threat of Loose Russian Nuclear Weapons and Fissile Material.* By Graham T. Allison, Owen Cote, Jr., Richard A. Falkenrath, and Steven E. Miller. CSIA Studies in International Security. John F. Kennedy School of Government, Harvard University, 1996.

Ferguson, Charles D. and Michele M. Smith. "Assessing Radiological Weapons: Attack Methods and Estimated Effects." In *Weapons of Mass Destruction and Terrorism.* 2nd ed. Edited by James J. F. Forest and Russell Howard. New York: McGraw-Hill, 2012.

Ferguson, Charles and William C. Potter. *Improvised Nuclear Devices and Nuclear Terrorism.* WMD Commission Report no. 2, 2009.

Forest, James J. F. and Russell Howard, eds. *Weapons of Mass Destruction and Terrorism.* 2nd ed. New York: McGraw-Hill, 2012.

Gottron, Frank, and Dana Shea. "Federal Efforts to Address the Threat of Bioterrorism," CRS Report to Congress. August 6, 2010.

Graham, Bob, Jim Talent, et al. *World at Risk: The Report of the Commission on the Prevention of Weapons of Mass Destruction Proliferation and Terrorism.* New York: Vintage Books, 2008.

Koblentz, Gregory. "Pathogens as Weapons: The International Security Implications of Biological Warfare." *International Security* 28, no. 3 (2003/2004).

Maerli, Morten Bremer, Annette Schaper, and Frank Barnaby. "The Characteristics of Nuclear Terrorist Weapons." In *Weapons of Mass Destruction and Terrorism.* Edited by Russell Howard and James J. F. Forest. New York: McGraw-Hill, 2007.

Medalia, Jonathan. "Terrorist 'Dirty Bombs': A Brief Primer." CRS Report for Congress. April 1,2004.

Stanley Foundation. "Future Weapons of Mass Destruction." *Policy Dialogue Brief* (December 1, 2006).

Tucker, Jonathan B. "Trafficking Networks for Chemical Weapons Precursors: Lessons from the Iran-Iraq War of the 1980s." James Martin Center for Nonproliferation Studies, Monterey Institute of International Studies. Occasional Paper no. 13. 2008.

Wittes, Benjamin. "Innovation's Darker Future: Biosecurity, Technologies of Mass Empowerment and the Constitution." Brookings Institution. December 8, 2010.

WEBSITES

Biological and Toxin Weapons Convention (BWC)
https://www.un.org/disarmament/wmd/bio

Carnegie Endowment for International Peace
http://www.carnegieendowment.org

Center for International Security & Cooperation
http://cisac.fsi.stanford.edu

Center for Nonproliferation Studies
http://www.nonproliferation.org

Centers for Disease Prevention & Control
http://www.cdc.gov

Chemical Weapons Convention (CWC)
http://www.opcw.org/chemical-weapons-convention

Defense Threat Reduction Agency
http://www.dtra.mil

Federation of American Scientists
http://www.fas.org

Global Threat Reduction Initiative
http://nnsa.energy.gov/gtri

Nuclear Non-Proliferation Treaty (NPT)
https://www.un.org/disarmament/wmd/nuclear/npt/

Nuclear Threat Initiative
http://www.nti.org

Proliferation Security Initiative
http://www.state.gov/t/isn/c10390.htm

NOTES

1. As defined in U.S. law, 18 U.S.C. § 2332a, http://www.fbi.gov/about-us/investigate/terrorism/wmd/wmd_faqs.

2. Incendiary devices have especially been a weapon of choice for environmental extremists, who have used them in attacks against logging companies, ski resorts, park ranger stations, and other such targets.

3. Centers for Disease Control and Prevention website on chemical agents, http://www.bt.cdc.gov/chemical.

4. See "Pulmonary Agents," Federation of American Scientists, http://www.fas.org/nuke/guide/usa/doctrine/army/mmcch/PulmAgnt.htm.

5. For example, see National Research Council, High Impact Terrorism (Washington, D.C.: National Academies Press, 2002): 115, http://goo.gl/GlhbS.

6. "VX Backgrounder," Council on Foreign Relations (January 2006), http://goo.gl/UJEKz.

7. See the CDC website on chemical agents at http://www.bt.cdc.gov/chemical.

8. See the CDC website on bioterrorism at http://www.bt.cdc.gov/bioterrorism.

9. For more information on these, see "Lab Aspects of Bioterrorism," http://goo.gl/f6xap. Also see the CDC website on bioterrorism (note 8).

10. Note: In any kind of chemical, biological or radiological contamination event, when you need to remove your shirt do not pull it off over your head. Cut it off instead.

11. Nuclear Threat Initiative, "Radiological Terrorism Tutorial," http://www.nti.org/h_learn more/radtutorial/index.html.

12. Ibid.

13. Ibid.

14. Jonathan Medalia, "Terrorist 'Dirty Bombs': A Brief Primer," CRS Report for Congress (April 1, 2004).

15. Ibid.

16. The two sources for this section are Medalia, "Terrorist 'Dirty Bombs'" and the NTI "Radiological Terrorism Tutorial."

17. For details, see Charles Ferguson, Tahseen Kazi and Judith Perera, *Radioactive Sources: Surveying the Security Risks* (Monterey, CA: Center for Nonproliferation Studies, 2003).

18. NTI, "Radiological Terrorism Tutorial."

19. Medalia, "Terrorist 'Dirty Bombs.'"

20. For more details, see: Morten Bremer Maerli, Annette Schaper, and Frank Barnaby, "The Characteristics of Nuclear Terrorist Weapons," in *Weapons of Mass Destruction and Terrorism*, ed. Russell Howard and James J. F. Forest (New York: McGraw-Hill, 2007); and Owen R. Cote, Jr., "A Primer on Fissile Materials and Nuclear Weapon Design," in *Avoiding Nuclear Anarchy: Containing the Threat of Loose Russian Nuclear Weapons and Fissile Material*, by Graham T. Allison, Owen Cote, Jr., Richard A. Falkenrath, and Steven E. Miller, CSIA Studies in International Security, John F. Kennedy School of Government, Harvard University (1996).

21. Ferguson et al., *Radioactive Sources*, 2.

18

Assessing the
WMD Terrorist Threat

In the previous lecture, we examined the basic aspects of chemical, biological, radiological and nuclear (CBRN) weapons. Now we will review the threat of terrorist groups acquiring and using these kinds of weapons, and then examine the threat of nuclear terrorism in particular.

Appreciating this threat requires that we first examine a bit of history. Many centuries ago, a form of biological warfare was seen in conflicts during which dead bodies infected with the plague were catapulted over an enemy's fortress walls. During an early period of America's history, British soldiers gave Native Americans blankets that were infected with the smallpox virus. Chemical weapons were first used in significant amounts during World War I. On April 22, 1915, the German army released chlorine gas in an attack against the French in Belgium, causing at least 2,800 casualties. The British retaliated later that year at the Battle of Loos, using the same gas against German troops. In total, about 124,000 tons of chemical weapons were used by all sides during World War I, inflicting over a million casualties (90,000 of them fatal). Attacks involving weapons of mass destruction (WMD) during World War II included the use of mustard gas by Italy against Ethiopians during its invasion of Abyssinia in 1936; the use of intestinal typhoid bacteria by the Japanese in poisoning a Soviet water supply near the former Mongolian border in 1939; and the spreading (by Japan, using air cargo drops) of rice and wheat mixed with plague-carrying fleas over China and Manchuria in 1940.

During the Cold War, the threat from WMD was largely focused on a small number of countries. We had a bipolar international system in which powerful countries held a fairly strong monopoly on nuclear, chemical, and biological weapons. While a handful of these countries tested various weapons, they were almost never used in any conflict. The most glaring exception was seen during the Iran-Iraq war of the 1980s. Specifically, Iraq began using mustard gas against Iran's human wave attacks in August 1983, and used the nerve agent tabun in 1984. The Iraqi military also used chemical weapons (particularly hydrogen cyanide and mustard gas) in its campaign against the Kurds during the late 1980s, most notably in the Halabja massacre of 1988. And while Iraq developed an offensive biological weapons capability including anthrax, botulinum toxin, and aflatoxin during the late 1980s, there is no evidence to indicate these weapons were ever deployed. Over the last few decades, the WMD threat vectors expanded considerably. New states became nuclear powers, like China, India, Pakistan, Israel, and North Korea, eventually creating a crisis of legitimacy for global nonproliferation norms and procedures—a crisis that has become particularly troubling with regard to Iran's uranium enrichment and nuclear energy program. And the rapid collapse of the Soviet Union created a somewhat chaotic situation where weapons and materials have allegedly gone unaccounted for. These and other events shape our understanding of the modern threat of states acquiring or using WMD.

Terrorists and other violent nonstate actors have also used—or at least tried to acquire and use—weapons of mass destruction on several occasions within the past three decades. For example, in 1981, a religious cult known as the Rajneeshees left India and relocated to a ranch in a town called the Dalles, Ore., about an hour's drive from Portland.[1] Around 4,000 cult members lived at the ranch, which was intended to be a self-contained commune, but a conflict ensued with county officials over a host of land-use issues. By 1984, the cult's leaders decided that the only solution was to gain control over the county commission, so they devised a plot to make a large number of local residents sick just before the November election, thus reducing voter turnout to the point where the cult could win. To carry out this plot, cult members working at the Rajneeshee medical clinic obtained samples from a diagnostic kit of the salmonella bacterium, a common cause of food poisoning, and cultivated the agent in laboratory glassware. In September of that year, cult members engineered a test run of their plan by using salmonella to contaminate salad bars in 10 restaurants in the area. As a result, 751 local residents became seriously ill and 45 were hospitalized with symptoms ranging from nausea and diarrhea, to headache and fever, although none died. Since many of these restaurants were located near an interstate highway, a number of out-of-state travelers may also have been infected at these restaurants, so the actual number of victims was probably much higher. The cult members eventually abandoned their plan to influence the election, and some of them even left the group altogether. Once investigators discovered what had happened, a couple of group members were arrested and sent to jail for the attack.[2]

In 1985, federal law enforcement authorities discovered that a small survivalist group in the Ozark Mountains of Arkansas known as The Covenant, The Sword, and The Arm of the Lord had acquired about 30 gallons of potassium cyanide, with the apparent intent to poison water supplies in New York, Chicago, and Washington, D.C. Led by a right-wing preacher named James Ellison, this group based its ideology on the Christian Identity movement, described in Lecture 10. The group's members devised a scheme to poison urban water supplies in the belief that such attacks would make the Messiah return more quickly by punishing unrepentant sinners. The plot failed when U.S. government agents, who were investigating the group for gun trafficking and racketeering, raided their compound and discovered the cyanide.

In June 1990, the Liberation Tigers of Tamil Eelam (LTTE) became the first official insurgent, guerrilla, or terrorist organization to stage a chemical weapons attack when it used chlorine gas in an assault on a Sri Lankan armed forces camp at East Kiran. This attack was relatively crude: several large drums of chlorine were transported from a nearby paper mill and positioned around the camp's perimeter, and when the wind currents were judged right, the attackers released the gas, which wafted into the camp. More than 60 military personnel were injured, and the LTTE captured the facility. However, while this was part of a first round in a renewed military offensive, the LTTE did not use a similar weapon in subsequent attacks, in part due to revulsion among their core supporters and constituencies.[3] As noted in the previous lecture, chlorine is a fairly common chemical, particularly in industrialized societies where it is used for a broad range of applications from municipal sewage treatment plants to plastics and other industries. In 2007, insurgents in Iraq tried to use chlorine gas in a small number of their attacks against U.S. and coalition forces, but the practice was short-lived, probably because of the same disadvantageous results the LTTE encountered and because overall the casualties from those attacks were not significantly greater than what we have seen from conventional roadside and suicide bombings.

On March 20, 1995, Aum Shinrikyo—a Japanese religious cult—launched an attack on the Tokyo subway using sarin nerve agent, killing nearly a dozen people and injuring thousands more. They used a rather crude delivery mechanism for this attack—plastic bags filled with sarin liquid were placed on the floor of subway cars, and members of the group then punctured the bags with the ends of their umbrellas. Its objective in this attack was to disrupt an anticipated effort by law enforcement authorities to arrest members of the group (it attacked subway lines leading to many government ministries). Had the group incorporated a more sophisticated attack plan, the death toll could have been much higher. Aum Shinrikyo had also used sarin in an attack the previous year in Matsumoto, this time using a truck with a sprayer to target officials involved in a judicial proceeding against it; this attack killed seven and injured 34 people. Aum also tried to use biological agents to inflict mass casualties. The cult had attracted university-trained biologists as members, and they obtained a veterinary vaccine strain of the anthrax bacterium, cultivated it, and released the resulting agents as a biological weapon in Tokyo on at least nine different occasions. However, the attacks were harmless because the veterinary vaccine strain is nonvirulent and does not have a significant impact on humans.

In October 2001, powdered anthrax was delivered by envelopes through the U.S. mail, killing five people and making dozens of others very sick. Investigators later determined that this was most likely the work of one individual, not a terrorist group.[4] But it certainly raised alarms about what terrorist groups worldwide might have learned from such an attack. In January 2003, British police raided an apartment in North London and found recipes and instructions in Arabic for making ricin as well as other toxins, along with a mortar and pestle that appeared to contain chemical residue, 20 castor beans (the raw ingredient needed to produce ricin), cherry and apple seeds (which are used in the production of cyanide), and a CD-ROM containing instructions for the fabrication of homemade explosives. In January 2004, U.S. forces discovered seven pounds of cyanide salt during a raid on a Baghdad house that was purportedly connected with al-Qaeda members, and in November of that year they discovered a "chemical laboratory" in Fallujah containing (among other items) potassium cyanide, hydrochloric acid, and sulfuric acid. In April 2004, Jordanian authorities announced that they had broken up an al-Qaeda plot to use large quantities of toxic chemicals—including sulfuric acid, cyanide, and insecticides—in attacks against the U.S. Embassy, the Jordanian prime minister's office, and the headquarters of Jordanian intelligence.

AT A GLANCE

Characteristics of a group interested in WMD may include:

- a belief in its ethnic, racial and/or religious superiority over the victims and targets of an attack
- a perception that conventional attacks haven't been effective
- a willingness to take risks with untested weapons
- an apocalyptic, doomsday ideology

And in a WMD terrorism plot much closer to home, on December 9, 2008, authorities in the small town of Belfast, Maine responded to a report of domestic violence. They arrived at the home of James Cummings to find that he had been shot dead by his wife, who they later learned had been suffering from years of horrible domestic abuse. But the other things they found led them to contact the FBI, which sent teams of investigators and forensic specialists to the home. There, the FBI compiled an inventory of materials that strongly suggest Cummings was attempting to assemble a radiological weapon.[5] The state police in Maine had already detected radiation emissions in six small jars in the home, and the FBI confirmed this in their official inventory, which lists four bottles of depleted uranium-238, purchased online from a nuclear supply company; two jars of thorium-232;[6] and a small sample of beryllium, purchased from a vendor in Colorado. All three of these radioactive metals—uranium, thorium, and beryllium—are highly toxic when ingested and cause cancer if inhaled as fine airborne particles. However, Cummings had none of them in large quantity, and all of the materials in his possession had a long half-life, meaning that they would not have made for a very effective radiological weapon.

In addition to the radioactive materials, Cummings had also purchased large quantities of commonly available 3% hydrogen peroxide and used his kitchen stove to concentrate this into 35% hydrogen peroxide. When combined with various acids, this concentrated form is used to make TATP and HMTD, which are very powerful explosives that have been used in a variety of terrorist attacks, including the July 2005 suicide bombings in London, and many attacks in Iraq, Afghanistan, Pakistan, Indonesia, and Turkey. He had also acquired significant amounts of lithium metal, thermite, aluminum powder, and other materials that can be used to detonate and increase the power of these explosives. Investigators also found a sketch of a workable design for constructing a dirty bomb, and a shopping list, with the title "best for dirty bombs," indicating he was trying to buy cobalt-60, cesium-137, and strontium-90. Naturally, the FBI wondered what his intentions were.

According to their interviews with a variety of witnesses, Cummings was a terribly angry man who expressed white supremacist sympathies, was obsessed with Adolf Hitler, and had recently filled out an application to join the National Socialist Movement. He was apparently incensed about the election of Barack Obama to the presidency, and his wife reported that his plan was to construct a dirty bomb, hide it in the undercarriage of their motor home, drive it to Washington, D.C., and kill the president. Of course, if only he had lived to see who was elected eight years later, he might be a very happy camper indeed, judging from the resurgence of right-wing extremism in the U.S. today. Cummings also had significant financial resources at his disposal, having received a $2 million real estate inheritance. He spent several months winning the confidence of online suppliers of radioactive materials, using a variety of cover stories, PayPal accounts, and shipping addresses. According to his wife, he convinced them that he was a professor conducting research. Overall, the FBI believes that Cummings was more advanced in his efforts than any previously known domestic threat involving a dirty bomb.[7]

More recently, the Islamic State in Iraq and Syria (ISIS, but often referred to as the so-called Islamic State) has used various chemical weapons in over 50 attacks, including sulfur mustard agents and munitions loaded with chlorine gas. It also set fire to a sulfur mine, creating a toxic cloud that sickened hundreds of civilians with nose bleeds, headaches, and choking fits.[8] Chemical weapons have also been used in Syria by government forces in attacks against rebel-held villages. According to a May 2017 report to Congress by the U.S. Director of National Intelligence, "the Syrian regime used the nerve agent sarin in an attack against the opposition in Khan Shaykhun on 4 April 2017 in what is probably the largest chemical weapons attack since August 2013."[9] Looking ahead to the future, one hopes that such frequent use of low-grade WMD in that conflict will not inspire other states or nonstate actors to follow in their footsteps.

ASSESSING THE WMD TERRORIST THREAT

These examples help to illustrate the diversity of potential WMD terrorist threats. But it is important to point out that there are only a handful of these cases, which has implications for our understanding of terrorism in general. To assess the WMD threat among the broader terrain of terrorist groups, we can use an analytical framework that examines two dimensions (as illustrated in Figure 18.1)—capabilities and opportunities is one dimension, and intentions is the other.

Most terrorist groups fall into the lower left quadrant of this diagram, having both low intentions and low capabilities for a WMD terrorist attack. Opposite this, in the upper right-hand quadrant, is where we place terrorist groups we worry about most—groups with both a proven capability to develop or acquire weapons of mass destruction and a high level of intention for using those weapons if and when they become available. For example, Aum Shinrikyo, the group that attacked the Tokyo subway in 1995 using the nerve agent sarin, is now a shadow of what it once was, but at its high point during the mid-1990s Aum would have been placed in the top right quadrant of this diagram—high intentions, high capabilities. At its compound near Tokyo, called Satian-7, Aum members built several high-tech facilities and developed a sophisticated program of manufacturing chemicals ostensibly for industrial use.[10] Sarin was just one of several chemical weapons programs that the group pursued. It also attempted to weaponize various bacteria, such as anthrax and botulinum, but was unsuccessful. Several reports indicate the cult had over ten thousand members

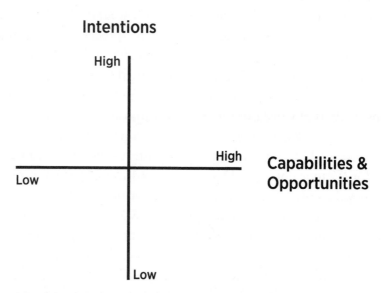

Figure 18.1: A framework for assessing the threat of WMD terrorism.
Source: Author.

in several countries and nearly $1 billion in assets, including "secular" businesses all across Japan and overseas. The combination of the group's resources, capabilities, and apocalyptic ideology (described in Lecture 11) produced a rare and deadly type of WMD terrorist threat.

Thankfully, there are very few groups today with a similar combination of capabilities and intentions. As noted above, the Islamic State has used chemical weapons in dozens of attacks in Iraq and Syria. Here, too, we find not only extensive resources at the group's disposal but also an apocalyptic ideology that motivates and guides its strategic and tactical decisions.[11] In contrast, groups like Hizballah in Lebanon or the FARC in Colombia may have the financial resources and possibly some involvement from a state government in developing or acquiring weapons of mass destruction, but to date these groups have not demonstrated an intention to do so. Thus we would put them in the lower right-hand quadrant of this diagram: high capabilities, but low intentions. And finally, we have the groups in the upper left-hand quadrant—groups like al-Qaeda or Jemmah Islamiyyah in Southeast Asia that have indicated a desire for WMD and an intention of using them, but, according to current intelligence, are constrained by limited capabilities.

What do we know about terrorist groups' intentions? In its 2008 report *World at Risk*, the Commission on the Prevention of WMD Proliferation and Terrorism predicted a high likelihood of some type of WMD terrorist attack by the year 2013.[13] In his 2012 "Worldwide Threat Assessment of the U.S. Intelligence Community" prepared for Congress, then-Director of National Intelligence James Clapper indicated that "we worry about a limited CBR attack in the United States or against our interests overseas in the next year because of the interest expressed in such a capability by some foreign groups, such as al-Qaeda in the Arabian Peninsula (AQAP)."[12] Lucky for us, as of this writing (April 2018) none of these dire predictions have come true, but we have certainly seen the U.S. government take the threat seriously: the FBI established a Directorate for Weapons of Mass Destruction, and the Department of Homeland Security has a new Countering Weapons of Mass Destruction Office.

Some analysts suggest that the most probable WMD scenarios involve the use of toxic industrial chemicals, biological poisons, or radioisotopes fabricated into an improvised dispersal device. The use of chemical warfare agents, biological warfare agents, and improvised nuclear devices are other possible scenarios, though they are considered less likely due to the difficulties in obtaining the necessary materials, technologies, and expertise.[14]

Our understanding of a group's views on WMD typically comes from its stated ideological goals, an articulation of the group's vision of the future, and the strategy through which it hopes to achieve that vision (as we have discussed in several lectures of this series). A terrorist group's vision of the future might include retribution for past injustices, changes in the policy directions of a local regime (or even a superpower), a world with greater socioeconomic equality, or even a world without certain types of people in it. Some may pursue a vision of a better world for their children; others may pursue a vision of salvation in the afterlife.

By extension, a group's ideology can be compared to others along a spectrum with regard to their views toward the use of violence in pursuit of their espoused future vision. At one end of this spectrum are groups that desire dramatic changes, but do not see the necessity of violent means to bring about those changes. At the other end of the spectrum are those who seek nothing less than the complete destruction of life as we know it. Between the two extreme ends of the spectrum are a variety of groups willing to use some level of violence in pursuit of their objectives.

At a certain point along the spectrum of ideologies there is a threshold of catastrophic terrorism, based on the amount of death and destruction generated by the true believers of the ideology, a threshold which relatively few groups have crossed. Indeed, there are relatively few groups or individuals whose ideologies articulate a desire for the end of the world, or at least the end of all mankind, and who can therefore be placed at this end of the spectrum. Examples include extreme environmentalist cults like the Voluntary Human Extinction Movement, which calls for the elimination of the human race in order to save the planet,[15] and apocalyptic doomsday or final judgment cults. Among the latter category, the most prominent in recent years have been Aum Shinrikyo and Islamic State, as mentioned earlier.

While this discussion is not meant to dismiss the threat of nuclear terrorism, the truth is that weapons of mass destruction really don't offer many strategically useful benefits to most terrorist groups, and certainly not commensurate with the level of costs and resource investments it would take to acquire a WMD capability. Further, a significant majority of terrorist groups have recognized the need to impose constraints on their violence, in order to maintain the popular support necessary for financing their operations and recruiting new members to their ranks. In fact, many terrorists throughout history have pursued a vision of the future in which they will someday be in charge of a particular governable space, and this vision may require them to overthrow an existing government but ensure that the space and people they seek to govern are left relatively undamaged. For example, the Marxist ideology of the FARC in Colombia or the Sendero Luminoso in Peru does not lend itself to a WMD attack, nor does the nationalist ideology of the Irish Republican Army.

However, if the envisioned governable space desired by a terrorist group is distinctly different from the larger population of a nation-state (like a separate Basque country, a Tamil homeland, a Chechen or Kurdish state, etc.), there are fewer constraints against a catastrophic terror attack against the governing regime and those who support it (e.g., in Madrid, Moscow, or Istanbul). Perhaps, then, Chechen rebels could determine it potentially beneficial to deploy a WMD against Moscow or some other densely populated city in Russia, if they felt that doing so would force the government to acquiesce to Chechnya's demands for an independent homeland. But they are likely constrained from pursuing this course of action by the likelihood that a WMD terror attack would produce the opposite effect—heavy-handed Russian military reprisals—coupled with inevitable international condemnation for crossing the threshold of catastrophic terrorism. This in turn could potentially impact their financial and logistics networks. Thus, as with most other groups, the lack of WMD terrorist attacks by Chechens may owe more to a lack of strategic benefit and intentions than a lack of capabilities.

As noted earlier, several groups that have already crossed the threshold of catastrophic terrorism, or at least intend to if given the capability and opportunity, appear unconstrained by earthly considerations, and instead see themselves as fulfilling the mandate of a higher power—in essence, the threat they pose is limited solely by the weapons they can acquire. A common thread among these groups is the need for mass destruction and death in order to bring about a better world envisioned and articulated through some form of catastrophic ideology. Most commonly, this future utopian world is envisioned through the lens of some type of religious interpretation (as seen in the cases of Aum Shinrikyo and Islamic State). Some religious extremists are seeking the end of the world, but most just want their religion to dominate the world by any means necessary. This is an apt description of al-Qaeda's ideology and its rationale for pursuing WMD.

Of course, it's fairly well known that al-Qaeda's leadership has long expressed an interest in WMD, as indicated in things like Osama bin Laden's fatwa of 1998 and training manuals like the *Encyclopedia of Afghan Jihad*. We also know from intelligence and media reports that since 9/11, al-Qaeda has sought to establish links with Pakistani nuclear scientists, obtain nuclear suitcase bombs from Russia, procure biological and chemical agents from the Czech Republic, Iraq, North Korea, and elsewhere, and develop the means for spreading diseases and poisons among a targeted population—for example, within major U.S. cities.

One of the main questions to grapple with, however, is *why* al-Qaeda would want to attack the United States or other Western countries using a weapon of mass destruction. Often, media and political leaders fail to convey a sophisticated understanding of this issue, instead opting for shorthand reasons like, "they want to destroy our way of life" or "they hate us for who we are." The reality, of course, is much more complex. On a strategic level, al-Qaeda's leaders want to economically damage the United States and the West at large. As discussed in Lecture 13, al-Qaeda has recognized that the center of gravity for the United States is its economy, and damaging it will thus have a severe impact on America's ability to project power in other areas, including militarily and politically.

Al-Qaeda's leaders want to change the course of history. The movement they claim to lead would get a huge morale boost if they could somehow diminish U.S. power and prestige particularly through the same kind of "war of attrition" that they claim led directly to the demise of the Soviet Union. Of course, in order to have an opportunity of establishing a global Islamic caliphate, they must do all they can to undermine the current Westphalian state-based system of international order and power brokering. In other words, they have to show how man-made systems and rules are inferior to the systems and rules proscribed by the Holy Quran. Further, attacking the West would provide a morale boost to affiliated ideological movements around the world by demonstrating how the militarily weak can defeat the militarily strong.

Al-Qaeda's leaders also believe that supporters of the global Salafi-jihadist movement want and expect a "spectacular" event that would be even bigger than 9/11. From this perspective, anything less than a WMD attack may be perceived as a sign of weakness on the part of al-Qaeda. As described in Lecture 12, al-Qaeda is in direct competition with other "voices" in the Muslim world, and a catastrophic terror attack will allow it to claim center stage in this global debate. The leaders of al-Qaeda have argued that America and the West have it coming; in essence, a WMD attack is necessary to "even the score." And they believe that a "nuclear 9/11" would cause a massive economic depression that could lead to the demise of the United States' position as the world's superpower. A nuclear attack would also be preferred over a chemical, biological, or radiological attack. As part of their efforts to promote a perception of al-Qaeda as a vanguard of the new global jihadist movement, they would prefer the visual impact of a mushroom cloud rather than news footage of people dying from chemical agents or biological pathogens.

This brings us to a central issue about the threat of WMD terrorism: what these kinds of weapons enable a terrorist group to achieve depends on the specific attributes of these weapons, which are quite different from each other (as noted in Lecture 17). For example, biological and chemical weapons can be deployed silently, possibly allowing a terrorist group to deploy the weapon and escape without detection or capture by law enforcement. However, because the effects produced by chemical and biological weapons are usually delayed and spread over time, they do not lend themselves to the type of dramatic news footage that most terrorist groups seek. Headline news stories of sick and dying people, with photos or film of hospital rooms, does not engender the same type of public response about terrorism as an explosion on a bus in Karachi or a hotel in Tel Aviv.

However, while attacking human populations with weaponized diseases is the primary focus of the literature and security policies in this area, there is a growing concern among some analysts that the real threat of bio-weapons is an attack against the agricultural sector. This is a fear rooted in historical experience. During World War I, German agents used anthrax and the equine disease glanders to infect livestock and feed for export to Allied forces. Incidents included the infection of Romanian sheep with anthrax and glanders for export to Russia, Argentinian mules with anthrax for export to Allied troops, and American horses and feed with glanders for export to France.

In a bio-terror attack against U.S. agricultural targets, the goal of the terrorist group would likely be to trigger large-scale economic fallout. Examples of this kind of attack might include the direct introduction of toxins or bacteria into the food chain. Small-scale processing facilities are viewed as particularly vulnerable to this type of attack, largely because many lack sophisticated security systems and often rely on a transient labor force. Another type of attack in this category could be a viral strike targeting the cattle industry. Weaponizing an agent such as foot and mouth disease is neither expensive nor technically demanding—in fact, it could be as easy as traveling to Africa or Central Asia, places where the disease can be easily found, then taking a handkerchief, wiping the nose of an infected animal, and carrying the disease in your pocket through airport security and to a U.S. state like Texas, Oklahoma, or Kansas, leaning over a fence and introducing the disease to livestock there. Attacks like these could potentially cripple U.S. meat and dairy industries, at least temporarily.

Like al-Qaeda, any terrorist groups interested in using a WMD would want it to produce a spectacular, massive impact, a shock and awe effect to garner instant worldwide publicity. Thus, a nuclear or radiological weapon may be far more attractive, but these are also significantly more difficult to acquire or to design and build.[16] The bottom line here is that understanding the attributes of different weapons contributes to our analysis of whether there is a significant likelihood of use, as well as what kind of groups would be most likely interested in using them. Overall, most analysts believe that the leaders of jihadist groups like al-Qaeda or Islamic State are very likely interested in acquiring small chemical, portable radiological or nuclear weapons, but are unlikely to have interest in acquiring or disseminating highly contagious viruses or diseases.

THE THREAT OF NUCLEAR TERRORISM

No terrorist attack scenario captures more imagination than those featuring a nuclear weapon, mainly because of their unequaled capacity for death and destruction. A nuclear terrorist attack has been prominent among Hollywood movies and television shows for years, and when policymakers or media refer to WMD, a nuclear weapon is frequently the first thing many people think of. Well-respected political leaders have frequently highlighted the threat of nuclear terrorism as the most serious danger facing the world today.[17] When President Obama convened the Nuclear Security Summit in Washington, D.C. in April 2016, he warned that "Just the smallest amount of plutonium—about the size of an apple—could kill and injure hundreds of thousands of innocent people."[18] Former International Atomic Energy Agency (IAEA) Director General Mohamed ElBaradei, Harvard Professor Graham Allison, and former Mexican President Ernesto Zedillo called nuclear terrorism "the biggest potential threat to civilization" adding that "the highly enriched uranium required to make an elementary nuclear bomb could be hidden inside a football."[19] Yet, despite all these dire warnings, a nuclear weapon is actually considered by experts to be the least likely type of WMD to be acquired and used by terrorist groups. In fact, we have actually seen almost no interest in nuclear weapons among the hundreds of terrorist groups that have come and gone since the creation of the first bombs dropped in Hiroshima and Nagasaki.

In his book *Will Terrorists Go Nuclear?*, Brian Jenkins noted that al-Qaeda is actually the world's first terrorist group to have a declared nuclear policy.[20] This group has actively sought to acquire nuclear weapons since the mid-1990s, and bin Laden publicly asserted al-Qaeda's right to acquire nuclear weapons. His 1998 statement "The Nuclear Bomb of Islam" called it a religious obligation of all faithful Muslims. U.S. military and intelligence officers investigating former al-Qaeda training camps in Afghanistan during the early 2000s found diagrams, instructional manuals, and notes from meetings with Pakistani scientists, further indicating this terrorist network's determination to acquire nuclear weapons. And on May 21, 2003, radical Saudi cleric Nasir al Fahd wrote a 26-page fatwa providing a source of religious justification for acquiring and using a nuclear weapon.

However, Jenkins also points to a number of significant challenges al-Qaeda or any other terrorist group would need to overcome before successful carrying out a nuclear attack. The first and perhaps most difficult problem they would face is acquiring an intact, usable nuclear weapon, or building one themselves. Most scholars agree that any nation-state in possession of nuclear weapons is very unlikely to give or sell them to a terrorist group. Obviously, it is equally in their best interests to prevent terrorists from stealing such weapons as well. These nations have invested massive amounts of resources over a long period of time, including special facilities, highly skilled scientific experts, complicated experiments and tests, expensive materials, and so forth. Such an investment is undoubtedly worth fiercely protecting. So, that leaves the terrorist group with the only alternative of building a nuclear weapon from scratch—something that even well-resourced nations have wanted to do at some point over the past century, but only a handful of them have succeeded. The specific details involved in such an effort are daunting indeed.

First, the terrorist group would need to acquire enough fissile material: at least 25kg of highly enriched uranium (HEU) or at least 8kg of weapons-grade plutonium.[21] Worldwide there are significant stockpiles of both, mainly at tightly guarded research labs and weapons facilities. If the group were somehow lucky enough to acquire the material in suitable format and quantity for making a bomb, their next challenge would be evading intelligence and law enforcement agencies during what would surely be a massive search. At the same time, they would need the scientific and physical capability to construct the weapon while avoiding detection. And of course they would need significant financial resources.

Assuming the terrorists had nuclear materials and the help of several competent scientists, engineers, machine technicians, and so forth, they would also need some way of protecting everyone from radiation exposure—and also ensuring that every single member of the group maintains the highest level of operational security and secrecy. If nothing went wrong throughout this entire lengthy, complex process, and by some evil miracle the group succeeded in fabricating a bomb, it would have to trust the bomb would function as desired because there would be no way to test it. The group would simply need a way to transport the weapon (which could weigh as much as a ton) safely to its intended target.

The sheer scope of these cumulative challenges leads most experts to agree that the sheer difficulties involved are likely a source of deterrence for terrorist groups to consider this kind of scenario. Even though Osama bin Laden actively sought nuclear weapons for many years, as Jenkins notes, his efforts were often amateurish and at times he fell prey to con artists. There are actually far more reasons for a terrorist group to avoid altogether the notion of a nuclear weapon than to pursue one. For example, there are so many other improvised explosive devices—like suicide belts and car bombs—that have proven to be cheaper, easier, and more reliable. For the terrorist group seeking to deploy a WMD for whatever reason, there are many possibilities in the chemical, biological, and radiological categories that look comparatively more feasible than a nuclear weapon.

A nuclear terrorist attack is thus widely considered to be a high consequence but low probability kind of event. Kind of like you or I winning a multimillion-dollar lottery jackpot, but of course with much different kinds of high consequences. Further, governments around the world are working hard—individually and collectively—to make the probability of nuclear terrorism even lower. For example, on April 28, 2004 the U.N. Security Council unanimously voted to adopt Resolution 1540, a measure aimed at preventing nonstate actors from acquiring nuclear, biological, and chemical weapons, their means of delivery, and related materials.[22] As Graham Allison has argued for many years, the most critical thing to do is eliminate nuclear materials before they wind up in the hands of terrorists. In his 2004 book on this topic, he states a clear and concise response to this threat: "No fissile material, no nuclear explosion, no nuclear terrorism. It is that simple."[23] Compared to the wide availability of industrial chemicals, radiological source materials, and biological pathogens, fissile material is exceedingly rare. Making it even more rare will diminish the threat of nuclear terrorism, to the benefit of everyone.

SUMMARY

To sum up, there is ample research and intelligence to suggest that the WMD terrorist threat is quite real, but within narrow parameters. The most important elements for understanding the true nature of this threat include the terrorist group's motivations; the availability of chemical, biological, radioactive, or fissile materials needed for such weapons; the quality of knowledge and personnel available within the group to properly assemble the weapons; their opportunities to acquire and transport required materials, or fully functioning weapons, across borders; and the attributes of the weapons themselves.

In the global landscape of terrorist groups, few have openly expressed an interest in acquiring these weapons or using them, and even fewer have the necessary capabilities to do so. Al-Qaeda is considered by most analysts as one of the few groups in the "high intentions" and "potential high capability" category. Its main peer competitor, the Islamic State, may have some intentions but limited (and decreasing) capabilities. Ethnonational separatist groups—like the Chechen rebels who are responsible for numerous suicide bombings against Russia—may be a likely candidate for orchestrating a chemical or radiological terrorist attack, primarily because those affected would be contained within a geographic location that is separate from the support population. Further, this reflects the kind of "othering" that was described in Lecture 8. And the dual use nature of many industrial chemicals and radioactive sources, particularly in an industrial society such as Russia, makes for a level of potential availability that is most worrisome.

Meanwhile, the threat of bioterrorism is of growing concern to many in the government and among academics. As mentioned in the previous lecture, there are currently 82 listed biological agents, pathogens, and toxins that the government believes may pose a severe threat to human or animal health.[23] More than 400 U.S. research entities are registered to work with these kinds of biological agents, and roughly 15,000 individuals are cleared for access to the materials that include anthrax, smallpox, and the Ebola virus.[24] That may not seem like very much in a country as big as ours, but we constantly worry about that one individual who becomes persuaded by a cult or terrorist organization to use their access to biological agents in ways that cause harm to U.S. citizens. Most analysts believe that an attack with bio-weapons is possible by apocalyptic cults like Aum Shinrikyo, which expressed interest in spurring an apocalypse to cleanse the world of evil. And a nuclear attack, however unlikely, would clearly have an enormous and lasting impact. Overall, preventing a terrorist attack using any kind of WMD will depend on coordination and information-sharing among all U.S. domestic agencies and the private sector, as well as international cooperation, vigilance, and perhaps a little bit of luck.

QUESTIONS FOR DISCUSSION

- What are the challenges associated with terrorist acquisition and use of CBRN weapons?
- Why would a terrorist group use a radiological weapon?
- How might a terrorist group acquire a radiological weapon?
- Under what circumstances would a well-funded terrorist group launch a WMD attack, and what kind of weapon would it use?
- Some analysts have argued that as long as high-yield explosives remain relatively easy to acquire or manufacture, the threat of a WMD terrorist attack is really exaggerated. Do you agree? Why or why not?
- What feasible counterterrorism tactics can countries employ to deter terrorists from acquiring and using these weapons?

RECOMMENDED READING

Ackerman, Gary A. and Lauren E. Pinson. "An Army of One: Assessing CBRN Pursuit and Use by Lone Wolves and Autonomous Cells." *Terrorism and Political Violence* 26, no. 1 (2014): 226–45.

Allison, Graham. *Nuclear Terrorism: The Ultimate Preventable Catastrophe*. New York: Times Books/ Henry Holt & Co., 2004.

Bunn, Matthew and Anthony Wier. "The Seven Myths of Nuclear Terrorism." In *Weapons of Mass Destruction and Terrorism*. 2nd ed. Edited by Russell Howard and James J. F. Forest. New York: McGraw-Hill, 2012.

Bunn, Matthew. *Securing the Bomb 2010: Securing All Nuclear Materials in Four Years*. Project on Managing the Atom, Belfer Center for Science and International Affairs, Harvard University, and the Nuclear Threat Initiative. 2010.

Cameron, Gavin and Natasha E. Bajema. "Assessing the Post-9/11 Threat of CBRN Terrorism." In *Terrorism and Counterterrorism*. Edited by Russell Howard and Bruce Hoffman. New York: McGraw-Hill, 2011.

Cameron, Gavin. "Nuclear Terrorism: Reactors and Radiological Attacks after September 11." In *Weapons of Mass Destruction and Terrorism*. 2nd ed. Edited by Russell Howard and James J. F. Forest. New York: McGraw-Hill, 2012.

Carter, Ashton B., Michael M. May and William J. Perry. "The Day After: Action Following a Nuclear Blast in a U.S. City." In *Weapons of Mass Destruction and Terrorism*. 2nd ed. Edited by Russell Howard and James J. F. Forest. New York: McGraw-Hill, 2012.

Chyba, Christopher F. and Alex L. Greninger. "Biotechnology and Bioterrorism: An Unprecedented World." In *Weapons of Mass Destruction and Terrorism*. 2nd ed. Edited by Russell Howard and James J. F. Forest. New York: McGraw-Hill, 2012.

Ferguson, Charles D. and William C. Potter. *Improvised Nuclear Devices and Nuclear Terrorism*. Weapons of Mass Destruction Commission, Report no. 2, 2009.

Hoffman, Bruce. "CBRN Terrorism Post-9/11." In *Weapons of Mass Destruction and Terrorism*. 2nd ed. Edited by Russell Howard and James J. F. Forest. New York: McGraw-Hill, 2012.

Jenkins, Brian M. *Will Terrorists Go Nuclear?* New York: Prometheus, 2008.

Maerli, Morton Bremer, Annette Schaper, and Frank Barnaby. "Characteristics of Nuclear Terrorist Weapons." In *Weapons of Mass Destruction and Terrorism*. 2nd ed. Edited by Russell Howard and James J. F. Forest. New York: McGraw-Hill, 2012.

Mowatt-Larssen, Rolf. *Al-Qaeda Weapons of Mass Destruction Threat: Hype or Reality?* Belfer Center for Science and International Affairs, Harvard University, 2010.

Mueller, John. The Atomic Terrorist? In *Weapons of Mass Destruction and Terrorism*. 2nd ed. Edited by Russell Howard and James J. F. Forest. New York: McGraw-Hill, 2012.

Parachini, John V. "The Making of Aum Shinrikyo's Chemical Weapons Program." In *The Making of a Terrorist*. Vol. 2. Edited by James J. F. Forest. Westport, CT: Praeger, 2005.

Tucker, Jonathan. "Chemical Terrorism: Assessing Threats and Responses." In *Weapons of Mass Destruction and Terrorism*. 2nd ed. Edited by Russell Howard and James J. F. Forest. New York: McGraw-Hill, 2012.

WEBSITES

Center for Nonproliferation Studies
http://www.nonproliferation.org

Centers for Disease Prevention & Control
http://www.cdc.gov

Nuclear Threat Initiative
http://www.nti.org

NOTES

1. For a full account of this event, see the special coverage by the *Oregonian* at http://www.oregonlive.com/rajneesh/.

2. Ibid.

3. Bruce Hoffman, *Inside Terrorism* (Columbia University Press, 2006): 361, note 29.

4. See the FBI's "Amerithrax Investigation" reports, http://www.fbi.gov/about-us/history/famous-cases/Anthrax-amerithrax.

5. Barton Gellma, "The Secret World of Extreme Militias," *Time*, September 30, 2010, http://goo.gl/GiEGu.

6. Cummings produced this at home using standard references and technical manuals that showed how to extract thorium from commercially available tungsten electrodes by soaking them in a peroxide bath.

7. Gellma, "The Secret World of Extreme Militias."

8. Thomas Gibbons-Neff, "Islamic State has used chemical weapons 52 times in Iraq and Syria since 2014," Washington Post, November 22, 2016, http://wapo.st/2zr3Z2s.

9. "Worldwide Threat Assessment of the U.S. Intelligence Community," Statement delivered to the Senate Select Comm. on Intelligence, (May 11, 2017) (statement of Daniel R. Coats), p. 7, http://bit.ly/2pE65Ul.

10. John V. Parachini, "The Making of Aum Shinrikyo's Chemical Weapons Program," in *The Making of a Terrorist*, vol. 2, ed. James J. F. Forest (Westport, CT: Praeger, 2005).

11. William McCants, The ISIS Apocalypse: The History, Strategy and Doomsday Vision of the Islamic State (New York: St. Martin's Press, 2015).

12. *Unclassified Statement for the Record on the Worldwide Threat Assessment of the U.S. Intelligence Community for the House Permanent Select Comm. on Intelligence*, (February 2, 2012) (statement of James R. Clapper).

13. Bob Graham, Jim Talent, et al., *World at Risk: The Report of the Commission on the Prevention of Weapons of Mass Destruction Proliferation and Terrorism* (New York: Vintage Books, 2008).

14. This is according to the FBI's WMD Directorate website at http://goo.gl/GblOA.

15. See its website at http://www.vhemt.org.

16. Jonathan Medalia, "Terrorist 'Dirty Bombs': A Brief Primer," CRS Report for Congress (April 1, 2004).

17. For example, see the list of quoted compiled by Graham Allison in "Nuclear Terrorism Fact Sheet," The Belfer Center, Harvard University, April 2010, http://bit.ly/2AQHuk2.

18. The White House, Office of the Press Secretary, "Remarks by President Obama and Prime Minister Rutte at Open Session of the Nuclear Summit," Washington, DC, April 1, 2016, http://bit.ly/2mlvxNZ.

19. Mohamed ElBaradei, Graham Allison, and Ernesto Zedillo, "Nuclear Security," New York Times, April 9, 2010, http://nyti.ms/2muXtQF.

20. See Brian Michael Jenkins, *Will Terrorists Go Nuclear?* (New York: Prometheus Books, 2008): 241–44.

21. Graham Allison, "Nuclear Terrorism Fact Sheet."

22. Kelsey Davenport, "UN Security Council Resolution 1540 At a Glance," Arms Control Association, August 2017, https://www.armscontrol.org/taxonomy/term/27.

23. Graham Allison,*Nuclear Terrorism: The Ultimate Preventable Catastrophe* (New York: Times Books/Henry Holt & Co., 2004).

24. Martin Matishak, "Possible Select Agent Reshuffle Adheres to Biosecurity Panel Findings," *Global Security Newswire* (October 6, 2011), http://goo.gl/0pL6e.

25. Ibid.

V

Concluding Thoughts

19

The Future of Terrorism

Okay, by now this lecture series has covered quite a lot of material about the history and key concepts of terrorism, a broad range of terrorist groups and their ideological motivations, and various political and socioeconomic factors that impact a terrorist group's operational environment. We have examined the many ways in which terrorism is a type of violent human behavior fueled by a mixture of push and pull factors (including a sense of identity, personal frustrations and aspirations, and contextual opportunities) that may lead an individual to support or directly engage in terrorist activity. And we have also explored various kinds of decisions that terrorists make, particularly regarding finances, tactics, weapons, and targets. There is of course much more than this in the vast landscape of terrorism studies, so I hope this book has inspired you to explore the work of other scholars, such as those I have recommended in the resource lists at the end of each lecture.

To conclude this lecture series, I'd like to do three things: first, I'll describe some recent trends in terrorist activity as this book goes to press (late 2018); then I'll provide some research-based observations about counterterrorism; and finally, I'll share with you a number of my own thoughts and concerns about the future of terrorism, particularly as it pertains to the United States.

CONTEMPORARY TRENDS IN TERRORIST ACTIVITY

One of the most interesting trends in the world of terrorism these days is how peer competition has intensified within the global jihadist movement between the followers and affiliates of Islamic State and the followers and affiliates of al-Qaeda. Following the death of Osama bin Laden in May 2011, Ayman al-Zawahiri was announced as the new leader of al-Qaeda, and he has been featured in a flurry of audio and video messages that seek to inspire Muslims everywhere to join the movement. Fortunately, these messages have found very limited resonance among his target audience. Furthermore, Islamic State propaganda has increasingly featured Zawahiri in its own propaganda as a target of ridicule and scorn. As Graeme Wood noted, "Dabiq publishes unflattering photographs of Zawahiri, which make him look decrepit, as if waiting for a bowl of Jell-O at a jihadist retirement home."[1]

Meanwhile, from the very day the Islamic State declared the establishment of a new Islamic caliphate in Iraq and Syria, the leadership cadre of al-Qaeda condemned the move as a mistake and has been highly critical of the self-proclaimed "caliph" Abu al-Baghdadi. Today, al-Baghdadi and his colleagues are no longer appealing for new recruits to come join them in defending their territory—they have no territory to defend. Instead, they have changed their tune and embraced the same kind of "think globally, act locally" propaganda strategy that al-Qaeda has been promoting for nearly two decades. Around the world, some affiliate groups (sometimes called wilayat) of al-Qaeda and Islamic State have switched allegiances, while others (like Boko Haram) have split into opposing factions, one declaring loyalty to al-Zawahiri and the other to al-Baghdadi. The core disagreement between leaders of al-Qaeda and Islamic State remains the question of who should be considered the true vanguard of the global jihadist movement, and it is very likely this intense peer competition will continue until one side gives way and is willing to compromise with the other.

Another important trend has been the rise of right-wing extremist attacks in Europe and North America. While the July 2011 attack by Anders Breivik in Oslo, Norway is perhaps the most dramatic example in recent years, we have seen right-wing attacks against Muslims leaving a place of worship (e.g. Quebec City, January 2017), against Hindus in a bar in Olathe, Kan. (February 2017), and against a crowd protesting a racist rally in Charlottesville, Va. (August 2017). In May 2017 right-wing extremists killed an African-American 23-year-old U.S. Army second lieutenant in Maryland and two people on a commuter train in Portland, Ore. who were simply trying to prevent the attacker from harassing a Muslim woman in a headscarf. These attackers have all been white nationalists and vocal supporters of right-wing extremist ideologies. Many are anti-global (or anti-"globalist" elites, as described by the far-right media outlet Breitbart), believing in conspiracy theories involving an imminent threat to national sovereignty and/or personal liberty. And as noted in Lecture 10, these right-wing extremists are motivated by a deep sense of "othering" that directs their anger and violence toward specific types of individuals based on ethnicity, religion, political beliefs, and other characteristics.

In April 2017, the U.S. Government Accountability Office released a report that examined domestic terrorist attacks between 9/11 and December 2016. The conclusions of this analysis were striking: "Of the 85 extremist incidents that resulted in death since September 12, 2001, far-right wing violent extremist groups were responsible for 62 (73%), while radical Islamist violent extremists were responsible for 23 (27%)."[2] A similar report published two months later by a nonprofit organization, looking at a different collection of data, found that there were almost twice as many terrorist incidents by right-wing extremists as by Islamist extremists in the U.S. from 2008 to 2016.[3]

Meanwhile, a report by two academics in North Carolina found that U.S. law enforcement agencies "consider anti-government violent extremists, not radicalized Muslims, to be the most severe threat of political violence that they face."[4] Among these anti-government extremists, the most worrisome are members of the so-called Sovereign Citizens movement, who have been responsible for dozens of attacks and plots against police officers and others over the past 10 years. According to Bob Paudert, a retired Arkansas police chief whose son was shot and killed during a traffic stop, "every state has sovereign citizens . . . [and] they are willing to kill and be killed for their beliefs."[5] Some attacks have involved elaborate plots to kill police officers responding to a fire (Florida, November 2014), wiring a house with explosives (Ohio, January 2014), and ambushing a patrol car (Louisiana, 2012), though the most common attacks have involved seemingly routine traffic stops, often when the patrol officer notices unusual, unofficial-looking license plates on a vehicle.

At the opposite end of the political spectrum we are also seeing an increase in violence associated with Antifa (an "antifascist" group) and other anti-authoritarian, left-wing movements. In January 2017, Antifa members protested Trump's inauguration in Washington, D.C. by smashing storefronts and bus stops. Two weeks later, other members of this movement attacked the student union center at UC Berkeley in protest of a scheduled speech by a prominent right-wing extremist. In March and April 2017, pro-Trump rallies were violently disrupted by black-clad protestors wielding makeshift weapons. And other political events in Texas, California, Oregon, and Virginia have also devolved into violence between left-wing and right-wing extremists.

But perhaps the most important trend we see in terrorism today is the increasing frequency of do-it-yourself (DIY) attacks throughout Europe, North America, and the Middle East. The list of recent attacks that can be described as examples of DIY terrorism include a wide variety of places: Tunis, Tunisia (March 2015), Ankara, Turkey (October 2015), San Bernardino, Calif. (December 2015), Orlando, Fla. (June 2016), St. Etienne, France (July 2016), and Quetta, Pakistan (August 2016). Increasingly, DIY terrorists have used ordinary cars or trucks in their attacks. On July 14, 2016, Mohamed Lahouaiej-Bouhlel used a delivery truck to mow down 86 people celebrating Bastille Day in Nice, France. On November 28, 2016, Abdul-Razak Ali Artan ran down several students at Ohio State University with his vehicle, then stabbed several others. In London, Khalid Masood drove a car into pedestrians on Westminster Bridge on March 22, 2017, killing five and injuring 45 others. Then on June 3, 2017, three attackers drove a car into pedestrians on London Bridge. And on August 12, 2017, James Fields, Jr. rammed his car into a crowd of anti-racism protestors in Charlottesville, Va., killing a young woman.

The good news, if there is any, is that most of the "wannabe terrorists" who try to carry out their own DIY attacks are amateurs, incapable of harming anyone but themselves. Some do not have the resources necessary to succeed, while others make key mistakes in the planning or execution of their attacks, resulting in an overall high failure rate among those "inspired" to do this kind of thing. Often, these attackers are limited to weapons of opportunity: guns, knives, vehicles, basic explosives, etc. rather than the kind of sophisticated suicide vests or improvised explosive devices engineered by al-Qaeda, Islamic State, or their affiliates.

Within the ideological sphere of global jihadists, this trend of DIY terrorism involves a relatively low investment by a group's leaders basically limited to producing and disseminating materials (primarily online) that are intended to provide instruction and motivation for these kinds of attacks. However, to date these attacks have had only a limited impact, particularly compared to the more lethal threat of well-trained cadres of terrorist operatives with battlefield experience in Afghanistan, Iraq, Syria, and elsewhere. It remains highly unlikely that DIY terrorist attacks will help the global jihadist movement achieve any significant goals or objectives. But regardless of ideological category or potential impact, we can also expect that this trend of terrorism will be a security challenge for many years to come.

RESPONDING TO TERRORISM

Of course, our journey through the study of terrorism would be incomplete if we did not focus some attention on the ways in which governments have responded to the terrorist threat, and the ways in which terrorist groups or movements have ended. For example, in some cases a terrorist group's leaders have been captured or killed. In Sri Lanka, the military launched an offensive in 2009 that finally defeated the Liberation Tigers of Tamil Eelam (LTTE), the ethnonationalist group that had caused death and destruction there for over two decades. Meanwhile, in other instances the ideology of the terrorists failed to resonate among successive generations, limiting their ability to attract support and recruits among a population. This was particularly notable among anarchist and left-wing terrorist movements of the past century. Some terrorists (like the Abu Sayyaf Group in the Philippines) became more interested in profitable kinds of criminal activities, which eventually eroded the community support upon which they were originally dependent.[6]

In several cases, terrorist groups have abandoned their armed struggle and embraced a political process. For example, after the Good Friday Agreement was signed in April 1998, Northern Ireland finally saw the end of political violence. Well, not entirely: a few months later; on August 15, 1998, a car bomb packed with 500 lbs. of explosives detonated in Omagh[7] and since then, Republican dissident groups have carried out a spate of terrorist attacks, including bombings in Londonderry and other parts of the country. But despite these attempts to demonstrate the "spoiler" strategic logic of terrorist attacks, it's at least a lot quieter these days in Northern Ireland than it was for many decades.[8]

Similarly, in Spain—as described in Lecture 8—the Basque terrorist group ETA (Euzkadi ta Askatasuna, which means "Basque Homeland and Freedom" in the Basque language),[9] declared a permanent ceasefire in January 2011 and the creation of a new political party called Sortu.[10] Then in April 2017, the group announced it would hand over all its weapons and explosives to local authorities, and in May 2018, the group issued a formal announcement that it had disbanded permanently. These and other developments indicate that we may finally be seeing a new commitment among the Basque communities toward engaging in the Spanish political process.

And in Colombia, a terrorist movement founded in 1964—the Revolutionary Armed Forces of Colombia (*Fuerzas Armadas Revolucionarias de Colombia*, or FARC)—announced a permanent ceasefire in 2016. In December of that year the Colombian government officially ratified the peace accord, and in June 2017 the group provided detailed information for where the United Nations monitoring team could locate their weapons storage bunkers. Then in September of that year, FARC's leaders announced the formation of a new political party and their intention to participate in the 2018 Colombian elections. Interestingly, they kept the same acronym, but changed their name to the Common Alternative Revolutionary Force (*Fuerza Alternativa Revolucionaria del Común,* or FARC), and their party's logo is now a red rose.

Overall, understanding the goals, decision-making, and operational challenges of terrorist groups can help counterterrorism professionals find ways to accelerate the demise of terrorist groups like these. Furthermore, there exists an increasing wealth of scholarly research on the strategies and practices used by governments in their response to terrorism (sometimes successful, sometimes not), often addressing questions of effectiveness, efficiency, and ethics. Much of this research is unfortunately ignored in most Hollywood portrayals of counterterrorism, which leads many in the general public to have a lot of misperceptions about how simple or easy it must be.

Alex Schmid defines counterterrorism as "a proactive effort to prevent, deter, and combat politically motivated violence directed at civilian and non-combatant targets, by the use of a broad spectrum of response measures—law enforcement, political, psychological, social, economic and paramilitary."[11] The complexities of counterterrorism are illustrated by the myriad ways in which these different response measures can be used, either separately or combined as components of a comprehensive security strategy. As a result, there exists no universal theory on "what works" and what does not in counterterrorism. Further, there is often a danger of political bias in research and analysis of counterterrorism, creating even greater diversity of opinions and disagreements in the scholarly literature. And when movies and television shows give the impression that countering terrorism merely involves "the good guys" finding and killing "the bad guys," it creates unreasonable expectations among the members of a society about the immediate effectiveness of any counterterrorism strategy.

What we do know is that because terrorism is a very contextual phenomenon, a counterterrorism strategy must be tailored to address the specific contexts, actions, and impacts of a particular terrorist threat. Further, there are specific attributes of a nation's power that can (and often should) be brought to bear against a terrorist threat: the use of force by military and law enforcement, and the supporting roles of diplomatic, information, economic, financial and intelligence activities.[12] And decades of research also show that none of these elements of national power can succeed on their own; as Korb and Boorstin argue, the integration of these elements is critical to the success of any counterterrorism effort.[13]

According to the 2002 *U.S. National Security Strategy*, "we must make use of every tool in our arsenal—military power, better homeland defenses, law enforcement, intelligence, and vigorous efforts to cut off terrorist financing."[14] The 2006 *U.S. National Strategy for Countering Terrorism* echoes this perspective: "the paradigm for combating terrorism now involves the application of all elements of our national power and influence. Not only do we employ military power, we use diplomatic, financial, intelligence, and law enforcement activities to protect the Homeland and extend our defenses, disrupt terrorist operations, and deprive our enemies of what they need to operate and survive."[15] And the 2011 *National Strategy for Counterterrorism* also carried this theme forward by declaring its intent to integrate "the capabilities and authorities of each department and agency, ensuring the right tools are applied at the right time to the right situation in a manner that is consistent with U.S. laws."[16]

The synthesis of these various dimensions of counterterrorism was also highlighted recently in a Brookings Doha Center report on the Islamic State (IS), which recommended that the regional and international response to the threat of IS should include "a series of policies aimed at 1) countering IS's financial strength and ability to fund the provision of governance and social services to civilians; 2) neutralizing IS's capacity for military mobility and the rapid re-deployment of manpower; 3) collecting and acting on intelligence relating to IS's senior leadership and military command and control structure; 4) weakening and delegitimizing IS's effective use of social media for recruitment and information operations; and 5) seeking to stabilize the existing conflict dynamics in both Syria and Iraq."[17]

Overall, integration of all the elements of national power is essential. However, it can be argued that none is more crucial to the success or failure of counterterrorism than intelligence. Unfortunately, there is some confusion about what is and is not considered intelligence, so let me say a few words about that before continuing. First of all, the purpose of intelligence is to reduce uncertainty about one's adversaries (and sometimes allies), in order to gain a decision advantage over them[18] (particularly in areas of strategy, operations, and tactics). Information is gathered for this purpose from a very broad range of activities, from human interaction to technology, and then the analysis of this information is conveyed to policymakers and decision-makers in the form of intelligence reports. Intelligence should not be viewed as predicting the future. It is neither a "best guess" based on a "gut feeling," nor is it perfect and infallible. In addition to mistakes (which all humans make), inaccurate intelligence is often the result of intentional efforts by our adversaries to mislead and deceive.

Accurate, high-quality intelligence is absolutely critical for determining where, when, and how to apply other instruments of national power. Effective action in military, diplomatic, law enforcement, financial interdiction, and all other areas of counterterrorism requires deep levels of knowledge, insight, and understanding—the intended products of any national intelligence service. Further, as explained in the beginning of this lecture, terrorism is a context-specific phenomenon. Thus, the success or failure of a counterterrorism strategy is often highly dependent on understanding and adapting to situational factors. For example, as research by Gregory Miller revealed, the attributes of a terrorist group impact the relative success of various counterterrorism policies.[19] There can be no one-size-fits-all approach to countering such a complex phenomenon as terrorism. A government must first determine *what kind of terrorist threat it is dealing with*—is it domestic or global in orientation? What do we know about the terrorists' motivating grievances, funding sources, support networks, leaders, operatives, and capabilities? What ideological category does it fall into (for example, left-wing, ethnonationalist, religious, right-wing, environmental extremism, etc.)? These are questions that must be answered before determining how and where a nation's resources should be committed.

A country's political climate will also affect the formulation, implementation, and assessment of counterterrorism strategies. The tendency to politicize certain components of a counterterrorism strategy (for example, surveillance and intelligence collection) can make objective assessment of successes or failures all the more difficult. Thus, when integrating all the elements of national power toward a comprehensive counterterrorism effort, we must be sure to pause and reflect on how well we understand our own intentions, capabilities, and biases about our enemies. One thing is certain: there is no place for prejudice, bloodthirst, or bigotry in effective counterterrorism.[20] Intelligence analysts, diplomats, policymakers, law enforcement, military personnel, and others involved in counterterrorism must be committed to objectivity, self-discipline, integrity, and attention to nuances and details of whatever terrorist threat their country is confronting.

As someone who has studied terrorism for many years now, I am an optimist; I have to be, in order to keep my sanity amid the dark realities of the world that I have

Figure 19.1: September 11 tribute lights. U.S. Coast Guard Photo by Public Affairs 2nd Class Mike Hvozda.

described within the pages of this book. Like many of you, I will never forget the attacks of September 11, 2001, nor will I underestimate the lethal threat posed by members of the global Salafi-jihadist movement. But I have also come to recognize the value of resilience as a powerful tool that societies can use to thwart the efforts of even the most well-resourced and motivated terrorists. As you've surely noticed by now, my perspective about terrorism differs considerably from those fear-mongering types who would have you believe there is a terrorist around every corner, waiting to strike. Instead, my understanding of terrorism gives me confidence that the global jihadists will someday, perhaps in our distant future, be nothing more than something we read about in history books.

The death of Osama bin Laden was clearly not a crippling blow to al-Qaeda, but it did inflict some damage to the global jihadist network. Really, all of al-Qaeda's remaining core leaders will eventually die, and when they do their replacements will probably be respected veteran jihadist fighters, but will not have the same mythical saga as the "founders" of the group, and as a result will be less able to influence others in the Muslim world. Of course, al-Qaeda's global "presence" is already relatively shallow and is under increasing financial pressures. Further, because al-Qaeda–related attacks killed an average of eight Muslims for every one non-Muslim during the 10 years immediately following the 9/11 attacks,[21] there was rapidly decreasing support in the Muslim world for the Salafi-jihadist ideology. But then along came Abu al-Baghdadi and the Islamic State, and we saw a resurgence in both foreign fighter recruitment and in do-it-yourself attacks described in Lecture 15. And yet, the Islamic State has now lost virtually all the territory it once controlled, and with it the group has lost significant legitimacy and influence within the broader jihadist movement. By early January 2018, the Iraqi government was claiming that its war against the Islamic State was over, Russia was announcing a partial withdrawal of its troops from Syria, and counterterrorism officials in both Europe and the U.S. were focusing significantly more attention on the flow of militants fleeing the conflict and returning home, or migrating to other conflict zones like Libya.[22]

The decline of the Islamic State's power over the past two years raises questions about whether there may have been too much hyperbole and hysteria about the threat to the U.S. homeland posed by this group. For example, after a 2016 attack in Brussels, Belgium, then-presidential candidate Ted Cruz called for stepped-up police patrols in Muslim neighborhoods in the United States, while the Department of State issued a warning against traveling to Europe. But the worst examples of overreaction in the

U.S. were seen among news media, who have often fueled a perception of the terrorist threat that is not supported by real evidence. As Stephen Walt argued in 2016, news media know that "hyping the danger will keep people reading, listening, and watching . . . [but] airing melodramatic news coverage makes the Islamic State far more dangerous than it really is."[23]

This leads me to my final thoughts about counterterrorism for today, which center on the critically important role of resilience in defeating terrorist movements. As explained early in this lecture series, terrorism at its core is an attempt to use violence and fear to influence a population in ways the terrorist group feels will help them achieve their goals and objectives. As Brian Jenkins explains, "the objective of terrorism is to create fear"[24] and they want to use our fear to their advantage—if we are fearful enough, the terrorists can use violence and the threat of violence to coerce our behavior. And unfortunately, after studying and teaching in this field for almost two decades, it strikes me that people seem more afraid of terrorism today than they were in the months immediately following the attacks of September 11, 2001. Yet the evidence shows that between 2001 and 2013, the likelihood of an American being killed in the U.S. by a terrorist attack was less than one in 56 million; in comparison, the chance of drowning in a bathtub was one in 1 million, and the chance of being the victim of an ordinary homicide in the U.S. was one in 20,000.[25] As noted in Lecture 2, there were far more terrorist attacks during the 1970s in the U.S. and Europe than there are today. But these risk assessment data and historical facts are largely ignored in contemporary discussions about terrorism.

When a society steadfastly refuses to be coerced by threats and violence, the terrorists fail to achieve anything. And the truth is, we know from historical evidence that the failure of a terrorist group is by far its most likely outcome. But it seems that in the current U.S. political environment, politicians are able to benefit from exploiting that fear, in some cases even with the most authoritarian instincts and awful prejudices. A variety of media also benefit from exploiting that fear, attracting viewers, building and sustaining a base of followers who buy into the narrative that terrorism is the most important security threat we all face. Within this environment, rational voices who—based on a study of the history of terrorism, and a research-based understanding of terrorist radicalization—call for us to keep terrorism in proper perspective are shouted down by both the fearful and those exploiting the fear to their advantage.

My perspective about community resilience is informed by watching how the British responded to recent terrorist attacks in London. Here we have a country, and

particularly a major city, that has endured a generational campaign of nationalist terrorism (IRA/PIRA) and more recently a campaign of Islamist-jihadist attacks. And
yet their continued resolve, their refusal to be coerced by terrorists, is worth taking to
heart. After the worst of those jihadist attacks (on July 7, 2005), the Queen of England
visited hospitals to meet victims and express sympathy. During a visit to the Royal
London Hospital, she stated, "Those who perpetrate these brutal acts against innocent
people should know that they will not change our way of life."[26] And indeed, the trains
throughout London were operating at normal capacity the very next day, people were
back to work, the economy did not grind to a halt, people did not stop traveling to or
through London. More noteworthy, very few political leaders in the U.K. made any
effort to try and exacerbate or exploit the fear of terrorism in ways that we have seen
here in the U.S. Most respectable media outlets followed the same norm, reporting the
facts as they became known instead of blaring headlines about impending doom. And
after the most recent jihadist attacks in London (like those described in Lecture 15),
we have again seen a similarly high level of resilience, an adamant refusal to be afraid,
and little interest in trying to profit from the fear of terrorism.

In Germany, too, we see a level of calm and resilience that perhaps our American
society can learn from. As noted in Lecture 9, Germans suffered a campaign of terrorism from the late 1960s through the 1970s, mainly by the left-wing Red Army Faction
(also known as the Baader-Meinhof Group). But the more recent terrorist attacks in
that country have been orchestrated by jihadists or by right-wing extremists. After a
series of four attacks within one week in July 2016, the spokesman for the Munich
police made a public appeal: "Give us the chance to report facts. Don't speculate, don't
copy from each other."[27] Most politicians and media services heeded his advice. Only
a small handful of fringe politicians—like the leader of the anti-immigrant Alternative for Germany party—tried to capitalize on the attacks, and was immediately condemned on social and broadcast media.[28]

Personally, I think each of us has a choice to make, though I recognize it's a very
difficult choice for most of us. On the one hand, we can choose to be fearful—as I
noted earlier, this is exactly what terrorists want. Apparently, being fearful is what
many politicians and media in the U.S. want as well. Fear is a very powerful emotion.
But we would do well to pause and ask ourselves: When we fear for our own personal
safety, or for the security of those we love and care about, how does that impact our
decision-making? And how can those decisions be manipulated by media and political
elites? Furthermore, how can we ever get to a place of comfort and relaxation where

that fear is no longer warranted, particularly if some members of society don't seem to want that to happen? Imposing new security procedures, physical barriers, displays of armed force, policies targeting members of a population deemed a threat based on demographic attributes—these all give the impression of "making us safer" but in 250 years of terrorist history, there is virtually no evidence that such things actually diminish the ability of terrorists to make a society afraid of further attacks.

On the other hand, a society like ours can choose to reject any and all attempts to make us fearful. We can refuse to be terrorized, by the terrorists or by those who might try to benefit from exploiting fear. We can examine the evidence (nonpartisan, factual data on terrorism is plentiful if you look for it), and study the true nature of terrorism in all its forms. When we recognize what this evidence shows—that terrorism is a rare event, especially when compared to the many other tragic and criminal things that could happen to us any day of the year—we have strong reason to question the intentions of those who apparently want us to fear. When each of us actively refuses to allow fear to coerce our behavior, this can strengthen our community resilience. Emergency preparedness and a sense of shared responsibility also strengthen our communities in ways that help us respond effectively in the event something happens (from natural disasters to terrorist attacks).

The historical record reveals how communities that are resilient, that refuse to be terrorized, will never be defeated by terrorists. As Stephen Walt noted, "terrorists cannot defeat us; we can only defeat ourselves."[29] If we embrace this perspective, putting terrorism in its proper place instead of exacerbating and overhyping the threat, the future will never look as bleak and scary as certain media or politicians would have us believe. With that in mind, let me wrap up this final lecture with some comments about the future (or more accurate, potential futures) of terrorism.

THE FUTURE OF TERRORISM

To begin with, the future doesn't really look that promising for terrorists. As we noted earlier in these lectures, terrorist groups have rarely achieved any of their intended goals. They have not brought down any national economies or political regimes. Even those that have been around the longest (IRA/PIRA, ETA, FARC, etc.) failed to acquire the power to make significant change. A colleague of mine, Max Abrahms, has in several of his research articles illustrated how the use of terrorism almost never succeeds.[30] So, will the scourge of terrorism just go away in time? Or, are terrorists fatally blinded by their own arrogance and perceived superiority—especially if they are motivated by a religiously-based ideology? Unfortunately, when we reflect on the broad history of terrorism, we see that it has been as much a part of the human condition as many other kinds of political conflict and violent crime, which leads to the conclusion that terrorism does have a future.

The fact that terrorism will continue to be a part of the human experience raises some questions for which there are relatively few answers. For example, will the Salafi-jihadist ideology be the leading motivation for terrorism 20–30 years from now? If it is, why? And if not, what will take its place as the most prominent ideological motivation of terrorist attacks? Will the future see incremental changes in terrorist tactics, or sudden new innovations similar to 9/11? What kinds of analysis help us anticipate future events?

In looking at the first question, I do believe that the Salafi-jihadist ideology will very likely be the leading motivation for terrorism 20–30 years from now. The reasons for this include several ideological and contextual factors. First, the ideological roots of Salafism and global jihadist ideologies are deeper and more sacred than the roots of many other ideologies (see Lecture 14). Believers of this ideology find theological resonance and perceived legitimacy in historical and contemporary events, from crusades of centuries ago to more recent conflicts in Muslim countries like Afghanistan and Iraq. They point to a perceived illegitimacy of apostate regimes in places like Egypt, Saudi Arabia, and Syria, and also argue that a secularizing, globalization agenda is being imposed by the West as a direct threat to Islamic law, traditions, and religious devotion. Further, the Salafi-jihadist ideology in particular is reinforced by deep animosity between Sunni and Shiite communities, punctuated by periods of bloodshed for well over two decades, including in countries like Iraq, Syria, Pakistan, Yemen, and others.

The central driving force behind the spread of this ideology is a powerful vision of the future, involving the re-establishment of an Islamist caliphate. The supporters of this vision see a caliphate as the only means by which legitimate governance and justice can be achieved for the Muslim world. This caliphate is seen by true believers as the physical manifestation of God's will. They believe this vision has been abandoned by apostates, and is being actively obstructed by infidels, enemies of God. With this kind of vision in mind, there is probably no possibility of reaching a negotiated compromise with the true believers.

Meanwhile, we know that strong Salafist networks have been established worldwide. In some cases, wealthy patrons in the Gulf (like Saudi Arabia) have helped promote and support the spread of Salafism. Now, we know that most Salafists reject the political agenda of the global jihadists; however, these networks would prove valuable to the global jihadists by laying the ideological foundations for attracting new recruits to wherever Jihadist-related conflict emerges next, and for attracting new sources of funding and logistical support. And finally, we know that over the past few years the Islamic State has worked to create an external operations network to promote and facilitate attacks in Europe (France, Belgium, Turkey, Russia, etc.).

In addition to these ideological dimensions, we also have to consider some contextual enablers, like the emerging "youth bulge" in the Middle East and North Africa coupled with economic stagnation and resource scarcity, resulting in limited opportunities to achieve a person's aspirations for a better life. These trends will only exacerbate longstanding grievances about local corruption, nepotism, and lack of fairness that are unlikely to be resolved soon. As well, some of the major unresolved conflicts that fuel animosity and unrest in the Muslim world are unlikely to end anytime soon. For example, future acts of terrorism could be motivated by the Israel-Palestinian conflict, the conflict that simmers beneath the surface between Saudi Arabia and Iran, or continued animosity between Pakistan and India.

And finally, we will certainly continue to see the global expansion of international communication technologies that are used to spread ideological inspiration and tactical knowledge, especially operational instructions. Since terrorism is largely an idea-driven phenomenon, this global communication technology dimension brings to Salafi-jihadism a sustaining power that previous kinds of terrorism never had. With these ideological and contextual factors as a backdrop, global Salafi-jihadism has become a network of jihadist networks, individuals, wannabes, ideological entrepreneurs, seekers, bomb-makers, facilitators, financiers, and many others. When looking at all these issues cumulatively, it leads to the conclusion that a network this complex, with ideological roots this deep and with so many different potential enabling environments, will not just vanish within the next 20 years.

Instead, this amorphous, decentralized structure may allow the movement to adapt organically to changes in the global operating environment, and to sustain and regenerate itself over multiple decades. It also encourages long-term competition between the various affiliates of al-Qaeda and the Islamic State, which will be competing for recruits, resources, and relevance over the next 20 years. This intra-network competition could very well lead to the rise of new affiliate groups for both al-Qaeda and the Islamic State, or perhaps an entirely new "brand" of global jihadism will emerge and capture the hearts and minds of those who believe in these ideological goals and objectives.

Meanwhile, beyond the Salafi-jihadist threat it would not surprise me if other ideologies also inspire new or renewed kinds of terrorist attacks. For example, when we reflect on David Rapoport's framework regarding the historical waves of terrorism, it's noteworthy that ecoterrorism has not yet had a wave. So, maybe we'll see new kinds of environmental terrorists (for example, a new Earth First! or Earth Liberation Front), launching attacks against corporate targets whom they accuse of damaging the environment. These extremists would likely be animated by the increasing physical effects of climate change and global warming, such as diminishing food and water supplies in some countries (with drought and famine in the most extreme cases); coral reef bleaching, glacial melting, increasing threats of flooding to low-lying islands, an increasing frequency of extreme weather events worldwide, and so forth. Additional sources of anger among environmentalists could include deforestation, toxic chemical dumping, and the masses of plastic waste floating in our oceans. Really, there are so many things today in our natural environment that could motivate anger, particularly among the youth of tomorrow, and this anger could lead some individuals to embrace a violent course of action. For example, what if some of them begin launching dirty bomb attacks against oil refineries, like at the Port of Houston, with the intention of causing a critical blow to the U.S. oil sector, sending oil prices skyrocketing and creating new demand for alternative energy sources? Perhaps they would begin attacking facilities that manufacture plastic bags and water bottles, or supermarkets where large quantities of these things are sold, in order to change the behavior of consumers regarding such products?

Or perhaps the future will bring a wave of terrorism associated with animal rights activists. Could we see some kind of group like the Animal Liberation Front (ALF) becoming ultra-violent, launching an all-out war to save dolphins, for example? In this scenario, a small cell of ALF members, enraged by the documentary *The Cove*, could begin attacking Japanese political and economic targets worldwide as well as SeaWorld and similar kinds of resorts. Or maybe we could see some kind of hybrid "act local" movement, in which members of ALF merge with anti-globalization activists or others to form violent groups that launch terrorist attacks against large commercial farms, or food engineering firms like Monsanto, or factories and research institutes that specialize in genetic modification of foods and animals.

Or maybe we'll see the emergence of economically oriented "defending the underprivileged" terrorists, motivated by extreme anger at structural disadvantages linked to globalization, tax breaks for corporations, and increasing concentration of wealth among a super-wealthy, while the gap widens between haves and have-nots. Certainly we have seen a lot of anti-elite angry rhetoric in recent years. Furthermore, it is widely agreed that underprivileged populations tend to be the ones who suffer the most from the kinds of environmental degradation that animates extremists like the ecoterrorists mentioned earlier. We may also see an escalation of ethnonationalist terror attacks by Kurdish separatists, perhaps even sometimes targeting the West. We can certainly expect the Kurds to have some major frustration at the continued denial of their dreams for independent statehood despite several years of Kurdish fighters working and sacrificing alongside Western coalition forces to defeat the Islamic State. We could also see an escalation of separatist attacks related to the situation in Kashmir, raising the threat (however unlikely) of a nuclear exchange between Pakistan and India.

Meanwhile, within the U.S. and Europe, it is entirely possible that today's rising nationalism, isolationism, and anti-globalization will become increasingly violent. Perhaps we'll see terrorist attacks against multinational corporations, foreign-owned banks, franchises, international university branches, or other entities that are perceived by locals as a threat to their country's sovereignty. On a similar note, the recent actions of the so-called Antifa movement could escalate. Incidents like what we saw in Berkeley, Charlottesville, Chicago, Portland, and Seattle in 2017 could perhaps encourage a violent response by right-wing extremists, sparking a campaign of domestic terrorist attacks by and against both ends of the political spectrum that may last for many years. It's also possible that the increase of "othering" and white nationalism in mainstream discourse will lead to a rise in attacks against immigrant populations or ethnic minority populations in Europe and North America. We've already seen some examples of this in recent years. Over time, in reaction to those attacks, we may see immigrant communities or ethnic minority groups deciding to use terrorism against majority population targets as a form of revenge. Just like we might see the emergence of new Shiite revenge terrorist groups targeting Sunni communities in the Middle East and Asia, we could see a rise of immigrant vs. anti-immigrant terrorist attacks in the U.S. and Europe. In essence, an escalation of terrorist violence between different segments of society is a very possible outcome of the kinds of "othering" we see today.

Beyond the dimension of ideological motivations, I'm sure that in the future we will want to devise new ideas about how to prevent or constrain future technological innovations by terrorists. For example, it is very likely we will see an increase in the use of drones to remotely deliver IEDs to targets. We have already seen Islamic State terrorists in Syria do this on a few occasions,[31] and multiple sources already indicate Hizballah has this capability.[32] As the skills for piloting drones meld with video gaming, smartphones, and virtual reality headsets, I can imagine a day when this kind of terrorist attack would become quite popular among young tech-savvy terrorists. Similarly, it's probably only a matter of time before we begin to see robots programmed to carry out terrorist attacks, either autonomously or with limited human control, particularly as robots and remote controlled devices become increasingly cheaper to buy.

Other areas of technology that interest me from a security perspective include the potential for terrorists to use cyberattacks as a way to amplify the fear and terror impact of kinetic attacks. These could include hacking into public utilities, like power stations, and causing them to shut down. Attacks on certain kinds of critical infrastructure could even turn them into weapons of their own. For example, Hurricane Katrina demonstrated how the failure of key levees can have a devastating effect on New Orleans. Terrorists with high explosives could destroy those levees and the deluge of water could cause mass destruction, while they also use misinformation about evacuation instructions to cause further chaos. Other examples could include a cyberattack against a dam in order to flood a nearby populated area, or shutting down the sewage system of a major city, where raw sewage in the streets could produce an outbreak of cholera or any number of other diseases. And there are concerns about the potential for a major cyberattack that causes a global financial market meltdown.

But cyberspace also allows the dissemination of misinformation, fake videos, hacked websites, and Twitter feeds used to manipulate perceptions, amplifying fear and panic before and after a terrorist attack. We are already seeing examples of how Facebook Live, Periscope, and other social media apps could be used for live streaming of terrorist attacks. In the future, it's possible that we'll see a group incorporate some kind of interactive potential, a sort of "choose the next victim" opportunity to encourage virtual participation in terrorism from the comfort of one's home.

I am also very concerned about the future potential for dual-use chemicals to be used by terrorists. We have already seen examples of this kind of WMD terrorism in Syria and Iraq, where Islamic State has allegedly used chlorine and sulfur mustard agents in dozens of attacks.[33] Throughout the U.S. there are thousands of industrial facilities where various kinds of chemicals are used to manufacture pesticides, cleaning agents, textiles, plastics, and much more. A terrorist might decide to attack a chemical storage depot, for example, in order to amplify the impact of the initial explosion by creating a toxic cloud that drifts into a nearby community. And in addition to the many facilities where such chemicals are found, we must also focus on the security of the trains and trucks that transport these chemicals every day.

And of course there are widespread concerns about the threat of biological weapons as well. For example, we know there are scientists working in areas of synthetic biology, like molecular manipulation, or new forms of potentially lethal biological agents. Is there potential for terrorists to take advantage of a laboratory accident, or an incident in which experiments go wrong? The scientific community is already concerned about the kind of "insider threat" portrayed by the Hollywood movie *12 Monkeys*, in which a lethal virus is unleashed by a biology lab assistant motivated by a belief in the apocalypse and a desire to destroy the human race. Guarding against these kinds of threats is something for which the government has only limited capabilities, particularly because most of the new and innovative biotechnology developments are taking place in the private sector. You can expect companies to screen those they hire to ensure scientific competence, but given America's protection for civil rights, liberties, and privacy, it is trickier to make sure those they hire aren't influenced by some extreme religious or political ideologies. A similar concern, of course, is found among companies that own and operate civilian nuclear power plants and research facilities across the U.S. and Europe.

These are just some random projections of what we might want to anticipate for the future based on a cursory analysis of history and current trends in terrorism. At the very least, our expectations for the future should be framed by what we know about the capabilities of modern terrorist organizations, and the many ways in which technologies are evolving. We can never underestimate the capabilities of smart, motivated individuals to come up with new and innovative ways to cause death and destruction. If we fall into the trap of thinking that terrorists are crazy or stupid, we are setting ourselves up for something awful in the future.

SUMMARY

So to sum up this brief look at the future, we have to keep in mind that there is a long history of terrorism, and everything seems to indicate that there is a future for terrorism as well, unfortunately. However, it is a future that we can manage successfully, through interagency coordination, international cooperation, sharing information throughout our intelligence and law enforcement communities, and investing in robust counterideology efforts. We should also try to ensure a moral and ethical legitimacy in everything the United States and other nations do to counter terror-ism. How we fight terrorism has a significant impact on perceptions of justice and legitimacy. When negative, perceptions in these areas can animate terrorist groups and supporters. As we have seen throughout history, a government's reaction to terrorism can be just as damaging as the attack itself. Our government leaders must have vision, nuance, vigilance, and an ability to adapt to the situation. And above all, we must avoid doing things that undermine our own resilience, as a society that refuses to be coerced through violence and fear will never be defeated by terrorists.

Earlier in this lecture, I mentioned how rare it is to find a group that has achieved its core strategic goals and objectives by using terrorism. However, despite the his-torical record of failure, I'm pretty confident that terrorism is going to be with us for the foreseeable future. It is unlikely that there will ever be a time when we don't have some group or individual who wants the power to make changes, and is convinced that violence is the only means to obtaining that power. Of course, to paraphrase for-mer Secretary of Defense Donald Rumsfeld, there are many things we know we don't know, and things we don't even know we don't know. For example, are there angry or marginalized groups in the United States or elsewhere today who have not engaged in terrorist activity, but under certain circumstances might embrace an agenda of political violence? Who are they, where are they, and under what circumstances could such a group begin a campaign of terrorism? As we engage these questions in the future, we must be open to answers that are unanticipated. Terrorism is, after all, a type of human behavior, and we surely know that human behavior is not always predictable.

Finally, let's wrap up on a relatively positive note. I believe that government agen-cies within the United States are doing better every year at cooperating with each other and with their foreign counterparts. Every day, millions of law enforcement, military, and intelligence professionals worldwide are working together in the relentless pursuit of terrorist leaders and to diminish their ability to organize or inspire future attacks. I also believe there are more people today than ever before who are interested in learning about the true nature of terrorism, rather than accepting at face value the superficial and often hysterical portrayal of the terrorist threat to our country. In turn, this learn-ing will contribute to a new level of resilience in our society. Instead of focusing exclu-sively on terrorists, we can also attack the terror by actively engaging citizens in their own preparedness and response.[34] Together, we will find new and increasingly effective ways to deal with the problem of terrorism, in whatever form it presents itself in the future. For now, best wishes for a safe and enjoyable rest of your day.

QUESTIONS FOR DISCUSSION

- Does terrorism have a future? If so, why?
- If terrorist groups have so very rarely achieved their stated objectives, why won't this problem just go away eventually?
- What kinds of analysis can help us anticipate future events?
- Will the future see incremental changes in terrorist tactics, or sudden new innovations like 9/11?
- What can we do to reduce the chances of terrorist attacks in the future?

RECOMMENDED READING

Abrahms, Max. "Why Terrorism Does Not Work." *International Security* 31, no. 2 (2006).

Cronin, Audrey. "How Al-Qaeda Ends: The Demise and Decline of Terrorist Groups." *International Security* 31 (2006).

Forest, James J. F. "An Introduction to the Study of Counterterrorism." In *Essentials of Counterterrorism*. Edited by James J. F. Forest (Westport, CT: Praeger, 2015): 1–32.

Gartenstein-Ross, Daveed. "Don't Get Cocky, America: Al-Qaeda is Still Deadly without Osama bin Laden." In *Terrorism and Counterterrorism*. Edited by Russell Howard and Bruce Hoffman. New York: McGraw-Hill, 2011.

Hoffman, Bruce. "Terrorism Today and Tomorrow." Chapter 9. In *Inside Terrorism*. New York: Columbia University Press, 2006.

Holmes, Jennifer. "Developing and Implementing a Counterterrorism Policy in a Liberal Democracy." In *Countering Terrorism and Insurgency in the 21st Century*. Vol. 1. Edited by James J. F. Forest. Westport, CT: Praeger, 2007.

Jenkins, Brian Michael. "The Land of the Fearful, or the Home of the Brave?" In The Long Shadow of 9/11: America's Response to Terrorism. Edited by Brian Michael Jenkins and John Paul Godges. Santa Monica, CA: RAND Corporation, 2011. Pp. 195–208.

Lansford, Tom. "Multinational Intelligence Cooperation." In *Countering Terrorism and Insurgency in the 21st Century*. Vol. 1. Edited by James J. F. Forest. Westport, CT: Praeger, 2007.

Liepman, Andrew and Philip Mudd. "Lessons from the Fifteen-Year Counterterrorism Campaign." *CTC Sentinel* 9, no. 10 (October 25, 2016). https://www.ctc.usma.edu/posts/october-2016.

Malvesti, Michele L. and Frances Fragos Townsend. "Special Operations Forces and the Raid against Bin Ladin: Policymaker Considerations in Combating Terrorism." In *Terrorism and Counterterrorism*. Edited by Russell Howard and Bruce Hoffman. New York: McGraw-Hill, 2011.

Miller, Gregory. "Confronting Terrorisms: Group Motivation and Successful State Policies." *Terrorism and Political Violence* 19, no. 3 (2007).

Moghadam, Assaf. "An Al-Qaeda Balance Sheet." *Military and Strategic Affairs* 2, no. 2 (2010).

Neumann, Peter R. "Options and Strategies for Countering Online Radicalization in the United States." *Studies in Conflict and Terrorism* 36, no. 6 (2013): 431–59.

Clapper, James R. *Statement for the Record on the Worldwide Threat Assessment of the U.S. Intelligence Committee for the Senate Committee on Armed Services.* March 20, 2011).

Stern, Jessica. "Deradicalization or Disengagement of Terrorists: Is it Possible?" In *Future Challenges in National Security and Law.* Edited by Peter Berkowitz. Stanford, CA: Hoover Institution Press, 2010.

Szrom, Charlie and Chris Harnisch. "Al-Qaeda's Operating Environments: A New Approach to the War on Terror." In *Terrorism and Counterterrorism.* Edited by Russell Howard and Bruce Hoffman. New York: McGraw-Hill, 2011.

U.K. Intelligence and Security Committee. "Could 7/7 Have Been Prevented?" Report from House of Commons Presented to Parliament. May 2009. http://goo.gl/fK2FS.

Walt, Stephen. "Monsters of Our Own Imaginings." *Foreign Policy* (March 24, 2016). http://atfp .co/1pK4IU5.

Warrick, Joby. "Inside the Economic War Against the Islamic State." *Washington Post*, December 31, 2016. https://goo.gl/IyZTCP.

Zirakzadeh, Cyrus Ernesto. "From Revolutionary Dreams to Organizational Fragmentation: Disputes over Violence Within ETA and Sendero Luminoso." *Terrorism and Political Violence* 14, no. 4 (2002).

WEBSITES

Center for Terrorism and Security Studies, UMass Lowell
http://www.uml.edu/ctss

Perspectives on Terrorism
http://www.terrorismanalysts.com/pt

Sentinel—a journal by the Combating Terrorism Center at West Point
https://ctc.usma.edu/ctc-sentinel/

NOTES

1. Graeme Wood, *The Way of the Strangers* (New York: Random House, 2016): 120.

2. U.S. Government Accountability Office, "Countering Violent Extremism," Washington, DC (April 2017), https://www.gao.gov/assets/690/683984.pdf.

3. David Neiwert et al. *Homegrown Terror.* Center for Investigative Reporting Reveal (June 22, 2017), https://apps.revealnews.org/homegrown-terror/.

4. Charles Kurzman and David Schanzer, *Law Enforcement Assessment of the Violent Extremist Threat*. Triangle Center on Homeland Security, Durham, NC (June 25, 2015), http://bit.ly/1oUeKBJ.

5. Caitlin Dickson, "Sovereign Citizens are America's Top Cop Killers," *Daily Beast*, November 25, 2014, http://thebea.st/2H2RlHJ.

6. See Audrey Cronin, "How Al Qaida Ends: The Demise and Decline of Terrorist Groups," *International Security* 31, no. 1 (Summer 2006):7–48; and Seth Jones and Martin Libiski, *How Terrorist Groups End* (Santa Monica, CA: RAND Corporation, 2008).

7. A vivid, detailed account of this event is available at http://bit.ly/2ECZjWp; Also, see the BBC News website at http://news.bbc.co.uk.

8. For an analysis of this phenomenon, see John Horgan and John F. Morrison, "Here to Stay? The Rising Threat of Violent Dissident Republicanism in Northern Ireland," *Terrorism and Political Violence* 23, no. 4 (2011).

9. A timeline of ETA's terrorist campaign is available on the BBC website at: http://www.bbc.co.uk/news/world-europe-11181982. Also, see the ETA group profile at: http://goo.gl/qtUwc; and Council on Foreign Relations, "Backgrounder: Basque Fatherland and Liberty (ETA)" (November 17, 2008), http://goo.gl/gOeF9.

10. "Basque Terrorism: Dying Spasms," *Economist*, August 7, 2009.

11. Alex Schmid, *The Routledge Handbook of Terrorism Research* (New York: Taylor & Francis, 2013): 620.

12. The next several paragraphs of this discussion previously appeared in the introductory chapter of my book *Essentials of Counterterrorism*, published by Praeger in 2015.

13. Lawrence Korb and Robert Boorstin, *Integrated Power: A National Security Strategy for the 21st Century* (New York: Center for American Progress, June 2005).

14. The White House, *The National Security Strategy of the United States of America* (September 17, 2002), http://www.whitehouse.gov/nsc/nss.html.

15. The White House, *National Strategy for Counterterrorism* (September, 2006): https://2001-2009.state.gov/s/ct/rls/wh/71803.htm.

16. The White House, *National Strategy for Counterterrorism* (May 1, 2011): 7, https://obamawhitehouse.archives.gov/sites/default/files/counterterrorism_strategy.pdf.

17. Charles Lister, "Profiling the Islamic State," Brookings Doha Center Analysis Paper No. 13 (November 2014): 3, at http://www.brookings.edu/doha.

18. Jennifer E. Sims, "The Contemporary Challenges of Counterterrorism Intelligence," in *Essentials of Counterterrorism*, ed. by James J. F.Forest (Westport, CT: Praeger, 2015).

19. Gregory D. Miller, "Confronting Terrorisms: Group motivation and successful state policies." *Terrorism and Political Violence* 19 (2007): 331–50.

20. Racism, or a belief in ethnic/racial/religious or other superiority undermines an agent's ability to understand one's adversary, appreciate the challenges faced by a terrorist, and how they might overcome those challenges to become a more lethal terrorist. For more on this, see Meg Stalcup and Joshua Craze, "How We Train Our Cops to Fear Islam," *Washington Monthly*, March/April 2011.

21. Muhammad al-Obaidi, Nassir Abdullah, and Scott Helfstein, "Deadly Vanguards: A Study of al Qaida's Violence Against Muslims," *Combating Terrorism Center* (December 1, 2009), http://goo.gl/qxGHq.

22. "Islamic State and the Crisis in Iraq and Syria in Maps," BBC News (January 10, 2018), http://bbc.in/1nbXXmb; and Greg Myre, "Where did the Islamic State Fighters Go?" NPR (January 1, 2018), /n.pr/2lEIzG7.

23. Stephen Walt, "Monsters of Our Own Imaginings," *Foreign Policy* (March 24, 2016), http://atfp.co/1pK4IU5.

24. Brian Michael Jenkins, "The Land of the Fearful, or the Home of the Brave?," in *The Long Shadow of 9/11: America's Response to Terrorism*, ed. Brian Michael Jenkins and John Paul Godges (Santa Monica: RAND Corporation, 2011): 207. Also, see Brian Michael Jenkins, "True Grit: To Counter Terror, We Must Conquer Our Own Fear," *RAND Review* 30, no. 2 (Summer 2006): 10–19.

25. "Learning to Live With It," *Economist*, September 3, 2016, http://econ.st/2yc7Mft.

26. "Queen condemns bombing outrage," BBC News (July 8, 2005), http://news.bbc.co.uk/2/hi/4665537.stm.

27. "Pure Reason: How Germans Handle Terror," *Economist*, July 30, 2016, http://econ.st/2EwwXQN.

28. Ibid.

29. Stephen Walt, "Monsters of Our Own Imaginings."

30. Max Abrahms, "Why Terrorism Does Not Work," *International Security* 31, no. 2 (2006): 42–78.

31. Joby Warrick, "Use of Weaponized Drones by ISIS Spurs Terrorism Fears," *Washington Post*, February 21, 2017, http://wapo.st/2Bn3kQ5.

32. For example, see "Hezbollah drone flies over Israel," BBC News (November 7, 2004), http://news.bbc.co.uk/2/hi/3990773.stm; and Ya'aqov Katz, "Hizballah Drone Shot Down was Carrying Explosives," *Jerusalem Post*, September 19,2006.

33. Eric Schmitt, "ISIS Used Chemical Arms at Least 52 Times in Syria and Iraq, Report Says," *New York Times*, November 21, 2016, http://nyti.ms/2oQkRut.

34. Brian Michael Jenkins, "True Grit," 10.

INDEX